Game Programming Using Qt

A complete guide to designing and building fun games with Qt and Qt Quick 2 using their associated toolsets

Witold Wysota

Lorenz Haas

BIRMINGHAM - MUMBAI

Game Programming Using Qt

First published: January 2016

Production Reference: 1210116

Published by Packt Publishing Ltd.
Livery Place
35 Livery Street
Birmingham B3 2PB, UK.

ISBN 978-1-78216-887-4

www.packtpub.com

Credits

Authors
Witold Wysota
Lorenz Haas

Reviewers
Simone Angeloni
Rahul De
Pooya Eimandar
Shaveen Kumar
M. Cihan Özer

Acquisition Editor
Vinay Argekar

Content Development Editor
Pooja Mhapsekar

Technical Editor
Mrunmayee Patil

Copy Editor
Neha Vyas

Project Coordinator
Sanjeet Rao

Proofreader
Safis Editing

Indexer
Monica Ajmera Mehta

Graphics
Disha Haria
Jason Monterio

Production Coordinator
Conidon Miranda

Cover Work
Conidon Miranda

About the Authors

Witold Wysota is a software architect and developer living in Poland. He started his adventure with Qt in 2004 when he joined QtForum.org and started answering questions about programming with Qt. Shortly afterwards, he became part of the moderator group of the forum. In 2006, together with the moderator team, he established QtCentre.org, which quickly became the largest community-driven support site devoted to Qt. For a number of years, he conducted commercial, academic, and public trainings and workshops and has been giving lectures on Qt, Qt Quick, and related technologies. He is a certified Qt developer and was a member of Qt Education Advisory Board with Nokia, where he helped prepare materials in order to use Qt in educational activities.

Witold was also a technical reviewer for *Foundations of Qt Development*, *Johan Thelin*, *Apress Publishing*, a book about Qt 4, and an author of a couple of articles on programming with Qt.

In real life, he is a passionate adept of Seven Star Praying Mantis, a traditional style of Chinese martial arts.

I would like to thank all the people who have worked on Qt's development over the years for creating such a great programming framework, which was the main force that helped me to shape my programming career.

I would also like to thank Lorenz for helping me with the book as well as the team at Packt Publishing for having a magnitude of patience for me during the process of the creation of this book.

Lorenz Haas is a passionate programmer who started his Qt career with Qt 3. Thrilled by Qt's great community, especially the one at QtCentre.org, he immersed himself in this framework, became one of the first certified Qt developers and specialists, and turned his love for Qt into his profession.

Lorenz is now working at a medium-sized IT company based in Erlangen, Germany, as a lead software architect. He mainly develops machine controls and their user interfaces as well as general solutions for the industry sector. Additionally, he runs his own small consultancy and programming business called Histomatics (`http://www.histomatics.de`).

A few years ago, he started contributing to Qt Creator. He added a couple of refactoring options that you probably rely on a regular basis if you use Qt Creator. He is also the author of the Beautifier plugin.

I would like to thank Witold who guided me through my first steps into the Qt world back in the days and who still assists me with any problems that arise. I am also very grateful to him for taking me on board for this book writing project. He's an excellent teacher and tutor!

Secondly, I would like to thank the team at Packt Publishing, who helped and guided us through the entire process of writing this book.

About the Reviewers

Simone Angeloni is a software developer and consultant with over a decade of experience in C++ and scripting languages. He is a passionate gamer, but an even more passionate modder and game designer.

He is currently working for Crytek GmbH and developing the UI of the free-to-play, award-winning video game Warface. Before this, he was realizing configuration systems for railway signaling and creating standalone applications with Qt. Later, he worked with universities and the National Institute of Nuclear Physics to realize fast data acquisition for particle accelerators.

Recently, he founded Clockwise Interactive, a game company that is currently working on the production of its first title.

Rahul De is a 23-year-old systems and server-side engineer from Kolkata, India. He recently graduated from the Vellore Institute of Technology with a bachelor of technology degree in computer science and now works with ThoughtWorks. Being a tech and open source enthusiast and a proper "geeks geek", Rahul took up programming at a very young age and quickly matured from developing small-time native applications for desktops to maintaining servers, writing compilers, building IDEs, and enhancing Qt. His latest pet projects involve Medusa—a JIT compiler for Python using Qt, which aims to provide up to a 1500 percent boost for Python projects.

Being an avid gamer, he has already dabbled quite a bit with various engines such as Unreal and Cry. He likes to play and develop games in his spare time.

Pooya Eimandar was born on 7th January 1986. He graduated in computer science and has a hardware engineering degree from Shomal University. He is also the author of *DirectX 11.1 Game Programming, Packt Publishing*.

He began his career working on various 3D simulation applications. In 2010, he founded BaziPardaz Game Studio, and since then, he has been leading an open source game engine (`https://persianengine.codeplex.com/`) at Bazipardaz.

He is currently working on a playout and CG editor tool for Alalam News Network. You can find more information about him at `http://PooyaEimandar.com/`.

Shaveen Kumar is a computer scientist and engineer. He graduated from Carnegie Mellon University in 2013 with a master's degree in entertainment technology and is working at Google. He works there as a graphics engineer and technical artist. His main interests are in GPU programming, parallel computing, game engine development, robotics, and computer vision.

More information about his work can be found at `http://www.shaveenk.com`.

M. Cihan Özer is a game developer and researcher in computer graphics. He started his career in game development and worked for several mobile and game companies.

He got his bachelor's degree from Ankara University, Turkey, and he is currently an MS student at Université de Montréal, Canada. Cihan's work focuses on realistic rendering and interactive techniques.

I would like to thank the authors of this book. It will help a lot of people who want to learn Qt and work with it. Also, I would like to thank the great people at Packt Publishing for giving me the opportunity to review this book.

www.PacktPub.com

Support files, eBooks, discount offers, and more

For support files and downloads related to your book, please visit www.PacktPub.com.

Did you know that Packt offers eBook versions of every book published, with PDF and ePub files available? You can upgrade to the eBook version at www.PacktPub.com and as a print book customer, you are entitled to a discount on the eBook copy. Get in touch with us at service@packtpub.com for more details.

At www.PacktPub.com, you can also read a collection of free technical articles, sign up for a range of free newsletters and receive exclusive discounts and offers on Packt books and eBooks.

https://www2.packtpub.com/books/subscription/packtlib

Do you need instant solutions to your IT questions? PacktLib is Packt's online digital book library. Here, you can search, access, and read Packt's entire library of books.

Why subscribe?

- Fully searchable across every book published by Packt
- Copy and paste, print, and bookmark content
- On demand and accessible via a web browser

Free access for Packt account holders

If you have an account with Packt at www.PacktPub.com, you can use this to access PacktLib today and view 9 entirely free books. Simply use your login credentials for immediate access.

Table of Contents

Preface

As a leading cross-platform toolkit for all significant desktop, mobile, and embedded platforms, Qt is becoming more popular by the day. This book will help you learn the nitty-gritty of Qt and will equip you with the necessary toolsets to build apps and games. This book is designed as a beginner's guide to take programmers that are new to Qt from the basics, such as objects, core classes, widgets, and so on, and new features in version 5.4, to a level where they can create a custom application with best practices when it comes to programming with Qt.

With a brief introduction on how to create an application and prepare a working environment for both desktop and mobile platforms, we will dive deeper into the basics of creating graphical interfaces and Qt's core concepts of data processing and display before you try to create a game. As you progress through the chapters, you'll learn to enrich your games by implementing network connectivity and employing scripting. Delve into Qt Quick, OpenGL, and various other tools to add game logic, design animation, add game physics, and build astonishing UIs for games. Toward the end of this book, you'll learn to exploit mobile device features, such as accelerators and sensors, to build engaging user experiences.

What this book covers

Chapter 1, Introduction to Qt, will familiarize you with the standard behavior that is required when creating cross-platform applications as well as show you a bit of history of Qt and how it evolved over time with an emphasis on the most recent architectural changes in Qt.

Chapter 2, Installation, will guide you through the process of installing a Qt binary release for desktop platforms, setting up the bundled IDE, and looking at various configuration options related to cross-platform programming.

Chapter 3, Qt GUI Programming, will show you how to create classic user interfaces with the Qt Widgets module. It will also familiarize you with the process of compiling applications using Qt.

Chapter 4, Qt Core Essentials, will familiarize you with the concepts related to data processing and display in Qt—file handling in different formats, Unicode text handling and displaying user-visible strings in different languages, and regular expression matching.

Chapter 5, Graphics with Qt, describes the whole mechanism related to creating and using graphics in Qt in 2D and 3D. It also presents multimedia capabilities for audio and video (capturing, processing, and output)

Chapter 6, Graphics View, will familiarize you with 2D-object-oriented graphics in Qt. You will learn how to use built-in items to compose the final results as well as create your own items supplementing what is already available and possibly animate them.

Chapter 7, Networking, will demonstrate the IP networking technologies that are available in Qt. It will teach you how to connect to TCP servers, implement a reliable server using TCP, and implement an unreliable server using UDP.

Chapter 8, Scripting, shows you the benefits of scripting in applications. It will teach you how to employ a scripting engine for a game by using JavaScript. It will also suggest some alternatives to JavaScript for scripting that can be easily integrated with Qt.

Chapter 9, Qt Quick Basics, will teach you to program resolution-independent fluid user interfaces using a QML declarative engine and Qt Quick 2 scene graph environment. In addition, you will learn how to implement new graphical items in your scenes.

Chapter 10, Qt Quick, will show you how to bring dynamics to various aspects of a UI. You will see how to create fancy graphics and animations in Qt Quick by using the particle engine, GLSL shaders and built-in animation, and state machine capabilities, and you will learn how to use these techniques in games.

Chapter 11, Miscellaneous and Advanced Concepts, covers the important aspects of Qt programming that didn't make it into the other chapters but may be important for game programming. This chapter is available online at the link `https://www.packtpub.com/sites/default/files/downloads/Advanced_Concepts.pdf`.

What you need for this book

All you need for this book is a Windows machine with the latest version of Qt installed. The examples presented in this book are based on Qt 5.4.

Qt can be downloaded from `http://www.qt.io/download-open-source/`.

Who this book is for

The expected readers of this book will be application and UI developers/programmers who have basic/intermediate functional knowledge of C++. The target audience also includes C++ programmers. No previous experience with Qt is required for you to read this book. Developers with up to a year of Qt experience will also benefit from the topics covered in this book.

Sections

In this book, you will find several headings that appear frequently (Time for action, What just happened?, Pop quiz, and Have a go hero).

To give clear instructions on how to complete a procedure or task, we use these sections as follows:

Time for action – heading

1. Action 1
2. Action 2
3. Action 3

Instructions often need some extra explanation to ensure they make sense, so they are followed with these sections:

What just happened?

This section explains the working of the tasks or instructions that you have just completed.

You will also find some other learning aids in the book, for example:

Pop quiz – heading

These are short multiple-choice questions intended to help you test your own understanding.

Have a go hero – heading

These are practical challenges that give you ideas to experiment with what you have learned.

Conventions

You will also find a number of text styles that distinguish between different kinds of information. Here are some examples of these styles and an explanation of their meaning.

Code words in text, database table names, folder names, filenames, file extensions, pathnames, dummy URLs, user input, and Twitter handles are shown as follows: "This API is centered on `QNetworkAccessManager`, which handles the complete communication between your game and the Internet."

A block of code is set as follows:

```
QNetworkRequest request;
request.setUrl(QUrl("http://localhost/version.txt"));
request.setHeader(QNetworkRequest::UserAgentHeader, "MyGame");
m_nam->get(request);
```

When we wish to draw your attention to a particular part of a code block, the relevant lines or items are set in bold:

```
void FileDownload::downloadFinished(QNetworkReply *reply) {
  const QByteArray content = reply->readAll();
  m_edit->setPlainText(content);
  reply->deleteLater();
}
```

Any command-line input or output is written as follows:

```
git clone git://code.qt.io/qt/qt5.git
cd qt5
perl init-repository
```

New terms and **important words** are shown in bold. Words that you see on the screen, in menus or dialog boxes for example, appear in the text like this: "On the **Select Destination Location** screen, click on **Next** to accept the default destination."

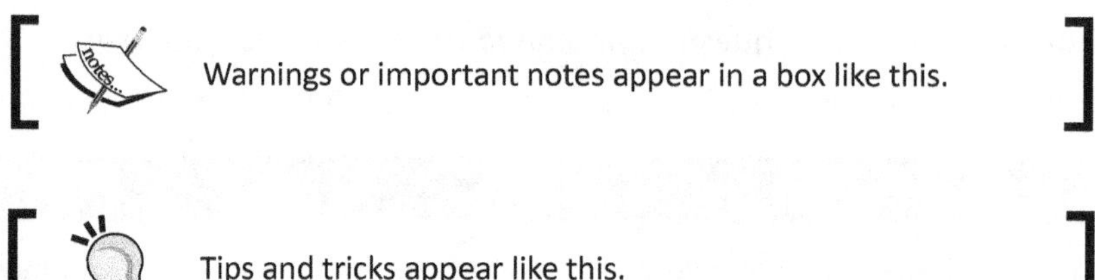

Warnings or important notes appear in a box like this.

Tips and tricks appear like this.

Reader feedback

Feedback from our readers is always welcome. Let us know what you think about this book—what you liked or disliked. Reader feedback is important for us as it helps us develop titles that you will really get the most out of.

To send us general feedback, simply e-mail `feedback@packtpub.com`, and mention the book's title in the subject of your message.

If there is a topic that you have expertise in and you are interested in either writing or contributing to a book, see our author guide at `www.packtpub.com/authors`.

Customer support

Now that you are the proud owner of a Packt book, we have a number of things to help you to get the most from your purchase.

Downloading the example code

You can download the example code files from your account at `http://www.packtpub.com` for all the Packt Publishing books you have purchased. If you purchased this book elsewhere, you can visit `http://www.packtpub.com/support` and register to have the files e-mailed directly to you.

Downloading the color images of this book

We also provide you with a PDF file that has color images of the screenshots/diagrams used in this book. The color images will help you better understand the changes in the output. You can download this file from `https://www.packtpub.com/sites/default/files/downloads/GameProgrammingUsingQt_ColoredImages.pdf`.

Errata

Although we have taken every care to ensure the accuracy of our content, mistakes do happen. If you find a mistake in one of our books—maybe a mistake in the text or the code—we would be grateful if you could report this to us. By doing so, you can save other readers from frustration and help us improve subsequent versions of this book. If you find any errata, please report them by visiting `http://www.packtpub.com/submit-errata`, selecting your book, clicking on the **Errata Submission Form** link, and entering the details of your errata. Once your errata are verified, your submission will be accepted and the errata will be uploaded to our website or added to any list of existing errata under the Errata section of that title.

To view the previously submitted errata, go to `https://www.packtpub.com/books/content/support` and enter the name of the book in the search field. The required information will appear under the **Errata** section.

Piracy

Piracy of copyrighted material on the Internet is an ongoing problem across all media. At Packt, we take the protection of our copyright and licenses very seriously. If you come across any illegal copies of our works in any form on the Internet, please provide us with the location address or website name immediately so that we can pursue a remedy.

Please contact us at `copyright@packtpub.com` with a link to the suspected pirated material.

We appreciate your help in protecting our authors and our ability to bring you valuable content.

Questions

If you have a problem with any aspect of this book, you can contact us at `questions@packtpub.com`, and we will do our best to address the problem.

1
Introduction to Qt

In this chapter, you will learn what Qt is and how it evolved. We will pay special attention to the differences between Qt's major versions 4 and 5. Finally, you will learn to decide on which of the available Qt licensing schemes to choose for our projects.

The cross-platform programming

Qt is an application programming framework that is used to develop cross-platform applications. What this means is that software written for one platform can be ported and executed on another platform with little or no effort. This is obtained by limiting the application source code to a set of calls to routines and libraries available to all the supported platforms, and by delegating all tasks that may differ between platforms (such as drawing on the screen and accessing system data or hardware) to Qt. This effectively creates a layered environment (as shown in the following figure), where Qt hides all platform-dependent aspects from the application code:

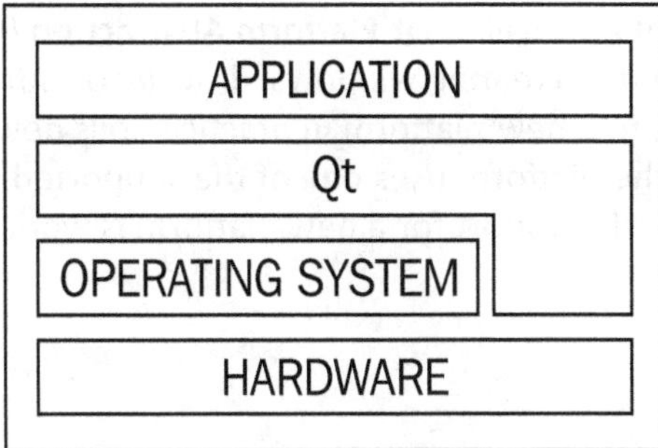

Of course, at times we need to use some functionality that Qt doesn't provide. In such situations, it is important to use conditional compilation like the one used in the following code:

```
#ifdef Q_OS_WIN32
// Windows specific code
#elif defined(Q_OS_LINUX) || defined(Q_OS_MAC)
// Mac and Linux specific code
#endif
```

Downloading the example code

You can download the example code files from your account at `http://www.packtpub.com` for all the Packt Publishing books you have purchased. If you purchased this book elsewhere, you can visit `http://www.packtpub.com/support` and register there to have the files e-mailed directly to you.

What just happened?

Before the code is compiled, it is first fed to a preprocessor that may change the final text that is going to be sent to a compiler. When it encounters a `#ifdef` directive, it checks for the existence of a label that will follow (such as `Q_OS_WIN32`), and only includes a block of code in compilation if the label is defined. Qt makes sure to provide proper definitions for each system and compiler so that we can use them in such situations.

You can find a list of all such macros in the Qt reference manual under the term "QtGlobal".

Qt Platform Abstraction

Qt itself is separated into two layers. One is the core Qt functionality that is implemented in a standard C++ language, which is essentially platform-independent. The other is a set of small plugins that implement a so-called **Qt Platform Abstraction** (**QPA**) that contains all the platform-specific code related to creating windows, drawing on surfaces, using fonts, and so on. Therefore, porting Qt to a new platform in practice boils down to implementing the QPA plugin for it, provided the platform uses one of the supported standard C++ compilers. Because of this, providing basic support for a new platform is work that can possibly be done in a matter of hours.

Supported platforms

The framework is available for a number of platforms, ranging from classical desktop environments through embedded systems to mobile phones. The following table lists down all the platforms and compiler families that Qt supports at the time of writing. It is possible that when you are reading this, a couple more rows could have been added to this table:

Platform	QPA plugins	Supported compilers
Linux	XCB (X11) and Wayland	GCC, LLVM (clang), and ICC
Windows XP, Vista, 7, 8, and 10	Windows	MinGW, MSVC, and ICC
Mac OS X	Cocoa	LLVM (clang) and GCC
Linux Embedded	DirectFB, EGLFS, KMS, and Wayland	GCC
Windows Embedded	Windows	MSVC
Android	Android	GCC
iOS	iOS	LLVM (clang) and GCC
Unix	XCB (X11)	GCC
RTOS (QNX, VxWorks, and INTEGRITY)	qnx	qcc, dcc, and GCC
BlackBerry 10	qnx	qcc
Windows 8 (WinRT)	winrt	MSVC
Maemo, MeeGo, and Sailfish OS	XCB (X11)	GCC
Google Native Client (unsupported)	pepper	GCC

A journey through time

The development of Qt was started in 1991 by two Norwegians—Eirik Chambe-Eng and Haavard Nord, who were looking to create a cross-platform GUI programming toolkit. The first commercial client of Trolltech (the company that created the Qt toolkit) was the European Space Agency. The commercial use of Qt helped Trolltech sustain further development. At that time, Qt was available for two platforms—Unix/X11 and Windows; however, developing with Qt for Windows required buying a proprietary license, which was a significant drawback in porting the existing Unix/Qt applications.

A major step forward was the release of Qt Version 3.0 in 2001, which saw the initial support for Mac as well as an option to use Qt for Unix and Mac under a liberal GPL license. Still, Qt for Windows was only available under a paid license. Nevertheless, at that time, Qt had support for all the important players in the market—Windows, Mac, and Unix desktops, with Trolltech's mainstream product and Qt for embedded Linux.

In 2005, Qt 4.0 was released, which was a real breakthrough for a number of reasons. First, the Qt API was completely redesigned, which made it cleaner and more coherent. Unfortunately, at the same time, it made the existing Qt-based code incompatible with 4.0, and many applications needed to be rewritten from scratch or required much effort to be adapted to the new API. It was a difficult decision, but from the time perspective, we can see it was worth it. Difficulties caused by changes in the API were well countered by the fact that Qt for Windows was finally released under GPL. Many optimizations were introduced that made Qt significantly faster. Lastly, Qt, which was a single library until now, was divided into a number of modules:

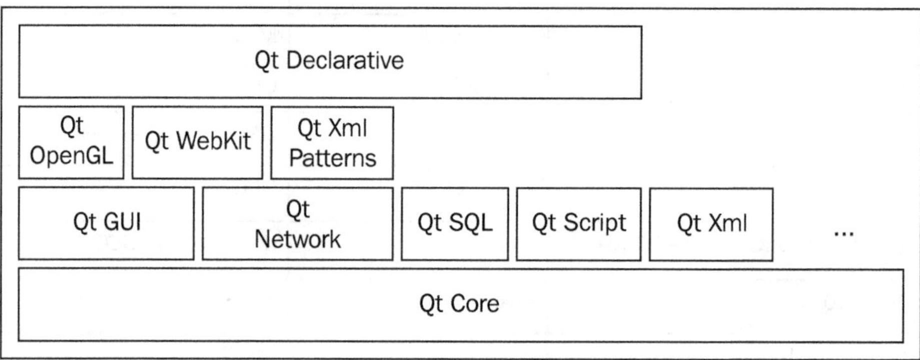

This allowed programmers to only link to the functionality that they used in their applications, reducing the memory footprint and dependencies of their software.

In 2008, Trolltech was sold to Nokia, which at that time was looking for a software framework to help it expand and replace its Symbian platform in the future. The Qt community became divided, some people were thrilled, others worried after seeing Qt's development get transferred to Nokia. Either way, new funds were pumped into Qt, speeding up its progress and opening it for mobile platforms—Symbian and then Maemo and MeeGo.

For Nokia, Qt was not considered a product of its own, but rather a tool. Therefore, they decided to introduce Qt to more developers by adding a very liberal LGPL license that allowed the usage of the framework for both open and closed source development.

Bringing Qt to new platforms and less powerful hardware required a new approach to create user interfaces and to make them more lightweight, fluid, and eye candy. Nokia engineers working on Qt came up with a new declarative language to develop such interfaces—the **Qt Modeling Language** (**QML**) and a Qt runtime for it called Qt Quick.

The latter became the primary focus of the further development of Qt, practically stalling all nonmobile-related work, channeling all efforts to make Qt Quick faster, easier, and more widespread. Qt 4 was already in the market for 7 years and it became obvious that another major version of Qt had to be released. It was decided to bring more engineers to Qt by allowing anyone to contribute to the project.

Nokia did not manage to finish working on Qt 5.0. As a result of an unexpected turn over of Nokia toward different technology in 2011, the Qt division was sold in mid-2012 to the Finnish company Digia that managed to complete the effort and release Qt 5.0 in December of the same year.

New in Qt 5

The API of Qt 5 does not differ much from that of Qt 4. Therefore, Qt 5 is almost completely source compatible with its predecessor, which means that we only need a minimal effort to port the existing applications to Qt 5. This section gives a brief introduction to the major changes between versions 4 and 5 of Qt. If you are already familiar with Qt 4, this can serve as a small compendium of what you need to pay attention to if you want to use the features of Qt 5 to their fullest extent.

Restructured codebase

The biggest change compared to the previous major release of Qt and the one that is immediately visible when we try to build an older application against Qt 5 is that the whole framework was refactored into a different set of modules. Because it expanded over time and became harder to maintain and update for the growing number of platforms that it supported, a decision was made to split the framework into much smaller modules contained in two module groups—Qt Essentials and Qt Add-ons. A major decision relating to the split was that each module could now have its own independent release schedule.

Qt Essentials

The Essentials group contains modules that are mandatory to implement for every supported platform. This implies that if you are implementing your system using modules from this group only, you can be sure that it can be easily ported to any other platform that Qt supports. Some of the modules are explained as follows:

- The QtCore module contains the most basic Qt functionality that all other modules rely on. It provides support for event processing, meta-objects, data I/O, text processing, and threading. It also brings a number of frameworks such as the animation framework, the State Machine framework, and the plugin framework.
- The Qt GUI module provides basic cross-platform support to build user interfaces. It is much smaller compared with the same module from Qt 4, as the support for widgets and printing has been moved to separate modules. Qt GUI contains classes that are used to manipulate windows that can be rendered using either the raster engine (by specifying `QSurface::RasterSurface` as the surface type) or OpenGL (`QSurface::OpenGLSurface`). Qt supports desktop OpenGL as well as OpenGL ES 1.1 and 2.0.
- The Qt Network module brings support for IPv4 and IPv6 networking using TCP and UDP as well as by controlling the device connectivity state. Compared to Qt 4, this module improves IPv6 support, adds support for opaque SSL keys (such as hardware key devices) and UDP multicast, and assembles MIME multipart messages to be sent over HTTP. It also extends support for DNS lookups.
- Qt Multimedia allows programmers to access audio and video hardware (including cameras and FM radio) to record and play multimedia content.
- Qt SQL brings a framework that is used to manipulate SQL databases in an abstract way.
- Qt WebKit is a port of the WebKit 2 web browser engine to Qt. It provides classes to display and manipulate web content and integrates with your desktop application.
- Qt Widgets extends the GUI module with the ability to create a user interface using widgets, such as buttons, edit boxes, labels, data views, dialog boxes, menus, and toolbars that are arranged using a special layout engine. It also contains the implementation of an object-oriented 2D graphics canvas called **Graphics View**. When porting Qt 4 applications to Qt 5, it is a good idea to start by enabling support of the widgets module (by adding *QT += widgets* to the project file) and then work your way down from here.
- Qt Quick is an extension of Qt GUI, which provides means to create lightweight fluid user interfaces using QML. It is described in more detail later in this chapter as well as in *Chapter 9, Qt Quick Basics*.

There are also other modules in this group, but we will not focus on them in this book. If you want to learn more about them, you can look them up in the Qt reference manual.

Qt Add-ons

This group contains modules that are optional for any platform. This means that if a particular functionality is not available on some platform or there is nobody willing to spend time working on this functionality for a platform, it will not prevent Qt from supporting this platform.

Some of the most important modules are QtConcurrent for parallel processing, Qt Script that allows us to use JavaScript in C++ applications, Qt3D that provides high-level OpenGL building blocks, and Qt XML Patterns that helps us to access XML data. Many others are also available, but we will not cover them here.

Qt Quick 2.0

The largest upgrade to Qt functionality-wise is Qt Quick 2.0. In Qt 4, the framework was implemented on top of Graphics View. This proved to be too slow when used with low-end hardware even with OpenGL ES acceleration enabled. This is because of the way Graphics View renders its content—it iterates all the items in sequence, calculates and sets its transformation matrix, paints the item, recalculates and resets the matrix for the next item, paints it, and so on. Since an item can contain any generic content drawn in an arbitrary order, it requires frequent changes to the GL pipeline, causing major slowdowns.

The new version of Qt Quick instead uses a scene-graph approach. It describes the whole scene as a graph of attributes and well-known operations. To paint the scene, information about the current state of the graph is gathered and the scene is rendered in a more optimal way. For example, it can first draw triangle strips from all items, then render fonts from all items, and so on. Furthermore, since the state of each item is represented by a subgraph, changes to each item can be tracked and it can be decided whether the visual representation of a particular item needs to be updated or not.

The old `QDeclarativeItem` class was replaced by `QQuickItem`, which has no ties to the Graphics View architecture. There is no routine available where you can directly paint the item, but there is a `QQuickPaintedItem` class available that aids in porting old code by rendering content based on `QPainter` to a texture and then rendering that texture using a scene-graph. Such items are, however, significantly slower than those directly using the graph approach, so if performance is important, they should be avoided.

Qt Quick plays an important role in Qt 5 and it is very useful to create games. We will cover this technology in detail in *Chapters 9, Qt Quick Basics* and *Chapter 10, Qt Quick*.

Meta-objects

In Qt 4, adding signals and slots to a class required the presence of a meta-object (that is, an instance of a class that describes another class) for that class. This was done by subclassing `QObject`, adding the `Q_OBJECT` macro to it, and declaring signals and slots in special scopes of the class. In Qt 5, this is still possible and advised in many situations, but we now have new interesting possibilities.

It is now acceptable to connect a signal to any compatible member function of a class or any callable entity, such as a standalone function or function object (`functor`). A side-effect is a compile-time compatibility check of the signal and the slot (as opposed to the runtime check of the "old" syntax).

C++11 support

In August 2011, ISO approved a new standard for C++, commonly referred to as C++11. It provides a number of optimizations and makes it easier for programmers to create effective code. While you could use C++11 together with Qt 4, it didn't provide any dedicated support for it. This has changed with Qt 5, which is now aware of C++11 and supports many of the constructs introduced by the new version of the language. In this book, we will sometimes use C++11 features in our code. Some compilers have C++11 support enabled by default, in others, you need to enable it. Don't worry if your compiler doesn't support C++11. Each time we use such features, I will make you aware of it.

Choosing the right license

Qt is available under two different licensing schemes—you can choose between a commercial license and an open source one. We will discuss both here to make it easier for you to choose. If you have any doubts regarding whether a particular licensing scheme applies to your use case, better consult a professional lawyer.

An open source license

The advantage of open source licenses is that we don't have to pay anyone to use Qt; however, the downside is that there are some limitations imposed on how it can be used.

When choosing the open source edition, we have to decide between GPL 3.0 and LGPL 2.1 or 3. Since LGPL is more liberal, in this chapter we will focus on it. Choosing LGPL allows you to use Qt to implement systems that are either open source or closed source—you don't have to reveal the sources of your application to anyone if you don't want to.

However, there are a number of restrictions you need to be aware of:

- Any modifications that you make to Qt itself need to be made public, for example, by distributing source code patches alongside your application binary.
- LGPL requires that users of your application must be able to replace Qt libraries that you provide them with other libraries with the same functionality (for example, a different version of Qt). This usually means that you have to dynamically link your application against Qt so that the user can simply replace Qt libraries with his own. You should be aware that such substitutions can decrease the security of your system, thus, if you need it to be very secure, open source might not be the option for you.
- LGPL is incompatible with a number of licenses, especially proprietary ones, so it is possible that you won't be able to use Qt with some commercial components.

The open source edition of Qt can be downloaded directly from `http://www.qt.io`.

A commercial license

All these restrictions are lifted if you decide to buy a commercial license for Qt. This allows you to keep the entire source code a secret, including any changes you may want to incorporate in Qt. You can freely link your application statically against Qt, which means fewer dependencies, a smaller deployment bundle size, and a faster startup. It also increases the security of your application, as end users cannot inject their own code into the application by replacing a dynamically loaded library with their own.

> To buy a commercial license, go to `http://qt.io/buy`.

Summary

In this chapter, you learned about the architecture of Qt. We saw how it evolved over time and we had a brief overview of what it looks like now. Qt is a complex framework and we will not manage to cover it all, as some parts of its functionality are more important for game programming than others that you can learn on your own in case you ever need them. Now that you know what Qt is, we can proceed with the next chapter where you will learn how to install Qt on your development machine.

2
Installation

In this chapter, you will learn how to install Qt on your development machine, including Qt Creator, an IDE tailored to use with Qt. You will see how to configure the IDE for your needs and learn the basic skills to use that environment. In addition to this, the chapter will describe the process of building Qt from the source code, which can be useful for customizing your Qt installation as well as getting a working Qt installation for embedded platforms. By the end of this chapter, you will be able to prepare your working environment for both desktop and embedded platforms using tools included in the Qt release.

Installing the Qt SDK

Before you can start using Qt on your machine, it needs to be downloaded and installed. Qt can be installed using dedicated installers that come in two flavors—the online installer, which downloads all the needed components on the fly, and a much larger offline installer, which already contains all the required components. Using an online installer is easier for regular desktop installs, so we will prefer this approach.

Time for action – installing Qt using an online installer

First, go to `http://qt.io` and click on **Download**. This should bring you to a page containing a list of options for different licensing schemes. To use the open source version, choose the Open Source edition licensed under GPL and LGPL. Then, you can click on the **Download Now** button to retrieve the online installer for the platform that you are currently running on or you can click on any of the header sections to reach a more comprehensive list of options. The links to online installers are at the beginning of the list, as shown in the following screenshot. Click and download the one suited to your host machine:

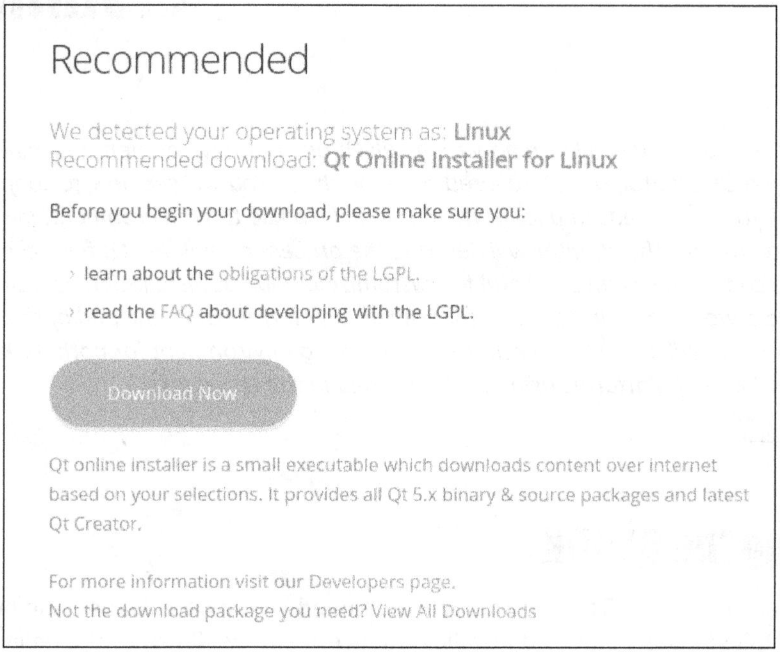

Recommended

We detected your operating system as: **Linux**
Recommended download: **Qt Online Installer for Linux**

Before you begin your download, please make sure you:

- learn about the obligations of the LGPL.
- read the FAQ about developing with the LGPL.

Download Now

Qt online installer is a small executable which downloads content over internet based on your selections. It provides all Qt 5.x binary & source packages and latest Qt Creator.

For more information visit our Developers page.
Not the download package you need? View All Downloads

When the download completes, run the installer, as shown:

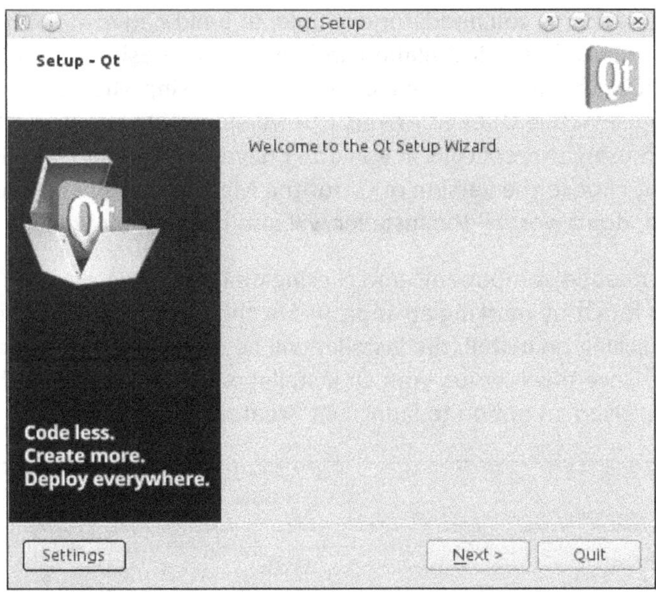

Click on **Next** and after a while of waiting as the downloader checks remote repositories, you'll be asked for the installation path. Be sure to choose a path where you have write access (it's best to put Qt into your personal directory unless you ran the installer as the system administrator user). Clicking on **Next** again will present you with choices of components that you wish to install, as shown in the following screenshot. You will be given different choices depending on your platform.

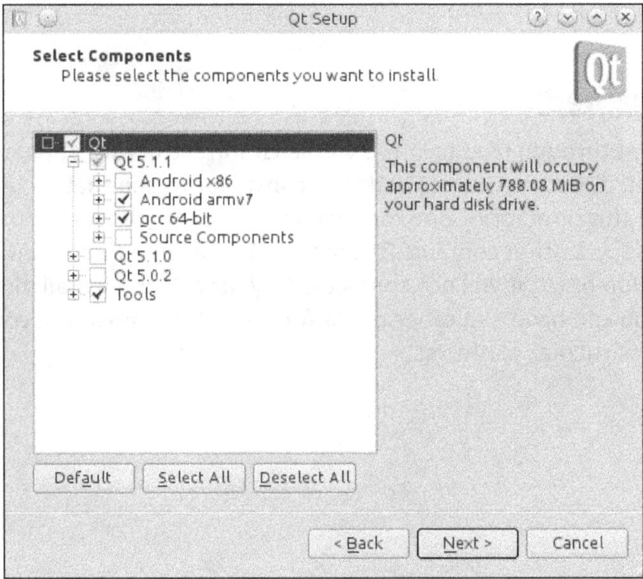

Choose whichever platforms you need, for example, to build native and Android applications on Linux, choose both gcc-based installation and one for the desired Android platform. When on Windows, you have to make additional choices. When using Microsoft compilers, you can choose whether to use native OpenGL drivers (the versions with the `OpenGL` suffix) or to emulate OpenGL ES using DirectX calls. If you don't have a Microsoft compiler or you simply don't want to use it, choose the version of Qt for the MinGW compiler. If you don't have a MinGW installation, don't worry—the installer will also install it for you.

After choosing the needed components and clicking on **Next** again, you will have to accept the licensing terms for Qt by marking an appropriate choice, as shown in the following screenshot. After clicking on **Install**, the installer will begin downloading and installing the required packages. Once this is done, your Qt installation will be ready. At the end of the process, you will be given an option to launch Qt Creator.

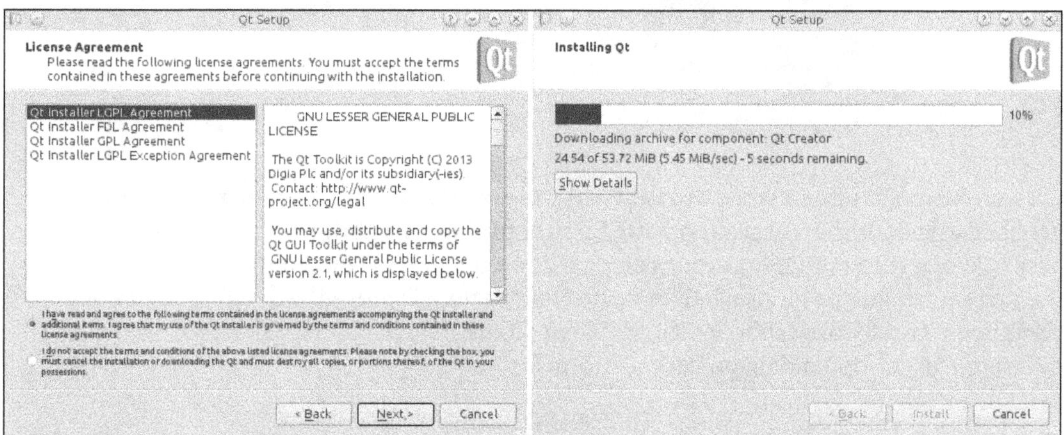

What just happened?

The process we went through results in the whole Qt infrastructure appearing on your disk. You can examine the directory you pointed to the installer to see that it created a number of subdirectories in this directory—one for each version of Qt chosen with the installer and another one called `Tools` that contains Qt Creator. You can see that if you ever decide to install another version of Qt, it will not conflict with your existing installation. Furthermore, for each version, you can have a number of platform subdirectories that contain the actual Qt installations for particular platforms.

Setting up Qt Creator

After Qt Creator starts, you should be presented with the following screen:

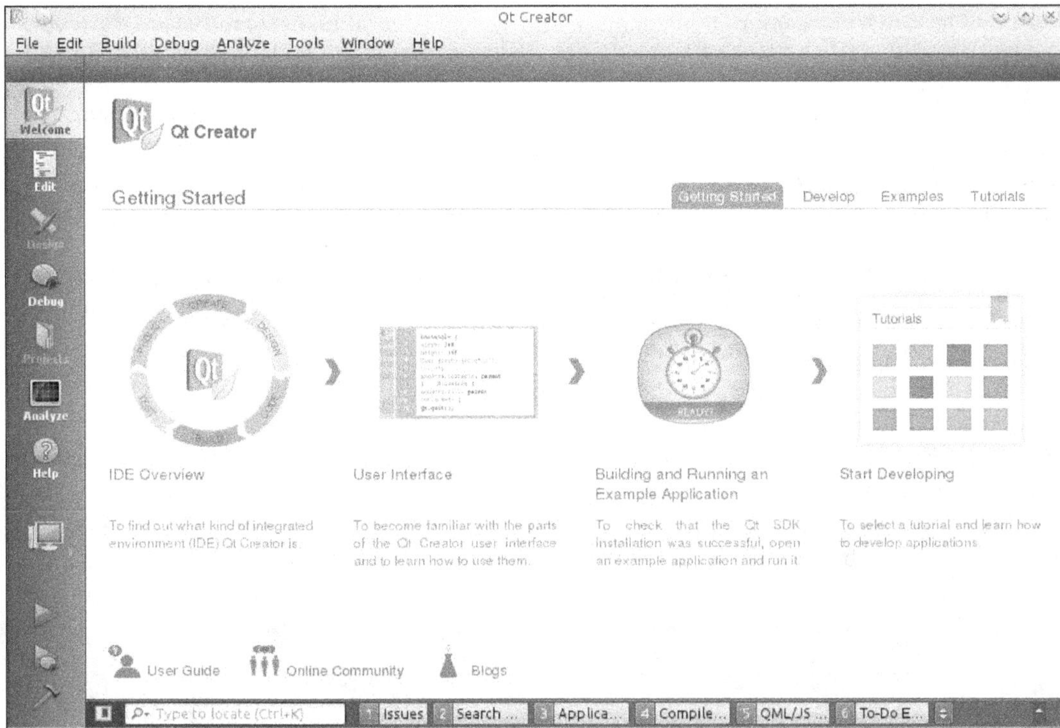

The program should already be configured properly for you to use the version of Qt and compiler that were just installed, but let's verify that anyway. From the **Tools** menu, choose **Options**. Once a dialog box pops up, choose **Build & Run** from the side list. This is the place where we can configure the way Qt Creator builds our project. A complete build configuration is called a **kit**. It consists of a Qt installation and a compiler that will be executed to perform the build. You can see tabs for all the three entities in the **Build & Run** section of the **Options** dialog box.

Let's start with the **Compilers** tab. If your compiler was not autodetected properly and is not in the list, click on the **Add** button, choose your compiler type from the list, and fill the name and path to the compiler. If the settings were entered correctly, Creator will autofill all the other details. Then, you can click on **Apply** to save the changes.

Next, you can switch to the **Qt Versions** tab. Again, if your Qt installation was not detected automatically, you can click on **Add**. This will open a file dialog box where you will need to find your Qt installation's directory wherein all the binary executables are stored (usually in the `bin` directory) and select a binary called `qmake`. Qt Creator will warn you if you choose a wrong file. Otherwise, your Qt installation and version should be detected properly. If you want, you can adjust the version name in the appropriate box.

The last tab to look at is the **Kits** tab. It allows you to pair a compiler with the Qt version to be used for compilation. In addition to this, for embedded and mobile platforms, you can specify a device to deploy to and a `sysroot` directory containing all the files needed to build the software for the specified embedded platform.

Time for action – loading an example project

Qt comes with a lot of examples. Let's try building one to check whether the installation and configuration were done correctly. In Qt Creator, click on the **Welcome** button on the top-left corner of the window to go the initial screen of the IDE. On the right-hand side of the page that appears (refer to the previous screenshot) there are a couple of tabs among which one of them happens to be called **Examples**. Clicking on that tab will open a list of examples with a search box. Make sure that the version of Qt you just installed is chosen in the list next to the search box. In the box, enter `aff` to filter the list of examples and click on **Affine Transformations** to open the project. If you are asked whether you want to copy the project to a new folder, agree. Qt Creator will then present you with the following window:

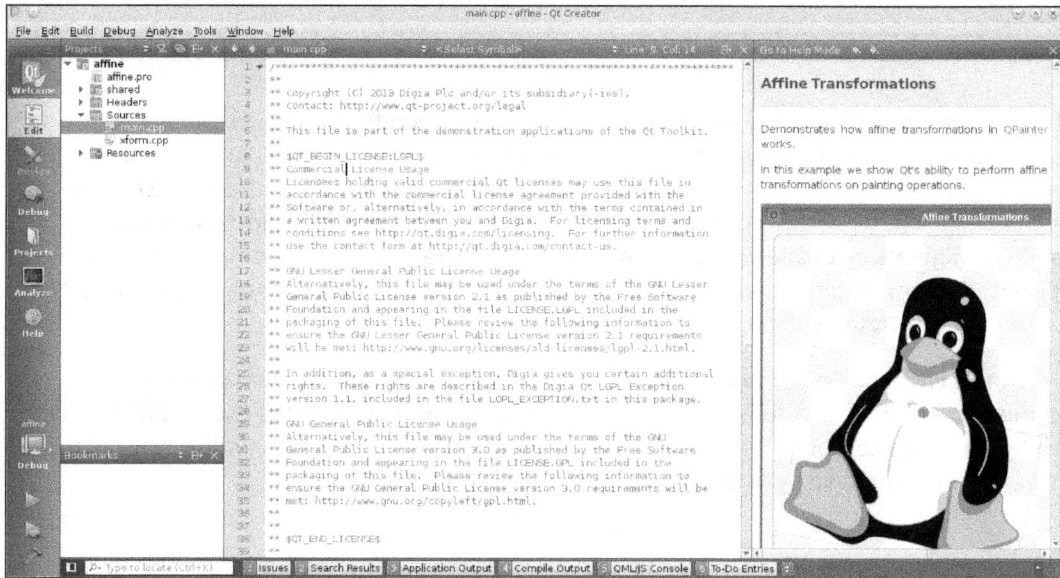

What just happened?

Qt Creator loaded the project and set a view that will help us to learn from example projects. The view is divided into four parts. Let's enumerate them starting from the left side. First there is Qt Creator's working mode selector that contains an action bar, which allows us to toggle between different modes of the IDE. Then, there is the project view that contains a list of files for the project. Next comes the source code editor, displaying the main part of the project's source code. Finally, far to the right, you can see the online help window displaying the documentation for the opened example.

Time for action – running the Affine Transformations project

Let's try building and running the project to check whether the building environment is configured properly. First, click on the icon in the action bar directly over the green triangle icon to open the build configuration popup, as shown in the following screenshot:

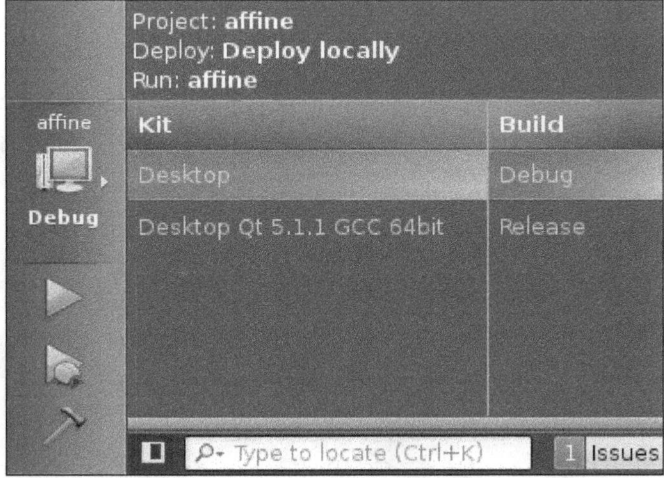

The exact content that you get may vary depending on your installation, but in general, on the left-hand side you will see the list of kits configured for the project and on the right-hand side you will see the list of build configurations defined for that kit. Choose a kit for your desktop installation and any of the configurations defined for that kit. You can adjust configurations by switching Qt Creator to the project management mode by clicking on the **Projects** button in the working mode selector bar. There, you can add and remove kits from the project and manage build configurations for each of the kits, as shown in the following screenshot:

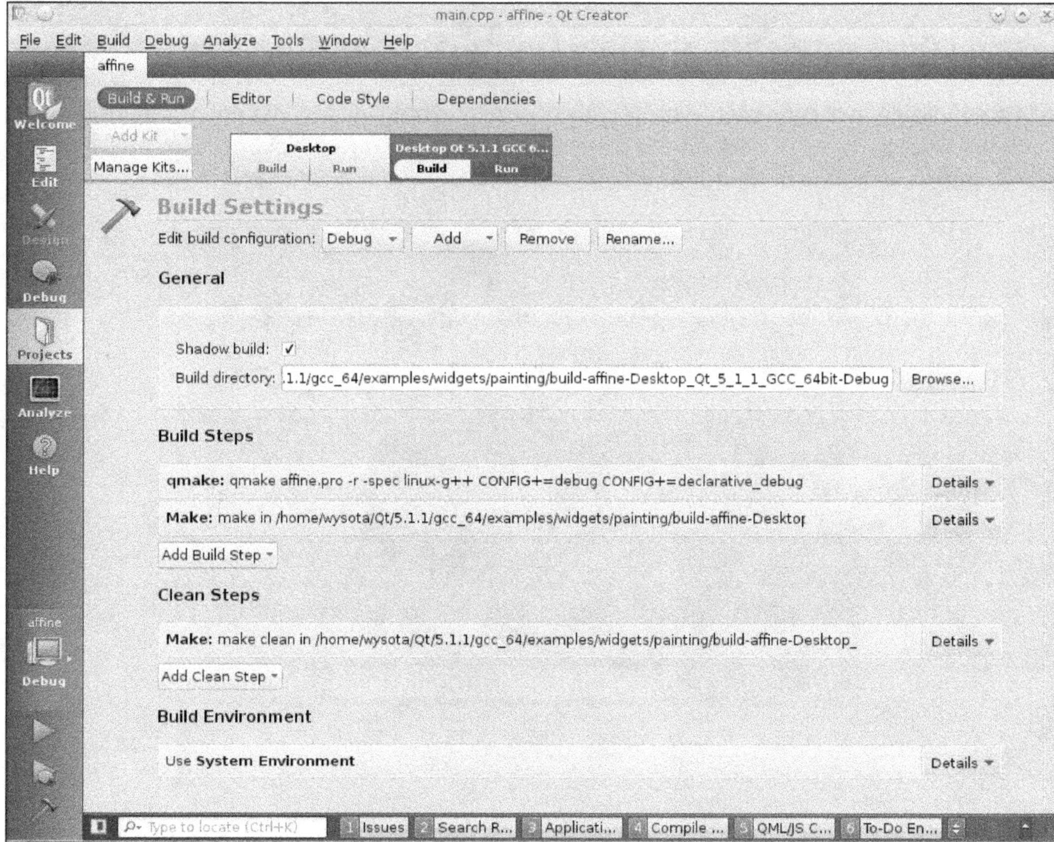

You can adjust, build, and clean steps, and toggle shadow building (that is, building your project outside the source code directory tree).

To build the project, click on the hammer icon at the bottom of the action bar. You can also click on the green triangle icon to build and run the project. If everything works, after some time, the application should be launched, as shown in the next screenshot:

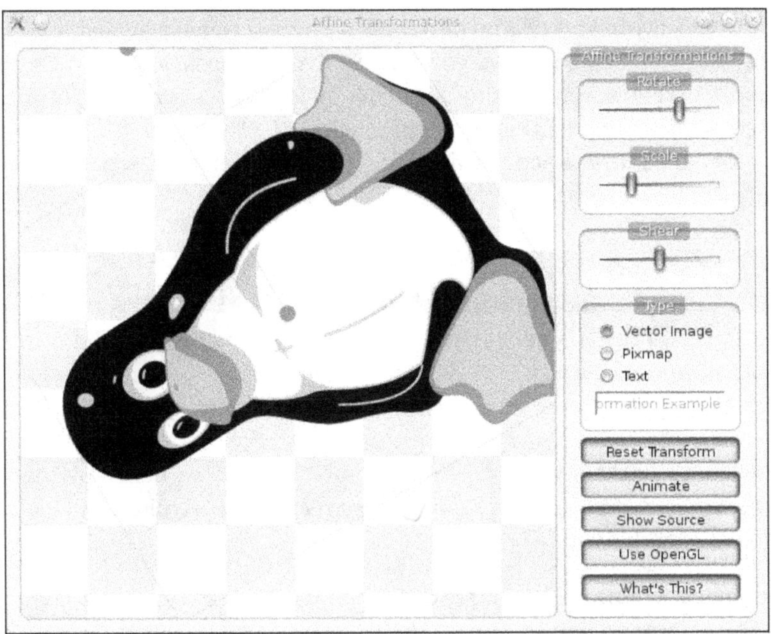

What just happened?

How exactly was the project built? If you open the **Projects** mode and look at **Build Settings** for a kit assigned to the project (as seen in one of the previous screenshots), you will notice that a number of build steps were defined. The first step for Qt projects is usually the `qmake` step, which runs a special tool that generates a `Makefile` for the project that is fed in the second step to a classic `make` tool. You can expand each of the steps by clicking on the respective **Details** button to see configuration options for each of the steps.

While `make` is considered as a standard tool for building software projects, `qmake` is a custom tool provided with Qt. If you go back to the **Edit** mode and see which files are listed in the project contents, you will notice a file with a `pro` extension. This is the main project file that contains a list of source and headers files in the project, definitions of Qt modules active for the project, and optionally, external libraries that the project needs to link against. If you want to learn the details of how such project files are managed, you can switch to the **Help** mode, choose **Index** from the drop-down list on the top of the window, and type `qmake Manual` to find the manual for the tool. Otherwise, just let Qt Creator manage your project for you. For self-contained Qt projects, you don't need to be a qmake expert.

Building Qt from sources

In most cases for desktop and mobile platforms, the binary release of Qt you download from the webpage is sufficient for all your needs. However, for embedded systems, especially for those ARM-based systems, there is no binary release available or it is too heavy resource-wise for such a lightweight system. In such cases, a custom Qt build needs to be performed. There are two ways to do such a build. One is to download the sources as a compressed archive just like the binary package. The other is to download the code directly from a Git repository. Since the first way is pretty much self-explanatory, we'll focus on the second approach.

Time for action – setting up Qt sources using Git

First, you need to install Git on your system if you don't already have it. How to do that depends on your operating system. For Windows, simply download an installer from `https://git-for-windows.github.io`. For Mac, the installer is available at `http://code.google.com/p/git-osx-installer`. For Linux, the simplest way is to use your system's package manager. For instance, on Debian-based distributions, just issue the `sudo apt-get install git` command on a terminal and wait until the installation gets completed.

Afterwards, you need to clone Qt's Git repository. Since Git is a command-line tool, we'll be using the command line from now on. To clone Qt's repository to a directory where you want to keep the sources, issue the following command:

```
git clone git://code.qt.io/qt/qt5.git
```

If all goes well, Git will download a lot of source code from the network and create a `qt5` directory, containing all the files that were downloaded. Then, change the current working directory to the one containing the freshly downloaded code:

```
cd qt5
```

Then you need to run a Perl script that will set up all the additional repositories for you. If you don't have Perl installed, you should do that now (you can get Perl for Windows from `http://www.activestate.com/activeperl/downloads`). Then, issue the following command:

```
perl init-repository
```

The script will start downloading all the modules required for Qt and should complete successfully after a period dependent on your network link speed.

What just happened?

At this point in the `qt5` directory, you have a number of subdirectories for different Qt modules (some of them were mentioned in *Chapter 1, Introduction to Qt*) each with a local Git repository containing the source code for the respective Qt modules and tools. Each of the modules can be updated separately if required.

Time for action – configuring and building Qt

Having the sources in place, we can start building the framework. To do that, in addition to a supported compiler, you will need Perl and Python (Version 2.7 or later) installed. For Windows, you will also need Ruby. If you are missing any of the tools, it's a good time to install them. Afterwards, open the command line and change the current working directory to the one containing the Qt source code. Then, issue the following command:

```
configure -opensource -nomake tests
```

This will launch a tool that detects whether all the requirements are met and will report any inconsistencies. It will also report the exact configuration of the build. You can customize the build (for example, if you need to enable or disable some features or cross-compile Qt for an embedded platform) by passing additional options to `configure`. You can see the available options by running `configure` with the `-help` switch.

If `configure` reports problems, you will have to fix them and restart the tool. Otherwise, start the build process by invoking `make` (or an equivalent like `mingw32-make` if using MinGW or `nmake` if using MSVC).

> Instead of `nmake`, you can use a tool called `jom` that is bundled with Qt. It will reduce the compilation time on multicore machines, which is what the default `nmake` tool can't do. For `make` and `mingw32-make`, you can pass the `-j N` parameter, where `N` stands for the number of cores in your machine.

What just happened?

After some time (usually less than an hour), if all goes well, the build should be complete and you will be ready to add the compiled framework to the list of kits available in Qt Creator.

> In Unix systems after the build gets completed, you can invoke a `make` install command with super-user privileges (obtained for example, with `sudo`) to copy the framework to a more appropriate place.

Summary

By now, you should be able to install Qt on your development machine. You can now use Qt Creator to browse the existing examples and learn from them or to read the Qt reference manual to gain additional knowledge. You can also just start a new C++ project and start writing code for it, build, and execute it. Once you become an experienced Qt developer, you will also be able to make your own custom build of Qt. In the next chapter, we will finally start using the framework and you will learn how to create graphical user interfaces by implementing our very first simple game.

3

Qt GUI Programming

This chapter will help you learn how to use Qt to develop applications with a graphical user interface using the Qt Creator IDE. We will get familiar with the core Qt functionality, property system, and the signals and slots mechanism that we will later use to create complex systems such as games. We will also cover the various actions and resource system of Qt. By the end of this chapter, you will be able to write your own programs that communicate with the user through windows and widgets.

Windows and dialogs

The most basic skill that you need to learn is creating windows, showing them on a screen, and managing their content.

Creating a Qt project

The first step to develop an application with Qt Creator is to create a project using one of the templates provided by the editor.

Time for action – creating a Qt Desktop project

When you first start Qt Creator, you will see a welcome screen. From the **File** menu, choose **New File or Project**. There are a number of project types to choose from. follow the given steps for creating a Qt Desktop project:

1. For a widget-based application, choose the **Applications** group and the **Qt Gui Application** template:

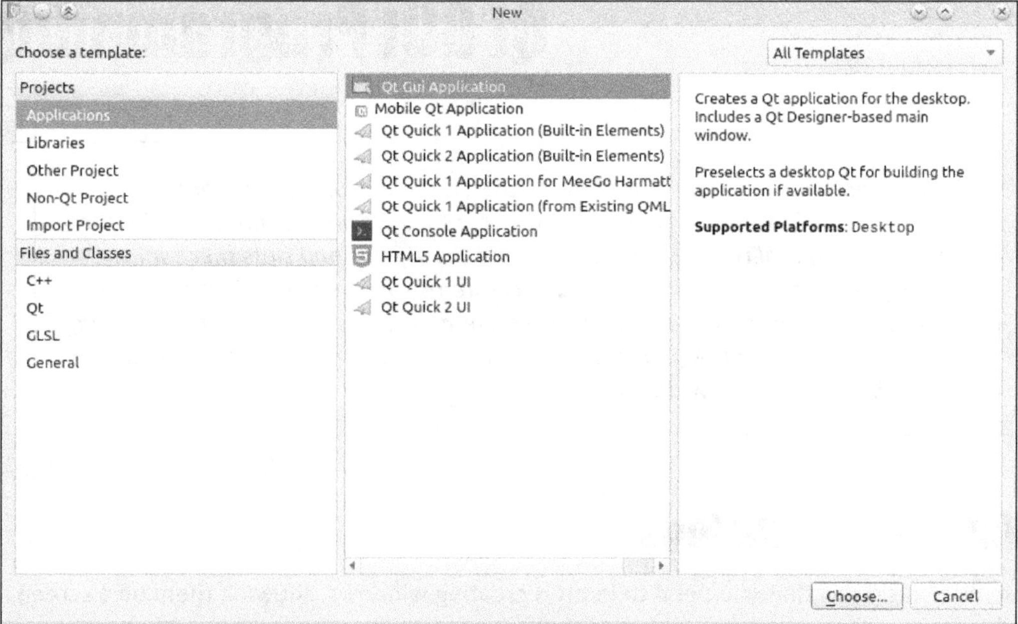

2. The next step is to choose a name and location for your new project:

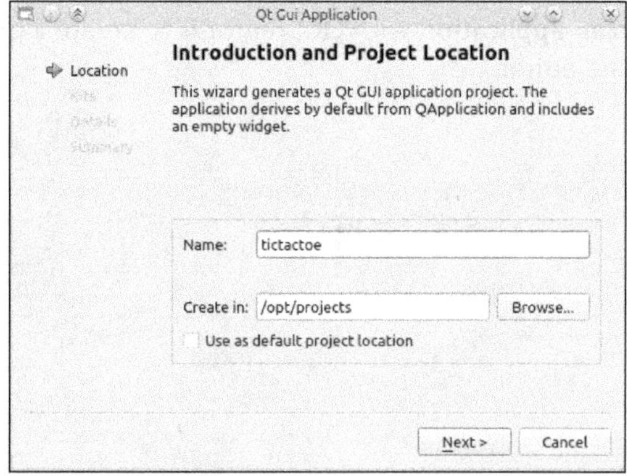

3. We are going to create a simple tic-tac-toe game, so we will name our project `tictactoe` and provide a nice location for it.

> If you have a common directory where you put all your projects, you can tick the **Use as default project location** checkbox for Creator to remember the location and suggest it the next time when you start a new project.

4. When you click on **Next**, you will be presented with a window that lets you choose one or more of the defined compilation kits for the project. Proceed to the next step without changing anything. You will be presented with the option of creating the first widget for your project. Fill in the data as shown in the following screenshot:

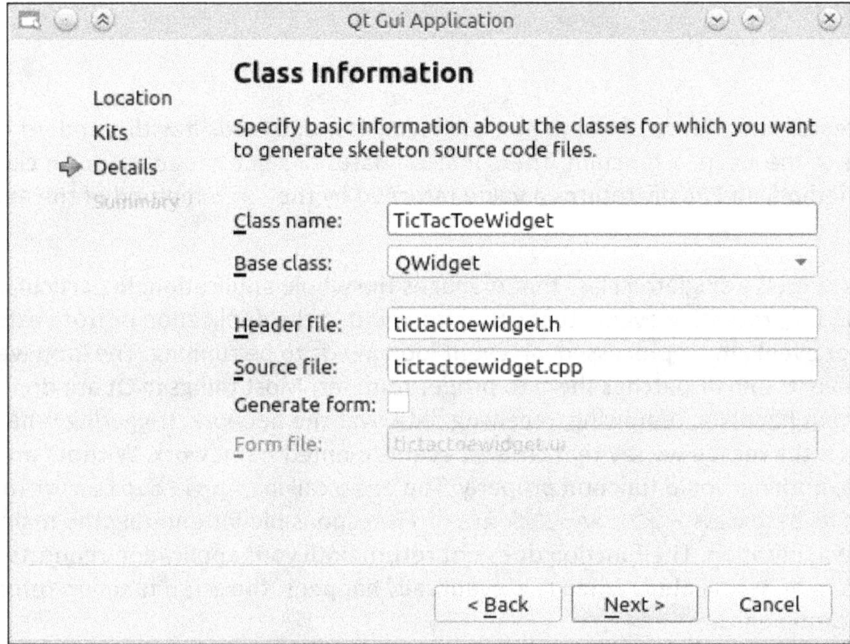

5. Then, click on **Next** and **Finish**.

What just happened?

Creator created a new subdirectory in the directory that you previously chose for the location of the project and where you put a number of files. Two of these files (`tictactoewidget.h` and `tictactoewidget.cpp`) implement the `TicTacToeWidget` class as the subclass of `QWidget`. The third file called `main.cpp` contains code for the entry point of the application:

```
#include "tictactoewidget.h"
#include <QApplication>

int main(int argc, char *argv[]) {
  QApplication a(argc, argv);
  TicTacToeWidget w;
  w.show();
  return a.exec();
}
```

This file creates an instance of the `QApplication` class and feeds it with standard arguments to the `main()` function. Then, it instantiates our `TicTacToeWidget` class, calls its `show` method, and finally returns a value returned by the `exec` method of the application object.

`QApplication` is a singleton class that manages the whole application. In particular, it is responsible for processing events that come from within the application or from external sources. For events to be processed, an event loop needs to be running. The loop waits for incoming events and dispatches them to proper routines. Most things in Qt are done through events—input handling, redrawing, receiving data over the network, triggering timers, and so on. This is the reason we say that Qt is an event-oriented framework. Without an active event loop, nothing would function properly. The `exec` call in `QApplication` (or to be more specific, in its base class—`QCoreApplication`) is responsible for entering the main event loop of the application. The function does not return until your application requests the event loop to be terminated. When this eventually happens, the `main` function returns and your application ends.

The final file that was generated is called `tictactoe.pro` and is the project configuration file. It contains all the information that is required to build your project using the tools Qt provides. Let's analyze this file:

```
QT += core gui
greaterThan(QT_MAJOR_VERSION, 4): QT += widgets
TARGET = tictactoe
TEMPLATE = app
SOURCES += main.cpp tictactoewidget.cpp
HEADERS += tictactoewidget.h
```

The first two lines enable Qt's core, gui, and widgets modules. The next two lines specify that your project file describes an application (as opposed to, for example, a library) and declares the name of the target that is executable to be tictactoe. The last two lines add files that Creator generated for us to build the process.

What we have now is a complete minimal Qt GUI project. To build and run it, simply choose the **Run** entry from the **Build** drop-down menu or click on the green triangle icon on the left-hand side of the Qt Creator window. After a while, you should see a window pop up. Since we didn't add anything to the window, it is blank.

Adding child widgets to a window

After we managed to get a blank window on screen, the next step is to add some content to it. To do this, you need to create widgets and tell Qt to position them in the window. The basic way to do this is to provide a parent to a widget.

In Qt, we group objects (such as widgets) into parent-child relationships. This scheme is defined in the superclass of QWidget—QObject, which is the most important class in Qt, and we will cover it in more detail later in this chapter. What is important now is that each object can have a parent object and an arbitrary number of children. In the case of widgets, there is a rule that a child occupies a subarea of its parent. If it doesn't have a parent, then it becomes a top-level window that can usually be dragged around, resized, and closed. We can set a parent for an object in two ways. One way is to call the setParent method defined in QObject that accepts a QObject pointer. Because of the rule mentioned earlier, QWidget wants to have other widgets as parents, so the method is overloaded in QWidget to accept a QWidget pointer. The other way is to pass a pointer to the parent object to the QWidget constructor of the child object. If you look at the code of the widget that was generated by Creator, you will notice that the constructor also accepts a pointer to a widget as its last (optional) argument:

```
TicTacToeWidget::TicTacToeWidget(QWidget *parent)
    : QWidget(parent)
{
}
```

It then passes that pointer to the constructor of its base class. Therefore, it is important that you always remember to create a constructor for your widgets that accepts a pointer to a QWidget instance and passes it up the inheritance tree. All standard Qt widgets also behave this way.

Managing widget content

Making a widget display as part of its parent is not enough to make a good user interface. You also need to set its position and size and react to the changes that happen to its content and to the content of its parent widget. In Qt, we do this using a mechanism called layouts.

Layouts allow us to arrange the content of a widget, making sure that its space is used efficiently. When we set a layout on a widget, we can start adding widgets and even other layouts, and the mechanism will resize and reposition them according to the rules that we specify. When something happens in the user interface that influences how widgets should be displayed (for example, the button text is replaced with longer text, which makes the button require more space to show its content; if not, one of the widgets gets hidden), the layout is triggered again, which recalculates all positions and sizes and updates widgets as necessary.

Qt comes with a predefined set of layouts that are derived from the `QLayout` class, but you can also create your own. Those that we already have at our disposal are `QHBoxLayout` and `QVBoxLayout`, which position items horizontally and vertically; `QGridLayout`, which arranges items in a grid so that an item can span across columns or rows; and `QFormLayout`, which creates two columns of items with item descriptions in one column and item content in the other. There is also `QStackedLayout`, which is rarely used directly and which makes one of the items assigned to it possess all the available space. You can see the most common layouts in action in the following figure:

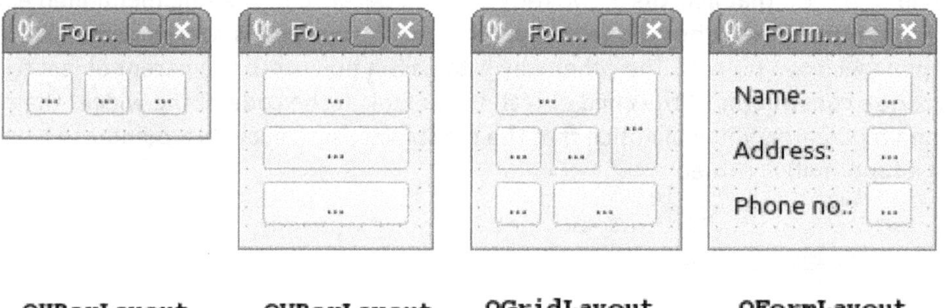

QHBoxLayout **QVBoxLayout** **QGridLayout** **QFormLayout**

To use a layout, we need to create an instance of it and pass a pointer to a widget that we want it to manage. Then, we can start adding widgets to the layout:

```
QHBoxLayout *layout = new QHBoxLayout(parentWidget);
QPushButton *button1 = new QPushButton;
QPushButton *button2 = new QPushButton;
layout->addWidget(button1);
layout->addWidget(button2);
```

We can even move widgets further from each other by setting spacing on the layout and setting custom margins on the layout:

```
layout->setSpacing(10);
layout->setMargins(10, 5, 10, 5); // left, top, right, bottom
```

After building and running this code, you see two buttons that are evenly distributed in their parent space. Note that, even though we didn't explicitly pass the parent widget pointer, adding a widget to a layout makes it reparent the newly added widget to the widget that the layout manages. Resizing the parent horizontally would also cause buttons to resize again, covering all the space available. However, if you resize `parentWidget` vertically, buttons will change their position but not their height.

This is because each widget has an attribute called a size policy, which decides how a widget is to be resized by a layout. You can set separate size policies for horizontal and vertical directions. A button has a vertical size policy of `Fixed`, which means that the height of the widget will not change from the default height regardless of how much space there is available. The following are the available size policies:

- `Ignore`: In this, the default size of the widget is ignored and the widget can freely grow and shrink
- `Fixed`: In this, the default size is the only allowed size of the widget
- `Preferred`: In this, the default size is the desired size, but both smaller and bigger sizes are acceptable
- `Minimum`: In this, the default size is the smallest acceptable size for the widget, but the widget can be made larger without hurting its functionality
- `Maximum`: In this, the default size is the largest size of the widget and the widget can be shrunk (even to nothing) without hurting its functionality
- `Expanding`: In this, the default size is the desired size; a smaller size (even zero) is acceptable but the widget is able to increase its usefulness when more and more space is assigned to it
- `MinimumExpanding`: This is a combination of `Minimum` and `Expanding`—the widget is greedy in terms of space and it cannot be made smaller than its default size

How do we determine the default size? The answer is by the size returned by the `sizeHint` virtual method. For layouts, the size is calculated based on the sizes and size policies of their child widgets and nested layouts. For basic widgets, the value returned by `sizeHint` depends on the content of the widget. In the case of a button, if it holds a line of text and an icon, `sizeHint` will return the size that is required to fully encompass the text, icon, some space between them, the button frame, and the padding between the frame and content itself.

Time for action – implementing a tic-tac-toe game board

We will now create a widget that implements a game board for tic-tac-toe using buttons.

Open the `tictactoewidget.h` file in Creator and update it by adding the highlighted code:

```
#ifndef TICTACTOEWIDGET_H
#define TICTACTOEWIDGET_H
#include <QWidget>
class QPushButton;

class TicTacToeWidget : public QWidget
{
  Q_OBJECT

public:
  TicTacToeWidget(QWidget *parent = 0);
  ~TicTacToeWidget();
private:
  QList<QPushButton*> board;
};
#endif // TICTACTOEWIDGET_H
```

Our additions create a list that can hold pointers to instances of the `QPushButton` class, which is the most commonly used button class in Qt. It will represent our game board. We have to teach the compiler to understand the classes that we use; thus, we add a forward declaration of the `QPushButton` class.

The next step is to create a method that will help us create all the buttons and use a layout to manage their geometries. Go to the header file again and add a `void setupBoard();` declaration in the `private` section of the class. To quickly implement a freshly declared method, we can ask Qt Creator to create the skeleton code for us by positioning the text cursor just before after the method declaration (before the semicolon), pressing *Alt* + *Enter* on the keyboard, and choosing **Add definition in tictactoewidget.cpp** from the pop-up.

It also works the other way around. You can write the method body first and then position the cursor on the method signature, press *Alt* + *Enter*, and choose **Add public declaration** from the quick fix menu. There are also various other context-dependent fixes that are available in Creator.

Because in the header file we only forward-declared `QPushButton`, we now need to provide a full class definition for it by including an appropriate header file. In Qt, all classes are declared in the header files that are called exactly the same as the classes themselves. Thus, to include a header file for `QPushButton`, we need to add a `#include <QPushButton>` line to the implementation file. We are also going to use the `QGridLayout` class to manage the space in our widget, so we need `#include <QGridLayout>` as well.

> From now on, this book will not remind you about adding the `include` directives to your source code—you will have to take care of this by yourself. This is really easy, just remember that to use a Qt class, you need to include a file named after that class.

Now, let's add the code to the body of the `setupBoard` method. First, let's create a layout that will hold our buttons:

```
QGridLayout *gridLayout = new QGridLayout;
```

Then, we can start adding buttons to the layout:

```
for(int row = 0; row < 3; ++row) {
  for(int column = 0; column < 3; ++column) {
    QPushButton *button = new QPushButton;
    button->setSizePolicy(QSizePolicy::Minimum,
      QSizePolicy::Minimum);
    button->setText(" ");
    gridLayout->addWidget(button, row, column);
    board.append(button);
  }
}
```

The code creates a loop over rows and columns of the board. In each iteration, it creates an instance of the `QPushButton` class and sets the button's size policy to `Minimum/Minimum` so that when we resize the widget, buttons also get resized. A button is assigned a single space as its content so that it gets the correct initial size. Then, we add the button to the layout in `row` and `column`. At the end, we store the pointer to the button in the list that was declared earlier. This lets us reference any of the buttons later on. They are stored in the list in such an order that the first three buttons of the first row are stored first, then the buttons from the second row, and finally those from the last row.

The last thing to do is to tell our widget that `gridLayout` is going to manage its size:

```
setLayout(gridLayout);
```

Alternatively, we might have passed this as a parameter to the layout's constructor.

Now that we have code that will prepare our board, we need to have it invoked somewhere. A good place to do this is the class constructor:

```
TicTacToeWidget::TicTacToeWidget(QWidget *parent)
        : QWidget(parent)
{
  setupBoard();
}
```

Now, build and run the program.

What just happened?

You should get a window containing nine buttons positioned in a grid-like fashion. If you start resizing the window, the buttons are going to be resized as well. This is because we set a grid layout with three columns and three rows that evenly distributes widgets in the managed area, as shown in the following figure:

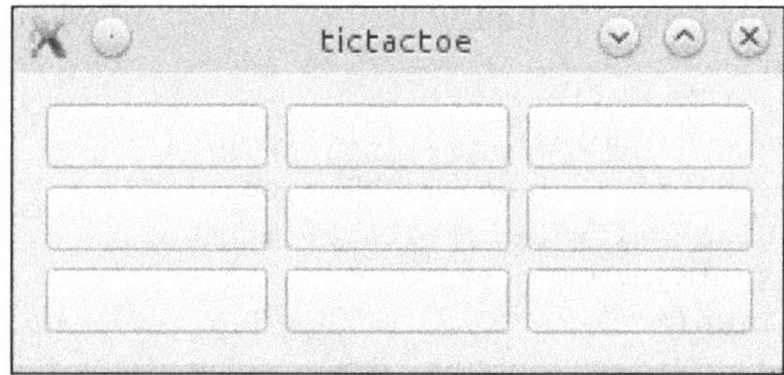

While we're here, add another `public` method to the class and name it `initNewGame`. We will use this method to clear the board when a new game is started. The body of the method should look as follows:

```
void TicTacToeWidget::initNewGame() {
  for(int i=0; i<9; ++i) board.at(i)->setText(" ");
}
```

> You might have noticed that although we created a number of objects in `setupBoard` using the `new` operator, we didn't destroy those objects anywhere (for example, in the destructor). This is because of the way the memory is managed by Qt. Qt doesn't do any garbage collecting (as Java does), but it has this nice feature related to `QObject` parent-child hierarchies. The rule is that whenever a `QObject` instance is destroyed, it also deletes all its children. Since both the layout object and the buttons are the children of the `TicTacToeWidget` instance, they will all be deleted when the main widget is destroyed. This is another reason to set parents to the objects that we create—if we do this, we don't have to care about explicitly freeing any memory.

Qt meta-objects

Most of the special functionality that Qt offers revolves around the `QObject` class and the meta-object paradigm that we will take a closer look at now. The paradigm says that with every `QObject` subclass, there is a special object associated that contains information about that class. It allows us to make runtime queries to learn useful things about the class—the class name, superclass, constructors, methods, fields, enumerations, and so on. The meta-object is generated for the class at compile time when three conditions are met:

- The class is a descendant of `QObject`
- It contains a special `Q_OBJECT` macro in a private section of its definition
- Code of the class is preprocessed by a special **Meta-Object Compiler** (**moc**) tool

We can comply to the first two conditions ourselves by writing proper code for the class just like Qt Creator does when we create a class derived from `QObject`. The last condition is met automatically when you use a tool chain that comes with Qt (and Qt Creator) to build your project. Then, it is enough to make sure that the file containing the class definition is added to the `HEADERS` variable of the project file and Qt will take care of the rest. What really happens is that moc generates some code for us that is later compiled in the main program.

All features discussed in this section of the chapter require a meta-object for the class. Therefore, it is essential to make sure that the three conditions I mentioned are met if you want a class to use any of those features.

Signals and slots

To trigger functionality as a response to something that happens in an application, Qt uses a mechanism of signals and slots. This is based on connecting a notification (which we call a **signal**) about a change of state in some object with a function or method (called a **slot**) that is executed when such a notification arises.

Signals and slots can be used with all classes that inherit `QObject`. A signal can be connected to a slot, member function, or functor (which includes a regular global function). When an object emits a signal, any of these entities that are connected to that signal will be called. A signal can also be connected to another signal in which case, emitting the first signal will make the other signal be emitted as well. You can connect any number of slots to a single signal and any number of signals to a single slot.

A signal slot connection is defined by the following four attributes:

- An object that changes its state (sender)
- A signal in the sender object
- An object that contains the function to be called (receiver)
- A slot in the receiver

To declare a signal, we put its declaration, that is, a regular member function declaration in a special class scope called signals. However, we don't implement such a function—this will be done automatically by moc. To declare a slot, we put the declaration in the class scope of either public slots, protected slots, or private slots. Slots are regular methods and can be called directly in code just like any other method. Contrary to signals, we need to provide bodies for slot methods.

A sample class implementing some signals and slots looks like as shown in the following code:

```
class ObjectWithSignalsAndSlots : public QObject {
  Q_OBJECT
public:
  ObjectWithSignalsAndSlots(QObject *parent = 0) : QObject(parent) {
  }
public slots:
  void setValue(int v) { … }
  void setColor(QColor c) { … }
private slots:
  void doSomethingPrivate();
signals:
```

```
    void valueChanged(int);
    void colorChanged(QColor);
};

void ObjectWithSignalsAndSlots::doSomethingPrivate() {
    // ...
}
```

Signals and slots can be connected and disconnected dynamically using the `connect()` and `disconnect()` statements.

The classic `connect` statement looks as follows:

```
connect(spinBox, SIGNAL(valueChanged(int)), dial,
  SLOT(setValue(int)));
```

This statement establishes a connection between `SIGNAL` of the `spinBox` object called `valueChanged` that carries an `int` parameter and a `setValue` slot in the `dial` object that accepts an `int` parameter. It is forbidden to put variable names or values in a `connect` statement. You can only make a connection between a signal and slot that have matching signatures, which means that they accept the same types of arguments (any type casts are not allowed, and type names have to match exactly) with the exception that the slot can omit an arbitrary number of last arguments. Therefore, the following `connect` statement is valid:

```
connect(spinBox, SIGNAL(valueChanged(int)), lineEdit,
  SLOT(clear()));
```

This is because the parameter of the `valueChanged` signal can be discarded before `clear` is called. However, the following statement is invalid:

```
connect(button, SIGNAL(clicked()), lineEdit,
  SLOT(setText(QString)));
```

There is nowhere to get the value that is to be passed to `setText`, so such a connection will fail.

It is important that you wrap signal and slot signatures into the `SIGNAL` and `SLOT` macros and that when you specify signatures, you only pass argument types and not values or variable names. Otherwise, the connection will fail.

Since Qt 5, there are a couple of different connect syntax available that don't require a meta-object for the class implementing the slot. The `QObject` legacy is still a requirement though, and the meta-object is still required for the class that emits the signal.

The first additional syntax that we can use is the one where we pass a pointer to the signal method and a pointer to the slot method instead of wrapping signatures in the `SIGNAL` and `SLOT` macros:

```
connect(button, &QPushButton::clicked, lineEdit,
  &QLineEdit::clear);
```

In this situation, the slot can be any member function of any `QObject` subclass that has argument types that match the signal or such that can be converted to match the signal. This means that you can, for example, connect a signal carrying a double value with a slot taking an int parameter:

```
class MyClass : public QObject {
  Q_OBJECT
public:
  MyClass(QObject *parent = 0) : QObject(parent) {
    connect(this, &MyClass::somethingHappened, this,
      &MyClass::setValue);
  }
  void setValue(int v) { … }
signals:
  void somethingHappened(double);
};
```

An important aspect is that you cannot freely mix meta-object-based and function-pointer-based approaches. If you decide to use pointers to member methods in a particular connection, you have to do that for both the signal and the slot.

We can even go a step further and have a signal connected to a standalone function:

```
connect(button, &QPushButton::clicked, &someFunction);
```

If you use C++11, the function can also be a lambda expression in which case, it is possible to write the body of the slot directly in the `connect` statement:

```
connect(pushButton, SIGNAL(clicked()), []()
  { std::cout << "clicked!" << std::endl; });
```

It is especially useful if you want to invoke a slot with a fixed argument value that can't be carried by a signal because it has less arguments. A solution is to invoke the slot from a lambda function (or a standalone function):

```
connect(pushButton, SIGNAL(clicked()), [label]()
  { label->setText("button was clicked"); });
```

A function can even be replaced with a function object (functor). To do this, we create a class for which we overload the call operator that is compatible with the signal that we wish to connect to, as shown in the following snippet:

```
class Functor {
public:
  Functor(Object *object, const QString &str) :
    m_object(object), m_str(str) {}
  void operator()(int x, int y) const {
    m_object->set(x, y, m_str);
  }
private:
  Object *m_object;
  QString m_str;
};

connect(obj1, SIGNAL(coordChanged(int, int)),
        Functor("Some Text"));
```

This is often a nice way to execute a slot with an additional parameter that is not carried by the signal, as this is much cleaner than using a lambda expression.

There are some aspects of signals and slots that we have not covered here. We will come back to them later when we deal with multithreading.

Pop quiz – making signal-slot connections

Q1. For which of the following do you have to provide your own implementation?

1. A signal
2. A slot
3. Both

Q2. Which of the following statements are valid?

1. `connect(sender, SIGNAL(textEdited(QString)), receiver, SLOT(setText("foo")))`
2. `connect(sender, SIGNAL(toggled(bool)), receiver, SLOT(clear()));`
3. `connect(sender, SIGNAL(valueChanged(7)), receiver, SLOT(setValue(int)));`
4. `connect(sender, &QPushButton::clicked, receiver, &QLineEdit::clear);`

Time for action – functionality of a tic-tac-toe board

We need to implement a function that will be called upon by clicking on any of the nine buttons on the board. It has to change the text of the button that was clicked on—either `X` or `O`—based on which player made the move; then, it has to check whether the move resulted in winning the game by the player (or a draw if no more moves are possible), and if the game ended, it should emit an appropriate signal, informing the environment about the event.

When the user clicks on a button, the `clicked()` signal is emitted. Connecting this signal to a custom slot lets us implement the mentioned functionality, but since the signal doesn't carry any parameters, how do we tell which button caused the slot to be triggered? We could connect each button to a separate slot but that's an ugly solution. Fortunately, there are two ways of working around this problem. When a slot is invoked, a pointer to the object that caused the signal to be sent is accessible through a special method in `QObject` called `sender()`. We can use that pointer to find out which of the nine buttons stored in the board list is the one that caused the signal to fire:

```
void TicTacToeWidget::someSlot() {
  QObject *btn = sender();
  int idx = board.indexOf(btn);
  QPushButton *button = board.at(idx);
  // ...
}
```

While `sender()` is a useful call, we should try to avoid it in our own code as it breaks some principles of object-oriented programming. Moreover, there are situations where calling this function is not safe. A better way is to use a dedicated class called `QSignalMapper`, which lets us achieve a similar result without using `sender()` directly. Modify the `setupBoard()` method in `TicTacToeWidget` as follows:

```
QGridLayout *gridLayout = new QGridLayout;
QSignalMapper *mapper = new QSignalMapper(this);
for(int row = 0; row < 3; ++row) {
  for(int column = 0; column < 3; ++column) {
    QPushButton *button = new QPushButton;
    button->setSizePolicy(QSizePolicy::Minimum,
                          QSizePolicy::Minimum);
    button->setText(" ");
    gridLayout->addWidget(button, row, column);
    board.append(button);
    mapper->setMapping(button, board.count()-1);
    connect(button, SIGNAL(clicked()), mapper, SLOT(map()));
  }
}
```

```
connect(mapper, SIGNAL(mapped(int)), this,
  SLOT(handleButtonClick(int)));
setLayout(gridLayout);
```

Here, we first created an instance of `QSignalMapper` and passed a pointer to the board widget as its parent so that the mapper is deleted when the widget is deleted. Then, when we create buttons, we "teach" the mapper that each of the buttons has a number associated with it—the first button will have the number `0`, the second one will be bound to the number `1`, and so on. By connecting the `clicked()` signal from the button to mapper's `map()` slot, we tell the mapper to do its magic upon receiving that signal. What the mapper will do is that it will then find the mapping of the sender of the signal and emit another signal—`mapped()`—with the mapped number as its parameter. This allows us to connect to that signal with a slot (`handleButtonClick`) that takes the index of the button in the board list.

Now it is time to implement the slot itself (remember to declare it in the header file!). However, before we do that, let's add a useful enum and a few helper methods to the class:

```
enum Player {
  Invalid, Player1, Player2, Draw
};
```

This enum lets us specify information about players in the game. We can use it immediately to mark whose move it is now. To do so, add a private field to the class:

```
Player m_currentPlayer;
```

Then, add the two public methods to manipulate the value of this field:

```
Player currentPlayer() const { return m_currentPlayer; }
void setCurrentPlayer(Player p) {
  if(m_currentPlayer == p) return;
  m_currentPlayer = p;
  emit currentPlayerChanged(p);
}
```

The last method emits a signal, so we have to add the signal declaration to the class definition along with another signal that we are going to use:

```
signals:
  void currentPlayerChanged(Player);
  void gameOver(TicTacToeWidget::Player);
```

Note that we only emit the `currentPlayerChanged` signal when the current player really changes. You always have to pay attention that you don't emit a "changed" signal when you set a value to a field to the same value that it had before the function was called. Users of your classes expect that if a signal is called changed, it is emitted when the value really changes. Otherwise, this can lead to an infinite loop in signal emissions if you have two objects that connect their value setters to the other object's changed signal.

Now let's declare the `handleButtonClick` slot:

```
public slots:
    void handleButtonClick(int);
```

And then implement it in the `.cpp` file:

```
void TicTacToeWidget::handleButtonClick(int index) {
  if(index < 0 || index >= board.size()) return;
    // out of bounds check
  QPushButton *button = board.at(index);
  if(button->text() != " ") return;
    // invalid move
  button->setText(currentPlayer() == Player1 ? "X" : "O");
  Player winner = checkWinCondition(index / 3, index % 3);
  if(winner == Invalid) {
    setCurrentPlayer(currentPlayer() == Player1 ? Player2 : Player1);
    return;
  } else {
    emit gameOver(winner);
  }
}
```

Here, we first retrieve a pointer to the button based on its index. Then, we check whether the button contains any text—if so, then this means that it doesn't participate in the game anymore, so we return from the method so that the player can pick another field in the board. Next, we set the current player's mark on the button. Then, we check whether the player has won the game, passing it the row (`index / 3`) and column (`index % 3`) index of the current move. If the game didn't end, we switch the current player and return. Otherwise, we emit a `gameOver()` signal, telling our environment who won the game. The `checkWinCondition()` method returns `Player1`, `Player2`, or `Draw` if the game has ended and `Invalid` otherwise. We will not show the implementation of this method here as it is quite complex. Try implementing it on your own and if you encounter problems, you can see the solution in the code bundle that accompanies this book.

Properties

Apart from signals and slots, Qt meta-objects also give programmers an ability to use the so-called properties that are essentially named attributes that can be assigned values of a particular type. They are useful to express important features of an object—like text of a button, size of a widget, player names in games, and so on.

Declaring a property

To create a property, we first need to declare it in a private section of a class that inherits `QObject` using a special `Q_PROPERTY` macro, which lets Qt know how to use the property. A minimal declaration contains the type of the property, its name, and information about a method name that is used to retrieve a value of the property. For example, the following code declares a property of the type `double` that is called `height` and uses a method called `height` to read the property value:

```
Q_PROPERTY(double height READ height)
```

The getter method has to be declared and implemented as usual. Its prototype has to comply with these rules: it has to be a public method that returns a value or constant reference of a type of the property, and it can't take any input parameters and the method itself has to be constant. Typically, a property will manipulate a private member variable of the class:

```
class Tower : public QObject {
  Q_OBJECT // enable meta-object generation
  Q_PROPERTY(double height READ height)
    // declare the property
  public:
    Tower(QObject *parent = 0) : QObject(parent)
      { m_height = 6.28; }
    double height() const { return m_height; }
    // return property value
  private:
    double m_height;
    // internal member variable holding the property value
};
```

Such a property is practically useless because there is no way to change its value. Luckily, we can extend the declaration to include the information about how to write a value to the property:

```
Q_PROPERTY(double height READ height WRITE setHeight)
```

Again, we have to declare and implement `setHeight` so that it behaves as the setter method for the property—it needs to be a public method that takes a value or constant reference of the type of the property and returns void:

```
void setHeight(double newHeight) { m_height = newHeight; }
```

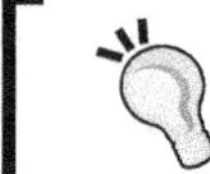

Property setters are good candidates for public slots so that you can easily manipulate property values using signals and slots.

We will learn about some of the other extensions to `Q_PROPERTY` declarations in the later chapters of this book.

Using a property

There are two ways in which you can access properties. One is of course, to use getter and setter methods that we declared with `READ` and `WRITE` keywords in the `Q_PROPERTY` macro—this will naturally work since they are regular C++ methods.

The other way is to use facilities offered by `QObject` and the meta-object system. They allow to us access properties by name using two methods that accept property names as strings. A generic property getter (which returns the property value) is a method called `property`. Its setter counterpart (that takes the value and returns void) is `setProperty`. Since we can have properties with different data types, what is the data structure that is used by those two methods that hold values for different kinds of properties? Qt has a special class for this called `QVariant`, which behaves a lot like a C union in the way that it can store values of different types. There are a couple of advantages to using a union though—the three most important are that you can ask the object what type of data it currently holds, you can convert some of the types to other types (for example, a string to an integer), and you can teach it to operate on your own custom types.

Time for action – adding properties to the board class

In this exercise, we will be adding a useful property to the board class. The property is going to hold information about the player who should make the next move. The type of the property is going to be the `TicTacToeWidget::Player` enumeration that we created earlier. For the getter and the setter methods, we are going to use the two functions that we created earlier: `currentPlayer()` and `setCurrentPlayer()`.

Open the header file for our class and modify the class definition as shown in the following code:

```
class TicTacToeWidget : public QWidget {
  Q_OBJECT
  Q_ENUMS(Player)
  Q_PROPERTY(Player currentPlayer READ currentPlayer
  WRITE setCurrentPlayer
  NOTIFY currentPlayerChanged)
public:
  enum Player { Invalid, Player1, Player2, Draw };
```

What just happened?

Since we want to use an enumeration as a type of a property, we have to inform Qt's meta-object system about the enum. This is done with the `Q_ENUMS` macro. Then, we declare a property called `currentPlayer` and mark our two existing methods as getter and setter for the property. We also use the `NOTIFY` keyword to mark `currentPlayerChanged` as a signal that is sent to inform about a change in the value of the property. We won't be using this extra information in our small game, and we don't require `currentPlayer` to be a property at all, but it is always a good idea to try and find good candidates for properties and expose them because some day, someone might want to use our class in a way we hadn't predicted and a particular property might become useful.

Designing GUIs

So far, we have coded all the user interfaces manually by writing C++ code that instantiates widgets, arranges them in layouts, and connects signals to slots. It is not that hard for simple widgets, but becomes tedious and time-consuming when the UI becomes more and more complex. Fortunately, Qt provides tools to do all this in a more pleasant way. Instead of writing C++ code, we can create forms using a graphical tool by dragging and dropping widgets on a canvas, applying layouts to them, and even establishing signal-slot connections using the point-and-click technique. Later during the compilation, such forms will get converted into C++ code for us and will be ready for applying onto a widget.

The tool is called Qt Designer and is integrated with Qt Creator. To use it, select **New File** or **Project** from the **File** menu and choose the **Qt Designer Form Class** template available after selecting Qt in the **Files and Classes** section of the dialog box. You get to choose a template for the form and configure details such as the names of the files to create. In the end, three files will get created—two of them implement a C++ class derived from `QWidget` or one of its subclasses and the last one contains data for the form itself.

After closing the wizard, we are taken to Qt Creator's **Design** mode that looks as shown in the following screenshot:

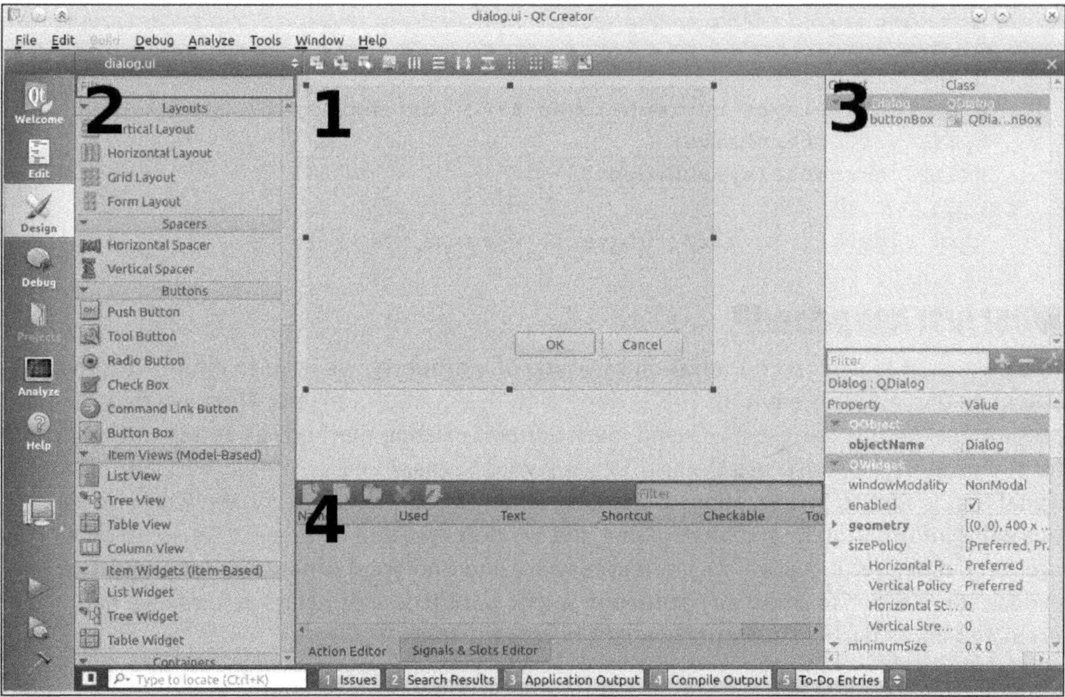

The **Design** mode consists of four major parts that are marked on the preceding figure with numbers.

The area marked as **1** is the main worksheet. It contains a graphical representation of the form being designed where you can move widgets around, compose them into layouts, and see how they react. It also allows further manipulation of the form using the point-and-click method that we will learn later.

The second area **2** is the widget box. It contains a list of available types of widget that are arranged into groups containing items with a related or similar functionality. Over the list, you can see a box that lets you filter widgets that are displayed in the list to only show those that match the entered expression. In the beginning of the list, there are also items that are not really widgets—one group contains layouts and the other one contains so-called spacers, which are a way to push other items away from each other.

The main purpose of the widget box is to add widgets to the form in the worksheet. You can do that by grabbing a widget from the list with the mouse, dragging it to the canvas, and releasing the mouse button. The widget will appear in the form and can be further manipulated with further tools in Creator's Design mode.

The next area **3**, which we are going to talk about, is situated on the right-hand side of the window and consists of two parts. At the top of the figure, you can see Object Inspector. It presents the parent-child relationship of all widgets that are currently present in the edited form. Each line contains the name of the object and the name of its class as seen by the meta-object system. If you click on an entry, a corresponding widget in the form gets selected (and vice versa).

The lower part of the figure shows the property editor. You can use it to change the values of all the properties that each object has. Properties are grouped by their classes that they have been declared in, starting from `QObject` (the base class implementing properties), which declares only one but an important property—`objectName`. Following `QObject`, there are properties declared in `QWidget`, which is a direct descendant of `QObject`. They are mainly related to the geometry and layout policies of the widget. Lower in the list, you can find properties that come from further derivations of `QWidget`. If you prefer a pure alphabetical order where properties are not grouped by their class, you can switch the view using a pop-up menu that becomes available after you click on the wrench icon positioned over the property list; however, once you get familiar with the hierarchy of Qt classes, it will be much easier to navigate the list when it is sorted by a class.

Having a closer look at the property editor, you can see that some of them have arrows beneath them that reveal new rows when clicked. These are composed properties where the complete property value is determined from more than one subproperty values; for example, if there is a property called `geometry` that defines a rectangle, it can be expanded to show four subproperties: `x`, `y`, `width`, and `height`. Another thing that you should quickly notice is that some property names are displayed in bold. This means that the property value was modified and is different from the default value for this property. This lets you quickly find those properties that you have modified.

The last group of functionality **4** that we will explain now is the one positioned in the lower part of the window. By default, you will see two tabs—**Action Editor** and **Signal/Slot Editor**. They allow us to create helper entities such as actions for the menus and toolbars or signal-slot connections between widgets using a clean tabular interface.

What was described here is the basic tool layout. If you don't like it, you can invoke the context menu from the main worksheet, uncheck the **Locked** entry, and rearrange all the windows to your liking or even close the ones you currently don't need.

Time for action – designing the game configuration dialog

Now, we will use Qt Designer forms to build a simple game configuration dialog that will let us choose names for our players.

First, invoke the new file dialog from the menu and choose to create a new **Qt Designer Form Class** as shown in the following screenshot:

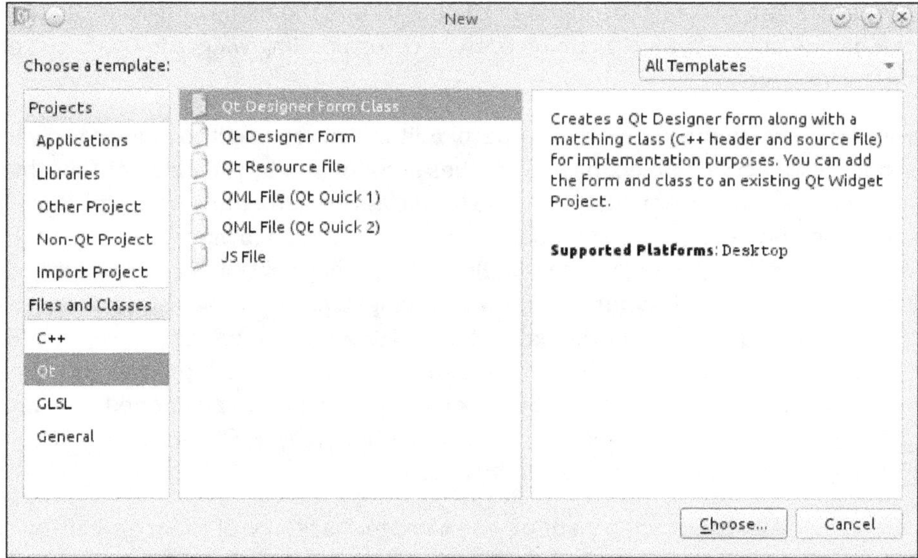

In the window that appears, choose **Dialog with Buttons Bottom**:

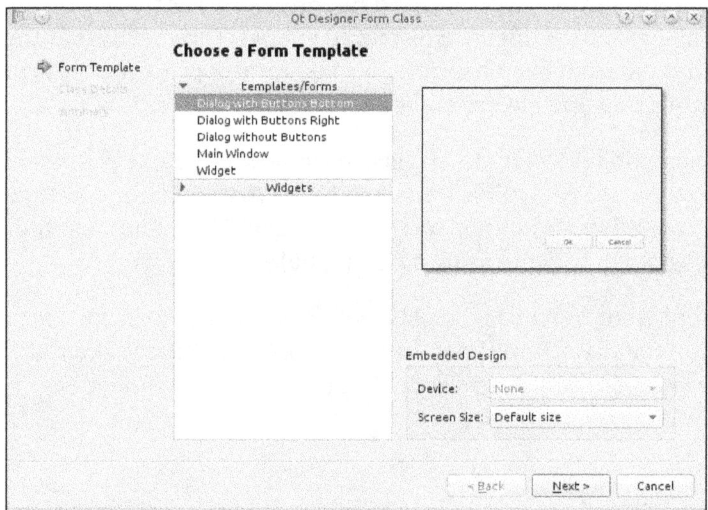

Adjust the class name to `ConfigurationDialog`, leave the rest of the settings at their default values, and complete the wizard.

Drag and drop two labels and two line edits on the form, position them roughly in a grid, double-click on each of the labels, and adjust their captions to receive a result similar to the following figure:

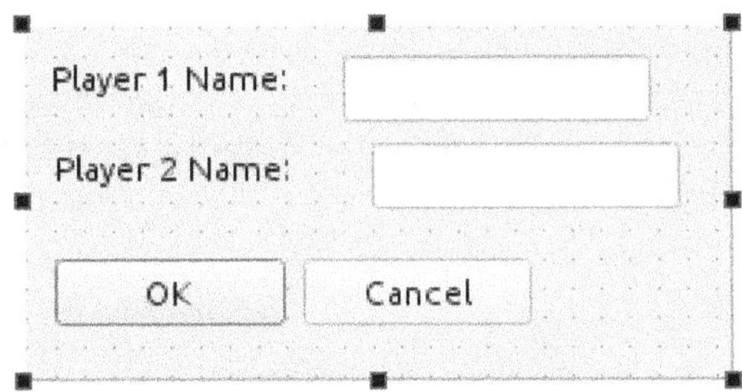

Select the first line to edit and look at the property editor. Find a property called `objectName` and change it to `player1Name`. Do the same for the other line and call it `player2Name`. Then, click on some empty space in the form and choose the **Layout in a grid** entry in the upper toolbar. You should see the widgets snap into place—that's because you have just applied a layout to the form. When you're done, open the **Tools** menu, go to the **Form Editor** submenu, and choose the **Preview** entry.

What just happened?

You can see a new window open that looks exactly like the form we just designed. You can resize the window and interact with the objects inside to monitor the behavior of the layouts and widgets. What really happened here is that Qt Creator built a real window for us based on the description that we provided in all the areas of the design mode. Without any compilation, in a blink of an eye we received a fully working window with all the layouts working and all the properties adjusted to our liking. This is a very important tool so make sure to use it often to verify that your layouts are controlling all the widgets as you intended them to—it is much faster than compiling and running the whole application just to check whether the widgets stretch or squeeze properly. It's all possible thanks to Qt's meta-object system.

Time for action – polishing the dialog

Now that the GUI itself works as we intended it to, we can focus on giving the dialog some more polish.

Accelerators and label buddies

The first thing we are going to do is add accelerators to our widgets. These are keyboard shortcuts that, when activated, cause particular widgets to gain keyboard focus or perform a predetermined action (for example, toggle a checkbox or push a button). Accelerators are usually marked by underlining them, as shown in the following figure:

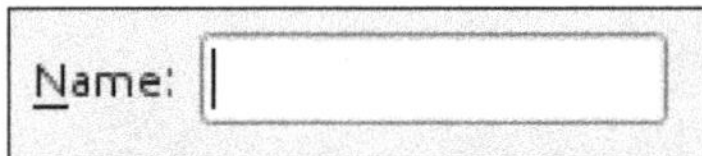

We will set accelerators to our line edits so that when the user activates an accelerator for the first field, it will gain focus. Through this we can enter the name of the first player, and similarly, when the accelerator for the second line edit is triggered, we can start typing in the name for the second player.

Start by selecting the label on the left-hand side of the first line edit. Press *F2* or double-click on the label (alternatively, find the text property of the label in the property editor and activate its value field). This enables us to change the text of the label. Navigate using cursor keys so that the text cursor is placed before the character `1` and type the `&` character. This character marks the character directly after it as an accelerator for the widget. For widgets that are composed of both text and the actual functionality (for example, a button), this is enough to make accelerators work. However, since `QLineEdit` does not have any text associated with it, we have to use a separate widget for that. This is why we have set the accelerator on the label. Now, we need to associate the label with the line edit so that the activation of the label's accelerator will forward it to the widget of our choice. This is done by setting a so-called buddy for the label. You can do this in code using the `setBuddy` method of the `QLabel` class or using Creator's form designer. Since we're already in the Design mode, we'll use the latter approach. For that, we need to activate a dedicated mode in the form designer.

Look at the upper part of Creator's window; directly above the form, you will find a toolbar containing a couple of icons. Click on the one labeled **Edit buddies** or just press *F5* on your keyboard. Now, move the mouse cursor over the label, press the mouse button, and drag from the label towards the line edit. When you drag the label over the line edit, you'll see a graphical visualization of a connection being set between the label and the line edit. If you release the button now, the association will be made permanent. You should notice that when such an association is made, the ampersand character (&) vanishes from the label and the character behind it gets an underscore. Repeat this for the other label and corresponding line edit. Now, you can preview the form again and check whether accelerators work as expected.

The tab order

While you're previewing the form, you can check another aspect of the UI design. Start by pressing the *Tab* key and see how the focus moves from widget to widget. There is a good chance that the focus will start jumping back and forth between buttons and line edits instead of a linear progress from top to bottom (which is an intuitive order for this particular dialog). To check and modify the order of focus, leave the preview and switch to the tab order editing mode by clicking on the icon called Edit Tab Order in the toolbar.

This mode associates a box with a number to each focusable widget. By clicking on the rectangle in the order you wish the widgets to gain focus, you can reorder values, thus reordering focus. Now, make it so that the order is as shown in the following figure:

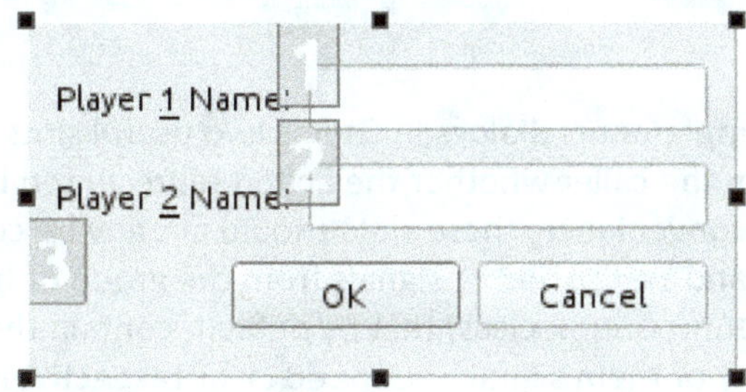

Enter the preview again and check whether the focus changes according to what you've set.

When deciding about the tab order, it is good to consider which fields in the dialog are mandatory and which are optional. It is a good habit to allow the user to tab through all the mandatory fields first, then to the dialog confirmation button (for example, one that says **OK** or **Accept**), and then cycle through all the optional fields. Thanks to this, the user will be able to quickly fill all the mandatory fields and accept the dialog without the need to cycle through all the optional fields that the user wants to leave at their default values.

Signals and slots

The last thing we are going to do right now is make sure that the signal-slot connections are set up properly. To do this, switch to the signal-slot editor mode by pressing *F4* or choosing **Edit Signals/Slots** from the toolbar. The **Dialog with Buttons Bottom** widget template predefines two connections for us, which should now become visible in the main canvas area:

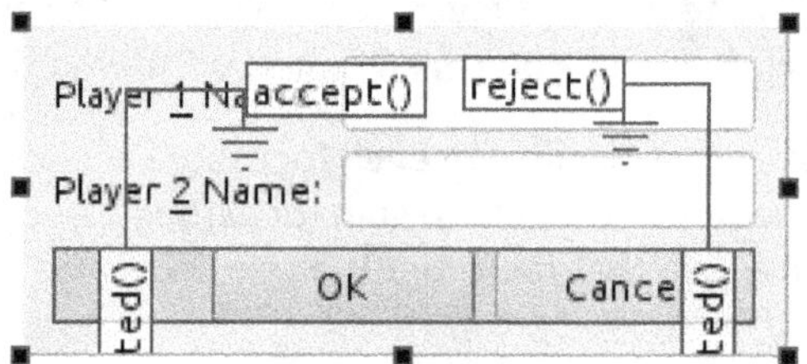

The `QDialog` class that implements dialogs in Qt has two useful slots—`accept()` and `reject()`—which inform the caller whether the action represented by the dialog was accepted or not. For our convenience, these slots should already be connected to the respective `accepted()` and `rejected()` signals from the group of buttons (which is an instance of the `QDialogButtonBox` class) that by default, contain the **OK** and **Cancel** buttons. If you click on any of them signal `accepted()` or respectively, `rejected()` will be emitted by the box.

At this point, we can add some more connections to make our dialog more functional. Let's make it such that the button to accept the dialog is only enabled when neither of the two line edits is empty (that is, when both the fields contain player names). While we will implement the logic itself later, we can now make connections to a slot that will perform the task.

Since no such slot exists by default, we need to inform the form editor that such a slot will exist at the time when the application is compiled. To do this, we need to switch back to the default mode of the form editor by pressing *F3* or choosing **Edit Widgets** from the toolbar. Then, you can invoke the form's context menu and choose **Change signals/slots**. A window will pop up such as the one shown in the following figure that lists the available signals and slots:

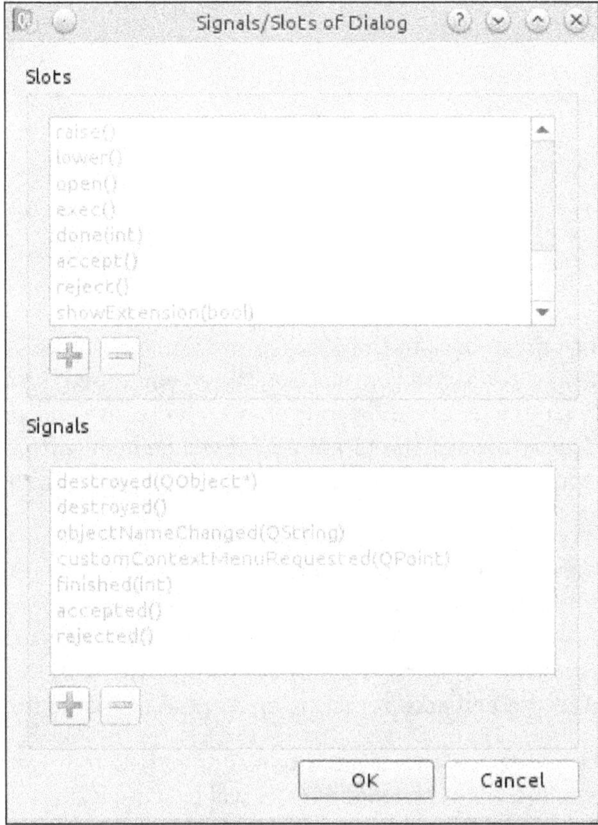

Click on the **+** button in the **Slots** group and create a slot called `updateOKButtonState()`:

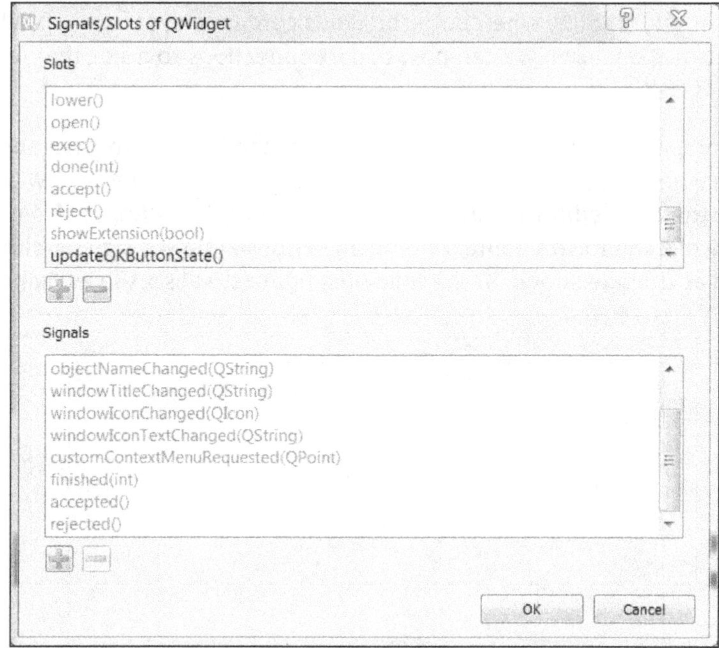

Then, accept the dialog and go back to the **Signals/Slots** mode. Create a new connection by grabbing one of the line edits with your mouse. When you move the cursor outside the widget, you will notice a red line following your pointer. If the line encounters a valid target, the line will change to an arrow and the target object will be highlighted. The form itself can also be a target (or a source); in this case, the line will end with a ground mark (two short horizontal lines).

When you release the mouse button, a window will pop up, listing all the signals of the source object and all the slots of the target object. Choose the `textChanged(QString)` signal. Note that when you do this, some of the available slots will disappear. This is because the tool only allows us to choose from slots that are compatible with the highlighted signal. Select our newly created slot and accept the dialog. Repeat the same for the other line edit.

What we have done here is that we've created two connections that will trigger when the text of either of the two line edits is changed. They will execute a slot that doesn't exist yet—by "creating" the slot, we only declared our intention to implement it in a `QDialog` subclass that was also created for us. You can now go ahead and save the form.

What just happened?

We performed a number of tasks that make our form follow standard behaviors known from many applications—this makes form navigation easy and shows the user which actions can be undertaken and which are currently not available.

Using designer forms

If you open the form in a text editor (for example, by switching to the Creator's **Edit** pane), you will notice that it is really an XML file. So how do we use this file?

As part of the build process, Qt calls a special tool called **User Interface Compiler** (**uic**) that reads the file and generates a C++ class that contains a `setupUi()` method. This method accepts a pointer to a widget and contains code, which instantiates all the widgets, sets their properties, and establishes signal-slot connections, and it is our responsibility to call it to prepare the GUI. The class itself, which is named after your form (that is after the value of the `objectName` property of the form object) with a `Ui` namespace prepended to it (for example, `Ui::MyForm`) is not derived from a widget class but is rather meant to be used with one. There are basically three ways of doing this.

Direct approach

The most basic way to use a Qt Designer form is to instantiate a widget and the form object and to call `setupUi` on the widget, like this:

```
QWidget *widget = new QWidget
Ui_form ui * = new Ui_form;
ui->setupUi(widget);
```

This approach has a number of flaws. First of all, it creates a potential memory leak of the `ui` object (remember, it is not `QObject`, so you can't set a parent to it so that it's deleted when the parent is deleted). Second, since all the widgets of the form are variables of the `ui` object that is not tied to the widget object, it breaks encapsulation, which is one of the most important paradigms of object-oriented programming. However, there is a situation when such a construct is acceptable. This is when you create a simple short-lived modal dialog. You surely need to remember that to show regular widgets, we have been using the `show()` method. This is fine for non-modal widgets, but for modal dialogs you should instead call the `exec()` method that is defined in the `QDialog` class. This is a blocking method that doesn't return until the dialog is closed. This allows us to modify the code so that it becomes:

```
QDialog dialog;
Ui_form ui;
ui.setupUi(&dialog);
dialog.exec();
```

Since we're creating objects on the stack, the compiler will take care of deleting them when the local scope ends.

The multiple-inheritance approach

The second way of using Designer forms is to create a class derived from both `QWidget` (or one of its subclasses) and the form class itself. We can then call `setupUi` from the constructor:

```
class Widget : public QWidget, private Ui::MyForm {
public:
  Widget(QWidget *parent = 0) : QWidget(parent) {
    setupUi(this);
  }
};
```

This way, we keep the encapsulation as our class inherits fields and methods from the `Ui` class, and we can call any of them directly from within the class code while restricting access from the outside world by using private inheritance. The drawback of this approach is that we pollute the class namespace, for example, if we had a name object in `Ui::MyForm`, we wouldn't be able to create a `name` method in `Widget`.

The single inheritance approach

Fortunately, we can work around this using the composition instead of inheritance. We can derive our widget class only from `QWidget` and instead of also subclassing `Ui::MyForm`, we can make an instance of it a private member of the new class:

```
class Widget : public QWidget {
public:
  Widget(QWidget *parent = 0) : QWidget(parent) {
    ui = new Ui::MyForm;
    ui->setupUi(this);
  }
  ~Widget() { delete ui; }
private:
  Ui::MyForm *ui;
};
```

At the cost of having to manually create and destroy the instance of `Ui::MyForm`, we can have the additional benefit of containing all variables and code of the form in a dedicated object, which prevents the aforementioned namespace pollution.

This is the recommended way of using Designer forms, and it's also the default mode of operation when you tell Qt Creator to generate a Designer form class for you.

Time for action – the logic of the dialog

Now, it is time to make our game settings dialog work. Earlier, we declared a signal-slot connection but now the slot itself needs to be implemented.

Open the form class generated by Creator. If you're still in the Design mode, you can quickly jump to the respective form class file using the *Shift* + *F4* keyboard shortcut. Create a public slots section of the class and declare a `void updateOKButtonState()` slot. Open the refactorization menu (*Alt* + *Enter*) and ask Creator to create the skeleton implementation of the slot for you. Fill the function body with the following code:

```
void ConfigurationDialog::updateOKButtonState() {
    bool pl1NameEmpty = ui->player1Name->text().isEmpty();
    bool pl2NameEmpty = ui->player2Name->text().isEmpty();
    QPushButton *okButton = ui->buttonBox
      ->button(QDialogButtonBox::Ok);
    okButton->setDisabled(pl1NameEmpty || pl2NameEmpty);
}
```

This code retrieves player names and checks whether either of them is empty. Then, it asks the button box that currently contains the **OK** and **Cancel** buttons to give a pointer to the button that accepts the dialog. Then, we set the button's disabled state based on whether both player names contain valid values or not. The button state also needs to be updated when we first create the dialog, so add invocation of `updateOKButtonState()` to the constructor of the dialog:

```
ConfigurationDialog::ConfigurationDialog(QWidget *parent) :
  QDialog(parent), ui(new Ui::ConfigurationDialog)
{
  ui->setupUi(this);
  updateOKButtonState();
}
```

The next thing to do is to allow to store and read player names from outside the dialog—since the `ui` component is private, there is no access to it from outside the class code. This is a common situation and one that Qt is also compliant with. Each data field in almost every Qt class is private and may contain accessors (a getter and optionally a setter), which are public methods that allow to read and store values for data fields. Our dialog has two such fields—the names for the two players. At this point, we should note that they are good candidates for properties so at the end, we'll declare them as such. But first, let's start by implementing the accessors.

Setter methods in Qt are usually named using the lowercase pattern, for example, `set` followed by the name of the property with the first letter converted to uppercase. In our situation, the two setters will be called `setPlayer1Name` and `setPlayer2Name` and they will both accept `QString` and return `void`. Declare them in the class header as shown in the following code snippet:

```
void setPlayer1Name(const QString &p1name);
void setPlayer2Name(const QString &p2name);
```

Implement their bodies in the `.cpp` file:

```
void ConfiguratiosDialog::setPlayer1Name(const QString &p1name) {
  ui->player1Name->setText(p1name);
}
void ConfigurationDialog::setPlayer2Name(const QString &p2name) {
 ui->player2Name->setText(p2name);
}
```

Getter methods in Qt are usually called the same as the property that they are related to—`player1Name` and `player2Name`. Put the following code in the header file:

```
QString player1Name() const;
QString player2Name() const;
```

Put the following code in the implementation file:

```
QString ConfigurationDialog::player1Name() const
  { return ui->player1Name->text(); }
QString ConfigurationDialog::player2Name() const
  { return ui->player2Name->text(); }
```

The only thing left to do now is to declare the properties. Add the highlighted lines to the class declaration:

```
class ConfigurationDialog : public QDialog {
  Q_OBJECT
  Q_PROPERTY(QString player1Name READ
    player1Name WRITE setPlayer1Name)
  Q_PROPERTY(QString player2Name READ
    player2Name WRITE setPlayer2Name)
public:
  ConfigurationDialog(QWidget *parent = 0);
```

Our dialog is now ready. You can test it by creating an instance of it in `main()` and calling `show()` or `exec()`.

An application's main window

We already have two major components in our game—the game board and configuration dialog. Now, we will need to bind them together. To do this, we will use another important component—the `QMainWindow` class. A "main window" represents the control center of an application. It can contain menus, toolbars, docking widgets, a status bar, and the actual widget content called a "central widget", as presented in the following diagram:

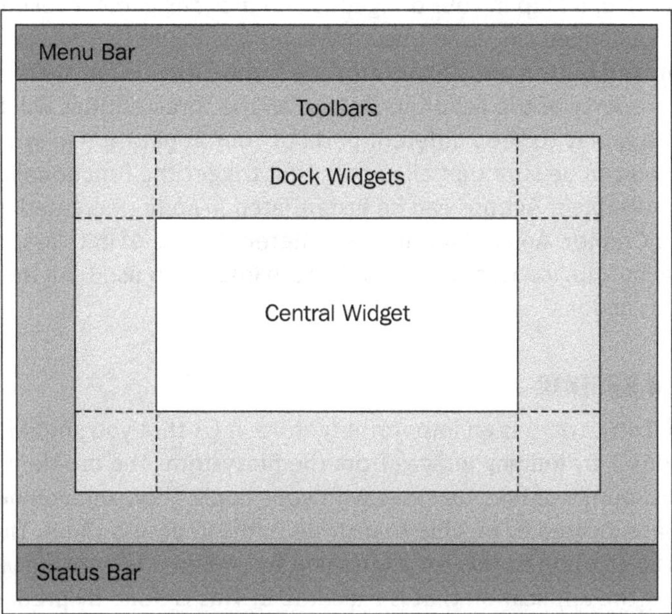

The central widget part doesn't need any extra explanation—it is a regular widget like any other. We will also not focus on dock widgets or the status bar here. They are useful components but they are so easy to master that you can learn about them yourself. Instead, we will spend some time mastering menus and toolbars. You have surely seen and used toolbars and menus in many applications and you know how important they are for good user experience.

The main hero shared by both these concepts is a class called `QAction`, which represents a functionality that can be invoked by a user. A single action can have more than one incarnation—it can be an entry in a menu (the `QMenu` instances), a toolbar (`QToolBar`), button, or keyboard shortcut (`QShortcut`). Manipulating the action (for example, changing its text) causes all its incarnations to update. For example, if you have a **Save** entry in the menu (with a keyboard shortcut bound to it), a Save icon in the toolbar, and maybe also a **Save** button somewhere else in your user interface and you want to disallow saving the document (for example, a map in your dungeons and dragons game level editor) because its contents haven't changed since the document was last loaded. In this case, if, the menu entry, toolbar icon, and button are all linked to the same `QAction` instance then, once you set the `enabled` property of the action to `false`, all the three entities will become disabled as well. This is an easy way to keep different parts of your application in sync—if you disable an action object, you can be sure that all entries that trigger the functionality represented by the action are also disabled. Actions can be instantiated in code or created graphically using **Action Editor** in Qt Creator. An action can have different pieces of data associated with it—a text, tooltip, status bar tip, icons, and others that are less often used. All these are used by incarnations of your actions.

The Qt resource system

While speaking of icons, there is an important feature in Qt that you should learn. A natural way of creating icons is by loading images from the filesystem. The problem with this is that you have to install a bunch of files together with your application and you need to always know where they are located to be able to provide paths to access them. This is difficult but fortunately, Qt has a solution to this—it allows you to embed arbitrary files (such as images for icons) directly in the application that is executable. This is done by preparing resource files that are later compiled in the binary. Fortunately, Qt Creator provides a graphical tool for this as well.

Time for action – the main window of the application

Create a new **Qt Designer Form Class** application. As a template, choose **Main Window**. Accept the default values for the rest of the wizard.

Create an action using the action editor and enter the following values in the dialog:

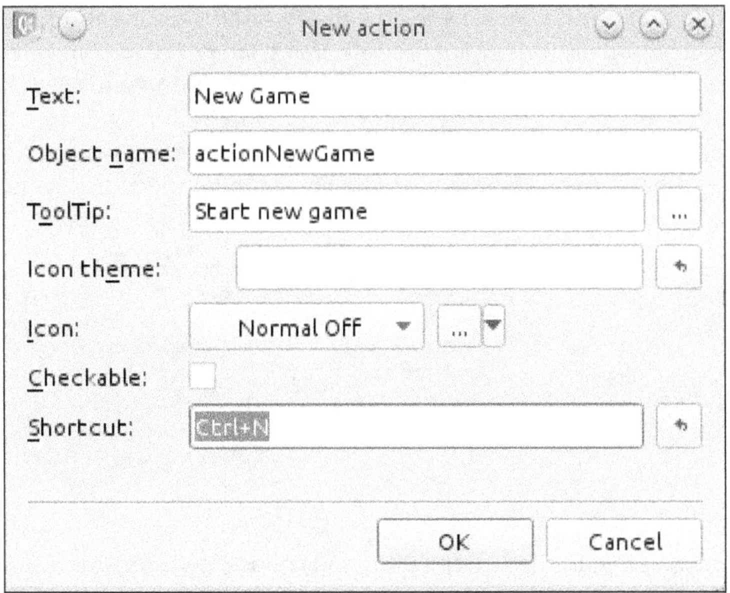

Now, create another action and fill it with the values shown in the following screenshot:

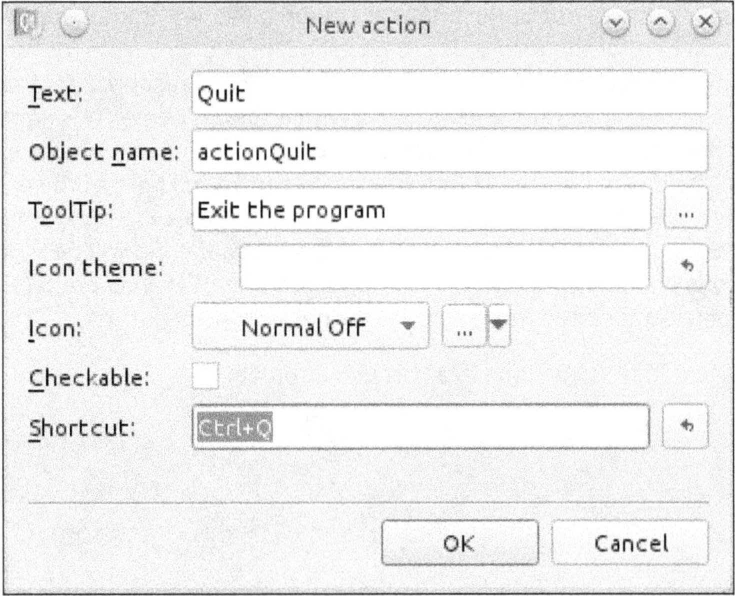

We want our game to look nice, so we will provide icons for the actions and we will embed images for them in our application using the resource system. Create a new file and make it **Qt Resource File**. Call it `resources.qrc`. Click on the **Add** button and choose **Add Prefix**. Change the value for the prefix to /. Then, click on the **Add** button again and choose **Add Files**. Find appropriate images for your actions and add them to the resource file. A dialog will appear asking whether you want to copy the files to the project directory. Agree by choosing **Copy**.

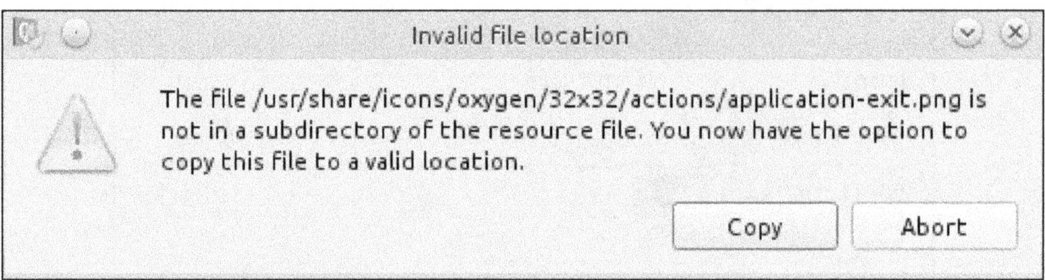

Now, edit the actions again in the Action Editor and choose icons for them.

What just happened?

We added a resource file to our project. In that resource file, we created entries for a number of images. Each of the images is put under a / prefix, which stands for the root node of the artificial filesystem that we create. Each entry in a resource file can be accessed directly from the manually written code as a file with a special name. This name is assembled from three components. First comes a colon character (`:`), which identifies the resource filesystem. This is followed by a prefix (for example, /) and a full path of the entry in the resource (for example, `exit.png`). This makes an image called `exit.png` accessible through the `:/exit.png` path. When we build the project, the file will be transformed into a C data array code and integrated with the application binary. Having prepared the resource file, we used images embedded there as icons for our actions.

The next step is to add these actions to a menu and toolbar.

Time for action – adding a pull-down menu

To create a menu for the window, double-click on the **Type Here** text on the top of the form and replace the text with `&File`. Then, drag the **New Game** action from the action editor over the newly created menu but do not drop it there yet. The menu should open now and you can drag the action so that a red bar appears in the submenu in the position where you want the menu entry to appear—now you can release the mouse button to create the entry. Afterwards, open the menu again by clicking on **File** and choose **Add Separator**. Then, repeat the drag-and-drop operation for the **Quit** action to insert a menu entry for it just below the separator in the **File** menu, as shown in the following figure:

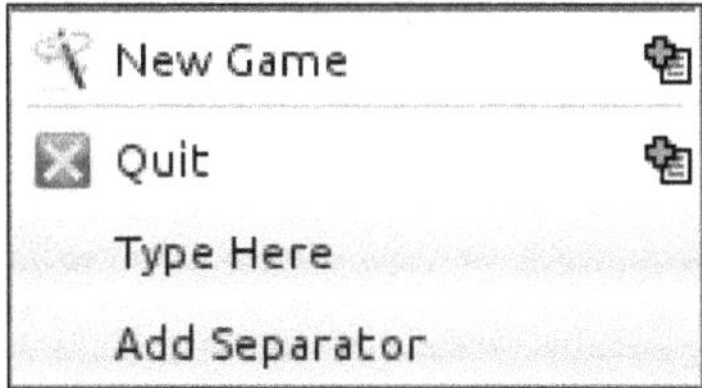

What just happened?

Using graphical tools, we created a menu for our program and added a number of actions (that were automatically transformed into menu items) to that menu. Each menu entry received some text and an icon specified by the action that was dropped in the menu.

> To create submenus, first create a menu entry by clicking on the **Type Here** line and entering the submenu name. Then, drag and hover an action over such a submenu. After a short time, a submenu will pop up and you will be able to drop your action there to create an entry in the second-level menu.

Time for action – creating a toolbar

To create a toolbar, invoke the context menu on the form and choose **Add Tool Bar**. Then, drag the **New Game** action over the toolbar and drop it there. Open a context menu for the toolbar and choose **Append Separator**. Then, drag the **Quit** action from the Action Editor and drop it in the toolbar behind the separator. The following figure presents the final layout that you should have now:

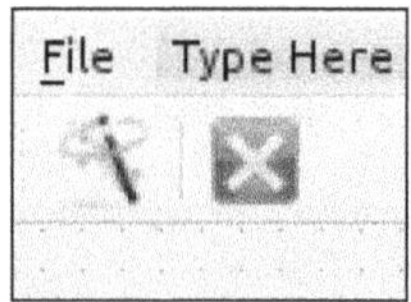

What just happened?

Creating toolbars is very similar to creating menus. You first create the container (the toolbar) and then drag-and-drop actions from the action editor. You can even drag an action from the menu bar and drop it on the toolbar and vice versa!

Time for action – filling in the central widget

Add two labels in the main window area—one at the top for the first player name and one at the bottom of the form for the second player name—and then change their `objectName` property to `player1` and `player2`, respectively. Clear their text property so that they don't display anything. Then, drag **Widget** from the widget box, drop it between the two labels' and set its object name to `gameBoard`. Invoke the context menu on the widget that you just dropped and choose **Promote to**. This allows us to substitute a widget in the form with another class; in our case, we will want to replace the empty widget with our game board. Fill the dialog that has just appeared with the values shown in the following figure:

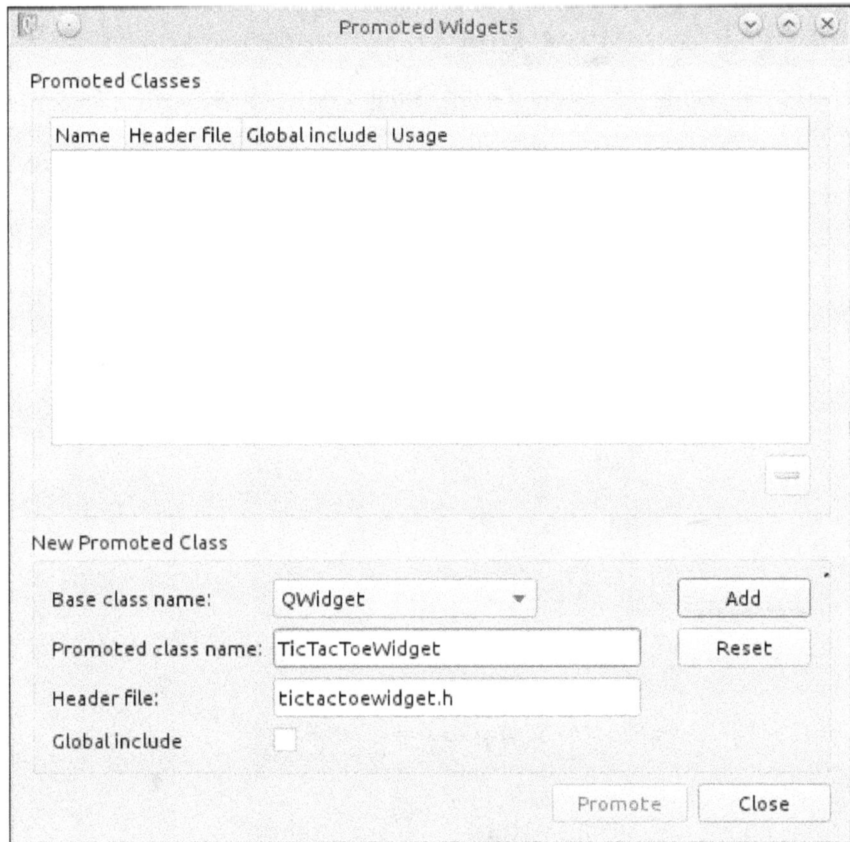

Then, click on the button labeled **Add** and then **Promote** to close the dialog and confirm the promotion. You will not notice any changes in the form because the replacement only takes place during compilation. Now, apply a vertical layout on the form so that the labels and the empty widget snap into place.

What just happened?

Not all widget types are directly available in the form designer. Sometimes, we need to use widget classes that will only be created in the project that is being built. The simplest way to be able to put custom widgets on a form is to ask the designer to replace class names with some of the objects when C++ code for the form is to be generated. By promoting an object to a different class, we saved a lot of work trying to otherwise fit our game board into the user interface.

Time for action – putting it all together

The visual part of the game is ready and what remains is to complete the logic of the main window and put all the pieces together. Add a public slot to the class and call it `startNewGame`. In the class constructor, connect the **New Game** action's triggered signal to this slot and connect the application's quit slot to the other action:

```
connect(ui->actionNewGame, SIGNAL(triggered()),
        this, SLOT(startNewGame()));
connect(ui->actionQuit, SIGNAL(triggered()),
        qApp, SLOT(quit()));
```

The `qApp` special macro represents a pointer to the application object instance, so the preceding code will call the `quit()` slot on the `QApplication` object created in `main()`, which in turn will eventually cause the application to end.

Let's implement the `startNewGame` slot as follows:

```
void MainWindow::startNewGame() {
  ConfigurationDialog dlg(this);
  if(dlg.exec() == QDialog::Rejected) {
    return; // do nothing if dialog rejected
  }
  ui->player1->setText(dlg.player1Name());
  ui->player2->setText(dlg.player2Name());
  ui->gameBoard->initNewGame();
  ui->gameBoard->setEnabled(true);
}
```

In this slot, we create the settings dialog and show it to the user, forcing him to enter player names. If the dialog was canceled, we abandon the creation of a new game. Otherwise, we ask the dialog for player names and set them on appropriate labels. Finally, we initialize the board and enable it so that users can interact with it.

While writing a turn-based board game, it is a good idea to always clearly mark whose turn it is now to make a move. We will do this by marking the moving player's name in bold. There is already a signal in the board class that tells us that a valid move was made, which we can react to in order to update the labels. Let's add an appropriate code into the constructor of the main window class:

```
connect(ui->gameBoard, SIGNAL(currentPlayerChanged(Player)),
        this, SLOT(updateNameLabels()));
```

Now for the slot itself; let add a private slot's section to the class and declare the slot there:

```
private slots:
  void updateNameLabels();
```

Now, we can implement it:

```
void MainWindow::updateNameLabels() {
  QFont f = ui->player1->font();
  f.setBold(ui->gameBoard->currentPlayer() ==
    TicTacToeWidget::Player1);
  ui->player1->setFont(f);
  f.setBold(ui->gameBoard->currentPlayer() ==
    TicTacToeWidget::Player2);
  ui->player2->setFont(f);
}
```

In addition to the slot being called after a signal is emitted, we can also use it to set the initial data for the labels when the game is starting. Since all the slots are also regular methods, we can simply call `updateNameLabels()` from `startNewGame()`—go ahead and invoke `updateNameLabels()` at the end of `startNewGame()`.

The last thing that needs to be done is to handle the situation when the game ends. Connect the `gameOver()` signal from the board to a new slot in the main window class. Implement the slot as follows:

```
void MainWindow::handleGameOver(TicTacToeWidget::Player winner) {
  ui->gameBoard->setEnabled(false);
  QString message;
  if(winner == TicTacToeWidget::Draw) {
    message = "Game ended with a draw.";
  } else {
    message = QString("%1 wins").arg(winner ==
      TicTacToeWidget::Player1
    ? ui->player1->text() : ui->player2->text());
  }
  QMessageBox::information(this, "Info", message);
}
```

What just happened?

Our code does two things. First, it disables the board so that players can no longer interact with it. Second, it checks who won the game, assembles the message (we will learn more about `QString` in the next chapter), and shows it using a static method `QMessageBox::information()` that shows a modal dialog containing the message and a button that allows us to close the dialog. The last thing that remains is to update the `main()` function in order to create an instance of our `MainWindow` class:

```
#include "mainwindow.h"
#include <QApplication>
int main(int argc, char *argv[])
{
  QApplication a(argc, argv);
  MainWindow w;
  w.show();
  return a.exec();
}
```

Now, you can run your first Qt game.

Have a go hero – extending the game

As an additional exercise, you can try to modify the code we have written in this chapter to allow playing the game on boards bigger than 3 x 3. Let the user decide about the size of the board (you can modify the game options dialog for that and use `QSlider` and `QSpinBox` to allow the user to choose the size of the board) and you can then instruct `TicTacToeWidget` to build the board based on the size it gets. Remember to adjust the game winning logic! If at any point you run into a dead end and do not know which classes and functions to use, consult the reference manual.

To quickly find the documentation for a class (or any other page in the docs), switch to the **Help** pane, choose **Index** from the drop-down list on top of the sidebar, and type in the search term, such as `QAction`. Also, the *F1* key is very helpful for browsing the manual. Position the mouse pointer or text cursor in the code editor over the name of a class, function, or object and press *F1* on your keyboard. By doing this, Qt Creator will happily show you the available help information on the chosen subject.

Pop quiz – using widgets

Q1. A method that returns the preferred size of a widget is called:

1. `preferredSize`
2. `sizeHint`
3. `defaultSize`

Q2. What is the name of a Qt class that can carry values for any property?

1. `QVariant`
2. `QUnion`
3. `QPropertyValue`

Q3. What is the purpose of the `QAction` object?

1. It represents a functionality that a user can invoke in the program.
2. It holds a key sequence to move the focus on a widget.
3. It is a base class for all forms generated using Qt Designer.

Summary

In this chapter, you learned how to create simple graphical user interfaces with Qt. We went through two approaches—creating user interface classes by writing all the code directly and designing the user interface with a graphical tool that generates most of the code for us. There is no telling which of the two approaches is better; each of them is better in some areas and worse in others. In general, you should prefer using Qt Designer forms to write code directly because it's faster and less prone to errors as most of the code is generated. However, if you want to retain more control over the code or your GUI is highly dynamic, writing all the code yourself will be easier, especially when you gain enough experience with Qt to avoid common pitfalls and learn to use advanced programming constructs.

We also learned how the heart of Qt—the meta-object system—works. You should now be able to create simple user interfaces and fill them with logic by connecting signals to slots—predefined ones as well as custom ones that you now know how to define and fill with code.

Qt contains many widget types but I didn't introduce them to you one by one. There is a really nice explanation of many widget types in the Qt manual called *Qt Widget Gallery*, which shows most of them in action.

If you have any doubts about using any of those widgets, you can check the example code and also look up the appropriate class in the Qt reference manual to learn more about them.

Using Qt is much more than just dragging-and-dropping widgets on forms and providing some code to glue the pieces together. In the next chapter, you will learn about some of the most useful functionalities that Qt has to offer; they do not relate to showing graphics on screen, but rather let you manipulate various kind of data. This is essential for any game that is more complicated than a simple tic-tac-toe.

4
Qt Core Essentials

This chapter will help you master Qt ways of basic data processing and storage. First of all, you will learn how to handle textual data and how to match text against regular expressions. Then, you will see how to store and fetch data from files and how to use different storage formats for text and binary data. By the end of this chapter, you will be able to implement non-trivial logic and data processing in your games efficiently. You will also know how to load external data in your games and how to save your own data in permanent storage for future use.

Text handling

Applications with a graphical user interface (and games surely fall into this category) are able to interact with users by displaying text and by expecting textual input from the user. We have already scratched the surface of this topic in the previous chapter by using the `QString` class. Now, we will go into more details.

Manipulating strings

Text in Qt is internally encoded using Unicode, which allows to represent characters in almost all languages spoken in the world and is de facto standard for native encoding of text in most modern operating systems. You have to be aware though that contrary to the `QString` class, the C++ language does not use Unicode by default. Thus, each string literal (that is, each bare text you wrap in quotation marks) that you enter in your code needs to be converted to Unicode first before it can be stored in any of Qt's string handling classes. By default, this is done implicitly assuming that the string literal is UTF-8 encoded, but `QString` provides a number of static methods to convert from other encodings such as `QString::fromLatin1()` or `QString::fromUtf16()`. This conversion is done at runtime, which adds an overhead to the program execution time, especially if you tend to do a lot of such conversions in your programs. Luckily, there is a solution for this:

```
QString str = QStringLiteral("I'm writing my games using Qt");
```

You can wrap your string literal in a call to `QStringLiteral`, as shown in the preceding code, which if your compiler supports, will perform the conversion at compile time. It's a good habit to wrap all your string literals into `QStringLiteral` but it is not required, so don't worry if you forget to do that.

We will not go into great detail here when describing the `QString` class, as in many aspects it is similar to `std::string`, which is part of the standard C++. Instead, we will focus on the differences between the two classes.

Encoding and decoding text

The first difference has already been mentioned—`QString` keeps the data encoded as Unicode. This has the advantage of being able to express text in virtually any language at the cost of having to convert from other encodings. Most popular encodings—UTF-8, UTF-16, and Latin1—have convenience methods in `QString` for converting from and to the internal representation. But, Qt knows how to handle many other encodings as well. This is done using the `QTextCodec` class.

You can list the codecs supported on your installation by using the `QTextCodec::availableCodecs()` static method. In most installations, Qt can handle almost 1,000 different text codecs.

Most Qt entities that handle text can access instances of this class to transparently perform the conversion. If you want to perform such conversion manually, you can ask Qt for an instance of a codec by its name and make use of the `fromUnicode()` and `toUnicode()` methods:

```
QByteArray big5Encoded = "你好";
QTextCodec *big5Codec = QTextCodec::codecForName("Big5");
QString text = big5Codec->toUnicode(big5Encoded);
QTextCodec *utf8Codec = QTextCodec::codecForMib(106); // UTF-8
QByteArray utf8Encoded = utf8Codec->fromUnicode(text);
```

Basic string operations

The most basic tasks that involve text strings are those where you add or remove characters from the string, concatenate strings, and access the string's content. In this regard, `QString` offers an interface that is compatible with `std::string`, but it also goes beyond that, exposing many more useful methods.

Adding data at the beginning or at the end of the string can be done using the `prepend()` and `append()` methods, which have a couple of overloads that accept different objects that can hold textual data, including the classic `const char*` array. Inserting data in the middle of a string can be done with the `insert()` method that takes the position of the character where we need to start inserting as its first argument and the actual text as its second argument. The `insert` method has exactly the same overloads as `prepend` and `append`, excluding `const char*`. Removing characters from a string is similar. The basic way to do this is to use the `remove()` method that accepts the position at which we need to delete characters and the number of characters to delete is as shown:

```
QString str = QStringLiteral("abcdefghij");
str.remove(2, 4); // str = "abghij"
```

There is also a remove overload that accepts another string. When called, all its occurrences are removed from the original string. This overload has an optional argument that states whether comparison should be done in the default case-sensitive (`Qt::CaseSensitive`) or case-insensitive (`Qt::CaseInsensitive`) way:

```
QString str = QStringLiteral("Abracadabra");
str.remove(QStringLiteral("ab"), Qt::CaseInsensitive);
// str = "racadra"
```

To concatenate strings, you can either simply add two strings together or you can append one string to the other:

```
QString str1 = QStringLiteral("abc");
QString str2 = QStringLiteral("def");
QString str1_2 = str1+str2;
QString str2_1 = str2;
str2_1.append(str1);
```

Accessing strings can be divided into two use cases. The first is when you wish to extract a part of the string. For this, you can use one of these three methods: `left()`, `right()`, and `mid()` that return the given number of characters from the beginning or end of the string or extract a substring of a specified length, starting from a given position in the string:

```
QString original = QStringLiteral("abcdefghij");
QString l = original.left(3); // "abc"
QString r = original.right(2); // "ij"
QString m = original.mid(2, 5); // "cdefg"
```

The second use case is when you wish to access a single character of the string. The use of the index operator works with `QString` in a similar fashion as with `std::string`, returning a copy or non-const reference to a given character that is represented by the `QChar` class, as shown in the following code:

```
QString str = "foo";
QChar f = str[0]; // const
str[0] = 'g'; // non-const
```

In addition to this, Qt offers a dedicated method—`at()`—that returns a copy of the character:

```
QChar f = str.at(0);
```

> You should prefer to use `at()` instead of the index operator for operations that do not modify the character, as this explicitly sets the operation.

The string search and lookup

The second group of functionality is related to searching for the string. You can use methods such as `startsWith()`, `endsWith()`, and `contains()` to search for substrings in the beginning or end or in an arbitrary place in the string. The number of occurrences of a substring in the string can be retrieved by using the `count()` method.

Be careful, there is also a `count()` method that doesn't take any parameters and returns the number of characters in the string.

If you need to know the exact position of the match, you can use `indexOf()` or `lastIndexOf()` to receive the position in the string where the match occurs. The first call works by searching forward and the other one searches backwards. Each of these calls takes two optional parameters—the second one determines whether the search is case-sensitive (similar to how `remove` works). The first one is the position in the string where the search begins. It lets you find all the occurrences of a given substring:

```
#include <QtDebug>
// ...
int pos = -1;
QString str = QStringLiteral("Orangutans like bananas.");
do {
  pos = str.indexOf("an", pos+1);
  qDebug() << "'an' found starts at position" << pos;
} while(pos!=-1);
```

Dissecting strings

There is one more group of useful string functionalities that makes `QString` different from `std::string`. That is, cutting strings into smaller parts and building larger strings from smaller pieces.

Very often, a string contains substrings that are glued together by a repeating separator. A common case is the **Comma-separated Values** (**CSV**) format where a data record is encoded in a single string where fields in the record are separated by commas. While you could extract each field from the record using functions that you already know (for example, `indexOf`), an easier way exists. `QString` contains a `split()` method that takes the separator string as its parameter and returns a list of strings that are represented in Qt by the `QStringList` class. Then, dissecting the record into separate fields is as easy as calling the following code:

```
QString record = "1,4,8,15,16,24,42";
QStringList fields = record.split(",");
for(int i=0; i< fields.count(); ++i){
  qDebug() << fields.at(i);
}
```

The inverse of this method is the `join()` method present in the `QStringList` class, which returns all the items in the list as a single string merged together with a given separator:

```
QStringList fields = { "1", "4", "8", "15", "16", "24", "42" };
  // C++11 syntax!
QString record = fields.join(",");
```

Converting between numbers and strings

`QString` also provides some methods for convenient conversion between textual and numerical values. Methods such as `toInt()`, `toDouble()`, or `toLongLong()` make it easy to extract numerical values from strings. Apart from `toDouble()`, they all take two optional parameters—the first one is a pointer to a `bool` variable that is set to `true` or `false` depending on whether the conversion was successful or not. The second parameter specifies the numerical base (for example, binary, octal, decimal, or hexadecimal) of the value. The `toDouble()` method only takes a `bool` pointer to mark the success or failure as shown in the following code:

```
bool ok;
int v1 = QString("42").toInt(&ok, 10);
  // v1 = 42, ok = true
long long v2 = QString("0xFFFFFF").toInt(&ok, 16);
  // v2 = 16777215, ok = true
double v3 = QString("not really a number").toDouble(&ok);
  //v3 = 0.0, ok = false
```

A static method called `number()` performs the conversion in the other direction—it takes a numerical value and number base and returns the textual representation of the value:

```
QString txt = QString::number(255, 16); // txt = "0xFF"
```

If you have to combine both `QString` and `std::string` in one program, `QString` offers you the `toStdString()` and `fromStdString()` methods to perform an adequate conversion.

> Some of the other classes that represent values also provide conversions to and from `QString`. An example of such a class is `QDate`, which represents a date and provides the `fromString()` and `toString()` methods.

Using arguments in strings

A common task is to have a string that needs to be dynamic in such a way that its content depends on the value of some external variable—for instance, you would like to inform the user about the number of files being copied, showing "copying file 1 of 2" or "copying file 2 of 5" depending on the value of counters that denote the current file and total number of files. It might be tempting to do this by assembling all the pieces together using one of the available approaches:

```
QString str = "Copying file " + QString::number(current)
  + " of "+QString::number(total);
```

There are a number of drawbacks to such an approach; the biggest of them is the problem of translating the string into other languages (this will be discussed later in this chapter) where in different languages their grammar might require the two arguments to be positioned differently than in English.

Instead, Qt allows us to specify positional parameters in strings and then replace them with real values. Positions in the string are marked with the `%` sign (for example, `%1`, `%2`, and so on) and they are replaced by making a call to `arg()` and passing it the value that is used to replace the next lowest marker in the string. Our file copy message construction code then becomes:

```
QString str = QStringLiteral("Copying file %1 of %2")
                                        .arg(current).arg(total);
```

The `arg` method can accept single characters, strings, integers, and real numbers and its syntax is similar to that of `QString::number()`.

Regular expressions

Let's briefly talk about **regular expressions**—usually shortened as **regex** or **regexp**. You will need these regular expressions whenever you have to check whether a string or parts of it matches a given pattern or when you want to find specific parts inside the text and possibly want to extract them. Both the validity check and the finding/extraction are based on the so-called pattern of the regular expression, which describes the format a string must have to be valid, to be found, or to be extracted. Since this book is focused on Qt, there is unfortunately no time to cover regular expressions in depth. This is not a huge problem, however, since you can find plenty of good websites that provide introductions to regular expressions on the Internet. A short introduction can be found in Qt's documentation of `QRegExp` as well.

Even though there are many flavors of the regular expression's syntax, the one that Perl uses has become the *de facto* standard. According to `QRegularExpression`, Qt offers Perl-compatible regular expressions.

> `QRegularExpression` was first introduced with Qt 5. In the previous versions, you'll find the older `QRegExp` class. Since `QRegularExpression` is closer to the Perl standard and since its execution speed is much faster compared to `QRegExp`, we advise you to use `QRegularExpression` whenever possible. Nevertheless, you can read the `QRegExp` documentation about the general introduction of regular expressions.

Time for action – a simple quiz game

To introduce you to the main usage of `QRegularExpression`, let's imagine this game: a photo, showing an object, is shown to multiple players and each of them has to estimate the object's weight. The player whose estimate is closest to the actual weight wins. The estimates will be submitted via `QLineEdit`. Since you can write anything in a line edit, we have to make sure that the content is valid.

So what does valid mean? In this example, we define that a value between 1 g and 999 kg is valid. Knowing this specification, we can construct a regular expression that will verify the format. The first part of the text is a number, which can be between 1 and 999. Thus, the corresponding pattern looks like `[1-9][0-9]{0,2}`, where `[1-9]` allows—and demands—exactly one digit, except zero, which is optionally followed by up to two digits including zero. This is expressed through `[0-9]{0,2}`. The last part of the input is the weight's unit. With a pattern such as `(mg|g|kg)`, we allow the weight to be input in **milligrams (mg)**, **grams (g)**, or **kilograms (kg)**. With `[ ]?`, we finally allow an optional space between the number and unit. Combined together, the pattern and construction of the related `QRegularExpression` object looks like this:

```
QRegularExpression regex("[1-9][0-9]{0,2}[ ]? (mg|g|kg)");
regex.setPatternOptions(QRegularExpression:: CaseInsensitiveOption);
```

What just happened?

In the first line, we constructed the aforementioned `QRegularExpression` object while passing the regular expression's pattern as a parameter to the constructor. We also could have called `setPattern()` to set the pattern:

```
QRegularExpression regex;
regex.setPattern("[1-9][0-9]{0,2}[ ]?(mg|g|kg)");
```

Both the approaches are equivalent. If you have a closer look at the unit, you can see that right now, the unit is only allowed to be entered in lowercase. We want, however, to also allow it to be in uppercase or mixed case. To achieve this, we can of course write `(mg|mG|Mg|MG|g|G|kg|kG|Kg|KG)`. Not only is this a hell of a work when you have more units, this is also very error-prone, and so we opt for a cleaner and more readable solution. On the second line of the initial code example, you see the answer: a pattern option. We used `setPatternOptions()` to set the `QRegularExpression::CaseInsensitiveOption` option, which does not respect the case of the characters used. Of course, there are a few more options that you can read about in Qt's documentation on `QRegularExpression::PatternOption`. Instead of calling `setPatternOptions()`, we could have also passed the option as a second parameter to the constructor of `QRegularExpression`:

```
QRegularExpression regex("[1-9][0-9]{0,2}[ ]?(mg|g|kg)",
           QRegularExpression::CaseInsensitiveOption);
```

Now, let's see how to use this expression to verify the validity of a string. For the sake of simplicity and better illustration, we simply declared a string called `input`:

```
QString input = "23kg";
QRegularExpressionMatch match = regex.match(input);
bool isValid = match.hasMatch();
```

All we have to do is call `match()`, passing the string we would like to check against it. In return, we get an object of the `QRegularExpressionMatch` type that contains all the information that is further needed—and not only to check the validity. With `QRegularExpressionMatch::hasMatch()`, we then can determine whether the input matches our criteria, as it returns `true` if the pattern could be found. Otherwise, of course, `false` is returned.

Attentive readers surely will have noticed that our pattern is not quite finished. The `hasMatch()` method would also return `true` if we matched it against "foo 142g bar". So, we have to define that the pattern is checked from the beginning to the end of the matched string. This is done by the `\A` and `\z` anchors. The former marks the start of a string and the latter the end of a string. Don't forget to escape the slashes when you use such anchors. The correct pattern would then look as follows:

```
QRegularExpression regex("\\A[1-9][0-9]{0,2}[ ]?(mg|g|kg)\\z",
           QRegularExpression::CaseInsensitiveOption);
```

Extracting information out of a string

After we have checked that the sent guess is well formed, we have to extract the actual weight from the string. In order to be able to easily compare the different guesses, we further need to transform all values to a common reference unit. In this case, it should be a milligram, the lowest unit. So, let's see what `QRegularExpressionMatch` can offer us for this task.

With `capturedTexts()`, we get a string list of the pattern's captured groups. In our example, this list would contain "23kg" and "kg". The first element is always the string that was fully matched by the pattern followed by all the sub strings captured by the used brackets. Since we are missing the actual number, we have to alter the pattern's beginning to `([1-9][0-9]{0,2})`. Now, the list's second element is the number and the third element is the unit. Thus, we can write the following:

```
int getWeight(const QString &input) {
  QRegularExpression regex("\\A([1-9][0-9]{0,2}) [ ]?(mg|g|kg)\\z");
  regex.setPatternOptions(QRegularExpression:: CaseInsensitiveOption);
  QRegularExpressionMatch match = regex.match(input);
  if(match.hasMatch()) {
    const QString number = match.captured(1);
    int weight = number.toInt();
    const QString unit = match.captured(2).toLower();
    if (unit == "g") {
      weight *= 1000;
    } else if (unit == "kg") {
      weight *= 1000000 ;
    }
    return weight;
  } else {
    return -1;
  }
}
```

In the function's first two lines, we set up the pattern and its option. Then, we match it against the passed argument. If `QRegularExpressionMatch::hasMatch()` returns `true`, the input is valid and we extract the number and unit. Instead of fetching the entire list of captured text with `capturedTexts()`, we query specific elements directly by calling `QRegularExpressionMatch::captured()`. The passed integer argument signifies the element's position inside the list. So, calling `captured(1)` returns the matched digits as a `QString`.

`QRegularExpressionMatch::captured()` also takes `QString` as the argument's type. This is useful if you have used named groups inside the pattern, for example, if you have written `(?<number>[1-9][0-9]{0,2})`, then you can get the digits by calling `match.captured("number")`. Named groups pay off if you have long patterns or when there is a high probability that further brackets will be added in future. Be aware that adding a group at a later time will shift the indices of all the following groups by `1` and you will have to adjust your code!

To be able to calculate using the extracted number, we need to convert `QString` into an integer. This is done by calling `QString::toInt()`. The result of this conversion is then stored in the `weight` variable. Next, we fetch the unit and transform it to lowercase characters on-the-fly. This way, we can, for example, easily determine whether the user's guess is expressed in grams by checking the unit against the lowercase "g". We do not need to take care of the capital "G" or the variants "KG", "Kg", and the unusual "kG" for kilogram.

To get the standardized weight in milligrams, we multiply `weight` by 1,000 or 1,000,000, depending on whether this was expressed in g or kg. Lastly, we return this standardized weight. If the string wasn't well formed, we return `-1` to indicate that the given guess was invalid. It is then the caller's duty to determinate which player's guess was the best.

Pay attention to whether your chosen integer type can handle the weight's value. For our example, 100,000,000 is the biggest possible value that can be held by a signed integer on a 32-bit system. If you are not sure whether your code will be compiled on a 32-bit system, use `qint32`, which is guaranteed to be a 32-bit integer on every system that Qt supports, allowing decimal notations.

As an exercise, try to extend the example by allowing decimal numbers so that 23.5g is a valid guess. To achieve this, you have to alter the pattern in order to enter decimal numbers and you also have to deal with `double` instead of `int` for the standardized weight.

Finding all pattern occurrences

Lastly, let's have a final look at how to find, for example, all numbers inside a string, even those leading with zeros:

```
QString input = "123 foo 09 1a 3";
QRegularExpression regex("\\b[0-9]+\\b");
QRegularExpressionMatchIterator i = regex.globalMatch(input);
while (i.hasNext()) {
  QRegularExpressionMatch match = i.next();
  qWarning() << match.capturedTexts();
}
```

The `input` QString instance contains an exemplary text in which we would like to find all numbers. The "foo" as well as "1a" variables should not be found by the pattern since these are not valid numbers. Therefore, we set up the pattern defining that we require at least one digit, `[0-9]+`, and that this digit—or these digits—should be wrapped by word boundaries, `\b`. Note that you have to escape the slash. With this pattern, we initiate the `QRegularExpression` object and call `globalMatch()` on it. Inside the passed argument, the pattern will be searched. This time, we do not get `QRegularExpressionMatch` back but, instead, an iterator of the `QRegularExpressionMatchIterator` type. Since `QRegularExpressionMatchIterator` behaves like a Java iterator, with `hasNext()`, we check whether there is a further match and if so we bring up the next match by calling `next()`. The type of the returned match is then `QRegularExpressionMatch`, which you already know.

If you need to know about the next match inside the `while` loop, you can use `QRegularExpressionMatchIterator::peekNext()` to receive it. The upside of this function is that it does not move the iterator.

This way, you can iterate all pattern occurrences in the string. This is helpful if you, for example, want to highlight a search string in text.

Our example would give the output: `("123"), ("09") and ("3").`

Taking into account that this was just a brief introduction to regular expressions, we would like to encourage you to read the *Detailed Description* section in the documentation to `QRegularExpression`, `QRegularExpressionMatch`, and `QRegularExpressionMatchIterator`. Regular expressions are very powerful and useful, so, in your daily programming life, you can benefit from the profound knowledge of regular expressions!

Data storage

When implementing games, you will often have to work with persistent data—you will need to store the saved game data, load maps, and so on. For that, you have to learn about the mechanisms that let you use the data stored on digital media.

Files and devices

The most basic and low-level mechanism that is used to access data is to save and load it from the files. While you can use the classic file access approaches provided by C and C++, such as `stdio` or `iostream`, Qt provides its own wrapper over the file abstraction that hides platform-dependent details and provides a clean API that works across all platforms in a uniform manner.

The two basic classes that you will work with when using files are `QDir` and `QFile`. The former represents the contents of a directory, lets you traverse filesystems, creates and remove directories, and finally, access all files in a particular directory.

Traversing directories

Traversing directories with `QDir` is really easy. The first thing to do is to have an instance of `QDir` in the first place. The easiest way to do this is to pass the directory path to the `QDir` constructor.

Qt handles file paths in a platform-independent way. Even though the regular directory separator on Windows is a backwards slash character (\) and on other platforms it is the forward slash (/), Qt accepts forward slash as a directory separator on Windows platforms as well. Therefore, you can always use / to separate directories when you pass paths to Qt functions.

You can learn the native directory separator for the current platform is by calling the `QDir::separator()` static function. You can transform between native and non-native separators with the `QDir::toNativeSeparators()` and `QDir::fromNativeSeparators()` functions.

Qt provides a number of static methods to access some special directories. The following table lists these special directories and functions that access them:

Access function	Directory
`QDir::current()`	The current working directory
`QDir::home()`	The home directory of the current user
`QDir::root()`	The root directory—usually / for Unix and `C:\` for Windows
`QDir::temp()`	The system temporary directory

When you already have a valid `QDir` object, you can start moving between directories. To do that, you can use the `cd()` and `cdUp()` methods. The former moves to the named subdirectory, while the latter moves to the parent directory.

To list files and subdirectories in a particular directory, you can use the `entryList()` method, which returns a list of entries in the directory that match the criteria passed to `entryList()`. This method has two overloads. The basic version takes a list of flags that correspond to the different attributes that an entry needs to have to be included in the result and a set of flags that determine the order in which entries are included in the set. The other overload also accepts a list of file name patterns in the form of `QStringList` as its first parameter. The most commonly used filter and sort flags are listed as follows:

Filter flags	
`QDir::Dirs, QDir::Files, QDir::Drives, QDir::AllEntries`	List directories, files, drives (or all) that match the filters
`QDir::AllDirs`	List all subdirectories regardless of whether they match the filter or not
`QDir::Readable, QDir::Writable, QDir::Executable`	List entries that can be read, written, or executed
`QDir::Hidden, QDir::System`	List hidden files and system files
Sort flags	
`QDir::Unsorted`	The order of entries is undefined
`QDir::Name, QDir::Time, QDir::Size, QDir::Type`	Sort by appropriate entry attributes
`QDir::DirsFirst, QDir::DirsLast`	Determines whether directories should be listed before or after files

Here is an example call that returns all JPEG files in the user's `home` directory sorted by size:

```
QDir dir = QDir::home();
QStringList nameFilters;
nameFilters << QStringLiteral("*.jpg") << QStringLiteral("*.jpeg");
QStringList entries = dir.entryList(nameFilters,
                      QDir::Files|QDir::Readable, QDir::Size);
```

The << operator is a nice and fast way to append entries to `QStringList`.

Getting access to the basic file

Once you know the path to a file (either by using `QDir::entryList()`, from some external source, or even by hardcoding the file path in code), you can pass it to `QFile` to receive an object that acts as a handle to the file. Before the file contents can be accessed, the file needs to be opened using the `open()` method. The basic variant of this method takes a mode in which we need to open the file. The following table explains the modes that are available:

Mode	Description
`ReadOnly`	This file can be read from
`WriteOnly`	This file can be written to
`ReadWrite`	This file can be read from and written to
`Append`	All data writes will be written at the end of the file
`Truncate`	If the file is present, its content is deleted before we open it
`Text`	Native line endings are transformed to `\n` and back
`Unbuffered`	The flag prevents the file from being buffered by the system

The `open()` method returns `true` or `false` depending on whether the file was opened or not. The current status of the file can be checked by calling `isOpen()` on the file object. Once the file is open, it can be read from or written to depending on the options that are passed when the file is opened. Reading and writing is done using the `read()` and `write()` methods. These methods have a number of overloads, but I suggest that you focus on using those variants that accept or return a `QByteArray` object, which is essentially a series of bytes—it can hold both textual and nontextual data. If you are working with plain text, then a useful overload for `write` is the one that accepts the text directly as input. Just remember that the text has to be null or terminated. When reading from a file, Qt offers a number of other methods that might come in handy in some situations. One of these methods is `readLine()`, which tries to read from the file until it encounters a new line character. If you use it together with the `atEnd()` method that tells you whether you have reached the end of the file, you can realize the line-by-line reading of a text file:

```
QStringList lines;
while(!file.atEnd()) {
  QByteArray line = file.readLine();
  lines.append(QString::fromUtf8(line));
}
```

Another useful method is `readAll()`, which simply returns the file content, starting from the current position of the file pointer until the end of the file.

You have to remember though that when using these helper methods, you should be really careful if you don't know how much data the file contains. It might happen that when reading line by line or trying to read the whole file into memory in one step, you exhaust the amount of memory that is available for your process (you can check the size of the file by calling `size()` on the `QFile` instance). Instead, you should process the file's data in steps, reading only as much as you require at a time. This makes the code more complex but allows us to better manage the available resources. If you require constant access to some part of the file, you can use the `map()` and `unmap()` calls that add and remove mappings of the parts of a file to a memory address that you can then use like a regular array of bytes:

```
QFile f("myfile");
if(!f.open(QFile::ReadWrite)) return;
uchar *addr = f.map(0, f.size());
if(!addr) return;
f.close();
doSomeComplexOperationOn(addr);
f.unmap(addr);
```

Devices

`QFile` is really a descendant class of `QIODevice`, which is a Qt interface that is used to abstract entities related to reading and writing. There are two types of devices: sequential and random access devices. `QFile` belongs to the latter group—it has the concepts of start, end, size, and current position that can be changed by the user with the `seek()` method. Sequential devices, such as sockets and pipes, represent streams of data—there is no way to rewind the stream or check its size; you can only keep reading the data sequentially—piece by piece, and you can check how far away you currently are from the end of data.

All I/O devices can be opened and closed. They all implement `open()`, `read()`, and `write()` interfaces. Writing to the device queues the data for writing; when the data is actually written, the `bytesWritten()` signal is emitted that carries the amount of data that was written to the device. If more data becomes available in the sequential device, it emits the `readyRead()` signal, which informs you that if you call `read` now, you can expect to receive some data from the device.

Time for action – implementing a device to encrypt data

Let's implement a really simple device that encrypts or decrypts the data that is streamed through it using a very simple algorithm—the Caesar cipher. What it does is that when encrypting, it shifts each character in the plaintext by a number of characters defined by the key and does the reverse when decrypting. Thus, if the key is `2` and the plaintext character is `a`, the ciphertext becomes `c`. Decrypting `z` with the key `4` will yield the value `v`.

We will start by creating a new empty project and adding a class derived from `QIODevice`. The basic interface of the class is going to accept an integer key and set an underlying device that serves as the source or destination of data. This is all simple coding that you should already understand, so it shouldn't need any extra explanation, as shown:

```
class CaesarCipherDevice : public QIODevice
{
    Q_OBJECT
    Q_PROPERTY(int key READ key WRITE setKey)
public:
    explicit CaesarCipherDevice(QObject *parent = 0)
    : QIODevice(parent) {
      m_key = 0;
      m_device = 0;
    }
    void setBaseDevice(QIODevice *dev) { m_device = dev; }
    QIODevice *baseDevice() const { return m_device; }
    void setKey(int k) { m_key = k; }
    inline int key() const { return m_key; }
private:
    int m_key;
    QIODevice *m_device;
};
```

The next thing is to make sure that the device cannot be used if there is no device to operate on (that is, when `m_device == 0`). For this, we have to reimplement the `QIODevice::open()` method and return `false` when we want to prevent operating on our device:

```
bool open(OpenMode mode) {
  if(!baseDevice())
    return false;
  if(baseDevice()->openMode() != mode)
    return false;
  return QIODevice::open(mode);
}
```

The method accepts the mode that the user wants to open the device with. We perform an additional check to verify that the base device was opened in the same mode before calling the base class implementation that will mark the device as open.

To have a fully functional device, we still need to implement the two protected pure virtual methods, which do the actual reading and writing. These methods are called by Qt from other methods of the class when needed. Let's start with `writeData()`, which accepts a pointer to a buffer containing the data and size of that a buffer:

```
qint64 CaesarCipherDevice::writeData(const char *data, qint64 len) {
    QByteArray ba(data, len);
    for(int i=0;i<len;++i)
      ba.data()[i] += m_key;
    int written = m_device->write(ba);
    emit bytesWritten(written);
    return written;
}
```

First, we copy the data into a local byte array. Then, we iterate the array, adding to each byte the value of the key (which effectively performs the encryption). Finally, we try to write the byte array to the underlying device. Before informing the caller about the amount of data that was really written, we emit a signal that carries the same information.

The last method that we need to implement is the one that performs decryption by reading from the base device and adding the key to each cell of the data. This is done by implementing `readData()`, which accepts a pointer to the buffer that the method needs to write to and the size of the buffer. The code is quite similar to that of `writeData()` except that we are subtracting the key value instead of adding it:

```
qint64 CaesarCipherDevice::readData(char *data, qint64 maxlen) {
  QByteArray baseData = m_device->read(maxlen);
  const int s = baseData.size();
  for(int i=0;i<s;++i)
    data[i] = baseData[i]-m_key;
  return s;
}
```

First, we read from the underlying device as much as we can fit into the buffer and store the data in a byte array. Then, we iterate the array and set subsequent bytes of data buffer to the decrypted value. Finally, we return the amount of data that was really read.

A simple `main()` function that can test the class looks as follows:

```
int main(int argc, char **argv) {
  QByteArray ba = "plaintext";
  QBuffer buf;
  buf.open(QIODevice::WriteOnly);
  CaesarCipherDevice encrypt;
  encrypt.setKey(3);
  encrypt.setBaseDevice(&buf);
  encrypt.open(buf.openMode());
  encrypt.write(ba);
  qDebug() << buf.data();

  CaesarCipherDevice decrypt;
  decrypt.setKey(3);
  decrypt.setBaseDevice(&buf);
  buf.open(QIODevice::ReadOnly);
  decrypt.open(buf.openMode());
  qDebug() << decrypt.readAll();
  return 0;
}
```

We use the `QBuffer` class that implements the `QIODevice` API and acts as an adapter for `QByteArray` or `QString`.

What just happened?

We created an encryption object and set its key to `3`. We also told it to use a `QBuffer` instance to store the processed content. After opening it for writing, we sent some data to it that gets encrypted and written to the base device. Then, we created a similar device, passing the same buffer again as the base device, but now, we open the device for reading. This means that the base device contains ciphertext. After this, we read all data from the device, which results in reading data from the buffer, decrypting it, and returning the data so that it can be written to the debug console.

Have a go hero – a GUI for the Caesar cipher

You can combine what you already know by implementing a full-blown GUI application that is able to encrypt or decrypt files using the Caesar cipher `QIODevice` class that we just implemented. Remember that `QFile` is also `QIODevice`, so you can pass its pointer directly to `setBaseDevice()`.

This is just a starting point for you. The `QIODevice` API is quite rich and contains numerous methods that are virtual, so you can reimplement them in subclasses.

Text streams

Much of the data produced by computers nowadays is based on text. You can create such files using a mechanism that you already know—opening `QFile` to write, converting all data into strings using `QString::arg()`, optionally encoding strings using `QTextCodec`, and dumping the resulting bytes to the file by calling `write`. However, Qt provides a nice mechanism that does most of this automatically for you in a way similar to how the standard C++ `iostream` classes work. The `QTextStream` class operates on any `QIODevice` API in a stream-oriented way. You can send tokens to the stream using the `<<` operator, where they get converted into strings, separated by spaces, encoded using a codec of your choice, and written to the underlying device. It also works the other way round; using the `>>` operator, you can stream data from a text file, transparently converting it from strings to appropriate variable types. If the conversion fails, you can discover it by inspecting the result of the `status()` method—if you get `ReadPastEnd` or `ReadCorruptData`, then this means that the read has failed.

While `QIODevice` is the main class that `QTextStream` operates on, it can also manipulate `QString` or `QByteArray`, which makes it useful for us to compose or parse strings.

Using `QTextStream` is simple—you just have to pass it the device that you want it to operate on and you're good to go. The stream accepts strings and numerical values:

```
QFile file("output.txt");
file.open(QFile::WriteOnly|QFile::Text);
QTextStream stream(&file);
stream << "Today is " << QDate::currentDate().toString() << endl;
QTime t = QTime::currentTime();
stream << "Current time is " << t.hour() << " h and " << t.minute()
       << "m." << endl;
```

Apart from directing content into the stream, the stream can accept a number of manipulators, such as `endl`, which have a direct or indirect influence on how the stream behaves. For instance, you can tell the stream to display a number as decimal and another as hexadecimal with uppercase digits using the following code (highlighted in the code are all manipulators):

```
for(int i=0;i<10;++i) {
  int num = qrand() % 100000;  // random number between 0 and 99999
  stream << dec << num << showbase << hex << uppercasedigits << num
         << endl;
}
```

This is not the end of the capabilities of `QTextStream`. It also allows us to display data in a tabular manner by defining column widths and alignments. Suppose that you have a set of records for game players that is defined by the following structure:

```
struct Player {
  QString name;
  qint64 experience;
  QPoint position;
  char direction;
};
QList<Player> players;
```

Let's dump such info into a file in a tabular manner:

```
QFile file("players.txt");
file.open(QFile::WriteOnly|QFile::Text);
QTextStream stream(&file);
stream << center;
stream << qSetFieldWidth(16) << "Player" << qSetFieldWidth(0) << " ";
stream << qSetFieldWidth(10) << "Experience"
       << qSetFieldWidth(0) << " ";
stream << qSetFieldWidth(13) << "Position"
       << qSetFieldWidth(0) << " ";
stream << "Direction" << endl;
for(int i=0;i<players.size();++i) {
  const Player &p = players.at(i);
  stream << left << qSetFieldWidth(16) << p.name
         << qSetFieldWidth(0) << " ";
  stream << right << qSetFieldWidth(10) << p.experience
         << qSetFieldWidth(0) << " ";
  stream << right << qSetFieldWidth(6) << p.position.x()
         << qSetFieldWidth(0) << " " << qSetFieldWidth(6)
         << p.position.y() << qSetFieldWidth(0) << " ";
```

```
    stream << center << qSetFieldWidth(10);
    switch(p.direction) {
      case 'n' : stream << "north"; break;
      case 's' : stream << "south"; break;
      case 'e' : stream << "east"; break;
      case 'w' : stream << "west"; break;
      default: stream << "unknown"; break;
    }
    stream << qSetFieldWidth(0) << endl;
  }
```

After running the program, you should get a result similar to the one shown in the following screenshot:

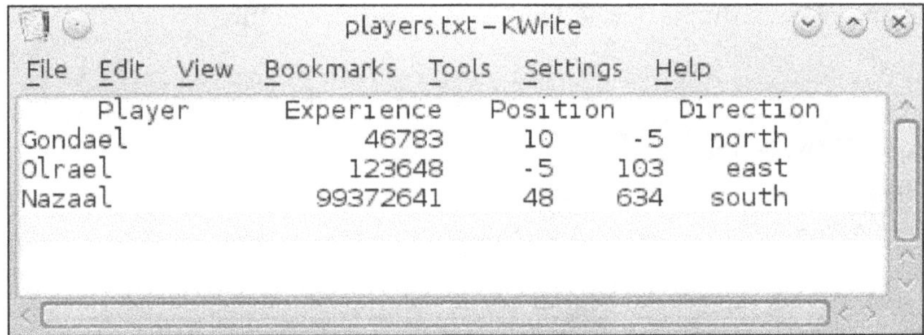

One last thing about `QTextStream` is that it can operate on standard C file structures, which makes it possible for us to use `QTextStream` to, for example, write to `stdout` or read from `stdin`, as shown in the following code:

```
QTextStream qout(stdout);
qout << "This text goes to process standard output." << endl;
```

Data serialization

More than often, we have to store object data in a device-independent way so that it can be restored later, possibly on a different machine with a different data layout and so on. In computer science, this is called serialization. Qt provides several serialization mechanisms and now we will have a brief look at some of them.

Binary streams

If you look at `QTextStream` from a distance, you will notice that what it really does is serialize and deserialize data to a text format. Its close cousin is the `QDataStream` class that handles serialization and deserialization of arbitrary data to a binary format. It uses a custom data format to store and retrieve data from `QIODevice` in a platform-independent way. It stores enough data so that a stream written on one platform can be successfully read on a different platform.

`QDataStream` is used in a similar fashion as `QTextStream`—the operators << and >> are used to redirect data into or out of the stream. The class supports most of the built-in Qt types so that you can operate on classes such as `QColor`, `QPoint`, or `QStringList` directly:

```
QFile file("outfile.dat");
file.open(QFile::WriteOnly|QFile::Truncate);
QDataStream stream(&file);
double dbl = 3.14159265359;
QColor color = Qt::red;
QPoint point(10, -4);
QStringList stringList = QStringList() << "foo" << "bar";
stream << dbl << color << point << stringList;
```

If you want to serialize custom data types, you can teach `QDataStream` to do that by implementing proper redirection operators.

Time for action – serialization of a custom structure

Let's perform another small exercise by implementing functions that are required to use `QDataStream` to serialize the same simple structure that contains the player information that we used for text streaming:

```
struct Player {
  QString name;
  qint64 experience;
  QPoint position;
  char direction;
};
```

For this, two functions need to be implemented, both returning a `QDataStream` reference that was taken earlier as an argument to the call. Apart from the stream itself, the serialization operator accepts a constant reference to the class that is being saved. The most simple implementation just streams each member into the stream and returns the stream afterwards:

```
QDataStream& operator<<(QDataStream &stream, const Player &p) {
  stream << p.name;
  stream << p.experience;
  stream << p.position;
  stream << p.direction;
  return stream;
}
```

Complementary to this, deserializing is done by implementing a redirection operator that accepts a mutable reference to the structure that is filled by data that is read from the stream:

```
QDataStream& operator>>(QDataStream &stream, Player &p) {
   stream >> p.name;
   stream >> p.experience;
   stream >> p.position;
   stream >> p.direction;
   return stream;
}
```

Again, at the end, the stream itself is returned.

What just happened?

We provided two standalone functions that define redirection operators for the `Player` class to and from a `QDataStream` instance. This lets your class be serialized and deserialized using mechanisms offered and used by Qt.

XML streams

XML has become one of the most popular standards that is used to store hierarchical data. Despite its verbosity and difficulty to read by human eye, it is used in virtually any domain where data persistency is required, as it is very easy to read by machines. Qt provides support for reading and writing XML documents in two modules. First, the `QtXml` module provides access using the **Document Object Model** (**DOM**) standard with classes such as `QDomDocument`, `QDomElement`, and others. We will not discuss this approach here, as now the recommended approach is to use streaming classes from the `QtCore` module. One of the downsides of `QDomDocument` is that it requires us to load the whole XML tree into the memory before parsing it. In some situations, this is compensated for by the ease of use of the DOM approach as compared to a streamed approach, so you can consider using it if you feel you have found the right task for it.

> If you want to use the DOM access to XML in Qt, remember to enable the `QtXml` module in your applications by adding a `QT += xml` line in the project configuration files.

As already said, we will focus on the stream approach implemented by the `QXmlStreamReader` and `QXmlStreamWriter` classes.

Time for action – implementing an XML parser for player data

In this exercise, we are going to create a parser to fill data that represents players and their inventory in an RPG game:

```
struct InventoryItem {
  enum Type { Weapon, Armor, Gem, Book, Other } type;
  QString subType;
  int durability;
};

struct Player {
  QString name;
  QString password;
  int experience;
  int hitPoints;
  QList<Item> inventory;
  QString location;
  QPoint position;
};

struct PlayerInfo {
  QList<Player> players;
};
```

Save the following document somewhere. We will use it to test whether the parser can read it:

```
<PlayerInfo>
    <Player hp="40" exp="23456">
        <Name>Gandalf</Name>
        <Password>mithrandir</Password>
        <Inventory>
            <InvItem type="weapon" durability="3">
                <SubType>Long sword</SubType>
            </InvItem>
            <InvItem type="armor" durability="10">
                <SubType>Chain mail</SubType>
```

```
            </InvItem>
        </Inventory>
        <Location name="room1">
            <Position x="1" y="0"/>
        </Location>
    </Player>
</PlayerInfo>
```

Let's create a class called `PlayerInfoReader` that will wrap `QXmlStreamReader` and expose a parser interface for the `PlayerInfo` instances. The class will contain two private members—the reader itself and a `PlayerInfo` instance that acts as a container for the data that is currently being read. We'll provide a `result()` method that returns this object once the parsing is complete, as shown in the following code:

```
class PlayerInfoReader {
public:
  PlayerInfoReader(QIODevice *);
  inline const PlayerInfo& result() const { return m_pinfo; }
private:
  QXmlStreamReader reader;
  PlayerInfo m_pinfo;
};
```

The class constructor accepts a `QIODevice` pointer that the reader is going to use to retrieve data as it needs it. The constructor is trivial, as it simply passes the device to the `reader` object:

```
PlayerInfoReader(QIODevice *device) {
    reader.setDevice(device);
}
```

Before we go into parsing, let's prepare some code to help us with the process. First, let's add an enumeration type to the class that will list all the possible tokens—tag names that we want to handle in the parser:

```
enum Token {
  T_Invalid = -1,
  T_PlayerInfo,                                   /* root tag */
  T_Player,                                       /* in PlayerInfo */
  T_Name, T_Password, T_Inventory, T_Location,    /* in Player */
  T_Position,                                     /* in Location */
  T_InvItem                                       /* in Inventory */
};
```

To use these tags, we'll add a static method to the class that returns the token type based on its textual representation:

```
static Token PlayerInfoReader::tokenByName(const QStringRef &r) {
  static QStringList tokenList = QStringList()
    << "PlayerInfo" << "Player"
    << "Name" << "Password"
    << "Inventory" << "Location"
    << "Position" << "InvItem";
  int idx = tokenList.indexOf(r.toString());
  return (Token)idx;
}
```

You can notice that we are using a class called `QStringRef`. It represents a string reference—a substring in an existing string—and is implemented in a way that avoids expensive string construction; therefore, it is very fast. We're using this class here because that's how `QXmlStreamReader` reports tag names. Inside this static method, we are converting the string reference to a real string and trying to match it against a list of known tags. If the matching fails, `-1` is returned, which corresponds to our `T_Invalid` token.

Now, let's add an entry point to start the parsing process. Add a public `read` method that initializes the data structure and performs initial checks on the input stream:

```
bool PlayerInfoReader::read() {
  m_pinfo = PlayerInfo();
  if(reader.readNextStartElement() &&
    tokenByName(reader.name()) == T_PlayerInfo) {
      return readPlayerInfo();
  } else {
    return false;
  }
}
```

After clearing the data structure, we call `readNextStartElement()` on the reader to make it find the starting tag of the first element, and if it is found, we check whether the root tag of the document is what we expect it to be. If so, we call the `readPlayerInfo()` method and return its result, denoting whether the parsing was successful. Otherwise, we bail out, reporting an error.

The `QXmlStreamReader` subclasses usually follow the same pattern. Each parsing method first checks whether it operates on a tag that it expects to find. Then, it iterates all the starting elements, handling those it knows and ignoring all others. Such an approach lets us maintain forward compatibility, since all tags introduced in newer versions of the document are silently skipped by an older parser.

Now, let's implement the `readPlayerInfo` method:

```
bool readPlayerInfo() {
  if(tokenByName(reader.name()) != T_PlayerInfo)
    return false;
  while(reader.readNextStartElement()) {
    if(tokenByName(reader.name()) == T_Player) {
      Player p = readPlayer();
      m_pinfo.players.append(p);
    } else
      reader.skipCurrentElement();
  }
  return true;
}
```

After verifying that we are working on a `PlayerInfo` tag, we iterate all the starting subelements of the current tag. For each of them, we check whether it is a `Player` tag and call `readPlayer()` to descend into the level of parsing data for a single player. Otherwise, we call `skipCurrentElement()`, which fast-forwards the stream until a matching ending element is encountered.

The structure of `readPlayer()` is similar; however, it is more complicated as we also want to read data from attributes of the `Player` tag itself. Let's take a look at the function piece by piece:

```
Player readPlayer() {
  if(tokenByName(reader.name()) != T_Player) return Player();
  Player p;
  const QXmlStreamAttributes& playerAttrs = reader.attributes();
  p.hitPoints = playerAttrs.value("hp").toString().toInt();
  p.experience = playerAttrs.value("exp").toString().toInt();
```

After checking for the right tag, we get the list of attributes associated with the opening tag and ask for values of the two attributes that we are interested in. After this, we loop all child tags and fill the `Player` structure based on the tag names. By converting tag names to tokens, we can use a `switch` statement to neatly structure the code in order to extract information from different tag types, as shown in the following code:

```
while(reader.readNextStartElement()) {
  Token t = tokenByName(reader.name());
  switch(t) {
  case Name:      p.name = reader.readElementText(); break;
  case Password:  p.password = reader.readElementText(); break;
  case Inventory: p.inventory = readInventory(); break;
```

If we are interested in the textual content of the tag, we can use `readElementText()` to extract it. This method reads until it encounters the closing tag and returns the text contained within it. For the `Inventory` tag, we call the dedicated `readInventory()` method.

For the `Location` tag, the code is more complex than before as we again descend into reading child tags, extracting the required information and skipping all unknown tags:

```
            case T_Location: {
                p.location = reader.attributes().
                  value("name").toString();
                while(reader.readNextStartElement()) {
                    if(tokenByName(reader.name()) == T_Position) {
                        const QXmlStreamAttributes& attrs
                          = reader.attributes();
                        p.position.setX(attrs.value("x")
                         .toString().toInt());
                        p.position.setY(attrs.value("y").
                          toString().toInt());
                        reader.skipCurrentElement();
                    } else
                        reader.skipCurrentElement();
                }
            }; break;
            default:
                reader.skipCurrentElement();
            }
        }
        return p;
    }
```

The last method is similar in structure to the previous one—iterate all the tags, skip everything that we don't want to handle (everything that is not an inventory item), fill the inventory item data structure, and append the item to the list of already parsed items, as shown in the following code:

```
    QList<InventoryItem> readInventory() {
      QList<InventoryItem> inventory;
      while(reader.readNextStartElement()) {
        if(tokenByName(reader.name()) != T_InvItem) {
          reader.skipCurrentElement();
          continue;
        }
        InventoryItem item;
        const QXmlStreamAttributes& attrs = reader.attributes();
```

```
      item.durability = attrs.value("durability").
      toString().toInt();
    QStringRef typeRef = attrs.value("type");
    if(typeRef == "weapon") {
      item.type = InventoryItem::Weapon;
    } else if(typeRef == "armor") {
      item.type = InventoryItem::Armor;
    } else if(typeRef == "gem") {
      item.type = InventoryItem::Gem;
    } else if(typeRef == "book") {
      item.type = InventoryItem::Book;
    } else item.type = InventoryItem::Other;
    while(reader.readNextStartElement()) {
      if(reader.name() == "SubType")
      item.subType = reader.readElementText();
      else
        reader.skipCurrentElement();
    }
    inventory << item;
  }
  return inventory;
}
```

In `main()` of your project, write some code that will check whether the parser works correctly. You can use the `qDebug()` statements to output the sizes of lists and contents of variables. Take a look at the following code for an example:

```
qDebug() << "Count:" << playerInfo.players.count();
qDebug() << "Size of inventory:"
         << playerInfo.players.first().inventory.size();
qDebug() << "Room: " << playerInfo.players.first().location
         << playerInfo.players.first().position;
```

What just happened?

The code you just wrote implements a full top-down parser of the XML data. First, the data goes through a tokenizer, which returns identifiers that are much easier to handle than strings. Then, each method can easily check whether the token it receives is an acceptable input for the current parsing stage. Based on the child token, the next parsing function is determined and the parser descends to a lower level until there is nowhere to descend to. Then, the flow goes back up one level and processes the next child. If at any point an unknown tag is found, it gets ignored. This approach supports a situation when a new version of software introduces new tags to the file format specification, but an old version of software can still read the file by skipping all the tags that it doesn't understand.

Have a go hero – an XML serializer for player data

Now that you know how to parse XML data, you can create the complementary part—a module that will serialize `PlayerInfo` structures into XML documents using `QXmlStreamWriter`. Use methods such as `writeStartDocument()`, `writeStartElement()`, `writeCharacters()`, and `writeEndElement()` for this. Verify that the documents saved with your code can be parsed with what we implemented together.

JSON files

JSON stands for **JavaScript Object Notation,** which is a popular lightweight textual format that is used to store object-oriented data in a human-readable form. It comes from JavaScript where it is the native format used to store object information; however, it is commonly used across many programming languages and a popular format for web data exchange. A simple JSON-formatted definition looks as follows:

```
{
    "name": "Joe",
    "age": 14,
    "inventory: [
        { "type": "gold; "amount": "144000" },
        { "type": "short_sword"; "material": "iron" }
    ]
}
```

JSON can express two kinds of entities: objects (enclosed in braces) and arrays (enclosed in square brackets) where an object is defined as a set of key-value pairs, where a value can be a simple string, an object, or array. In the previous example, we had an object containing three properties—name, age, and inventory. The first two properties are simple values and the last property is an array that contains two objects with two properties each.

Qt can create and read JSON descriptions using the `QJsonDocument` class. A document can be created from the UTF-8-encoded text using the `QJsonDocument::fromJson()` static method and can later be stored in a textual form again using `toJson()`. Since the structure of JSON closely resembles that of `QVariant` (which can also hold key-value pairs using `QVariantMap` and arrays using `QVariantList`), conversion methods to this class also exist using a set of `fromVariant()` and `toVariant()` calls. Once a JSON document is created, you can check whether it represents an object or an array using one of the `isArray` and `isObject` calls. Then, the document can be transformed into `QJsonArray` or `QJsonObject` using the `toArray` and `toObject` methods.

QJsonObject is an iterable type that can be queried for a list of keys (using keys()) or asked for a value of a specific key (with a value() method). Values are represented using the QJsonValue class, which can store simple values, an array, or object. New properties can be added to the object using the insert() method that takes a key as a string, a value can be added as QJsonValue, and the existing properties can be removed using remove().

QJsonArray is also an iterable type that contains a classic list API—it contains methods such as append(), insert(), removeAt(), at(), and size() to manipulate entries in the array, again working on QJsonValue as the item type.

Time for action – the player data JSON serializer

Our next exercise is to create a serializer of the same PlayerInfo structure as we used for the XML exercise, but this time the destination data format is going to be JSON.

Start by creating a PlayerInfoJSON class and give it an interface similar to the one shown in the following code:

```
class PlayerInfoJSON {
public:
  PlayerInfoJSON(){}
  QByteArray writePlayerInfo(const PlayerInfo &pinfo) const;
};
```

All that is really required is to implement the writePlayerInfo method. This method will use QJsonDocument::fromVariant() to perform the serialization; thus, what we really have to do is convert our player data to a variant. Let's add a protected method to do that:

```
QVariant PlayerInfoJSON::toVariant(const PlayerInfo &pinfo) const {
  QVariantList players;
  foreach(const Player &p, pinfo.players) players << toVariant(p);
  return players;
}
```

Since the structure is really a list of players, we can iterate the list of players, serialize each player to a variant, and append the result to QVariantList. Having this function ready, we can descend a level and implement an overload for toVariant() that takes a Player object:

```
QVariant PlayerInfoJSON::toVariant(const Player &player) const {
  QVariantMap map;
  map["name"]       = player.name;
  map["password"]   = player.password;
  map["experience"] = player.experience;
  map["hitpoints"]  = player.hitPoints;
```

```
    map["location"]    = player.location;
    map["position"]    = QVariantMap({ {"x", player.position.x()},
                                       {"y", player.position.y()} });
    map["inventory"]   = toVariant(player.inventory);
    return map;
}
```

Qt's `foreach` macro takes two parameters—a declaration of a variable and a container to iterate. At each iteration, the macro assigns subsequent elements to the declared variable and executes the statement located directly after the macro. A C++11 equivalent of `foreach` is a range that is based for construct:

```
for(const Player &p: pinfo.players)
  players << toVariant(p);
```

This time, we are using `QVariantMap` as our base type, since we want to associate values with keys. For each key, we use the index operator to add entries to the map. The position key holds a `QPoint` value, which is supported natively by `QVariant`; however, such a variant can't be automatically encoded in JSON, so we convert the point to a variant map using the C++11 initializer list. The situation is different with the inventory—again, we have to write an overload for `toVariant` that will perform the conversion:

```
QVariant PlayerInfoJSON::toVariant(const QList<InventoryItem> &items)
const {
  QVariantList list;
  foreach(const InventoryItem &item, items) list << toVariant(item);
  return list;
}
```

The code is almost identical to the one handling `PlayerInfo` objects, so let's focus on the last overload of `toVariant`—the one that accepts `Item` instances:

```
QVariant PlayerInfoJSON::toVariant(const InventoryItem &item) const {
  QVariantMap map;
  map["type"] = (int)item.type;
  map["subtype"] = item.subType;
  map["durability"] = item.durability;
  return map;
}
```

There is not much to comment here—we add all keys to the map, treating the item type as an integer for simplicity (this is not the best approach in a general case, as if we serialize our data and then change the order of values in the original enumeration, we will not get the proper item types after deserialization).

What remains is to use the code we have just written in the writePlayerInfo method:

```
QByteArray PlayerInfoJSON::writePlayerInfo(const PlayerInfo &pinfo)
const {
  QJsonDocument doc = QJsonDocument::fromVariant(toVariant(pinfo));
  return doc.toJson();
}
```

Time for action – implementing a JSON parser

Let's extend the PlayerInfoJSON class and equip it with a reverse conversion:

```
PlayerInfo PlayerInfoJSON::readPlayerInfo(const QByteArray &ba) const
{
  QJsonDocument doc = QJsonDocument::fromJson(ba);
  if(doc.isEmpty() || !doc.isArray()) return PlayerInfo();
  return readPlayerInfo(doc.array());
}
```

First, we read the document and check whether it is valid and holds the expected array. Upon failure, an empty structure is returned; otherwise, readPlayerInfo is called and is given QJsonArray to work with:

```
PlayerInfo PlayerInfoJSON::readPlayerInfo(const QJsonArray &array)
const {
  PlayerInfo pinfo;
  foreach(QJsonValue value, array)
    pinfo.players << readPlayer(value.toObject());
  return pinfo;
}
```

Since the array is iterable, we can again use foreach to iterate it and use another method—readPlayer—to extract all the needed data:

```
Player PlayerInfoJSON::readPlayer(const QJsonObject &object) const {
  Player player;
  player.name = object.value("name").toString();
  player.password = object.value("password").toString();
  player.experience = object.value("experience").toDouble();
  player.hitPoints = object.value("hitpoints").toDouble();
  player.location = object.value("location").toString();
```

```
    QVariantMap positionMap = object.value("position")
                             .toVariant().toMap();
    player.position = QPoint(positionMap["x"].toInt(),
                      positionMap["y"].toInt());
    player.inventory = readInventory(
                       object.value("inventory").toArray());
    return player;
}
```

In this function, we used `QJsonObject::value()` to extract data from the object and then we used different functions to convert the data to the desired type. Note that in order to convert to `QPoint`, we first converted it to `QVariantMap` and then extracted the values before using them to build `QPoint`. In each case, if the conversion fails, we get a default value for that type (for example, an empty string). To read the inventory, we employ a custom method:

```
QList<InventoryItem> PlayerInfoJSON::readInventory(const QJsonArray
&array) const {
  QList<InventoryItem> inventory;
  foreach(QJsonValue value, array)
    inventory << readItem(value.toObject());
  return inventory;
}
```

What remains is to implement `readItem()`:

```
InventoryItem PlayerInfoJSON::readItem(const QJsonObject &object)
const {
  Item item;
  item.type = (InventoryItem::Type)object.value("type").toDouble();
  item.subType = object.value("subtype").toString();
  item.durability = object.value("durability").toDouble();
  return item;
}
```

What just happened?

The class that was implemented can be used for bidirectional conversion between `Item` instances and a `QByteArray` object, which contains the object data in the JSON format. We didn't do any error checking here; instead, we relied on automatic type conversion handling in `QJsonObject` and `QVariant`.

QSettings

While not strictly a serialization issue, the aspect of storing application settings is closely related to the described subject. A Qt solution for this is the `QSettings` class. By default, it uses different backends on different platforms, such as system registry on Windows or INI files on Linux. The basic use of `QSettings` is very easy—you just need to create the object and use `setValue()` and `value()` to store and load data from it:

```
QSettings settings;
settings.setValue("windowWidth", 80);
settings.setValue("windowTitle", "MySuperbGame");
// ...
int windowHeight = settings.value("windowHeight").toInt();
```

The only thing you need to remember is that it operates on `QVariant`, so the return value needs to be converted to the proper type if needed as shown in the last line of the preceding code. A call to `value()` can take an additional argument that contains the value to be returned if the requested key is not present in the map. This allows you to handle default values, for example, in a situation when the application is first started and the settings are not saved yet:

```
int windowHeight = settings.value("windowHeight", 800);
```

The simplest scenario assumes that settings are "flat" in the way that all keys are defined on the same level. However, this does not have to be the case—correlated settings can be put into named groups. To operate on a group, you can use the `beginGroup()` and `endGroup()` calls:

```
settings.beginGroup("Server");
QString srvIP = settings.value("host").toString();
int port = settings.value("port").toInt();
settings.endGroup();
```

When using this syntax, you have to remember to end the group after you are done with it. An alternative to using the two mentioned methods is to pass the group name directly to invocation of `value()`:

```
QString srvIP = settings.value("Server/host").toString();
int port = settings.value("Server/port").toInt();
```

As was mentioned earlier, `QSettings` can use different backends on different platforms; however, we can have some influence on which is chosen and which options are passed to it by passing appropriate options to the constructor of the `settings` object. By default, the place where the settings for an application are stored is determined by two values—the organization and the application name. Both are textual values and both can be passed as arguments to the `QSettings` constructor or defined a priori using appropriate static methods in `QCoreApplication`:

```
QCoreApplication::setOrganizationName("Packt");
QCoreApplication::setApplicationName("Game Programming using Qt");
QSettings settings;
```

This code is equivalent to:

```
QSettings settings("Packt", "Game Programming using Qt");
```

All of the preceding code use the default backend for the system. However, it is often desirable to use a different backend. This can be done using the `Format` argument, where we can pass one of the two options—`NativeFormat` or `IniFormat`. The former chooses the default backend, while the latter forces the INI-file backend. When choosing the backend, you can also decide whether settings should be saved in a system-wide location or in the user's settings storage by passing one more argument—the scope of which can be either `UserScope` or `SystemScope`. This can extend our final construction call to:

```
QSettings settings(QSettings::IniFormat, QSettings::UserScope,
                   "Packt", "Game Programming using Qt");
```

There is one more option available for total control of where the settings data resides—tell the constructor directly where the data should be located:

```
QSettings settings(
  QStandardPaths::writableLocation(
    QStandardPaths::ConfigLocation
  ) +"/myapp.conf", QSettings::IniFormat
);
```

The `QStandardPaths` class provides methods to determine standard locations for files depending on the task at hand.

`QSettings` also allows you to register your own formats so that you can control the way your settings are stored—for example, by storing them using XML or by adding on-the-fly encryption. This is done using `QSettings::registerFormat()`, where you need to pass the file extension and two pointers to functions that perform reading and writing of the settings, respectively, as follows:

```
bool readCCFile(QIODevice &device, QSettings::SettingsMap &map) {
  CeasarCipherDevice ccDevice;
  ccDevice.setBaseDevice(&device);
  // ...
  return true;
}
bool writeCCFile(QIODevice &device, const QSettings::SettingsMap &map)
{ ... }
const QSettings::Format CCFormat = QSettings::registerFormat
  ("ccph", readCCFile, writeCCFile);
```

Pop quiz – Qt core essentials

Q1. What is the closest equivalent `std::string` in Qt?

1. `QString`
2. `QByteArray`
3. `QStringLiteral`

Q2. Which regular expression can be used to validate an IPv4 address, which is an address composed of four dot-separated decimal numbers with values ranging from 0 to 255?

Q3. Which do you think is the best serialization mechanism to use if you expect the data structure to evolve (gain new information) in future versions of the software?

1. JSON
2. XML
3. QDataStream

Summary

In this chapter, you learned a number of core Qt technologies ranging from text manipulation, to accessing devices that can be used to transfer or store data using a number of popular technologies such as XML or JSON. You should be aware that we have barely scratched the surface of what Qt offers and there are many other interesting classes you should familiarize yourself with but this minimum amount of information should give you a head start and show you the direction to follow with your future research.

In the next chapter, we will switch from describing data manipulation, which can be visualized using text or only in your imagination, to a more appealing media. We will start talking about graphics and how to transfer what you can see in your imagination to the screen of your computer.

5
Graphics with Qt

When it comes to graphics, we have so far been using only ready-made widgets for the user interface, which resulted in the crude approach of using buttons for a tic-tac-toe game. In this chapter, you will learn about much of what Qt has to offer with regard to custom graphics. This will let you not only create your own widgets, incorporating content that is entirely customized, but also integrate multimedia in your programs. You will also learn about employing your OpenGL skills to display fast 3D graphics. If you are not familiar with OpenGL, this chapter should give you a kick-start for further research in this topic. By the end of the chapter, you will be able to create 2D and 3D graphics for your games using classes offered by Qt and integrate them with the rest of the user interface.

When it comes to graphics, Qt splits this domain into two separate parts. One of them is raster graphics (used by widgets, for example). This part focuses on using high-level operations (such as drawing lines or filling rectangles) to manipulate colors of a grid of points that can be visualized on different devices, such as images or the display of your computer device. The other is vector graphics, which involves manipulating vertices, triangles, and textures. This is tailored for maximum speed of processing and display using hardware acceleration provided by modern graphics cards. Qt abstracts graphics by using the concept of a surface that it draws on. The surface (represented by the `QSurface` class) can be of one of two types—`RasterSurface` or `OpenGLSurface`. The surface can be further customized using the `QSurfaceFormat` class, but we will talk about that later as it is not important right now.

Raster painting

When we talk about GUI frameworks, raster painting is usually associated with drawing on widgets. However, since Qt is something more than a GUI toolkit, the scope of raster painting that it offers is much broader.

In general, Qt's drawing architecture consists of three parts. The most important part is the device the drawing takes place on, represented by the `QPaintDevice` class. Qt provides a number of paint device subclasses such as `QWidget` or `QImage` and `QPrinter` or `QPdfWriter`. You can see that the approach for drawing on a widget and printing on a printer will be quite the same. The difference is in the second component of the architecture—the paint engine (`QPaintEngine`). The engine is responsible for performing the actual paint operations on a particular paint device. Different paint engines are used to draw on images and to print on printers. This is completely hidden from you as a developer, so you really don't need to worry about it.

For you, the most important piece is the third component—`QPainter`—which is an adapter for the whole painting framework. It contains a set of high-level operations that can be invoked on the paint device. Behind the scenes, the whole work is delegated to an appropriate paint engine. While talking about painting, we will be focusing solely on the painter object as any painting code can be invoked on any of the target devices only by using a painter initialized on a different paint device. This effectively makes painting in Qt device agnostic, like in the following example:

```
void doSomePainting(QPainter *painter) {
  painter->drawLine(QPoint(0,0), QPoint(100, 40));
}
```

The same code can be executed on a painter working on any possible `QPaintDevice` class, be it a widget, an image, or an OpenGL context (through the use of `QOpenGLPaintDevice`).

Painter attributes

The `QPainter` class has a rich API that can basically be divided into three groups of methods. The first group contains setters and getters for attributes of the painter. The second group consists of methods, with names starting with `draw` and `fill` that perform drawing operations on the device. The last group has other methods, mostly ones that allow manipulating the coordinate system of the painter.

Let's start with the attributes. The three most important ones are the font, pen, and brush. The first is an instance of the `QFont` class. It contains a large number of methods for controlling such font parameters as font family, style (italic or oblique), font weight, and font size (either in points or device-dependent pixels). All the parameters are self-explanatory, so we will not discuss them here in detail. It is important to note that `QFont` can use any font installed on the system. In case more control over fonts is required or a font that is not installed in the system needs to be used, one can take advantage of the `QFontDatabase` class. It provides information about available fonts (such as whether a particular font is scalable or bitmap or what writing systems it supports) and allows adding new fonts into the registry by loading their definitions directly from files.

An important class, when it comes to fonts, is the `QFontMetrics` class. It allows calculating how much space is needed to paint particular text using a font or calculates text eliding. The most common use case is to check how much space to allocate for a particular user-visible string, for example:

```
QFontMetrics fm = painter.fontMetrics();
QRect rect = fm.boundingRect("Game Programming using Qt");
```

This is especially useful when trying to determine `sizeHint` for a widget.

The pen and brush are two attributes that define how different drawing operations are performed. The pen defines the outline, and the brush fills the shapes drawn using the painter. The former is represented by the `QPen` class and the latter by `QBrush`. Each of them is really a set of parameters. The most simple one is the color defined either as a predefined global color enumeration value (such as `Qt::red` or `Qt::transparent`) or an instance of the `QColor` class. The effective color is made up of four attributes—three color components (red, green, and blue) and an optional alpha channel value that determines transparency of the color (the larger the value, the more opaque the color). By default, all components are expressed as 8-bit values (0 to 255) but can also be expressed as real values representing a percentage of the maximum saturation of the component; for example, 0.6 corresponds to 153 (*0.6*255*). For convenience, one of the `QColor` constructors accepts hexadecimal color codes used in HTML (with `#0000FF` being an opaque blue color) or even bare color names (for example, `blue`) from a predefined list of colors returned by a static function `QColor::colorNames()`. Once a color object is defined using RGB components, it can be queried using different color spaces (for example, CMYK or HSV). Also, a set of static methods are available that act as constructors for colors expressed in different color spaces. For example, to construct a clear magenta color, any of the following expressions can be used:

- `QColor("magenta")`
- `QColor("#FF00FF")`
- `QColor(255, 0, 255)`
- `QColor::fromRgbF(1, 0, 1)`
- `QColor::fromHsv(300, 255, 255)`
- `QColor::fromCmyk(0, 255, 0, 0)`
- `Qt::magenta`

Apart from the color, QBrush has two additional ways of expressing the fill of a shape. You can use QBrush::setTexture() to set a pixmap that will be used as a stamp or QBrush::setGradient() to make the brush use a gradient to do the filling. For example, to use a gradient that goes diagonally and starts yellow in the top-left corner of the shape, becomes red in the middle of the shape, and ends magenta at the bottom-right corner of the shape, the following code can be used:

```
QLinearGradient gradient(0, 0, width, height);
gradient.setColorAt(0,   Qt::yellow);
gradient.setColorAt(0.5, Qt::red);
gradient.setColorAt(1.0, Qt::magenta);
QBrush brush = gradient;
```

When used with drawing a rectangle, this code will give the following output:

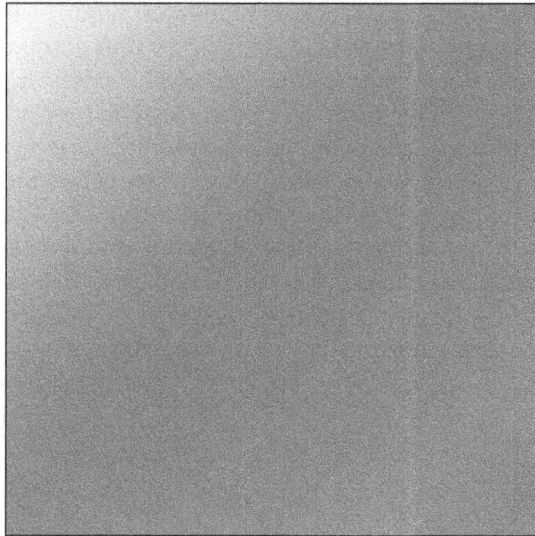

Qt can handle linear (QLinearGradient), radial (QRadialGradient), and conical (QConicalGradient) gradients. It comes with a sample (shown in the following screenshot) where you can see different gradients in action. This sample is located in examples/widgets/painting/gradients.

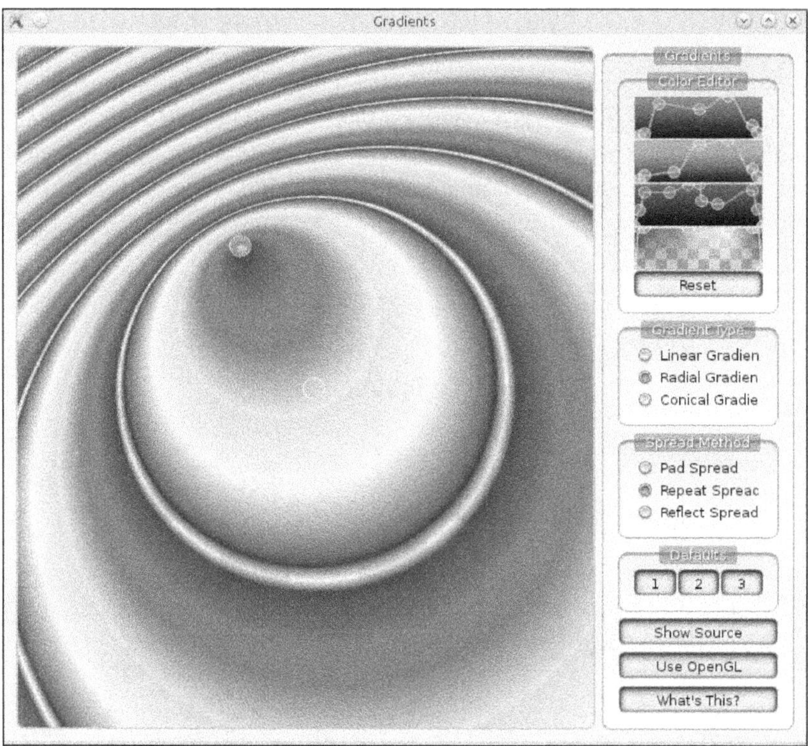

As for the pen, its main attribute is its width (expressed in pixels), which determines the thickness of the shape outline. A special width setting is `0`, which constitutes a so-called cosmetic pen that is always drawn as a 1 pixel-wide line no matter what transformations are applied to the painter (we'll cover this later). A pen can of course have a color set but, in addition to that, you can use any brush as a pen. The result of such an operation is that you can draw thick outlines of shapes using gradients or textures.

There are three more important properties for a pen. The first of them is the pen style, set using `QPen::setStyle()`. It determines whether lines drawn by the pen are continuous or somehow divided (dashes, dots, and so on). You can see available line styles together with their corresponding constants in the following diagram:

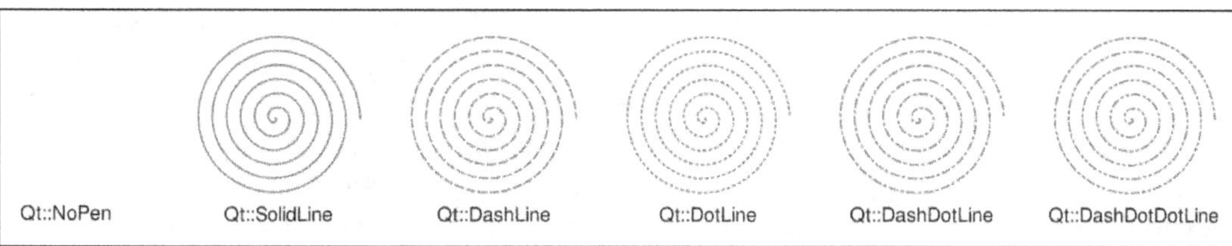

The second attribute is the cap style, which can be flat, square, or round. The third attribute—the join style—is important for polyline outlines and dictates how different segments of the polyline are connected. You can make the joins sharp (with `Qt::MiterJoin`), round (`Qt::RoundJoin`), or a hybrid of the two (`Qt::BevelJoin`). You can see the different pen attribute configurations (including different join and cap styles) in action by launching the pathstroke example shown in the following screenshot:

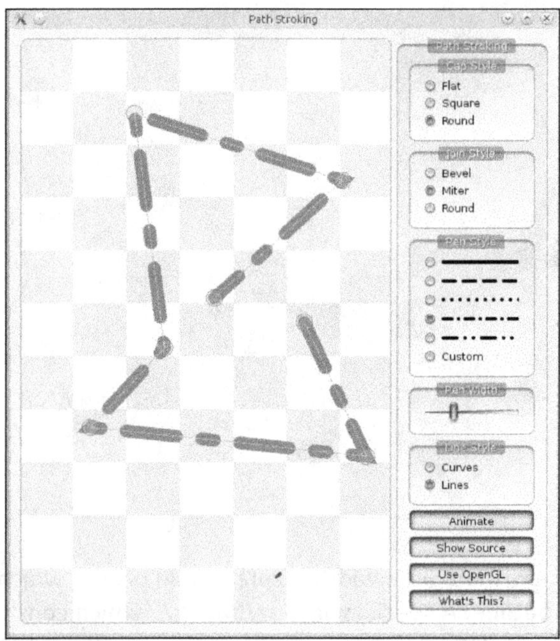

The next important aspect of the painter is its coordinate system. The painter in fact has two coordinate systems. One is its own logical coordinate system that operates on real numbers, and the other is the physical coordinate system of the device the painter operates on. Each operation on the logical coordinate system is mapped to physical coordinates in the device and applied there. Let's start with explaining the logical coordinate system first, and then we'll see how this relates to physical coordinates.

The painter represents an infinite Cartesian canvas with the horizontal axis pointing right and the vertical axis pointing down by default. The system can be modified by applying affine transformations to it—translating, rotating, scaling, and shearing. This way, you can draw an analog clock face that marks each hour with a line by executing a loop that rotates the coordinate system by 30 degrees for each hour and draws a line that is vertical in the newly obtained coordinate system. Another example is when you wish to draw a simple plot with *x* axis going right and *y* axis going up. To obtain the proper coordinate system, you would scale the coordinate system by `-1` in the vertical direction, effectively reversing the direction of the vertical axis.

What we described here modifies the world transformation matrix for the painter represented by an instance of the `QTransform` class. You can always query the current state of the matrix by calling `transform()` on the painter and you can set a new matrix by calling `setTransform()`. `QTransform` has methods such as `scale()`, `rotate()`, and `translate()` that modify the matrix, but `QPainter` has equivalent methods for manipulating the world matrix directly. In most cases, using these would be preferable.

Each painting operation is expressed in logical coordinates, goes through the world transformation matrix, and reaches the second stage of coordinate manipulation, which is the view matrix. The painter has the concept of `viewport()` and `window()` rectangles. The `viewport` rectangle represents the physical coordinates of an arbitrary rectangle while the `window` rectangle expresses the same rectangle but in logical coordinates. Mapping one to another gives a transformation that needs to be applied to each drawn primitive to calculate the area of the physical device that is to be painted. By default, the two rectangles are identical to the rectangle of the underlying device (thus no `window-viewport` mapping is done). Such transformation is useful if you wish to perform painting operations using measurement units other than the pixels of the target device. For example, if you want to express coordinates using percentages of the width and height of the target device, you would set the window width and height both to `100`. Then, to draw a line starting at 20% of the width and 10% of the height and ending at 70% of the width and 30% of the height, you would tell the painter to draw the line between (`20, 10`) and (`70, 30`). If you wanted those percentages to apply not to the whole area of an image but rather to its left half, you set the viewport rectangle only to the left half of the image.

> Setting the `window` and `viewport` rectangles only defines coordinate mapping; it does not prevent drawing operations from painting outside the `viewport` rectangle. If you want such behavior, you have to set a `clipping` rectangle on the painter.

Once you have the painter properly set, you can start issuing painting operations. `QPainter` has a rich set of operations for drawing different kinds of primitives. All of these operations have the prefix `draw` in their names, followed by the name of the primitive that is to be drawn. Thus, such operations as `drawLine`, `drawRoundedRect`, and `drawText` are available with a number of overloads that usually allow us to express coordinates using different data types. These may be pure values (either integer or real), Qt's classes, such as `QPoint` and `QRect`, or their floating point equivalents—`QPointF` and `QRectF`. Each operation is performed using current painter settings (font, pen, and brush).

To see the list of all drawing operations available, switch to the **Help** pane in Qt Creator. From the drop-down list on top of the window, choose **Index** and then type in `qpainter`. After confirming the search, you should see the reference manual for the `QPainter` class with all the drawing operations listed.

Before you start drawing, you have to tell the painter what device you wish to draw on. This is done using the `begin()` and `end()` methods. The former accepts a pointer to a `QPaintDevice` instance and initializes the drawing infrastructure, and the latter marks the drawing as complete. Usually, we don't have to use these methods directly as the constructor of `QPainter` calls `begin()` for us and the destructor invokes `end()`. Thus, the typical workflow is to instantiate a painter object, passing it the device, then do the drawing by calling `set` and `draw` methods, and finally let the painter be destroyed by going out of scope, as follows:

```
{
  QPainter painter(this); // paint on the current object
  QPen pen = Qt::red;
  pen.setWidth(2);
  painter.setPen(pen);
  painter.setBrush(Qt::yellow);
  painter.drawRect(0, 0, 100, 50);
}
```

We will cover more methods from the `draw` family in the following sections of this chapter.

Widget painting

It is time to actually get something onto the screen by painting on a widget. A widget is repainted as a result of receiving an event called `QEvent::Paint`, which is handled by reimplementing the virtual method `paintEvent()`. This method accepts a pointer to the event object of type `QPaintEvent` that contains various bits of information about the repaint request. Remember that you can only paint on the widget from within that widget's `paintEvent()` call.

Time for action – custom-painted widgets

Let's immediately use our new skills in practice!

Start by creating a new **Qt Widgets Application** in Qt Creator, choosing `QWidget` as the base class, and making sure the **Generate Form** box is unchecked.

Switch to the header file for the newly created class, add a protected section to the class and type void `paintEvent` for the section. Then press *Ctrl* + spacebar on your keyboard and Creator will suggest the parameters for the method. You should end up with the following code:

```
protected:
    void paintEvent(QPaintEvent *);
```

Creator will leave the cursor positioned right before the semicolon. Pressing *Alt* + *Enter* will open the refactoring menu, letting you add the definition in the implementation file. The standard code for a paint event is one that instantiates a painter on the widget, as shown:

```
void Widget::paintEvent(QPaintEvent *)
{
  QPainter painter(this);
}
```

If you run this code, the widget will remain blank. Now we can start adding the actual painting code there:

```
void Widget::paintEvent(QPaintEvent *)
{
  QPainter painter(this);
  QPen pen(Qt::black);
  pen.setWidth(4);
  painter.setPen(pen);
  QRect r = rect().adjusted(10, 10, -10, -10);
  painter.drawRoundedRect(r, 20, 10);
}
```

Build and run the code, and you'll obtain the following output:

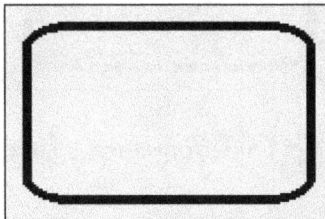

What just happened?

First we set a 2 pixel-wide black pen for the painter. Then we called `rect()` to retrieve the geometry rectangle of the widget. By calling `adjusted()`, we received a new rectangle with its coordinates (in left, top, right, and bottom order) modified by the given arguments, effectively giving us a rectangle with a 10 pixel margin on each side.

> Qt usually offers two methods that allow us to work with modified data. Calling `adjusted()` returns a new object with its attributes modified, while if we had called `adjust()`, the modification would have been done in place. Pay special attention to which method you use to avoid unexpected results. It's best to always check the return value for a method—whether it returns a copy or void.

Finally we call `drawRoundedRect()`, which paints a rectangle with its corners rounded by the number of pixels (in *x*, *y* order) given as the second and third argument. If you look closely, you will notice that the rectangle has nasty jagged rounded parts. This is caused by the effect of aliasing, where a logical line is approximated using the limited resolution of the screen; due to this, a pixel is either fully drawn or not drawn at all. Qt offers a mechanism called antialiasing to counter this effect by using intermediate pixel colors where appropriate. You can enable this mechanism by setting a proper render hint on the painter before you draw the rounded rectangle, as shown:

```
void Widget::paintEvent(QPaintEvent *)
{
  QPainter painter(this);
  painter.setRenderHint(QPainter::Antialiasing, true);
  // …
}
```

Now you'll get the following output:

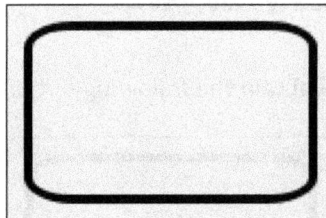

Of course, this has a negative impact on performance, so use antialiasing only where the aliasing effect is noticeable.

Time for action – transforming the viewport

Let's extend our code so that all future operations focus only on drawing within the border boundaries after the border is drawn. Use the `window` and `viewport` transformation as follows:

```
void Widget::paintEvent(QPaintEvent *) {
  QPainter painter(this);
  painter.setRenderHint(QPainter::Antialiasing, true);
  QPen pen(Qt::black);
  pen.setWidth(4);
  painter.setPen(pen);
  QRect r = rect().adjusted(10, 10, -10, -10);
  painter.drawRoundedRect(r, 20, 10);
  painter.save();
  r.adjust(2, 2, -2, -2);
  painter.setViewport(r);
  r.moveTo(0, -r.height()/2);
  painter.setWindow(r);
  drawChart(&painter, r);
  painter.restore();
}
```

Also create a protected method called `drawChart()`:

```
void Widget::drawChart(QPainter *painter, const QRect &rect) {
  painter->setPen(Qt::red);
  painter->drawLine(0, 0, rect.width(), 0);
}
```

Let's take a look at our output:

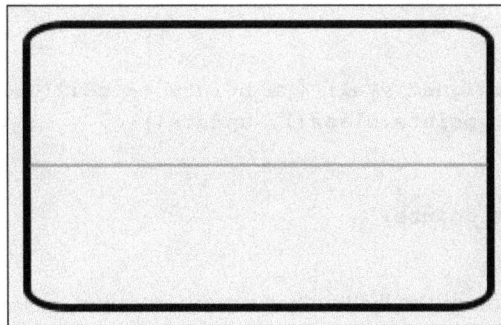

What just happened?

The first thing we did in the newly added code is call `painter.save()`. This call stores all parameters of the painter in an internal stack. We can then modify the painter state (by changing its attributes, applying transformations, and so on) and then, if at any point we want to go back to the saved state, it is enough to call `painter.restore()` to undo all the modifications in one go.

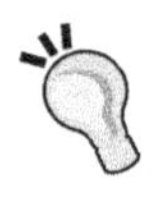

> The `save()` and `restore()` methods can be called as many times as needed. Just remember to always pair a call to `save()` with a similar call to `restore()`, or the internal painter state will get corrupted. Each call to `restore()` will revert the painter to the last saved state.

After the state is saved, we modify the rectangle again by adjusting for the width of the border. Then, we set the new rectangle as the viewport, informing the painter about the physical range of coordinates to operate on. Then we move the rectangle by half its height and set that as the painter window. This effectively puts the origin of the painter at half the height of the widget. Then, the `drawChart()` method is called whereby a red line is drawn on the *x* axis of the new coordinate system.

Time for action – drawing an oscillogram

Let's further extend our widget to become a simple oscillogram renderer. For that we have to make the widget remember a set of values and draw them as a series of lines.

Let's start by adding a `QList<quint16>` member variable that holds a list of unsigned 16-bit integer values. We will also add slots for adding values to the list and for clearing the list, as shown:

```
class Widget : public QWidget
{
  // ...
public slots:
  void addPoint(unsigned yVal) { m_points << qMax(0u, yVal); update(); }
  void clear() { m_points.clear(); update(); }
protected:
  // ...
  QList<quint16> m_points;
};
```

Note that each modification of the list invokes a method called `update()`. This schedules a paint event so that our widget can be redrawn with the new values.

Drawing code is also easy; we just iterate over the list and draw symmetric blue lines based on the values from the list. Since the lines are vertical, they don't suffer from aliasing and so we can disable this render hint, as shown:

```
void Widget::drawChart(QPainter *painter, const QRect &rect) {
  painter->setPen(Qt::red);
  painter->drawLine(0, 0, rect.width(), 0);
  painter->save();
  painter->setRenderHint(QPainter::Antialiasing, false);
  painter->setPen(Qt::blue);
  for(int i=0;i < m_points.size(); ++i) {
    painter->drawLine(i, -m_points.at(i), i, m_points.at(i));
  }
  painter->restore();
}
```

To see the result add a loop to `main` as follows. This fills the widget with data:

```
for(int i=0;i<450;++i) w.addPoint(qrand() % 120);
```

This loop takes a random number between `0` and `119` and adds it as a point to the widget. A sample result from running such code can be seen in the following screenshot:

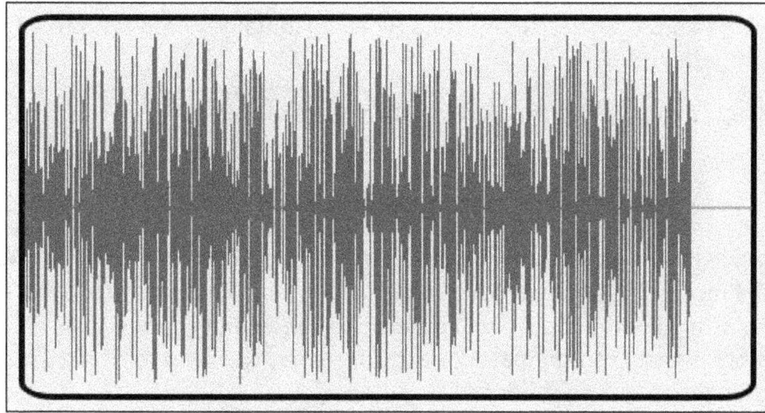

If you scale down the window, you will notice that the oscillogram extends past the boundaries of the rounded rectangle. Remember about clipping? You can use it now to constrain drawing by adding a simple `painter.setClipRect(r)` call just before you call `drawChart()`.

Input events

So far, the custom widget was not interactive at all. Although the widget content could be manipulated from within the source code (say by adding new points to the plot), the widget was deaf to any user actions (apart from resizing the widget, which caused a repaint). In Qt, any interaction between the user and the widget is done by delivering events to the widget. Such a family of events is generally called input events and contains events such as keyboard events and different forms of pointing-device events—mouse, tablet, and touch events.

In a typical mouse event flow, a widget first receives a mouse press event, then a number of mouse move events (when the user moves the mouse around while the mouse button is kept pressed), and finally, a mouse release event. The widget can also receive an additional mouse double-click event in addition to these events. It is important to remember that, by default, mouse move events are only delivered if a mouse button is pressed when the mouse is moved. To receive mouse move events when no button is pressed, a widget needs to activate a feature called **mouse tracking**.

Time for action – making oscillograms selectable

It's time to make our oscillogram widget interactive. We will teach it to add a couple of lines of code to it that let the user select part of the plot. Let's start with storage for the selection. We'll need two integer variables that can be accessed via read-only properties; therefore, add the following two properties to the class (you can initialize them both to `-1`) and implement their getters:

```
Q_PROPERTY(int selectionStart READ selectionStart
                              NOTIFY selectionChanged)
Q_PROPERTY(int selectionEnd READ selectionEnd
                            NOTIFY selectionChanged)
```

The user can change the selection by dragging the mouse cursor over the plot. When the user presses the mouse button over some place in the plot, we'll mark that place as the start of the selection. Dragging the mouse will determine the end of the selection. The scheme for naming events is similar to the paint event; therefore, we need to declare and implement the following two protected methods:

```
void Widget::mousePressEvent(QMouseEvent *mouseEvent) {
  m_selectionStart = m_selectionEnd = mouseEvent->pos().x() - 12;
  emit selectionChanged();
  update();
}
void Widget::mouseMoveEvent(QMouseEvent *mouseEvent) {
  m_selectionEnd = mouseEvent->pos().x() - 12;
  emit selectionChanged();
  update();
}
```

The structure of both event handlers is similar. We update the needed values, taking into consideration the left padding (12 pixels) of the plot, similar to what we do while drawing. Then, a signal is emitted and `update()` is called to schedule a repaint of the widget.

What remains is to introduce changes to the drawing code. I suggest you add a `drawSelection()` method similar to `drawChart()` but that is called from the paint event handler immediately before `drawChart()`, as shown:

```
void Widget::drawSelection(QPainter *painter, const QRect &rect) {
  if(m_selectionStart < 0 ) return;
  painter->save();
  painter->setPen(Qt::NoPen);
  painter->setBrush(palette().highlight());
  QRect selectionRect = rect;
  selectionRect.setLeft(m_selectionStart);
  selectionRect.setRight(m_selectionEnd);
  painter->drawRect(selectionRect);
  painter->restore();
}
```

First we check if there is any selection to be drawn at all. Then, we save the painter state and adjust the pen and brush of the painter. The pen is set to `Qt::NoPen`, which means the painter should not draw any outline. To determine the brush, we use `palette()`; this returns an object of type `QPalette` holding basic colors for a widget. One of the colors held in the object is the color of the highlight often used for marking selections. If you use an entry from the palette instead of manually specifying a color, you gain an advantage that when the user of the class modifies the palette, this modification is taken into account by our widget code.

> You can use other colors from the palette in the widget for other things we draw in the widget. You can even define your own `QPalette` object in the constructor of the widget to provide default colors for it.

Finally, we adjust the rectangle to be drawn and issue the drawing call.

When you run this program, you will notice that the selection color doesn't contrast very well with the plot itself. To overcome this, a common approach is to draw the "selected" content with a different (often inverted) color. This can easily be applied in this situation by modifying the `drawChart()` code slightly:

```
for(int i=0; i < m_points.size(); ++i) {
  if(m_selectionStart <= i && m_selectionEnd >=i) {
    painter->setPen(Qt::white);
```

```
    } else
      painter->setPen(Qt::blue);
    painter->drawLine(i, -m_points.at(i), i, m_points.at(i));
  }
```

Now you see the following output:

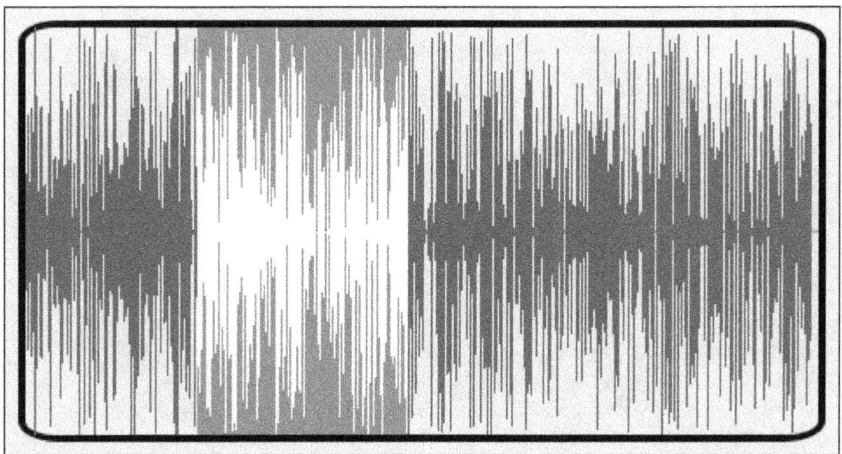

Have a go hero – reacting only to the left mouse button

As an exercise, you can modify the event handling code so that it only changes the selection if the mouse event was triggered by the left mouse button. To see which button triggered the mouse press event, you can use the `QMouseEvent::button()` method, which returns `Qt::LeftButton` for the left button, `Qt::RightButton` for the right, and so on.

Handling touch events is different. For any such event, you receive a call to the `touchEvent()` virtual method. The parameter of such a call is an object that can retrieve a list of points currently touched by the user with additional information regarding the history of user interaction (whether the touch was just initiated or the point was pressed earlier and moved) and what force is applied to the point by the user. Note that this is a low-level framework that allows you to precisely follow the history of touch interaction. If you are more interested in higher-level gesture recognition (pan, pinch, and swipe), there is a separate family of events available for it.

Handling gestures is a two-step procedure. First you need to activate gesture recognition on your widget by calling `grabGesture()` and passing in the type of gesture you want to handle. A good place for such code is the widget constructor.

Then your widget will start receiving gesture events. There are no dedicated handlers for gesture events but, fortunately, all events for an object flow through its `event()` method, which we can reimplement. Here is some example code that handles pan gestures:

```
bool Widget::event(QEvent *e) {
  if(e->type() == QEvent::Gesture) {
    QGestureEvent *gestureEvent = static_cast<QGestureEvent*>(e);
    QGesture *pan  = gestureEvent->gesture(Qt::PanGesture);
    if(pan) {
      handlePanGesture(static_cast<QPanGesture*>(pan));
    }
  }
  return QWidget::event(e);
}
```

First, a check for the event type is made; if it matches the expected value, the event object is cast to `QGestureEvent`. Then, the event is asked if `Qt::PanGesture` was recognized. Finally, a `handlePanGesture` method is called. You can implement such a method to handle your pan gestures.

Working with images

Qt has two classes for handling images. The first one is `QImage`, more tailored towards direct pixel manipulation. You can check the size of the image or check and modify the color of each pixel. You can convert the image into a different internal representation (say from 8-bit color map to full 32-bit color with a premultiplied alpha channel). This type, however, is not that fit for rendering. For that, we have a different class called `QPixmap`. The difference between the two classes is that `QImage` is always kept in the application memory, while `QPixmap` can only be a handle to a resource that may reside in the graphics card memory or on a remote *X* server. Its main advantage over `QImage` is that it can be rendered very quickly at the cost of the inability to access pixel data. You can freely convert between the two types but bear in mind that, on some platforms, this might be an expensive operation. Always consider which class serves your particular situation better. If you intend to crop the image, tint it with some color, or paint over it, `QImage` is a better choice. But if you just want to render a bunch of icons, it's best to keep them as `QPixmap` instances.

Loading

Loading images is very easy. Both `QPixmap` and `QImage` have constructors that simply accept a path to a file containing the image. Qt accesses image data through plugins that implement reading and writing operations for different image formats. Without going into the details of plugins, it is enough to say that the default Qt installation supports reading the following image types:

Type	Description
BMP	Windows bitmap
GIF	Graphics Interchange Format
ICO	Windows icon
JPEG	Joint Photography Experts Group
MNG	Multiple-image Network Graphics
PNG	Portable Network Graphics
PPM/PBM/PGM	Portable anymap
SVG	Scalable Vector Graphics
TIFF	Tagged Image File Format
XBM	X Bitmap
XPM	X Pixmap

As you can see, most popular image formats are available. The list can be further extended by installing additional plugins.

You can ask Qt for a list of supported image types by calling a static method, `QImageReader::supportedImageFormats()`, which returns a list of formats that can be read by Qt. For a list of writable formats, call `QImageWriter::supportedFileFormats()`.

An image can also be loaded directly from an existing memory buffer. This can be done in two ways. The first one is to use the `loadFromData()` method (it exists in both `QPixmap` and `QImage`), which behaves the same as when loading an image from a file—you pass it a data buffer and the size of the buffer and based on that, the loader determines the image type by inspecting the header data and loads the picture into `QImage` or `QPixmap`. The second situation is when you don't have images stored in a "filetype" such as JPEG or PNG but rather you have raw pixel data itself. In such a situation, `QImage` offers a constructor that takes a pointer to a block of data together with the size of the image and format of the data. The format is not a file format such as the ones listed earlier but rather a memory layout for data representing a single pixel.

The most popular format is `QImage::Format_ARGB32`, which means that each pixel is represented by 32-bits (4 bytes) of data divided equally between alpha, red, green, and blue channels—8-bits per channel. Another popular format is `QImage::Format_ARGB32_Premultiplied`, where values for the red, green, and blue channels are stored after being multiplied by the value of the alpha channel, which often results in faster rendering. You can change the internal data representation using a call to `convertToFormat()`. For example, the following code converts a true-color image to 256 colors, where color for each pixel is represented by an index in a color table:

```
QImage trueColor(image.png);
QImage indexed = trueColor.convertToFormat(QImage::Format_Indexed8);
```

The color table itself is a vector of color definitions that can be fetched using `colorTable()` and replaced using `setColorTable()`. The simplest way to convert an indexed image to grayscale is to adjust its color table as follows:

```
QImage indexed = …;
QVector<QRgb> ct = indexed.colorTable();
for(int i=0;i<ct.size();++i) ct[i] = qGray(ct[i]);
indexed.setColorTable(ct);
```

Modifying

There are two ways to modify image pixel data. The first one works only for `QImage` and involves direct manipulation of pixels using the `setPixel()` call, which takes the pixel coordinates and color to be set for that pixel. The second one works for both `QImage` and `QPixmap` and makes use of the fact that both these classes are subclasses of `QPaintDevice`. Therefore, you can open `QPainter` on such objects and use its drawing API. Here is an example of obtaining a pixmap with a blue rectangle and red circle painted over it:

```
QPixmap px(256, 256);
px.fill(Qt::transparent);
QPainter painter(&px);
painter.setPen(Qt::NoPen);
painter.setBrush(Qt::blue);
QRect r = px.rect().adjusted(10, 10, -10, -10);
painter.drawRect(r);
painter.setBrush(Qt::red);
painter.drawEllipse(r);
```

First we create a 256 x 256 pixmap and fill it with transparent color. Then we open a painter on it and invoke a series of calls that draws a blue rectangle and red circle.

`QImage` also offers a number of methods for transforming the image, including `scaled()`, `mirrored()`, `transformed()`, and `copy()`. Their API is intuitive so we won't discuss them here.

Painting

Painting images in its basic form is as simple as calling `drawImage()` or `drawPixmap()` from the `QPainter` API. There are different variants of the two methods, but basically all of them allow one to specify which portion of a given image or pixmap is to be drawn and where. It is worth noting that painting pixmaps is preferred to painting images as an image has to first be converted into a pixmap before it can be drawn.

If you have a lot of pixmaps to draw, a class called `QPixmapCache` may come in handy. It provides an application-wide cache for pixmaps. By using it, you can speed up pixmap loading while introducing a cap on memory usage.

Painting text

Drawing text using `QPainter` deserves a separate explanation, not because it is complicated but rather because Qt offers much flexibility in this regard. In general, painting text takes place by calling `QPainter::drawText()` or `QPainter::drawStaticText()`. Let's focus on the former first, which allows the drawing of generic text.

The most basic call to paint some text is a variant of this method, which takes *x* and *y* coordinates and the text to draw:

```
painter.drawText(10, 20, "Drawing some text at (10, 20)");
```

The preceding call draws the given text at position 10 horizontally and places the baseline of the text at position 20 vertically. The text is drawn using the painter's current font and pen. The coordinates can alternatively be passed as `QPoint` instances instead of being given *x* and *y* values separately. The problem with this method is that it allows little control over how the text is drawn. A much more flexible variant is one that lets us give a set of flags and expresses the position of the text as a rectangle instead of a point. The flags can specify alignment of the text within the given rectangle or instruct the rendering engine about wrapping and clipping the text. You can see the result of giving a different combination of flags to the call in the following image:

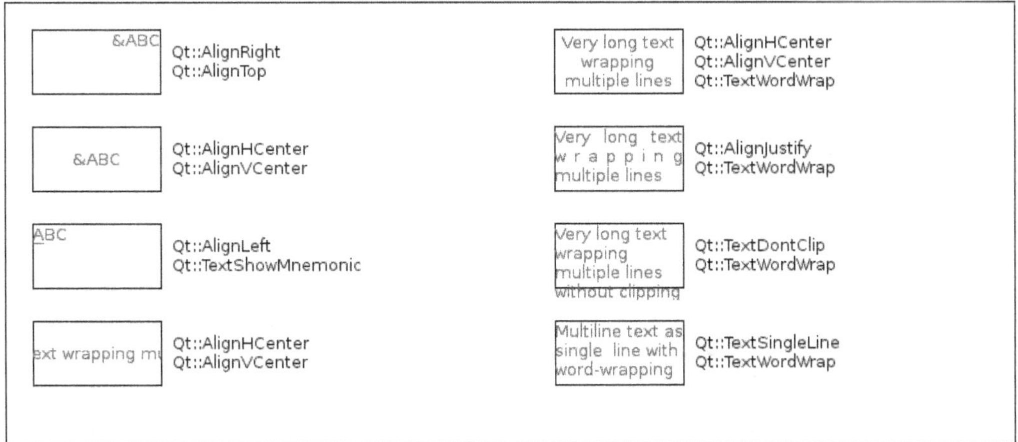

In order to obtain each of the preceding results, run code similar to the following:

```
painter.drawText(rect, Qt::AlignLeft|Qt::TextShowMnemonic, "&ABC");
```

You can see that, unless you set the `Qt::TextDontClip` flag, the text is clipped to the given rectangle; setting `Qt::TextWordWrap` enables line wrapping and `Qt::TextSingleLine` makes the engine ignore any newline characters encountered.

Static text

Qt has to perform a number of calculations when laying out the text, and this has to be done each time the text is rendered. This will be a waste of time if the text and its attributes have not changed since the last time. To avoid the need to recalculate the layout, the concept of static text was introduced.

To use it, instantiate `QStaticText` and initialize it with text you want to render along with any options you might want it to have (kept as the `QTextOption` instance). Then, store the object somewhere and, whenever you want the text to be rendered, just call `QPainter::drawStaticText()`, passing the static text object to it. If the layout of the text has not changed since the previous time the text was drawn, it will not be recalculated, resulting in improved performance. Here is an example of a custom widget that simply draws text using the static text approach:

```
class TextWidget : public QWidget {
public:
  TextWidget(QWidget *parent = 0) : QWidget(parent) {}
  void setText(const QString &txt) {
    m_staticText.setText(txt);
    update();
  }
```

```
protected:
  void paintEvent(QPaintEvent *) {
    QPainter painter(this);
    paitner.drawStaticText(0, 0, m_staticText);
  }
private:
  QStaticText m_staticText;
};
```

Rich text

So far, we have seen how to draw text where all the glyphs were rendered using the same attributes (font, color, and style) and laid out as a contiguous flow of characters. While useful, this doesn't handle situations where we want to mark out portions of the text using a different color or align it differently. To make it work, we would have to execute a series of `drawText` calls with modified painter attributes and with manually calculated text positions. Fortunately, there are better solutions.

Qt supports complex document formatting using its `QTextDocument` class. With this we can manipulate the text in a fashion similar to that of a text processor, applying formatting to paragraphs of text or individual characters. Then we can lay out and render the resulting document according to our needs.

While useful and powerful, building `QTextDocument` is too complicated if all we want is to draw a small amount of text with simple customizations applied. The authors of Qt have thought about that as well and have implemented a rich text mode for rendering text. After enabling this mode, you can specify the formatted text to `drawText` directly using a subset of HTML tags to obtain formatting effects such as changing the color of the text, underlining it, or making it superscript. Drawing a centered underlined caption followed by a fully justified description in a given rectangle is as easy as issuing the following call:

```
painter.drawText(rect,
  "<div align='center'><b>Disclaimer</b></div>"
  "<div align='justify'>You are using <i>this software</i> "
  "at your own risk. The authors of the software do not give "
  "any warranties that using this software will not ruin your "
  "business.</div>");
```

Qt's rich text engine does not implement the full HTML specification; it will not handle cascading style sheets, hyperlinks, tables, or JavaScript. The *Supported HTML Subset* page in the Qt reference manual describes what parts of the HTML 4 standard are supported. If you require full HTML support, you will have to use Qt's web page and web browser classes contained in the `webkitwidgets` (classes `QWebPage` and `QWebView`) or `webenginewidgets` (classes `QWebEnginePage` and `QWebEngineView`) modules.

Optimized drawing

During game programming, performance is often a bottleneck. Qt tries its best to be as efficient as possible, but sometimes the code needs additional tweaking to work even faster. Using static text instead of regular text is one such tweak; use it whenever possible.

Another important trick is to avoid re-rendering the whole widget unless really required. One thing is that the `QPaintEvent` object passed to `paintEvent()` contains information about the region of the widget that needs to be redrawn. If the logic of your widget allows it, you can optimize the process by rendering only the required part.

Time for action – optimizing oscillogram drawing

As an exercise, we will modify our oscillogram widget so that it only re-renders the part of its data that is required. The first step is to modify the paint event handling code to fetch information about the region that needs updating and pass it to the method drawing the chart. The changed parts of the code have been highlighted here:

```
void Widget::paintEvent(QPaintEvent *pe)
{
  QRect exposedRect = pe->rect();
  ...
  drawSelection(&painter, r, exposedRect);
  drawChart(&painter, r, exposedRect);
  painter.restore();
}
```

The next step is to modify `drawSelection()` to only draw the part of the selection that intersects with the exposed rectangle. Luckily, `QRect` offers a method to calculate the intersection for us:

```
void Widget::drawSelection(QPainter *painter, const QRect &rect,
const QRect &exposedRect)
{
    // ...
    QRect selectionRect = rect;
    selectionRect.setLeft(m_pressX);
    selectionRect.setRight(m_releaseX);
    painter->drawRect(selectionRect.intersected(exposedRect));
    painter->restore();
}
```

Finally, `drawChart` needs to be adjusted to omit the values outside the exposed rectangle:

```
void Widget::drawChart(QPainter *painter, const QRect &rect,
const QRect &exposedRect)
{
  painter->setPen(Qt::red);
  painter->drawLine(exposedRect.left(), 0, exposedRect.width(), 0);
  painter->save();
  painter->setRenderHint(QPainter::Antialiasing, false);
  const int lastPoint = qMin(m_points.size(),
    exposedRect.right()+1);
  for(int i=exposedRect.left(); i < lastPoint; ++i) {
    if(m_selectionStart <= i && m_selectionEnd >=i) {
      painter->setPen(Qt::white);
    } else
    painter->setPen(Qt::blue);
    painter->drawLine(i, -m_points.at(i), i, m_points.at(i));
  }
    painter->restore();
}
```

What just happened?

By implementing these changes, we have effectively reduced the painted area to the rectangle received with the event. In this particular situation, we will not save much time as drawing the plot is not that time-consuming; in many situations, however, you will be able to save a lot of time using this approach. For example, if we were to plot a very detailed aerial map of a game world, it would be very expensive to replot the whole map if only a small part of it were modified. We can easily reduce the number of calculations and drawing calls by taking advantage of the information about the exposed area.

Making use of the exposed rectangle is already a good step towards efficiency, but we can go a step further. The current approach requires that we redraw each and every line of the plot within the exposed rectangle, which still takes some time. Instead, we can paint those lines only once into a pixmap, and then, whenever the widget needs repainting, tell Qt to render part of the pixmap to the widget. This approach is usually called "double-buffering" (the second buffer being the pixmap acting as a cache).

Have a go hero – implementing a double-buffered oscillogram

It should be very easy for you now to implement this approach for our example widget. The main difference is that each change to the plot contents should not result in a call to `update()` but rather in a call that will re-render the pixmap and then call `update()`. The `paintEvent` method then becomes simply this:

```
void Widget::paintEvent(QPaintEvent *pe)
{
  QRect exposedRect = pe->rect();
  QPainter painter(this);
  painter.drawPixmap(exposedRect, pixmap(), exposedRect);
}
```

You'll also need to re-render the pixmap when the widget is resized. This can be done from within the void `resizeEvent(QResizeEvent*)` method.

At this point, you are ready to employ your newly gained skills in rendering graphics with Qt to create a game that uses widgets with custom graphics. The hero of today is going to be chess and other chess-like games.

Time for action – developing the game architecture

Create a new **Qt Widgets Application** project. After the project infrastructure is ready, choose **New File or Project** from the **File** menu and choose to create a **C++ Class**. Call the new class `ChessBoard` and set `QObject` as its base class. Repeat the process to create a `GameAlgorithm` class derived from `QObject` and another one called `ChessView` but, this time, choose `QWidget` as the base class. You should end up with a file named `main.cpp` and four classes—`MainWindow`, `ChessView`, `ChessBoard`, and `ChessAlgorithm`.

Now navigate to the header file for `ChessAlgorithm` and add the following methods to the class:

```
public:
  ChessBoard* board() const;
```

```
public slots:
  virtual void newGame();
signals:
  void boardChanged(ChessBoard*);
protected:
  virtual void setupBoard();
  void setBoard(ChessBoard *board);
```

Also, add a private `m_board` field of type `ChessBoard*`. Remember to either include `chessboard.h` or forward-declare the `ChessBoard` class. Implement `board()` as a simple getter method for `m_board`. The `setBoard()` method is going to be a protected setter for `m_board`:

```
void ChessAlgorithm::setBoard(ChessBoard *board)
{
    if(board == m_board) return;
    if(m_board) delete m_board;
    m_board = board;
    emit boardChanged(m_board);
}
```

Next, let's provide a base implementation for `setupBoard()` to create a default chess board with eight ranks and eight columns:

```
void ChessAlgorithm::setupBoard()
{
    setBoard(new ChessBoard(8,8, this));
}
```

The natural place to prepare the board is in a function executed when a new game is started:

```
void ChessAlgorithm::newGame()
{
    setupBoard();
}
```

The last addition to this class for now is to extend the provided constructor to initialize `m_board` to a null pointer.

In the last method shown, we instantiated a `ChessBoard` object so let's focus on that class now. First extend the constructor to accept two additional integer parameters besides the regular parent argument. Store their values in private `m_ranks` and `m_columns` fields (remember to declare the fields themselves in the class header file).

In the header file, just under the `Q_OBJECT` macro, add the following two lines as property definitions:

```
Q_PROPERTY(int ranks READ ranks NOTIFY ranksChanged)
Q_PROPERTY(int columns READ columns NOTIFY columnsChanged)
```

Declare signals and implement getter methods to cooperate with those definitions. Also add two protected methods:

```
protected:
    void setRanks(int newRanks);
    void setColumns(int newColumns);
```

These will be setters for ranks and columns properties, but we don't want to expose them to the outside world so we will give them `protected` access scope.

Put the following code into the `setRanks()` method body:

```
void ChessBoard::setRanks(int newRanks)
{
    if(ranks() == newRanks) return;
    m_ranks = newRanks;
    emit ranksChanged(m_ranks);
}
```

Next, in a similar way, you can implement `setColumns()`.

The last class we will deal with now is our custom widget, `ChessView`. For now, we will provide only a rudimentary implementation for one method, but we will expand it later as our implementation grows. Add a public `setBoard(ChessBoard *)` method with the following body:

```
void ChessView::setBoard(ChessBoard *board)
{
    if(m_board == board) return;

    if(m_board) {
    // disconnect all signal-slot connections between m_board and this
        m_board->disconnect(this);
    }
    m_board = board;
    // connect signals (to be done later)
    updateGeometry();
}
```

Now let's declare the `m_board` member. Because we are not the owners of the board object (the algorithm class is responsible for managing it) we will use the `QPointer` class, which tracks the lifetime of `QObject` and sets itself to null once the object is destroyed:

```
private:
  QPointer<ChessBoard> m_board;
```

`QPointer` initializes its value to null, so we don't have to do it ourselves in the constructor. For completeness, let's provide a getter method for the board:

```
ChessBoard *ChessView::board() const { return m_board; }
```

What just happened?

In the last exercise, we defined the base architecture for our solution. We can see that there are three classes involved: `ChessView` acting as the user interface, `ChessAlgorithm` for driving the actual game, and `ChessBoard` as a data structure shared between the view and the engine. The algorithm is going to be responsible for setting up the board (through `setupBoard()`), making moves, checking win conditions, and so on. The view will be rendering the current state of the board and will signal user interaction to the underlying logic.

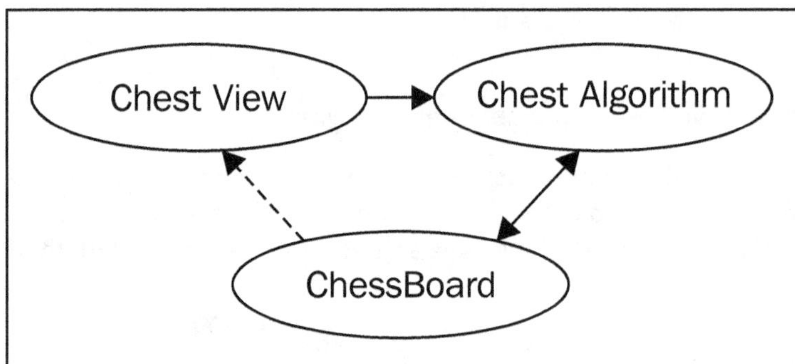

Most of the code is self-explanatory. You can see in the `ChessView::setBoard()` method that we are disconnecting all signals from an old board object, attaching the new one (we will come back to connecting the signals later when we have already defined them), and finally telling the widget to update its size and redraw itself with the new board.

Time for action – implementing the game board class

Now we will focus on our data structure. Add a new private member to `ChessBoard`, a vector of characters that will contain information about pieces on the board:

```
QVector<char> m_boardData;
```

Consider the following table that shows the piece type and the letters used for it:

Piece type		White	Black
	King	K	k
	Queen	Q	q
	Rook	R	r
	Bishop	B	b
	Knight	N	n
	Pawn	P	P

You can see that white pieces use upper-case letters and black pieces use lower-case variants of the same letters. In addition to that, we will use a space character (0x20 ASCII value) to denote that a field is empty. We will add a protected method for setting up an empty board based on the number of ranks and columns on the board and a `boardReset()` signal to inform that the position on the board has changed:

```
void ChessBoard::initBoard()
{
  m_boardData.fill(' ', ranks()*columns());
  emit boardReset();
}
```

We can update our methods for setting rank and column counts to make use of that method:

```
void ChessBoard::setRanks(int newRanks)
{
  if(ranks() == newRanks) return;
  m_ranks = newRanks;
  initBoard();
  emit ranksChanged(m_ranks);
}

void ChessBoard::setColumns(int newColumns)
{
  if(columns() == newColumns) return;
  m_columns = newColumns;
  initBoard();
  emit columnsChanged(m_columns);
}
```

The `initBoard()` method should also be called from within the constructor, so place the call there as well.

Next, we need a method to read which piece is positioned in the particular field of the board.

```
char ChessBoard::data(int column, int rank) const
{
  return m_boardData.at((rank-1)*columns()+(column-1));
}
```

Ranks and columns have indexes starting from 1, but the data structure is indexed starting from 0; therefore, we have to subtract 1 from both the rank and column index. It is also required to have a method to modify the data for the board. Implement the following public method:

```
void ChessBoard::setData(int column, int rank, char value)
{
  if(setDataInternal(column, rank, value))
    emit dataChanged(column, rank);
}
```

The method makes use of another one that does the actual job. However, this method should be declared with `protected` access scope. Again we adjust for index differences.

```
bool ChessBoard::setDataInternal(int column, int rank, char value)
{
  int index = (rank-1)*columns()+(column-1);
```

```
    if(m_boardData.at(index) == value) return false;
    m_boardData[index] = value;
    return true;
}
```

Since `setData()` makes use of a signal, we have to declare it as well:

```
signals:
  void ranksChanged(int);
  void columnsChanged(int);
  void dataChanged(int c, int r);
  void boardReset();
```

The signal will be emitted every time there is a successful change to the situation on the board. We delegate the actual work to the protected method to be able to modify the board without emitting the signal.

Having defined `setData()`, we can add another method for our convenience:

```
void ChessBoard::movePiece(int fromColumn, int fromRank, int toColumn,
int toRank)
{
  setData(toColumn, toRank, data(fromColumn, fromRank));
  setData(fromColumn, fromRank, ' ');
}
```

Can you guess what it does? That's right! It moves a piece from one field to another one leaving an empty space behind.

There is still one more method worth implementing. A regular chess game contains 32 pieces, and there are variants of the game where starting positions for the pieces might be different. Setting the position of each piece through a separate call to `setData()` would be very cumbersome. Fortunately, there is a neat chess notation called the **Forsyth-Edwards Notation (FEN)**, with which the complete state of the game can be stored as a single line of text. If you want the complete definition of the notation, you can look it up yourself. In short, we can say that the textual string lists piece placement rank by rank, starting from the last rank where each position is described by a single character interpreted as in our internal data structure (`K` for white king, `q` for black queen, and so on). Each rank description is separated by a / character. If there are empty fields on the board, they are not stored as spaces but rather as a digit specifying the number of consecutive empty fields. Therefore, the starting position for a standard game can be written as follows:

```
"rnbqkbnr/pppppppp/8/8/8/8/PPPPPPPP/RNBQKBNR"
```

This can be interpreted visually as follows:

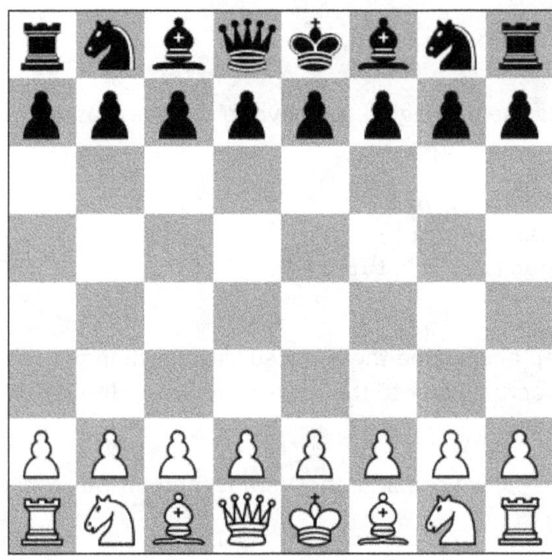

Let's write a method called `setFen()` to set up the board based on an FEN string:

```
void ChessBoard::setFen(const QString &fen)
{
  int index = 0;
  int skip = 0;
  const int columnCount = columns();
  QChar ch;
  for(int rank = ranks(); rank >0; --rank) {
    for(int column = 1; column <= columnCount; ++column) {
      if(skip > 0) {
        ch = ' ';
        skip--;
      } else {
        ch = fen.at(index++);
        if(ch.isDigit()) {
          skip = ch.toLatin1()-'0';
          ch = ' ';
          skip--;
        }
      }
      setDataInternal(column, rank, ch.toLatin1());
    }
```

```
        QChar next = fen.at(index++);
        if(next != '/' && next != ' ') {
          initBoard();
          return; // fail on error
        }
      }
      emit boardReset();
    }
```

The method iterates over all fields on the board and determines whether it is currently in the middle of inserting empty fields on the board or should rather read the next character from the string. If a digit is encountered, it is converted into an integer by subtracting the ASCII value of the 0 character (that is, *7-0 = 7*). After setting each rank, we require that a slash or a space be read from the string. Otherwise, we reset the board to an empty one and bail out of the method.

What just happened?

We taught the `ChessBoard` class to store simple information about chess pieces using a one-dimensional array of characters. We also equipped it with methods that allow querying and modifying game data. We implemented a fast way of setting the current state of the game by adopting the FEN standard. The game data itself is not tied to classic chess. Although we comply with a standard notation for describing pieces, it is possible to use other letters and characters outside the well-defined set for chess pieces. This creates a versatile solution for storing information about chess-like games, such as checkers, and possibly any other custom game played on a two-dimensional board of any size with ranks and columns. The data structure we came up with is not a stupid one—it communicates with its environment by emitting signals when the state of the game is modified.

Time for action – understanding the ChessView class

This is a chapter about doing graphics, so it is high time to focus on displaying our chess game. Our widget currently displays nothing, and our first task is going to be to show a chess board with rank and column symbols and fields colored appropriately.

By default, the widget does not have any proper size defined and we will have to fix that by implementing `sizeHint()`. However, to be able to calculate the size, we have to decide how big a single field on the board is going to be. Therefore, in `ChessView`, you should declare a property containing the size of the field, as shown:

```
Q_PROPERTY(QSize fieldSize
           READ fieldSize WRITE setFieldSize
           NOTIFY fieldSizeChanged)
```

To speed up coding, you can position the cursor over the property declaration, hit the *Alt* + *Enter* combination, and choose the **Generate missing Q_PROPERTY members** fixup from the pop-up menu. Creator will provide minor implementations for the getter and setter for you. You can move the generated code to the implementation file by positioning the cursor over each method, hitting *Alt* + *Enter,* and choosing the **Move definition to chessview.cpp file** fixup. While the generated getter method is fine, the setter needs some adjusting. Modify it by adding the following highlighted code:

```
void ChessView::setFieldSize(QSize arg)
{
    if (m_fieldSize == arg)
        return;

    m_fieldSize = arg;
    emit fieldSizeChanged(arg);
    updateGeometry();
}
```

This tells our widget to recalculate its size whenever the size of the field is modified. Now we can implement `sizeHint()`:

```
QSize ChessView::sizeHint() const
{
    if(!m_board) return QSize(100,100);
    QSize boardSize = QSize(fieldSize().width()
      * m_board->columns() +1,
    m_fieldSize.height() * m_board->ranks()   +1);
    int rankSize = fontMetrics().width('M')+4;
    int columnSize = fontMetrics().height()+4;
    return boardSize+QSize(rankSize, columnSize);
}
```

First we check if we have a valid board definition and if not, return a sane size of 100 x 100 pixels. Otherwise, the method calculates the size of all the fields by multiplying the size of each of the fields by the number of columns or ranks. We add one pixel to each dimension to accommodate the right and bottom border. A chess board not only consists of not only the fields themselves but also displays rank symbols on the left edge of the board and column numbers on the bottom edge of the board. Since we use letters to enumerate ranks, we check the width of the widest letter in the alphabet using the `QFontMetrics` class. We use the same class to check how much space is required to render a line of text using the current font so that we have enough space to put column numbers. In both cases, we add 4 to the result to make a 2 pixel margin between the text and the edge of the board and another 2 pixel margin between the text and the edge of the widget.

It is very useful to define a helper method for returning a rectangle that contains a particular field, as shown:

```
QRect ChessView::fieldRect(int column, int rank) const
{
  if(!m_board) return QRect();
  const QSize fs = fieldSize();
  QRect fRect = QRect(QPoint((column-1)*fs.width(),
    (m_board->ranks()-rank)*fs.height()), fs);
  // offset rect by rank symbols
  int offset = fontMetrics().width('M');
    // 'M' is the widest letter
  return fRect.translated(offset+4, 0);
}
```

Since rank numbers decrease from the top towards the bottom of the board, we subtract the desired rank from the maximum rank there is while calculating `fRect`. Then, we calculate the horizontal offset for rank symbols just like we did in `sizeHint()` and translate the rectangle by that offset before returning the result.

Finally, we can move on to implementing the event handler for the paint event. Declare the `paintEvent()` method (the fixup menu available under the *Alt* + *Enter* keyboard shortcut will let you generate a stub implementation of the method) and fill it with the following code:

```
void ChessView::paintEvent(QPaintEvent *event)
{
  if(!m_board) return;
  QPainter painter(this);
  for(int r = m_board->ranks(); r>0; --r) {
    painter.save();
    drawRank(&painter, r);
    painter.restore();
  }
  for(int c = 1; c<=m_board->columns();++c) {
    painter.save();
    drawColumn(&painter, c);
    painter.restore();
  }
  for(int r = 1; r<=m_board->ranks();++r) {
    for(int c = 1; c<=m_board->columns();++c) {
      painter.save();
      drawField(&painter, c, r);
      painter.restore();
    }
  }
}
```

The handler is quite simple. First we instantiate the `QPainter` object that operates on the widget. Then we have three loops—the first one iterates over ranks, the second over columns, and the third over all fields. The body of each loop is very similar: there is a call to a custom draw method that accepts a pointer to the painter and index of the rank, column, or both of them, respectively. Each of the calls is surrounded by executing `save()` and `restore()` on our `QPainter` instance. What are the calls for here? The three draw methods—`drawRank()`, `drawColumn()`, and `drawField()`—are going to be virtual methods responsible for rendering the rank symbol, the column number, and the field background. It will be possible to subclass `ChessView` and provide custom implementations for those renderers so that it is possible to provide a different look of the chess board. Since each of these methods takes the painter instance as its parameter, overrides of these methods could alter attribute values of the painter behind our back. Calling `save()` before handing the painter over to such override stores its state on an internal stack, and calling `restore()` after returning from the override resets the painter to what was stored with `save()`. This effectively gives us a failsafe to avoid breaking the painter in case the override does not clean up after itself if it modifies the painter.

Calling `save()` and `restore()` very often introduces a performance hit, so you should avoid saving and restoring painter states too often in time-critical situations. As our painting is very simple, we don't have to worry about that when painting our chess board.

Having introduced our three methods, we can start implementing them. Let's start with `drawRank` and `drawColumn`. Remember to declare them as virtual and put them in protected access scope (that's usually where Qt classes put such methods), as shown:

```
void ChessView::drawRank(QPainter *painter, int rank)
{
  QRect r = fieldRect(1, rank);
  QRect rankRect = QRect(0, r.top(), r.left(),
    r.height()).adjusted(2, 0, -2, 0);
  QString rankText = QString::number(rank);
  painter->drawText(rankRect,
    Qt::AlignVCenter|Qt ::AlignRight, rankText);
}

void ChessView::drawColumn(QPainter *painter, int column)
{
  QRect r = fieldRect(column, 1);
  QRect columnRect = QRect(r.left(), r.bottom(),
    r.width(), height()-r.bottom()).adjusted(0, 2, 0, -2);
  painter->drawText(columnRect,
    Qt:: AlignHCenter|Qt::AlignTop, QChar('a'+column-1));
}
```

Both methods are very similar. We use fieldRect() to query for the left-most column and bottom-most rank and based on that, we calculate where rank symbols and column numbers should be placed. The call to QRect::adjusted() is to accommodate the 2 pixel margin around the text to be drawn. Finally, we use drawText() to render appropriate text. For the rank, we ask the painter to align the text to the right edge of the rectangle and center the text vertically. In a similar way, when drawing the column we align to the top edge and center the text horizontally.

Now we can implement the third draw method. It should also be declared protected and virtual. Place the following code in the method body:

```
void ChessView::drawField(QPainter *painter, int column, int rank)
{
  QRect rect = fieldRect(column, rank);
  QColor fillColor = (column+rank) % 2 ? palette().
    color(QPalette::Light) : palette().color(QPalette::Mid);
  painter->setPen(palette().color(QPalette::Dark));
  painter->setBrush(fillColor);
  painter->drawRect(rect);
}
```

In this method, we use the QPalette object coupled with each widget to query for Light (usually white) and Mid (darkish) color depending on whether the field we are drawing on the chess board is considered white or black. We do that instead of hardcoding the colors to make it possible to modify colors of the tiles without subclassing simply by adjusting the palette object. Then we use the palette again to ask for the Dark color and use that as a pen for our painter. When we draw a rectangle with such settings, the pen will stroke the border of the rectangle to give it a more elegant look. Note how we modify attributes of the painter in this method and we do not set them back afterwards. We can get away with it because of the save() and restore() calls surrounding the drawField() execution.

We are ready now to see the results of our work. Let's switch to the MainWindow class and equip it with the following two private variables:

```
ChessView *m_view;
ChessAlgorithm *m_algorithm;
```

Then modify the constructor by adding the following highlighted code to set up the view and the game engine:

```
MainWindow::MainWindow(QWidget *parent) :
  QMainWindow(parent),
  ui(new Ui::MainWindow)
{
```

```
    ui->setupUi(this);
    m_view = new ChessView;
    m_algorithm = new ChessAlgorithm(this);
    m_algorithm->newGame();
    m_view->setBoard(m_algorithm->board());
    setCentralWidget(m_view);
    m_view->setSizePolicy(QSizePolicy::Fixed, QSizePolicy::Fixed);
    m_view->setFieldSize(QSize(50,50));
    layout()->setSizeConstraint(QLayout::SetFixedSize);
}
```

Afterwards, you should be able to build the project. When you run it, you should see a result similar to the one in the following screenshot:

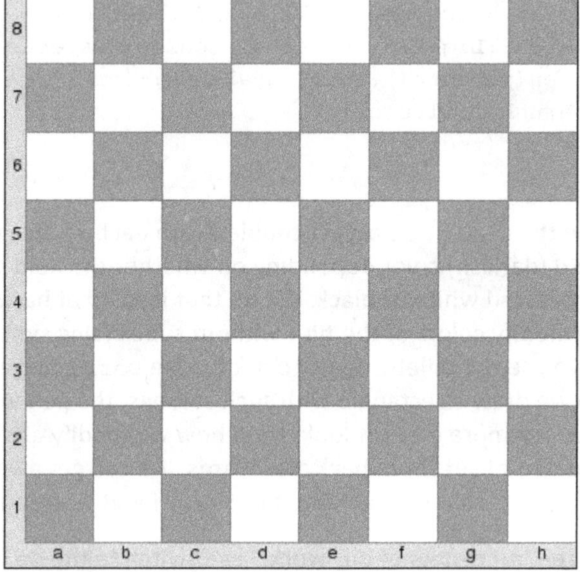

What just happened?

In this exercise, we did two things. First we provided a number of methods for calculating the geometry of important parts of the chess board and the size of the widget. Second, we defined three virtual methods for rendering visual primitives of a chess board. By making the methods virtual, we provided an infrastructure to let the look be customized by subclassing and overriding base implementations. Furthermore, by reading color from `QPalette`, we allowed customizing the colors of the primitives even without subclassing.

The last line of the main window constructor tells the layout of the window to force a fixed size of the window equal to what the size hint of the widget inside it reports.

Time for action – rendering the pieces

Now that we can see the board, it is time to put the pieces on it. We are going to use images for that purpose. In my case, we found a number of SVG files with chess pieces and decided to use them. SVG is a vector graphics format where all curves are defined not as a fixed set of points but rather as mathematic curves. Their main benefit is that they scale very well without causing an aliasing effect.

Let's equip our view with a registry of images to be used for "stamping" a particular piece type. Since each piece type is identified with char, we can use it to generate keys for a map of images. Let's put the following API into `ChessView`:

```
public:
  void setPiece(char type, const QIcon &icon);
  QIcon piece(char type) const;
private:
  QMap<char,QIcon> m_pieces;
```

For the image type, we do not use `QImage` or `QPixmap` but rather `QIcon`. This is because `QIcon` can store many pixmaps of different sizes and use the most appropriate one when we request an icon of a given size to be painted. This doesn't matter if we use vector images, but it does matter if you choose to use PNG or other types of image. In such cases, you can use `addFile()` to add many images to a single icon.

Going back to our registry, the implementation is very simple. We just store the icon in a map and ask the widget to repaint itself:

```
void ChessView::setPiece(char type, const QIcon &icon)
{
  m_pieces.insert(type, icon);
  update();
}

QIcon ChessView::piece(char type) const
{
  return m_pieces.value(type, QIcon());
}
```

Now we can fill the registry with actual images right after we create the view inside the `MainWindow` constructor. Note that we stored all the images in a resource file, as shown:

```
m_view->setPiece('P', QIcon(":/pieces/Chess_plt45.svg")); // pawn
m_view->setPiece('K', QIcon(":/pieces/Chess_klt45.svg")); // king
m_view->setPiece('Q', QIcon(":/pieces/Chess_qlt45.svg")); // queen
m_view->setPiece('R', QIcon(":/pieces/Chess_rlt45.svg")); // rook
m_view->setPiece('N', QIcon(":/pieces/Chess_nlt45.svg")); // knight
m_view->setPiece('B', QIcon(":/pieces/Chess_blt45.svg")); // bishop

m_view->setPiece('p', QIcon(":/pieces/Chess_pdt45.svg")); // pawn
m_view->setPiece('k', QIcon(":/pieces/Chess_kdt45.svg")); // king
m_view->setPiece('q', QIcon(":/pieces/Chess_qdt45.svg")); // queen
m_view->setPiece('r', QIcon(":/pieces/Chess_rdt45.svg")); // rook
m_view->setPiece('n', QIcon(":/pieces/Chess_ndt45.svg")); // knight
m_view->setPiece('b', QIcon(":/pieces/Chess_bdt45.svg")); // bishop
```

The next thing to do is to extend the `paintEvent()` method of the view to actually render our pieces. For that, we will introduce another protected virtual method called `drawPiece()`. We'll call it when iterating over all the ranks and columns of the board, as shown:

```
void ChessView::paintEvent(QPaintEvent *event)
{
  // ...
  for(int r = m_board->ranks(); r>0; --r) {
    for(int c = 1; c<=m_board->columns();++c) {
      drawPiece(&painter, c, r);
    }
  }
}
```

It is not a coincidence that we start drawing from the highest (top) rank to the lowest (bottom) one. By doing that, we allow a pseudo-3D effect: if a piece drawn extends past the area of the field, it will intersect the field from the next rank (which is possibly occupied by another piece). By drawing higher rank pieces first, we cause them to be partially covered by pieces from the lower rank, which imitates the effect of depth. By thinking ahead, we allow reimplementations of `drawPiece()` to have more freedom in what they can do.

The final step is to provide a base implementation for this method, as follows:

```
void ChessView::drawPiece(QPainter *painter, int column, int rank)
{
  QRect rect = fieldRect(column, rank);
  char value = m_board->data(column, rank);
  if(value != ' ') {
    QIcon icon = piece(value);
    if(!icon.isNull()) {
      icon.paint(painter, rect, Qt::AlignCenter);
    }
  }
}
```

The method is very simple, it queries for the rectangle of a given column and rank, then asks the `ChessBoard` instance about the piece occupying the given field. If there is a piece there, we ask the registry for the proper icon; if we get a valid one, we call its `paint()` routine to draw the piece centered in the field's rect. The image drawn will be scaled to the size of the rectangle. It is important that you only use images with a transparent background (such as PNG or SVG files and not JPEG files) so that the color of the field can be seen through the piece.

What just happened?

To test the implementation, you can modify the algorithm to fill the board with the default piece set up by introducing the following change to the `ChessAlgorithm` class:

```
void ChessAlgorithm::newGame()
{
  setupBoard();
  board()->setFen(
    "rnbqkbnr/pppppppp/8/8/8/8/PPPPPPPP/RNBQKBNR w KQkq - 0 1"
  );
}
```

Running the program should show the following result:

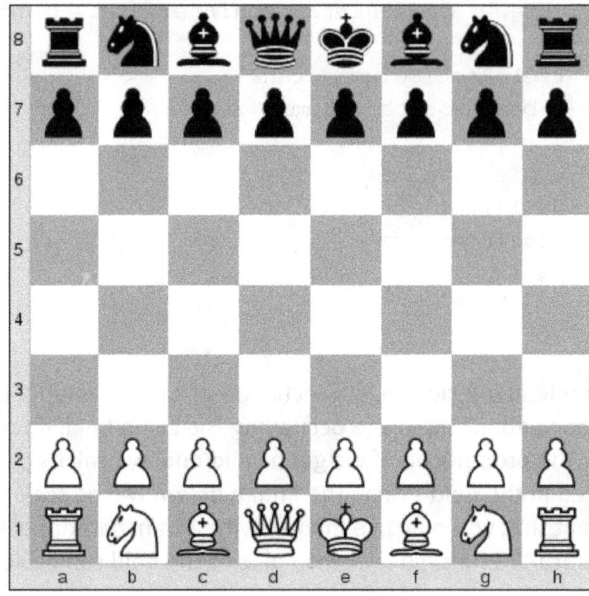

The modification we did in this step was very simple. First we provided a way to tell the board what each piece type looks like. This includes not only standard chess pieces but anything that fits into char and can be set inside the `ChessBoard` class's internal data array. Second, we made an abstraction for drawing the pieces with the simplest possible base implementation: taking an icon from the registry and rendering it to the field. By making use of `QIcon`, we can add several pixmaps of different sizes to be used with different sizes of a single field. Alternatively, the icon can contain a single vector image that scales very well all by itself.

Time for action – making the chess game interactive

We have managed to display the chess board but to actually play a game, we have to tell the program what moves we want to play. We could do that by adding the `QLineEdit` widget where we would input the move in algebraic form (for example, `Nf3` to move a knight to `f3`), but a more natural way is to click a piece with the mouse cursor (or tap it with a finger) and then click again on the destination field. To obtain such functionality, the first thing to do is to teach `ChessView` to detect mouse clicks. Therefore, add the following method:

```
QPoint ChessView::fieldAt(const QPoint &pt) const
{
  if(!m_board) return QPoint();
  const QSize fs = fieldSize();
```

```
    int offset = fontMetrics().width('M')+4;
      // 'M' is the widest letter
    if(pt.x() < offset) return QPoint();
    int c = (pt.x()-offset) / fs.width();
    int r = pt.y()/fs.height();
    if(c < 0 || c >= m_board->columns() || r<0 ||
      r >= m_board->ranks())
        return QPoint();
    return QPoint(c+1, m_board->ranks() - r);
      // max rank - r
}
```

The code looks very similar to the implementation of `fieldRect()`. This is because `fieldAt()` implements its reverse operation—it transforms a point in the widget coordinate space to the column and rank index of a field the point is contained in. The index is calculated by dividing point coordinates by the size of the field. You surely remember that, in the case of columns, the fields are offset by the size of the widest letter and a margin of 4 and we have to consider that in our calculations here as well. We do two checks: first we check the horizontal point coordinate against the offset to detect if the user clicked on the part of the widget where column symbols are displayed, and then we check if the rank and column calculated fit the range represented in the board. Finally, we return the result as a `QPoint` value since this is the easiest way in Qt to represent a two-dimensional value.

Now we need to find a way to make the widget notify its environment that a particular field was clicked. We can do this through the signal-slot mechanism. Switch to the header file of `ChessView` (if you currently have chessview.cpp opened in Qt Creator, you can simply push the *F4* key to be transferred to the corresponding header file) and declare a `clicked(const QPoint &)` signal:

```
signals:
  void clicked(const QPoint &);
```

To detect mouse input, we have to override one of the mouse event handlers a widget has, either `mousePressEvent` or `mouseReleaseEvent`. It seems obvious we should choose the former event; this would work, but it is not the best decision. Just think about the semantics of a mouse click: it is a complex event composed of pushing and releasing the mouse button. The actual "click" takes place after the mouse is released. Therefore let's use `mouseReleaseEvent` as our event handler:

```
void ChessView::mouseReleaseEvent(QMouseEvent *event)
{
  QPoint pt = fieldAt(event->pos());
  if(pt.isNull()) return;
  emit clicked(pt);
}
```

The code is simple; we use the method we just implemented and pass it the position read from the `QMouseEvent` object. If the returned point is invalid, we quietly return from the method. Otherwise, `clicked()` is emitted with the obtained column and rank values.

We can make use of the signal now. Go to the constructor of `MainWindow` and add the following line to connect the widget's clicked signal to a custom slot:

```
connect(m_view, SIGNAL(clicked(QPoint)),
  this, SLOT(viewClicked(QPoint)));
```

Declare the slot and implement it as follows:

```
void MainWindow::viewClicked(const QPoint &field)
{
  if(m_clickPoint.isNull()) {
    m_clickPoint = field;
  } else {
  if(field != m_clickPoint) {
    m_view->board()->movePiece(
      m_clickPoint.x(), m_clickPoint.y(),
      field.x(), field.y()
    );
    }
    m_clickPoint = QPoint();
  }
}
```

The function uses a class member variable `m_clickPoint` to store the clicked field. The variable value is made invalid after a move is made. Thus we can detect whether the click we are currently handling has "select" or "move" semantics. In the first case, we store the selection in `m_clickPoint`; in the other case, we ask the board to make a move using the helper method we implemented some time ago. Remember to declare `m_clickPoint` as a private member variable of `MasinWindow`.

All should be working now. However, if you build the application, run it, and start clicking around on the chess board, you will see that nothing happens. This is because we forgot to tell the view to refresh itself when the game position on the board is changed. We have to connect the signals the board emits to the `update()` slot of the view. Open the `setBoard()` method of the widget class and fix it as follows:

```
void ChessView::setBoard(ChessBoard *board)
{
  // ...
  m_board = board;
  // connect signals
  if(board){
    connect(board, SIGNAL(dataChanged(int,int)),
      this, SLOT(update()));
```

```
        connect(board, SIGNAL(boardReset()), this, SLOT(update()));
    }
    updateGeometry();
}
```

If you run the program now, moves you make will be reflected in the widget, as shown:

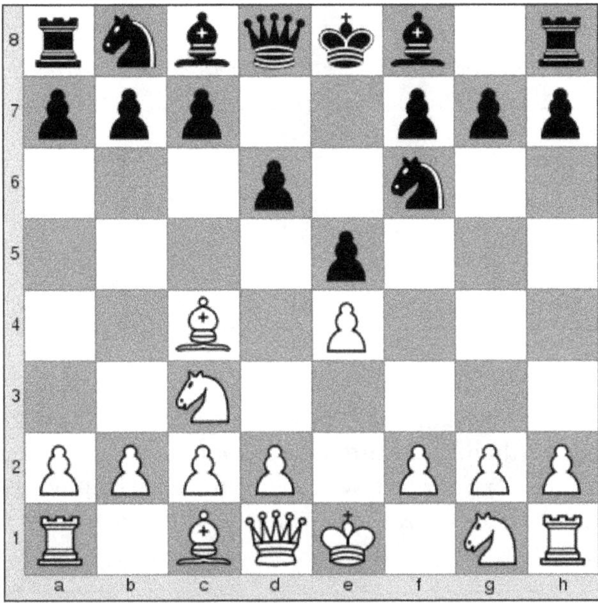

At this point, we might consider the visual part of the game as finished, but there is still one problem you might have spotted while testing our latest additions. When you click on the board, there is no visual hint that any piece was actually selected. Let's fix that now by introducing the ability to highlight any field on the board.

To do that, we will develop a generic system for different highlights. Begin by adding a `Highlight` class as an internal class to `ChessView`:

```
class ChessView : public QWidget
    // ...
public:
    class Highlight {
    public:
        Highlight() {}
        virtual ~Highlight() {}
        virtual int type() const { return 0; }
    };
// ...
};
```

It is a minimalistic interface for highlights and only exposes a method returning the type of the highlight using a virtual method. In our exercise, we will focus on just a basic type that marks a single field with a given color. Such a situation is going to be represented by the `FieldHighlight` class:

```
class FieldHighlight : public Highlight {
public:
  enum { Type = 1 };
  FieldHighlight(int column, int rank, QColor color)
    : m_field(column, rank), m_color(color) {}
  inline int column() const { return m_field.x(); }
  inline int rank() const { return m_field.y(); }
  inline QColor color() const { return m_color; }
  int type() const { return Type; }
private:
  QPoint m_field;
  QColor m_color;
};
```

You can see we provided a constructor that takes the column and rank indices and a color for the highlight and stores them in private member variables. Also, `type()` is redefined to return `FieldHighlight::Type`, which we can use to easily identify the type of highlight. The next step is to extend `ChessView` with abilities to add and remove highlights. As the container declares a private `QList<Highlight*> m_highlights` member variable, add method declarations:

```
public:
  void addHighlight(Highlight *hl);
  void removeHighlight(Highlight *hl);
  inline Highlight *highlight(int index)
    const {return m_highlights.at(index); }
  inline int highlightCount() const { return m_highlights.size(); }
```

Next provide implementations for non-inline methods:

```
void ChessView::addHighlight(ChessView::Highlight *hl)
{ m_highlights.append(hl); update(); }

void ChessView::removeHighlight(ChessView::Highlight *hl)
{ m_highlights.removeOne(hl); update(); }
```

Drawing the highlights is really easy: we will use yet another virtual `draw` method. Place the following call in the `paintEvent()` implementation right before the loop that is responsible for rendering pieces:

```
drawHighlights(&painter);
```

The implementation simply iterates over all the highlights and renders those it understands.

```
void ChessView::drawHighlights(QPainter *painter)
{
  for(int idx=0; idx < highlightCount(); ++idx) {
    Highlight *hl = highlight(idx);
    if(hl->type() == FieldHighlight::Type) {
      FieldHighlight *fhl = static_cast<FieldHighlight*>(hl);
      QRect rect = fieldRect(fhl->column(), fhl->rank());
      painter->fillRect(rect, fhl->color());
    }
  }
}
```

By checking the type of the highlight, we know which class to cast the generic pointer to. Then we can query the object for the needed data. Finally, we use `QPainter::fillRect()` to fill the field with the given color. As `drawHighlights()` is called before the piece painting loop and after the field painting loop, the highlight will cover the background but not the piece.

That's the basic highlighting system. Let's make our `viewClicked()` slot use it:

```
void MainWindow::viewClicked(const QPoint &field)
{
  if(m_clickPoint.isNull()) {
    if(m_view->board()->data(field.x(), field.y()) != ' ') {
      m_clickPoint = field;
      m_selectedField = new ChessView::FieldHighlight(
        field.x(), field.y(), QColor(255, 0, 0, 50)
      );
      m_view->addHighlight(m_selectedField);
    }
  } else {
    if(field != m_clickPoint) {
      m_view->board()->movePiece(
        m_clickPoint.x(), m_clickPoint.y(), field.x(), field.y()
```

```
            );
        };
        m_clickPoint = QPoint();
        m_view->removeHighlight(m_selectedField);
        delete m_selectedField;
        m_selectedField = 0;
    }
}
```

Notice how we check that a field can only be selected if it is not empty (that is, there is an existing piece occupying that field)?

You should also add a `ChessView::FieldHighlight *m_selectedField` private member variable and initialize it with a null pointer in the constructor. You can now build the game, execute it, and start moving pieces around.

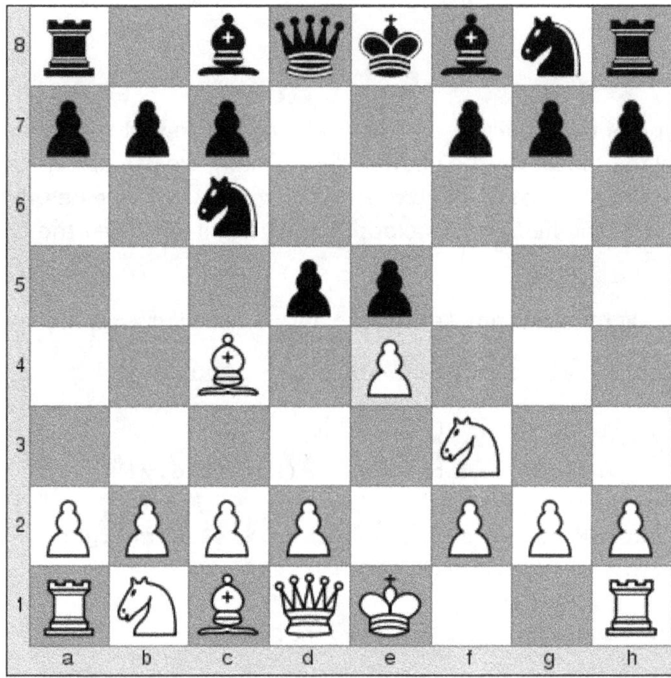

What just happened?

By adding a few lines of code, we managed to make the board clickable. We connected a custom slot that reads which field was clicked and can highlight it with a semi-transparent red color. Clicking on another field will move the highlighted piece there. The highlighting system we developed is very generic. We use it to highlight a single field with a solid color, but you can mark as many fields as you want with a number of different colors, for example, to show valid moves after selecting a piece. The system can easily be extended with new types of highlights; for example, you can draw arrows on the board using `QPainterPath` to have a complex hinting system (say showing the player the suggested move).

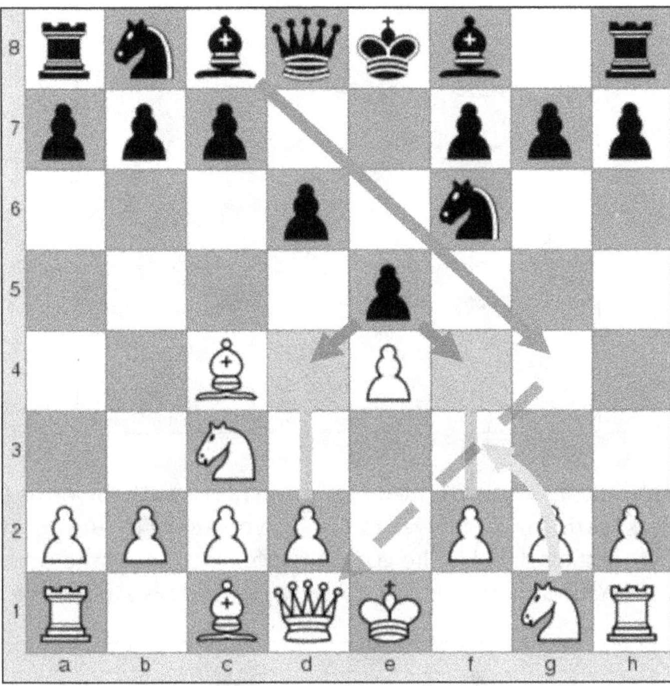

Time for action – connecting the game algorithm

It would take us too long to implement a full chess game algorithm here, so we will instead settle for a much simpler game called Fox and Hounds. One of the players has four pawns (hounds) which can only move over black fields and the pawn can only move in a forward fashion (toward higher ranks). The other player has just a single pawn (fox) which starts from the opposite side of the board.

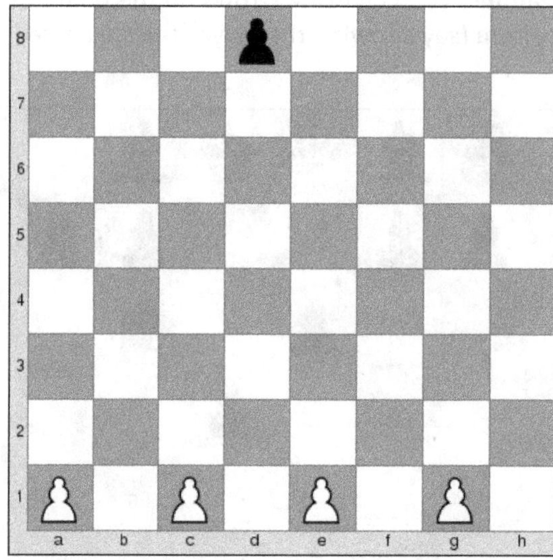

It can also move only over black fields; however it can move both forwards (toward higher ranks) as well as backwards (toward lower ranks). Players move in turns by moving their pawn by to a neighboring black field. The goal of the fox is to reach the opposite end of the board; the goal of the hounds is to trap the fox so that it can't make a move.

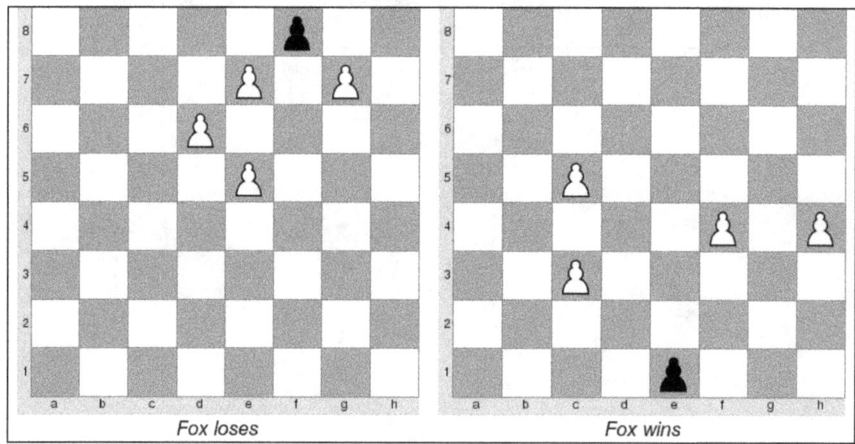

Fox loses   Fox wins

Time to get to work! First we will extend the `ChessAlgorithm` class with the required interface:

```
class ChessAlgorithm : public QObject
{
  Q_OBJECT
  Q_ENUMS(Result Player)
  Q_PROPERTY(Result result READ result)
  Q_PROPERTY(Player currentPlayer
             READ currentPlayer
             NOTIFY currentPlayerChanged)
public:
  enum Result { NoResult, Player1Wins, Draw, Player2Wins };
  enum Player { NoPlayer, Player1, Player2 };

  explicit ChessAlgorithm(QObject *parent = 0);
  ChessBoard* board() const;
  inline Result result() const { return m_result; }
  inline Player currentPlayer() const { return m_currentPlayer; }

signals:
  void boardChanged(ChessBoard*);
  void gameOver(Result);
  void currentPlayerChanged(Player);

public slots:
  virtual void newGame();
  virtual bool move(int colFrom, int rankFrom, int colTo, int rankTo);
  bool move(const QPoint &from, const QPoint &to);

protected:
  virtual void setupBoard();
  void setBoard(ChessBoard *board);
  void setResult(Result);
  void setCurrentPlayer(Player);
private:
  ChessBoard *m_board;
  Result m_result;
  Player m_currentPlayer;
};
```

There are two sets of members here. First we have a number of enums, variables, signals, and methods that are related to the state of the game: which player should make his move now and what is currently the result of the game. The `Q_ENUMS` macro is used to register enumerations in Qt's meta-type system so that they can be used as values for properties or arguments in signals. Property declarations and getters for them don't need any extra explanation. We have also declared protected methods for setting the variables from within subclasses. Here is their suggested implementation:

```
void ChessAlgorithm::setResult(Result value)
{
  if(result() == value) return;
  if(result() == NoResult) {
     m_result = value;
     emit gameOver(m_result);
  } else { m_result = value; }
}

void ChessAlgorithm::setCurrentPlayer(Player value)
{
  if(currentPlayer() == value) return;
  m_currentPlayer = value;
  emit currentPlayerChanged(m_currentPlayer);
}
```

Remember about initializing `m_currentPlayer` and `m_result` to `NoPlayer` and `NoResult` in the constructor of the `ChessAlgorithm` class.

The second group of functions is methods that modify the state of the game—the two variants of `move()`. The virtual variant is meant to be reimplemented by the real algorithm to check whether a given move is valid in the current game state and if that is the case, to perform the actual modification of the game board. In the base class, we can simply reject all possible moves:

```
bool ChessAlgorithm::move(int colFrom, int rankFrom,
  int colTo, int rankTo)
{
  Q_UNUSED(colFrom)
  Q_UNUSED(rankFrom)
  Q_UNUSED(colTo)
  Q_UNUSED(rankTo)
  return false;
}
```

Q_UNUSED is a macro to prevent the compiler from issuing warnings during compilation if the enclosed local variable is never used in the scope.

The overload is simply a convenience method that accepts two QPoint objects instead of four integers.

```
bool ChessAlgorithm::move(const QPoint &from, const QPoint &to)
{
  return move(from.x(), from.y(), to.x(), to.y());
}
```

The interface for the algorithm is ready now and we can implement it for the Fox and Hounds game. Subclass ChessAlgorithm to create a FoxAndHounds class:

```
class FoxAndHounds : public ChessAlgorithm
{
public:
  FoxAndHounds(QObject *parent = 0);
  void newGame();
  bool move(int colFrom, int rankFrom, int colTo, int rankTo);
};
```

The implementation of newGame() is pretty simple: we set up the board, place pieces on it, and signal that it is time for the first player to make their move.

```
void FoxAndHounds::newGame()
{
  setupBoard();
  board()->setFen("3p4/8/8/8/8/8/8/P1P1P1P1 w");
  // 'w' - white to move
  m_fox = QPoint(5,8);
  setResult(NoResult);
  setCurrentPlayer(Player1);
}
```

The algorithm for the game is quite simple. Implement move() as follows:

```
bool FoxAndHounds::move(int colFrom, int rankFrom,
  int colTo, int rankTo)
{
  if(currentPlayer() == NoPlayer) return false;
```

```
    // is there a piece of the right color?
    char source = board()->data(colFrom, rankFrom);
    if(currentPlayer() == Player1 && source != 'P') return false;
    if(currentPlayer() == Player2 && source != 'p') return false;

    // both can only move one column right or left
    if(colTo != colFrom+1 && colTo != colFrom-1) return false;

    // do we move within the board?
    if(colTo < 1 || colTo > board()->columns()) return false;
    if(rankTo < 1 || rankTo > board()->ranks()) return false;

    // is the destination field black?
    if((colTo + rankTo) % 2) return false;

    // is the destination field empty?
    char destination = board()->data(colTo, rankTo);
    if(destination != ' ') return false;

    // is white advancing?
    if(currentPlayer() == Player1 && rankTo <= rankFrom) return false;

    board()->movePiece(colFrom, rankFrom, colTo, rankTo);
    // make the move
    if(currentPlayer() == Player2) {
      m_fox = QPoint(colTo, rankTo);       // cache fox position
    }
    // check win condition
    if(currentPlayer() == Player2 && rankTo == 1){
      setResult(Player2Wins);              // fox has escaped
    } else if(currentPlayer() == Player1 && !foxCanMove()) {
      setResult(Player1Wins);        // fox can't move
    } else {
      // the other player makes the move now
      setCurrentPlayer(currentPlayer() == Player1 ? Player2 : Player1);
    }
    return true;
  }
```

Declare a protected `foxCanMove()` method and implement it using the following code:

```
bool FoxAndHounds::foxCanMove() const
{
  if(emptyByOffset(-1, -1) || emptyByOffset(-1, 1)
  || emptyByOffset( 1, -1) || emptyByOffset( 1, 1)) return true;
  return false;
}
```

Then do the same with `emptyByOffset()`:

```
bool FoxAndHounds::emptyByOffset(int x, int y) const
{
  const int destCol = m_fox.x()+x;
  const int destRank = m_fox.y()+y;
  if(destCol < 1 || destRank < 1
  || destCol > board()->columns()
  || destRank > board()->ranks()) return false;
    return (board()->data(destCol, destRank) == ' ');
}
```

Lastly declare a private `QPoint m_fox` member variable.

The simplest way to test the game is to make two changes to the code. First, in the constructor of the main window class, replace `m_algorithm = new ChessAlgorithm(this)` with `m_algorithm = new FoxAndHounds(this)`. Second, modify the `viewClicked()` slot as follows:

```
void MainWindow::viewClicked(const QPoint &field)
{
  if(m_clickPoint.isNull()) {
    // ...
  } else {
    if(field != m_clickPoint) {
      m_algorithm->move(m_clickPoint, field);
    }
    // ...
  }
}
```

You can also connect signals from the algorithm class to custom slots of the view or window to notify about the end of the game and provide a visual hint as to which player should make his move now.

What just happened?

We created a very simplistic API for implementing chess-like games by introducing the `newGame()` and `move()` virtual methods to the algorithm class. The former method simply sets everything up. The latter uses simple checks to determine whether a particular move is valid and if the game has ended. We use the `m_fox` member variable to track the current position of the fox to be able to quickly determine if it has any valid moves. When the game ends, the `gameOver()` signal is emitted and the result of the game can be obtained from the algorithm. You can use the exact same framework for implementing all chess rules.

Have a go hero – implementing the UI around the chess board

During the exercise, we focused on developing the game board view and necessary classes to make the game actually run. But we completely neglected the regular user interface the game might possess, such as toolbars and menus. You can try designing a set of menus and toolbars for the game. Make it possible to start a new game, save a game in progress (say by implementing a FEN serializer), load a saved game (say by leveraging the existing FEN string parser), or choose different game types that will spawn different `ChessAlgorithm` subclasses. You can also provide a settings dialog for adjusting the look of the game board. If you feel like it, you can add chess clocks or implement a simple tutorial system that will guide the player through the basics of chess using text and visual hints via the highlight system we implemented.

Have a go hero – connecting a UCI-compliant chess engine

If you really want to test your skills, you can implement a `ChessAlgorithm` subclass that will connect to a **Universal Chess Interface** (UCI) chess engine such as StockFish (`http://stockfishchess.org`) and provide a challenging artificial intelligence opponent for a human player. UCI is the de facto standard for communication between a chess engine and a chess frontend. Its specification is freely available, so you can study it on your own. To talk to a UCI-compliant engine you can use `QProcess`, which will spawn the engine as an external process and attach itself to its standard input and standard output. Then you can send commands to the engine by writing to its standard input and read messages from the engine by reading its standard output. To get you started, here is a short snippet of code that starts the engine and attaches to its communication channels:

```
class UciEngine : public QObject {
  Q_OBJECT
```

```
public:
  UciEngine(QObject *parent = 0) : QObject(parent) {
    m_uciEngine = new QProcess(this);
    m_uciEngine->setReadChannel(QProcess:StandardOutput);
    connect(m_uciEngine, SIGNAL(readyRead()), SLOT(readFromEngine()));
  }
public slots:
  void startEngine(const QString &enginePath) {
    m_uciEngine->start(enginePath);
  }
  void sendCommand(const QString &command) {
    m_uciEngine->write(command.toLatin1());
  }
private slots:
  void readFromEngine() {
    while(m_uciEngine->canReadLine()) {
      QString line = QString::fromLatin1(m_uciEngine->readLine());
      emit messageReceived(line);
    }
  }
signals:
  void messageReceived(QString);
private:
  QProcess *m_uciEngine;
};
```

OpenGL

We are not experts on OpenGL, so in this part of the chapter we will not teach you to do any fancy stuff with OpenGL and Qt but rather will show you how to enable the use of your OpenGL skills in Qt applications. There are a lot of tutorials and courses on OpenGL out there so if you're not that skilled with OpenGL, you can still benefit from what is described here by employing the knowledge gained here to more easily learn fancy stuff. You can use external materials and a high-level API offered by Qt, which is going to speed up many of the tasks described in the tutorials.

Introduction to OpenGL with Qt

There are basically two ways you can use OpenGL in Qt. The first approach is to use `QOpenGLWidget`. This is mostly useful if your application heavily depends on other widgets (for example. the 3D view is only one of the views in your application and is controlled using a bunch of other widgets surrounding the main view). The other way is to use `QOpenGLWindow`; this is most useful when the GL window is the dominant or even the only part of the program. Both APIs are very similar; they use instances of the `QOpenGLContext` class to access the GL context. The difference is practically only in how they render the scene to the window. `QOpenGLWindow` renders directly to the given window, while `QOpenGLWidget` first renders to an offscreen buffer that is then rendered to the widget. The advantage of the latter approach is that `QOpenGLWidget` can be part of a more complex widget layout while `QOpenGLWindow` is usually used as the sole, often fullscreen, window. In this chapter we will be using the more direct approach (`QOpenGLWindow`); however, bear in mind that you can do everything described here using the widget too. Just replace the window classes with their widget equivalents and you should be good to go.

We said that the whole API revolves around the `QOpenGLContext` class. It represents the overall state of the GL pipeline, which guides the process of data processing and rendering to a particular device.

A related concept that needs explanation is the idea of a GL context being "current" in a thread. The way OpenGL calls work is that they do not use any handle to any object containing information on where and how to execute the series of low-level GL calls. Instead, it is assumed that they are executed in the context of the current machine state. The state may dictate whether to render a scene to a screen or to a frame buffer object, which mechanisms are enabled, or the properties of the surface OpenGL is rendering on. Making a context "current" means that all further OpenGL operations issued by a particular thread will be applied to this context. To add to that, a context can be "current" only in one thread at the same time; therefore, it is important to make the context current before making any OpenGL calls and then marking it as available after you are done accessing OpenGL resources.

`QOpenGLWindow` has a very simple API that hides most of the unnecessary details from the developer. Apart from constructors and a destructor, it provides a small number of very useful methods. First there are auxiliary methods for managing the OpenGL context: `context()`, which returns the context, and `makeCurrent()` as well as `doneCurrent()` for acquiring and releasing the context. The remaining methods of the class are a number of virtual methods we can reimplement to display OpenGL graphics.

The first method is called `initializeGL()`, and it is invoked by the framework once before any painting is actually done so that you can prepare any resources or initialize the context in any way you require.

Then there are two most important methods: `resizeGL()` and `paintGL()`. The first is a callback invoked every time the window is resized. It accepts the width and height of the window as parameters. You can make use of that method by reimplementing it so that you can prepare yourself for the fact that the next call to the other method, `paintGL()`, renders to a viewport of a different size. Speaking of `paintGL()`, this is the equivalent of `paintEvent()` for the widget classes; it gets executed whenever the window needs to be repainted. This is the function where you should put your OpenGL rendering code.

Time for action – drawing a triangle using Qt and OpenGL

For the first exercise, we will create a subclass of `QOpenGLWindow` that renders a triangle using simple OpenGL calls. Create a new project starting with **Empty qmake Project** from the **Other Projects** group as the template. In the project file, put the following content:

```
QT = core gui
TARGET = triangle
TEMPLATE = app
```

Having the basic project setup ready, let's define a `SimpleGLWindow` class as a subclass of `QOpenGLWindow` and override the `initializeGL()` method to set white as the clear color of our scene. We do this by calling an OpenGL function called `glClearColor`. Qt provides a convenience class called `QOpenGLFunctions` that takes care of resolving most commonly used OpenGL functions in a platform-independent way. This is the recommended approach to access OpenGLES functions in a platform-independent manner. Our window is going to inherit not only `QOpenGLWindow` but also `QOpenGLFunctions`. However, since we don't want to allow external access to those functions, we use protected inheritance.

```
class SimpleGLWindow : public QOpenGLWindow,
protected QOpenGLFunctions {
public:
  SimpleGLWindow(QWindow *parent = 0) :
    QOpenGLWindow(NoPartialUpdate, parent) { }
protected:
  void initializeGL() {
    initializeOpenGLFunctions();
    glClearColor(1,1,1,0);
  }
```

In `initializeGL()`, we first call `initializeOpenGLFunctions()`, which is a method of the `QOpenGLFunctions` class, one of the base classes of our window class. The method takes care of setting up all the functions according to the parameters of the current GL context (thus it is important to first make the context current, which luckily is done for us behind the scenes before `initializeGL()` is invoked). Then we set the clear color of the scene to white.

The next step is to reimplement `paintGL()` and put the actual drawing code there:

```
    void paintGL() {
      glClear(GL_COLOR_BUFFER_BIT);
      glViewport(0, 0, width(), height());
      glBegin(GL_TRIANGLES);
        glColor3f(1, 0, 0);
        glVertex3f( 0.0f, 1.0f, 0.0f);
        glColor3f(0, 1, 0);
        glVertex3f( 1.0f,-1.0f, 0.0f);
        glColor3f(0, 0, 1);
        glVertex3f(-1.0f,-1.0f, 0.0f);
      glEnd();
    }
};
```

This function first clears the color buffer and sets the GL viewport of the context to be the size of the window. Then we tell OpenGL to start drawing using triangles with the `glBegin()` call and passing `GL_TRIANGLES` as the drawing mode. Then we pass three vertices along with their colors to form a triangle. Finally, we inform the pipeline by invoking `glEnd()` that we are done drawing using the current mode.

What is left is a trivial `main()` function that sets up the window and starts the event loop. Add a new **C++ Source File**, call it main.cpp, and implement `main()` as follows:

```
int main(int argc, char **argv) {
  QGuiApplication app(argc, argv);
  SimpleGLWindow window;
  window.resize(600,400);
  window.show();
  return app.exec();
}
```

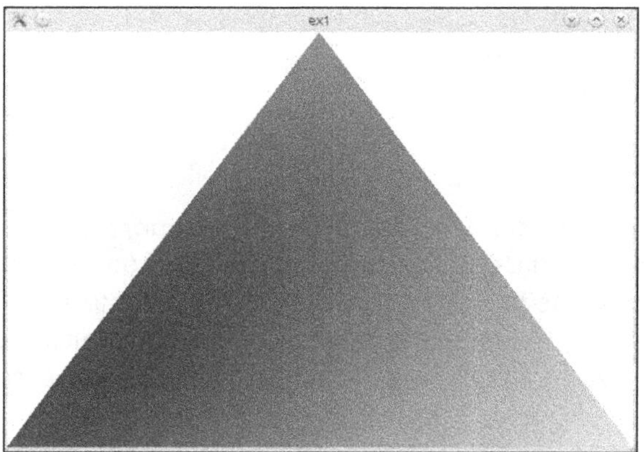

You can see the triangle has jagged edges. That's because of the aliasing effect. You can counter it by enabling multisampling for the window, which will make OpenGL render the contents multiple times and then average the result, which acts as antialiasing. To do that, add the following code to the constructor of the window:

```
QSurfaceFormat fmt = format();
fmt.setSamples(16); // multisampling set to 16
setFormat(fmt);
```

Drawing colored triangles is fun, but drawing textured cubes is even more fun so let's see how we can use OpenGL textures with Qt.

Time for action – scene-based rendering

Let's take our rendering code to a higher level. Putting OpenGL code directly into the `window` class requires subclassing the window class and makes the window class more and more complex. Let's follow good programming practice and separate rendering code from window code.

Create a new class and call it `AbstractGLScene`. It is going to be the base class for definitions of OpenGL scenes. You can derive the class (with protected scope) from `QOpenGLFunctions` to make accessing different GL functions easier. Make the scene class accept a pointer to `QOpenGLWindow`, either in the constructor or through a dedicated setter method. Make sure the pointer is stored in the class for easier access as we are going to rely on that pointer for accessing physical properties of the window. Add methods for querying the window's OpenGL context. You should end up with code similar to the following:

```
class AbstractGLScene : protected QOpenGLFunctions {
public:
  AbstractGLScene(QOpenGLWindow *wnd = 0) { m_window = wnd; }
  QOpenGLWindow* window() const { return m_window; }
  QOpenGLContext* context() {
    return window() ? window()->context() : 0;
  }
  const QOpenGLContext* context() const {
      return window() ? window()->context() : 0;
  }
private:
  QOpenGLWindow *m_window = nullptr; // C++11 required for assignment
};
```

Now the essential part begins. Add two pure virtual methods called `paint()` and `initialize()`. Also remember about adding a virtual destructor.

> Instead of making `initialize()` a pure virtual function, you can implement its body in such a way that it will call `initializeOpenGLFunctions()` to fulfill the requirements of the `QOpenGFunctions` class. Then, subclasses of `AbstractGLScene` can make sure the functions are initialized properly by calling the base class implementation of `initialize()`.

Next, create a subclass of `QOpenGLWindow` and call it `SceneGLWindow`. Equip it with setter and getter methods to allow the object to operate on an `AbstractGLScene` instance.

Then reimplement the `initializeGL()` and `paintGL()` methods and make them call appropriate equivalents in the scene:

```
void SceneGLWindow::initializeGL() { if(scene())
  scene()->initialize(); }
void SceneGLWindow::paintGL() { if(scene()) scene()->paint(); }
```

What just happened?

We have just set up a class chain that separates the window code from the actual OpenGL scene. The window forwards all calls related to scene contents to the scene object so that when the window is requested to repaint itself, it delegates the task to the scene object. Note that prior to doing that, the window will make the GL context current; therefore, all OpenGL calls the scene makes will be related to that context. You can store the code created in this exercise for later reuse in further exercises and your own projects.

Time for action – drawing a textured cube

Subclass `AbstractGLScene` and implement the constructor to match the one from `AbstractGLScene`. Add a method to store a `QImage` object in the scene that will contain texture data for the cube. Add a `QOpenGLTexture` pointer member as well, which will contain the texture, initialize it to 0 in the constructor, and delete it in the destructor. Let's call the image object `m_tex` and the texture `m_texture`. Now add a protected `initializeTexture()` method and fill it with the following code:

```
void initializeTexture() {
  m_texture = new QOpenGLTexture(m_tex.mirrored());
  m_texture->setMinificationFilter(QOpenGLTexture::LinearMipMapLinear);
  m_texture->setMagnificationFilter(QOpenGLTexture::Linear);
}
```

The function first mirrors the image vertically. This is because OpenGL expects the texture to be "upside down". Then we create a QOpenGLTexture object, passing it our image. Then we set minification and magnification filters so that the texture looks better when it is scaled.

We are now ready to implement the initialize() method that will take care of setting up the texture and the scene itself.

```
void initialize() {
  AbstractGLScene::initialize();
  m_initialized = true;
  if(!m_tex.isNull()) initializeTexture();
  glClearColor(1,1,1,0);
  glShadeModel(GL_SMOOTH);
}
```

We make use of a flag called m_initialized. This flag is needed to prevent the texture from being set up too early (when no GL context is available yet). Then we check if the texture image is set (using the QImage::isNull() method); if so, we initialize the texture. Then we set some additional properties of the GL context.

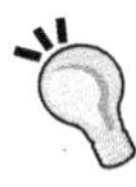

In the setter for m_tex, add code that checks if m_initialized is set to true and if so, calls initializeTexture(). This is to make certain that the texture is properly set regardless of the order in which the setter and initialize() are called. Also remember to set m_initialized to false in the constructor.

The next step is to prepare the cube data. We will define a special data structure for the cube that groups vertex coordinates and texture data in a single object. To store coordinates, we are going to use classes tailored to that purpose—QVector3D and QVector2D.

```
struct TexturedPoint {
  QVector3D coord;
  QVector2D uv;
  TexturedPoint(const QVector3D& pcoord, const QVector2D& puv) {
  coord = pcoord; uv = puv; }
};
```

QVector<TexturedPoint> will hold information for the whole cube. The vector is initialized with data using the following code:

```
void CubeGLScene::initializeCubeData() {
  m_data = {
    // FRONT FACE
    {{-0.5, -0.5,  0.5}, {0, 0}}, {{ 0.5, -0.5,  0.5}, {1, 0}},
```

```
        {{ 0.5,  0.5,  0.5}, {1, 1}}, {{-0.5,  0.5,  0.5}, {0, 1}},

        // TOP FACE
        {{-0.5,  0.5,  0.5}, {0, 0}}, {{ 0.5,  0.5,  0.5}, {1, 0}},
        {{ 0.5,  0.5, -0.5}, {1, 1}}, {{-0.5,  0.5, -0.5}, {0, 1}},

        // BACK FACE
        {{-0.5,  0.5, -0.5}, {0, 0}}, {{ 0.5,  0.5, -0.5}, {1, 0}},
        {{ 0.5, -0.5, -0.5}, {1, 1}}, {{-0.5, -0.5, -0.5}, {0, 1}},

        // BOTTOM FACE
        {{-0.5, -0.5, -0.5}, {0, 0}}, {{ 0.5, -0.5, -0.5}, {1, 0}},
        {{ 0.5, -0.5,  0.5}, {1, 1}}, {{-0.5, -0.5,  0.5}, {0, 1}},

        // LEFT FACE
        {{-0.5, -0.5, -0.5}, {0, 0}}, {{-0.5, -0.5,  0.5}, {1, 0}},
        {{-0.5,  0.5,  0.5}, {1, 1}}, {{-0.5,  0.5, -0.5}, {0, 1}},

        // RIGHT FACE
        {{ 0.5, -0.5,  0.5}, {0, 0}}, {{ 0.5, -0.5, -0.5}, {1, 0}},
        {{ 0.5,  0.5, -0.5}, {1, 1}}, {{ 0.5,  0.5,  0.5}, {0, 1}},
    };
}
```

The code uses C++11 syntax to operate on the vector. If you have an older compiler, you will have to use `QVector::append()` instead.

```
m_data.append(TexturedPoint(QVector3D(...), QVector2D(...)));
```

The cube consists of six faces and is centered on the origin of the coordinate system. The following image presents the same data in graphical form. Purple figures are texture coordinates in UV coordinate space.

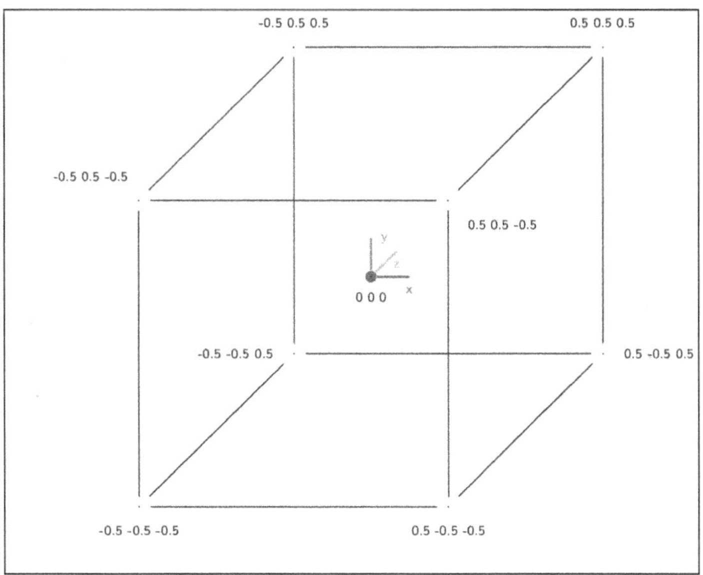

`initializeCubeData()` should be called from the scene constructor or from the `initialize()` method. What remains is the painting code.

```
void CubeGLScene::paint() {
  glClear(GL_COLOR_BUFFER_BIT| GL_DEPTH_BUFFER_BIT);
  glViewport(0, 0, window()->width(), window()->height());
  glLoadIdentity();

  glRotatef( 45, 1.0, 0.0, 0.0 );
  glRotatef( 45, 0.0, 1.0, 0.0 );

  glEnable(GL_DEPTH_TEST);
  glEnable(GL_CULL_FACE);
  glCullFace(GL_BACK);
  paintCube();
}
```

First we set up the viewport and then we rotate the view. Before calling `paintCube()`, which is going to render the cube itself, we enable depth testing and face culling so that only visible faces are drawn. The `paintCube()` routine looks as follows:

```
void CubeGLScene::paintCube() {
  if(m_texture)
    m_texture->bind();
  glEnable(GL_TEXTURE_2D);
  glBegin(GL_QUADS);
```

```
    for(int i=0;i<m_data.size();++i) {
      const TexturedPoint &pt = m_data.at(i);
      glTexCoord2d(pt.uv.x(), pt.uv.y());
      glVertex3f(pt.coord.x(), pt.coord.y(), pt.coord.z());
    }
    glEnd();
    glDisable(GL_TEXTURE_2D);
  }
```

First the texture is bound and texturing is enabled. Then we enter the quad drawing mode and stream in data from our data structure. Finally, we disable texturing again.

For completeness, here is a `main()` function that executes the scene:

```
int main(int argc, char **argv) {
  QGuiApplication app(argc, argv);
  SceneGLWindow window;
  QSurfaceFormat fmt;
  fmt.setSamples(16);
  window.setFormat(fmt);
  CubeGLScene scene(&window);
  window.setScene(&scene);
  scene.setTexture(QImage(":/texture.jpg"));
  window.resize(600,600);
  window.show();
  return app.exec();
}
```

Please note the use of `QSurfaceFormat` to enable multisample antialiasing for the scene. We have also put the texture image into a resource file to avoid problems with the relative path to the file.

Have a go hero – animating a cube

Try modifying the code to make the cube animated. To do that, have the scene inherit `QObject`, add an angle property of type `float` to it (remember about the `Q_OBJECT` macro). Then modify one of the `glRotatef()` lines to use the angle value instead of a constant value. Put the following code in `main()` right before calling `app.exec()`:

```
QPropertyAnimation anim(&scene, "angle");
anim.setStartValue(0);
anim.setEndValue(359);
anim.setDuration(5000);
anim.setLoopCount(-1);
anim.start();
```

Remember to put a call to `window()->update()` in the setter for the angle property so that the scene is redrawn.

Modern OpenGL with Qt

OpenGL code shown in the previous section uses a very old technique of streaming vertices one by one into a fixed OpenGL pipeline. Nowadays, modern hardware is much more feature rich and not only does it allow faster processing of vertex data but it also offers the ability to adjust different processing stages with the use of reprogrammable units called shaders. In this section, we will take a look at what Qt has to offer in the domain of a "modern" approach to using OpenGL.

Shaders

Qt can make use of shaders through a set of classes based around `QOpenGLShaderProgram`. This class allows compiling, linking, and executing shader programs written in GLSL. You can check if your OpenGL implementation supports shaders by inspecting the result of a static `QOpenGLShaderProgram::hasOpenGLShaderPrograms()` call that accepts a pointer to a GL context. All modern hardware and all decent graphics drivers should have some support for shaders. A single shader is represented by an instance of the `QOpenGLShader` class. Using it, you can decide on the type of shader, associate, and shader source code. The latter is done by calling `QOpenGLShader::compileSourceCode()`, which has a number of overloads for handling different input formats.

Qt supports all kinds of shaders, with the most common being vertex and fragment shaders. These are both part of the classic OpenGL pipeline. You can see an illustration of the pipeline on the following diagram:

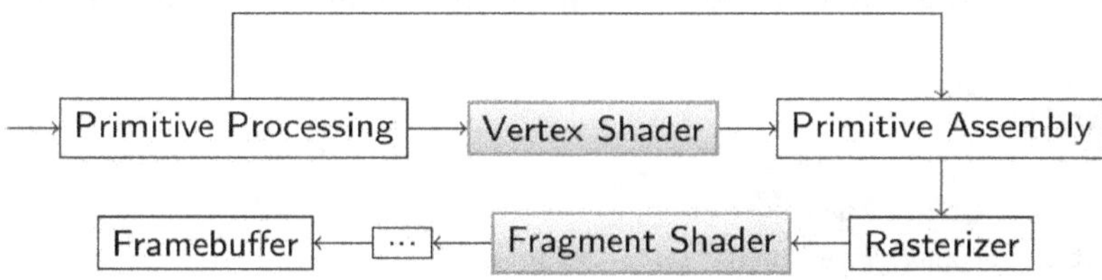

When you have a set of shaders defined, you can assemble a complete program by using `QOpenGLShaderProgram::addShader()`. After all shaders are added, you can `link()` the program and `bind()` it to the current GL context. The program class has a number of methods for setting values of different input parameters—uniforms and attributes both in singular and array versions. Qt provides mappings between its own types (such as `QSize` or `QColor`) to GLSL counterparts (for example, `vec2` and `vec4`) to make the programmer's life even easier.

A typical code flow for using shaders for rendering is as follows (first a vertex shader is created and compiled):

```
QOpenGLShader vertexShader(QOpenGLShader::Vertex);
QByteArray code = "uniform vec4 color;\n"
    "uniform highp mat4 matrix;\n"
    "void main(void) { gl_Position = gl_Vertex*matrix; }";
vertexShader.compileSourceCode(code);
```

The process is repeated for a fragment shader:

```
QOpenGLShader fragmentShader(QOpenGLShader::Fragment);
code = "uniform vec4 color;\n"
    "void main(void) { gl_FragColor = color; }";
fragmentShader.compileSourceCode(code);
```

Then shaders are linked into a single program in a given GL context:

```
QOpenGLShaderProgram program(context);
program.addShader(vertexShader);
program.addShader(fragmentShader);
program.link();
```

Whenever the program is used, it should be bound to the current GL context and filled with required data:

```
program.bind();
QMatrix4x4 m = …;
QColor color = Qt::red;
program.setUniformValue("matrix", m);
program.setUniformValue("color", color);
```

After that, calls activating the render pipeline are going to use the bound program:

```
glBegin(GL_TRIANGLE_STRIP);
…
glEnd();
```

Time for action – shaded objects

Let's convert our last program so that it uses shaders. To make the cube better, we will implement a smooth lighting model using the Phong algorithm. At the same time, we will learn to use some helper classes that Qt offers for use with OpenGL.

The basic goals for this mini-project are as follows:

- Use vertex and fragment shaders for rendering a complex object
- Handle model, view, and projection matrices
- Use attribute arrays for faster drawing

Start by creating a new subclass of `AbstractGLScene`. Let's give it the following interface:

```
class ShaderGLScene : public QObject, public AbstractGLScene {
  Q_OBJECT
public:
  ShaderGLScene(SceneGLWindow *wnd);
  void initialize();
  void paint();
protected:
  void initializeObjectData();
private:
  struct ScenePoint {
    QVector3D coords;
    QVector3D normal;
    ScenePoint(const QVector3D &c, const QVector3D &n);
  };
  QOpenGLShaderProgram m_shader;
  QMatrix4x4 m_modelMatrix;
  QMatrix4x4 m_viewMatrix;
  QMatrix4x4 m_projectionMatrix;
  QVector<ScenePoint> m_data;
};
```

Significant changes to the class interface in comparison with the previous project have been highlighted. We're not using textures in this project so `TexturedPoint` was simplified to `ScenePoint` with UV texture coordinates removed.

We can start implementing the interface with the `initializeObjectData()` function. We're not going to go line by line explaining what the body of the method does. You can implement it as you want; it is important that the method fill the `m_data` member with information about vertices and their normals.

In the sample code that comes with this book, you can find code that loads data from a file in PLY format generated with the Blender 3D program. To export a model from Blender, make sure it consists of just triangles (for that, select the model, go into the Edit mode by pressing *Tab*, open the **Faces** menu with *Ctrl* + *F*, and choose **Triangulate Faces**). Then click on **File** and **Export**; choose **Stanford (.ply)**. You will end up with a text file containing vertex and normal data as well as face definitions for the vertices.

You can always reuse the cube object from the previous project. Just be aware that its normals are not calculated properly for smooth shading; thus, you will have to correct them.

Before we can set up the shader program, we have to be aware of what the actual shaders look like. Shader code is going to be loaded from external files, so the first step is to add a new file to the project. In Creator, click on **File** and choose **New File or Project**; from the bottom pane, choose **GLSL**, and from the list of available templates choose **Vertex Shader (Desktop OpenGL)**. Call the new file `phong.vert` and input the following code:

```
uniform highp mat4 modelViewMatrix;
uniform highp mat3 normalMatrix;
uniform highp mat4 projectionMatrix;
uniform highp mat4 mvpMatrix;

attribute highp vec4 Vertex;
attribute mediump vec3 Normal;

varying mediump vec3 N;
varying highp vec3 v;

void main(void) {
  N = normalize(normalMatrix * Normal);
  v = vec3(modelViewMatrix * Vertex);
  gl_Position = mvpMatrix*Vertex;
}
```

The code is very simple. We declare four matrices representing different stages of coordinate mapping for the scene. We also define two input attributes—`Vertex` and `Normal`—which contain the vertex data. The shader is going to output two pieces of data—a normalized vertex normal and a transformed vertex coordinate as seen by the camera. Of course, apart from that we set `gl_Position` to be the final vertex coordinate. In each case, we want to be compliant with the OpenGL/ES specification so we prefix each variable declaration with a precision specifier.

Next, add another file, call it `phong.frag`, and make it a Fragment Shader (Desktop OpenGL). The content of the file is a typical ambient, diffuse, and specular calculation:

```
struct Material {
  lowp vec3 ka;
  lowp vec3 kd;
  lowp vec3 ks;
  lowp float shininess;
};

struct Light {
  lowp vec4 position;
  lowp vec3 intensity;
};

uniform Material mat;
uniform Light light;
varying mediump vec3 N;
varying highp vec3 v;

void main(void) {
  mediump vec3 n = normalize(N);
  highp vec3 L = normalize(light.position.xyz - v);
  highp vec3 E = normalize(-v);
  mediump vec3 R = normalize(reflect(-L, n));

  lowp float LdotN = dot(L, n);
  lowp float diffuse = max(LdotN, 0.0);
  lowp vec3 spec = vec3(0,0,0);

  if(LdotN > 0.0) {
    float RdotE = max(dot(R, E), 0.0);
    spec = light.intensity*pow(RdotE, mat.shininess);
  }
  vec3 color = light.intensity
             * (mat.ka + mat.kd*diffuse + mat.ks*spec);
  gl_FragColor = vec4(color, 1.0);
}
```

Apart from using the two varying variables to obtain the interpolated normal (`N`) and fragment (`v`) position, the shader declares two structures for keeping light and material information. Without going into the details about how the shader itself works, it calculates three components—ambient light, diffused light, and specular reflection—adds them together, and sets that as the fragment color. Since all the per vertex input data is interpolated for each fragment, the final color is calculated individually for each pixel.

Once we know what the shaders expect, we can set up the shader program object. Let's go through the `initialize()` method:

```
void initialize() {
  AbstractGLScene::initialize();
  glClearColor(0,0,0,0);
```

First we call the base class implementation and set the background color of the scene to black, as shown in the following code:

```
  m_shader.addShaderFromSourceCode
    (QOpenGLShader::Vertex, fileContent("phong.vert"));
  m_shader.addShaderFromSourceCode
    (QOpenGLShader::Fragment, fileContent("phong.frag"));
  m_shader.link();
```

Then we add two shaders to the program reading their source code from external files with the use of a custom helper function called `fileContent()`. This function essentially opens a file and returns its content. Then we link the shader program. The `link()` function returns a Boolean value but for simplicity we skip the error check here. The next step is to prepare all the input data for the shader, as shown:

```
  m_shader.bind();
  m_shader.setAttributeArray("Vertex",
    GL_FLOAT, m_data.constData(), 3, sizeof(ScenePoint));
  m_shader.enableAttributeArray("Vertex");
  m_shader.setAttributeArray("Normal",
    GL_FLOAT, &m_data[0].normal, 3, sizeof(ScenePoint));
  m_shader.enableAttributeArray("Normal");
  m_shader.setUniformValue("material.ka", QVector3D(0.1, 0, 0.0));
  m_shader.setUniformValue("material.kd",
    QVector3D(0.7, 0.0, 0.0));
  m_shader.setUniformValue("material.ks",
    QVector3D(1.0, 1.0, 1.0));
  m_shader.setUniformValue("material.shininess", 128.0f);
  m_shader.setUniformValue("light.position", QVector3D(2, 1, 1));
  m_shader.setUniformValue("light.intensity", QVector3D(1,1,1));
```

First the shader program is bound to the current context so that we can operate on it. Then we enable the setup of two attribute arrays—one for vertex coordinates and the other for their normals. We inform the program that an attribute called `Vertex` consists of three values of type `GL_FLOAT`. The first value is located at `m_data.constData()`, and data for the next vertex is located `sizeof(ScenePoint)` bytes later than data for the current point. Then we have a similar declaration for the `Normal` attribute, with the only exception that the first piece of data is placed at `&m_data[0].normal`. By informing the program about layout of the data, we allow it to quickly read all the vertex information when needed.

After attribute arrays are set, we pass values for uniform variables to the shader program, which concludes the shader program setup. You will notice that we didn't set values for uniforms representing the various matrices; we will do that separately for each repaint. The `paint()` method takes care of setting up all the matrices:

```
void ObjectGLScene::paint() {
  m_projectionMatrix.setToIdentity();
  qreal ratio = qreal(window()->width())
                / qreal(window()->height());
  m_projectionMatrix.perspective(90, ratio,
    0.5, 40); // angle, ratio, near plane, far plane
  m_viewMatrix.setToIdentity();
  QVector3D eye = QVector3D(0,0,2);
  QVector3D center = QVector3D(0,0,0);
  QVector3D up = QVector3D(0, 1, 0);
  m_viewMatrix.lookAt(eye, center, up);
```

In this method, we make heavy use of the `QMatrix4x4` class that represents a 4 x 4 matrix in so-called row-major order, which is suited to use with OpenGL. At the beginning, we reset the projection matrix and use the `perspective()` method to give it a perspective transformation based on current window size. Afterwards, the view matrix is also reset and the `lookAt()` method is used to prepare the transformation for the camera; center value indicates the center of the view eye is looking at. The `up` vector dictates the vertical orientation of the camera (with respect to the eye position).

The next couple of lines are similar to what we had in the previous project:

```
  glClear(GL_COLOR_BUFFER_BIT | GL_DEPTH_BUFFER_BIT);
  glViewport(0, 0, window()->width(), window()->height());
  glEnable(GL_DEPTH_TEST);
  glEnable(GL_CULL_FACE);
  glCullFace(GL_BACK);
```

After that, we do the actual painting of the object:

```
    m_modelMatrix.setToIdentity();
    m_modelMatrix.rotate(45, 0, 1, 0);
    QMatrix4x4 modelViewMatrix = m_viewMatrix*m_modelMatrix;
    paintObject(modelViewMatrix);
  }
```

We start by setting the model matrix, which dictates where the rendered object is positioned relative to the center of the world (in this case, we say it is rotated 45 degrees around the *y* axis). Then we assemble the model-view matrix (denoting the position of the object relative to the camera) and pass it to the `paintObject()` method, as shown:

```
  void paintCube(const QMatrix4x4& mvMatrix) {
    m_shader.bind();
    m_shader.setUniformValue("projectionMatrix",
      m_projectionMatrix);
    m_shader.setUniformValue("modelViewMatrix",
      mvMatrix);
    m_shader.setUniformValue("mvpMatrix",
      m_projectionMatrix*mvMatrix);
    m_shader.setUniformValue("normalMatrix",
      mvMatrix.normalMatrix());
    const int pointCount = m_data.size();
    glDrawArrays(GL_TRIANGLES, 0, pointCount);
  }
```

This method is very easy since most of the work was done when setting up the shader program. First the shader program is activated. Then all required matrices are set as uniforms for the shader. Included is the normal matrix calculated from the model-view matrix. Finally, a call to `glDrawArrays()` is issued telling it to render with the `GL_TRIANGLES` mode using active arrays, starting from the beginning of the array (offset `0`) and reading in the `pointCount` entities from the array.

After you run the project, you should get a result similar to the following one, which happens to contain the Blender monkey, Suzanne:

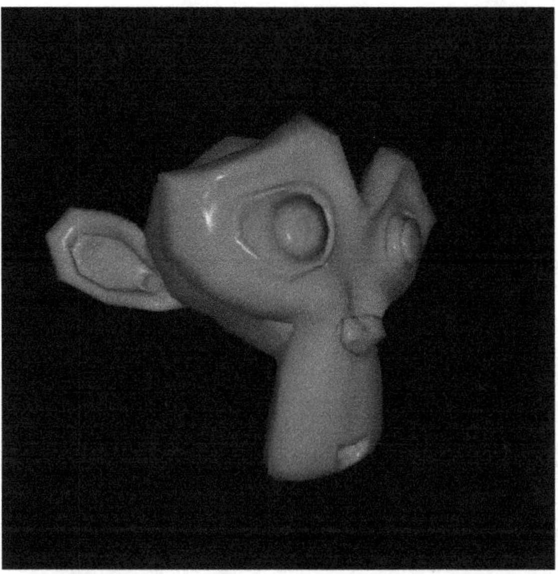

GL buffers

Using attribute arrays can speed up programming, but for rendering, all data still requires to be copied to the graphics card on each use. This can be avoided with OpenGL buffer objects. Qt provides a neat interface for such objects with its `QOpenGLBuffer` class. Currently supported buffer types are vertex buffers (where the buffer contains vertex information), index buffers (where the content of the buffer is a set of indexes to other buffers that can be used with `glDrawElements()`), and also less commonly used pixel pack buffers and pixel unpack buffers. The buffer is essentially a block of memory that can be uploaded to the graphics card and stored there for faster access. There are different usage patterns available that dictate how and when the buffer is transferred between the host memory and GPU memory. The most common pattern is a one-time upload of vertex information to the GPU that can later be referred to during rendering as many times as needed. Changing an existing application that uses an attribute array to use vertex buffers is very easy. First a buffer needs to be instantiated:

```
QOpenGLBuffer vbo(QOpenGLBuffer::VertexBuffer);
```

Then its usage pattern needs to be set. In case of a one-time upload, the most appropriate type is `StaticDraw`, as shown:

```
vbo.setUsagePattern(QOpenGLBuffer::StaticDraw);
```

Then the buffer itself has to be created for the current context:

```
context->makeCurrent(this);
vbo.create();
```

The next step is to actually allocate some memory for the buffer:

```
vbo.allocate(vertexCount*sizeof(ScenePoint));
```

To write data to the buffer, there are two options. First you can attach the buffer to the application's memory space using a call to `map()` and then fill the data using a returned pointer:

```
ScenePoint *buffer =
  static_cast<ScenePoint*>(vbo.map(QOpenGLBuffer::WriteOnly));
assert(buffer!=0);
for(int i=0;i<vbo.size();++i) { buffer[i] = m_data[i]; }
vbo.unmap();
```

An alternative approach is to write to the buffer directly using `write()`:

```
const int spSize = sizeof(ScenePoint);
for(int i=0;i<vbo.size();++i) {
  vbo.write (i*spSize, &m_data[i], spSize); }
```

Finally, the buffer can be used in the shader program in a way similar to an attribute array:

```
vbo.bind();
m_shader.setAttributeBuffer("Vertex"", GL_FLOAT, 0, 3,
  sizeof(ScenePoint));
m_shader.setAttributeBuffer("Normal"", GL_FLOAT,
  sizeof(QVector3D), 3, sizeof(ScenePoint));
```

The result is that all the data is uploaded to the GPU once and then used as needed by the current shader program or other OpenGL call supporting buffer objects.

Off-screen rendering

Sometimes, it is useful to render a GL scene not to the screen but rather to some image that can be later processed externally or used as a texture in some other part of rendering. For that, the concept of **Framebuffer Objects** (**FBO**) was created. An FBO is a rendering surface that behaves like the regular device frame buffer, with the only exception that the resulting pixels do not land on the screen. An FBO target can be bound as a texture in an existing scene or dumped as an image to regular computer memory. In Qt, such an entity is represented by a `QOpenGLFramebufferObject` class.

Once you have a current OpenGL context, you can create an instance of `QOpenGLFramebufferObject` using one of the available constructors. A mandatory parameter to pass is the size of the canvas (either as a `QSize` object or as a pair of integers describing the width and height of the frame). Different constructors accept other parameters such as the type of texture the FBO is to generate or a set of parameters encapsulated in `QOpenGLFramebufferObjectFormat`.

When the object is created, you can issue a `bind()` call on it, which switches the OpenGL pipeline to render to the FBO instead of the default target. A complementary method is `release()`, which restores the default rendering target. Afterwards, the FBO can be queried to return the ID of the OpenGL texture (using the `texture()` method) or to convert the texture to `QImage` (by invoking `toImage()`).

Summary

In this chapter, we learned about using graphics with Qt. You should be aware we have only scratched the surface of Qt capabilities in this regard. What was presented in this chapter will let you implement custom widgets, do some basic painting on images, and render OpenGL scenes. There are many more functionalities that we didn't go through, such as composition modes, paths, SVG handling, and many others. We will come back to some of these features in subsequent chapters, but we will leave most for you to discover on your own.

In the next chapter, we will learn a more object-oriented approach to do graphics, called Graphics View.

6
Graphics View

Widgets are great for designing graphical user interfaces. However, you will run into problems if you wish to animate multiple widgets at the same time by constantly moving them around in the application. For these situations, or in general for frequently transforming 2D graphics, Qt offers you Graphics View. In this chapter, you will learn the basics of the Graphics View architecture and its items. You also will learn how to combine widgets with Graphics View items. Once you have acquired a basic understanding, we are next going to develop a simple jump-and-run game illustrating how to animate the items. Finally, we'll look into some possibilities for optimizing Graphics View's performance.

Graphics View architecture

Three components form the core of Graphics View: an instance of `QGraphicsView`, which is referred to as **view**; an instance of `QGraphicsScene`, which is referred to as **scene**; and usually multiple instances of `QGraphicsItem`, which are referred to as **items**. The usual workflow is to first create a couple of items, then add them to a scene, and finally set that scene on a view.

In the following section, we will be discussing all three parts of the Graphics View architecture one after the other, beginning with the items, followed by the scene, and concluding with the view.

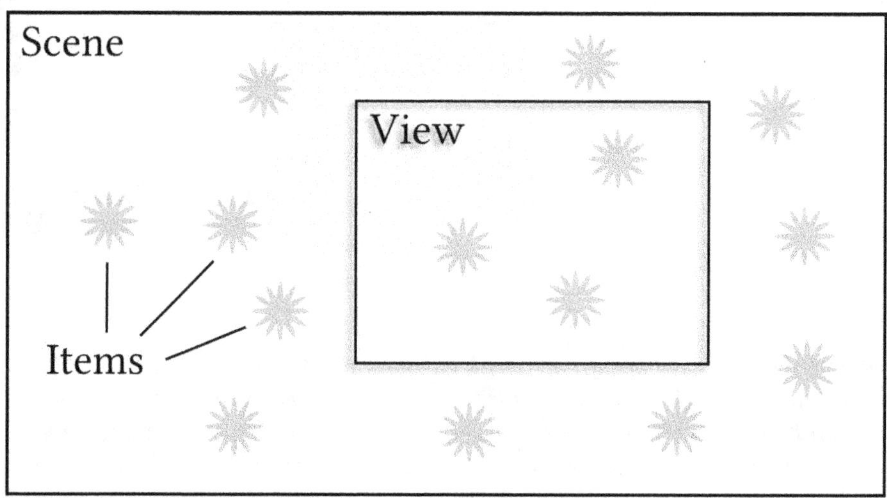

An illustration of Graphics View components

However, because it is not possible to deal with one component as entirely separate from the others, you need to get the big picture up front. This will help you to better understand the description of the three single parts. And do not worry if you do not understand all the details on their first occurrence. Be patient, work through the three parts, and all issues will hopefully become clear in the end.

Think of the items as Post-it notes. You take a note and write a message on it, paint an image on it, both write and paint on it or, quite possibly, just leave it blank. This is equivalent to creating an item with a defined paint function, whether it is a default one or you have customized it. Since the items do not have a predetermined size, you define a bounding rectangle inside which all the painting of the item is done. As with a note, which does not care where it is positioned or from which angle it is being looked at, the item always draws its content as if it were in an untransformed state, where a length unit corresponds to 1 pixel. The item exists in its own coordinate system. Although you can apply various transformations to the item, such as rotating and scaling, it's not the job of the item's paint function to take that into account; that's the scene's job.

What is the scene, then? Well, think of it as a larger sheet of paper onto which you attach your smaller Post-its, that is, the notes. On the scene, you can freely move the items around while applying funny transformations to them. It is the scene's responsibility to correctly display the items' position and any transformations applied to them. The scene further informs the items about any events that affect them and it has—as with the items—a bounding rectangle within which the items can be positioned.

Last but not least, let's turn our attention to the view. Think of the view as an inspection window or a person who holds the paper with the notes in their hands. You can watch the paper as a whole or you can only look at specific parts. And as a person can rotate and shear the paper with their hands, so the view can rotate and shear the scene and do a lot more transformations with it.

You may look at the preceding diagram and be worried about all the items being outside the view. Aren't they wasting GPU render time? Don't you need to take care of them by adding a so-called "view frustum culling" mechanism (to detect which item not to draw/render because it is not visible)? Well, the short answer is "no" because Qt is already taking care of this.

Items

So, let's look at the items. The most fundamental characteristic of items in Graphics View is their object-oriented approach. All items in the scene must inherit `QGraphicsItem`, which is an abstract class with—amongst numerous other public functions—two pure virtual functions called `boundingRect()` and `paint()`. Because of this simple and clear fact, there are principles which apply to each item.

Parent child relationship

The constructor of `QGraphicsItem` takes a pointer to another item that is set as the item's parent. If the pointer is `0`, the item has no parent. This gives you the opportunity to organize items in a tree structure similar to the `QObject` object even though the `QGraphicsItem` element does not inherit from the `QObject` object. You can change the relationship of items at any given time by calling the `setParentItem()` function. It takes the new parent as an argument. If you want to remove a child item from its parent, simply call the `setParentItem(0)` function on the child. The following code illustrates both possibilities for creating a relationship between items. (Please note that this code will not compile since `QGraphicsItem` is an abstract class. Here, it is just for the purpose of illustration, but it will work with a real item class.)

```
QGraphicsItem *parentItem = new QGraphicsItem();
QGraphicsItem *firstChildItem = new QGraphicsItem(parentItem);
QGraphicsItem *secondChildItem = new QGraphicsItem();
secondChildItem->setParentItem(parentItem);
delete parentItem;
```

First we create an item called `parentItem`, and since we do not use the constructor's argument, the item has no parent or child. Next, we create another item called `firstChildItem` and pass a pointer to the `parentItem` item as an argument. Thus, it has the `parentItem` item as its parent, and the `parentItem` item now has the `firstChildItem` item as its child. Next we create a third item called `secondChildItem`, but since we do not pass anything to its constructor, it has no parent at this point. In the next line, however, we change that by calling the `setParentItem()` function. Now it is also a child of the `parentItem` item.

> You can always check whether an item has a parent using the `parentItem()` function and check the returned `QGraphicsItem` pointer against `0`, which means that the item does not have a parent. To figure out if there are any children, call the `childItems()` function on the item. A `QList` method with the `QGraphicsItem` pointers to all child items is returned.

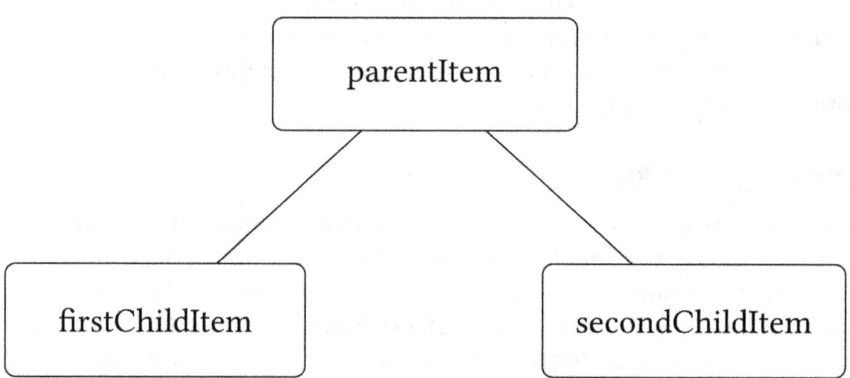

The parent-child relationship

The benefit of this parent-child relationship is that specific actions performed on a parent item also affect associated child items. For example, when you delete a parent item, all child items will also be deleted. For that reason, it is sufficient to delete the `parentItem` item in the preceding code. The destructors of the `firstChildItem` and `secondChildItem` items are called implicitly. The same applies when you add or remove a parent item from a scene. All child items will then get added or removed as well. The same applies when you hide a parent item or when you move a parent item. In both cases, the child items will behave the same way the parent does. Think of the earlier example of Post-it notes; they would behave the same. If you have a note with other notes attached to it, they will also move when you move the parent note.

If you are not sure whether a function call on the parent item is propagated to its child items, you can always have a look at the sources. You will find them in your Qt installation if you checked the option to also install the sources at the time of installation. You can also find them online at `https://github.com/qtproject/qtbase`.

Even if there isn't a meaningful comment, you can spot the relevant code easily. Just look for a `children` variable addressed through the d-pointer. Inside the destructor of the `QGraphicsItem` item, the relevant code fragment is as follows:

```
if (!d_ptr->children.isEmpty()) {
  while (!d_ptr->children.isEmpty())
    delete d_ptr->children.first();
  Q_ASSERT(d_ptr->children.isEmpty());
}
```

Appearance

You are probably wondering what a `QGraphicsItem` item looks like. Well, since it is an abstract class (and unfortunately the paint function is a pure virtual one), it does not look like anything. You will have to do all the painting yourself. Luckily, since the paint function of the `QGraphicsItem` item offers you a technique you already know, the `QPainter` pointer, this is not very difficult.

Don't panic! You don't have to draw all items yourself though. Qt offers a lot of standard shaped items you can use just out-of-the-box. You'll find them discussed in an upcoming section titled *Standard items*. However, since we need to draw a custom item once in a while, we go through this process.

Time for action – creating a black, rectangular item

As a first approach, let's create an item that paints a black rectangle:

```
class BlackRectangle : public QGraphicsItem {
public:
  explicit BlackRectangle(QGraphicsItem *parent = 0)
    : QGraphicsItem(parent) {}
  virtual ~BlackRectangle() {}

  QRectF boundingRect() const {
    return QRectF(0, 0, 75, 25);
  }
```

```
    void paint(QPainter *painter, const QStyleOptionGraphicsItem
               *option, QWidget *widget) {
      Q_UNUSED(option)
      Q_UNUSED(widget)
      painter->fillRect(boundingRect(), Qt::black);
    }
  };
```

What just happened?

First, we subclass `QGraphicItem` and call the new class `BlackRectangle`. The class' constructor accepts a pointer to a `QGraphicItem` item. This pointer is then passed to the constructor of the `QGraphicItem` item. We do not have to worry about it; `QGraphicItem` will take care of it and establish the parent-child relationship for our item, among other things. Next, the virtual destructor makes sure that it gets called even if the class is getting deleted through a base class pointer. This is a crucial point, as you will learn later when we talk about the scene.

Next, we define the `boundingRect()` function of our item, where we return a rectangle 75 pixels wide and 25 pixels high. This returned rectangle is the canvas for the `paint` method and simultaneously the promise to the scene that the item will only paint in this area. The scene relies on the correctness of that information, so you should strictly obey that promise. Otherwise, the scene will become cluttered up with relics of your drawing!

Lastly, we do the actual painting from `QPainter` in conjunction with a `QWidget` item. There is nothing different here except that the painter is already initialized with the appropriate values given to us through the first argument. Even if it is not needed, I would suggest that the painter be kept in the same state at the end of the function as it was in the beginning. If you follow that advice, and if you only use custom items in the scene, you can later optimize the render speed enormously. This especially applies to scenes with many items. But let us go back to what we were actually doing. We have taken the painter and called the `fillRect()` function, which does not touch the painter's internal state. As arguments, we used the `boundingRect()` function, which defines the area to fill, and the `Qt::black` parameter, which defines the fill color. Thus, by only filling the bounding rectangle of the item, we obeyed the bounding rectangle promise.

In our example, we have not used the two other arguments of the `paint` function. To suppress the compiler warnings about unused variables, we used Qt's `Q_UNUSED` macro.

Time for action – reacting to an item's selection state

The assigned pointer to a `QStyleOptionGraphicsItem` item might become handy if you want to alter the appearance of the item related to its state. For example, say you want to fill the rectangle with red when it gets selected. To do so, you only have to type this:

```
void paint(QPainter *painter, const QStyleOptionGraphicsItem *option,
           QWidget *widget) {
  Q_UNUSED(widget)
  if (option->state & QStyle::State_Selected)
    painter->fillRect(boundingRect(), Qt::red);
  else
    painter->fillRect(boundingRect(), Qt::black);
}
```

What just happened?

The `state` variable is a bitmask holding the possible states of the item. You can check its value against the values of the `QStyle::StateFlag` parameter by using bitwise operators. In the preceding case, the `state` variable is checked against the `State_Selected` parameter. If this flag is set, the rectangle is painted red.

The type of state is `QFlags<StateFlag>`. So, instead of using the bitwise operator to test if a flag is set, you can use the convenient function `testFlag()`. Used with the preceding example it would be as follows:

```
if (option->state.testFlag(QStyle::State_Selected))
```

The most important states you can use with items are described in the following table:

State	Description
`State_Enabled`	Indicates that the item is enabled. If the item is disabled, you may want to draw it as grayed out.
`State_HasFocus`	Indicates that the item has the input focus. To receive this state, the item needs to have the `ItemIsFocusable` flag set.
`State_MouseOver`	Indicates that the cursor is currently hovering over the item. To receive this state the item needs to have the `acceptHoverEvents` variable set to `true`.
`State_Selected`	Indicates that the item is selected. To receive this state, the item needs to have the `ItemIsSelectable` flag set. The normal behavior would be to draw a dashed line around the item as a selection marker.

Besides the state, `QStyleOptionGraphicsItem` offers much more information about the currently used style, such as the palette and the font used, accessible through the `QStyleOptionGraphicsItem::palette` and `QStyleOptionGraphicsItem::fontMetrics` parameters, respectively. If you aim for style-aware items, have a deeper look at this class in the documentation.

Time for action – making the item's size definable

Let's push the example of the black rectangle a step further. So far, `BlackRectangle` draws a fixed rectangle of size 75 x 25 pixels. It would be nice if one could define this size, so let us add the ability to define the size of the rectangle. Remember, only painting the rectangle larger does not help here because then you would break the promise regarding the bounding rectangle. So we need also to change the bounding rectangle as follows:

```
class BlackRectangle : public QGraphicsItem {
public:
  BlackRectangle(QGraphicsItem *parent = 0)
    : QGraphicsItem(parent), m_rect(0, 0, 75, 25) {}
//...
  QRectF boundingRect() const {
    return m_rect;
  }
//...
  QRectF rect() const {
    return m_rect;
  }
  void setRect(const QRectF& rect) {
    if (rect == m_rect)
      return;
    prepareGeometryChange();
    m_rect = rect;
}
private:
  QRectF m_rect;
};
```

What just happened?

Since the destructor and the `paint` function are unchanged, they are omitted. What exactly have we done here? First, we introduced a private member called `m_rect` to save the current rectangle's value. In the initialization list, we set `m_rect` to a default value of `QRectF(0, 0, 75, 25)` like we hard-coded it in the first example. Since the bounding rectangle should be the same as `m_rect`, we altered `boundingRect()` to return `m_rect`. The same value is returned by the getter function `rect()`. For now it seems redundant to have two functions returning the same value, but as soon as you draw a border around the rectangle, you need to return a different bounding rectangle. It needs to be increased by the used pen's width. Therefore, we leave this redundancy in place in order to make further improvements easier. The last new part is the setter function, which is pretty standard. We check if the value has changed, and if not we exit the function. Otherwise, we set a new value, but this has to happen after the `prepareGeometryChange()` call. This call is important to inform the scene about the coming geometry change. Then, the scene will ask the item to redraw itself. We do not need to handle that part.

Have a go hero – customizing the item

As an exercise, you can try to add an option to change the background color. You can also create a new item that allows you to set an image. If doing so, keep in mind that you have to change the item's bounding rectangle according to the size of the image.

Standard items

As you have seen, creating your own item involves some work, but overall it is not that difficult. A big advantage is that you can use `QPainter` to draw the item, the same technique you use to paint widgets. So there is nothing new you need to learn. Indeed, even if it is easy to draw filled rectangles or any other shape, it is a lot of work to subclass `QGraphicsItem` each time you need to create an item that does such basic tasks. And that's the reason why Qt comes with the following standard items that make your life as a developer much easier:

Standard item	Description
`QGraphicsLineItem`	Draws a simple line. You can define the line with `setLine(const QLineF&)`.
`QGraphicsRectItem`	Draws a rectangle. You can define the rectangle's geometry with `setRect(const QRectF&)`.

Standard item	Description
`QGraphicsEllipseItem`	Draws an ellipse. You can define the rectangle within which the ellipse is being drawn with `setRect(const QRectF&)`. Additionally, you can define whether only a segment of the ellipse should be drawn by calling `setStartAngle(int)` and `setSpanAngle(int)`. The arguments of both functions are in 16ths of a degree.
`QGraphicsPolygonItem`	Draws a polygon. You can define the polygon with `setPolygon(const QPolygonF&)`.
`QGraphicsPathItem`	Draws a path. You can define the path with `setPath(const QPainterPath&)`.
`QGraphicsSimpleTextItem`	Draws a simple text path. You can define the text with `setText(const QString&)` and the font with `setFont(const QFont&)`. This item is only for drawing *plain* text without any modification.
`QGraphicsTextItem`	Draws text. Unlike `QGraphicsSimpleTextItem`, this item can display HTML or render a `QTextDocument` element. You can set HTML with `setHtml(const QString&)` and the document with `setDocument(QTextDocument*)`. `QGraphicsTextItem` can even interact with the displayed text so that text editing or URL opening is possible.
`QGraphicsPixmapItem`	Draws a pixmap. You can define the pixmap with `setPixmap(const QPixmap&)`.

Since the drawing of these items is done by a `QPainter` pointer you can also define which pen and which brush should be used. The pen is set with `setPen(const QPen&)` and the brush with `setBrush(const QBrush&)`. These two functions, however, do not exist for `QGraphicsTextItem` and `QGraphicsPixmapItem`. To define the appearance of a `QGraphicsTextItem` item you have to use `setDefaultTextColor()` or HTML tags supported by Qt. Note that pixmaps usually do not have a pen or a brush.

Use `QGraphicsSimpleTextItem` wherever possible and try to avoid `QGraphicsTextItem` if it is not absolutely necessary. The reason is that `QGraphicsTextItem` lugs a `QTextDocument` object around and it is, besides being a subclass of `QGraphicsItem`, also a subclass of `QObject`. This is definitely too much overhead and has too high a performance cost for displaying simple text.

A word on how you set up items. Instead of writing two expressions, one for the initialization of the item and one for setting up its key information such as the rectangle for a `QGraphicsRextItem` item or the pixmap for a `QGraphicsPixmapItem`, almost all standard items offer you the option to pass that key information as a first argument to their constructors—besides the optional last argument for setting the item's parent. Say you would have written the following code:

```
QGraphicsRectItem *item = new QGraphicsRectItem();
item->setRect(QRectF(0, 0, 25, 25));
```

You can now simply write this:

```
QGraphicsRectItem *item = new QGraphicsRectItem(QRectF(0, 0, 25, 25));
```

You can even just write this:

```
QGraphicsRectItem *item = new QGraphicsRectItem(0, 0, 25, 25);
```

This is very convenient, but keep in mind that compact code may be harder to maintain than code that sets all variables through setter methods.

Coordinate system of the items

A last but very important note on the used coordinate system. Altogether, Graphics View deals with three different but connected coordinate systems. There is the item's coordinate system, the scene's coordinate system, and the view's coordinate system. All three coordinate systems differ from the Cartesian coordinate systems regarding the *y* axis: in Graphics View, like in `QPainter` pointer's coordinate system, the *y* axis is orientated and measured from the origin to the bottom. This means that a point below the origin has a positive *y* value. For now, we only care about the item's coordinate system. Since Graphics View is for 2D graphics, we have an *x* coordinate and a *y* coordinate with the origin at (0, 0). All points, lines, rectangles, and so on are specified in the item's own coordinate system. This applies to almost all occasions where you deal with values representing coordinates within the `QGraphicsItem` class or its derived classes. If you define, for example, the rectangle of a `QGraphicsRectItem` item, you use item coordinates. If an item receives a mouse press event, `QGraphicsSceneMouseEvent::pos()` is expressed in item coordinates. But there are some easy-to-identify exceptions to this statement. The return value of `scenePos()` and `sceneBoundingRect()` is expressed in scene coordinates. Pretty obvious, isn't it? The one thing that is a little bit tricky to identify is the returned `QPointF` pointer of `pos()`. The coordinates of this point are expressed in the item's parent coordinate system. This can be either the parent item's coordinate system or, more likely, the scene's coordinate system when the item does not have a parent item.

For a better understanding of `pos()` and the involved coordinate systems, think of Post-it notes again. If you put a note on a larger sheet of paper and then had to determine its exact position, how would you do it? Probably somewhat like this: "The note's upper left corner is positioned 3 cm to the right and 5 cm to the bottom from the paper's top left edge". In the Graphics View world, this would correspond to a parentless item whose `pos()` function returns a position in scene coordinates since the item's origin is directly pinned to the scene. On the other hand, say you put a note A on top of a (larger) note B, which is already pinned on a paper, and you have to determine A's position; how would you describe it this time? Probably by saying that note A is placed on top of note B or "2 cm to the right and 1 cm to the bottom from the top-left edge of note B". You most likely wouldn't use the underlying paper as a reference since it is not the next point of reference. This is because, if you move note B, A's position regarding the paper will change whereas A's relative position to B still remains unchanged. To switch back to Graphics View, the equivalent situation is an item that has a parent item. In this case, the `pos()` function's returned value is expressed in the coordinate system of its parent. So `setPos()` and `pos()` specify the position of the item's origin in relation to the next (higher) point of reference. This could be the scene or the item's parent item.

Keep in mind, however, that changing an item's position does not affect the item's internal coordinate system.

Time for action – creating items with different origins

Let's have a closer look at these three items defined by the following code snippet:

```
QGraphicsRectItem *itemA = QGraphicsRectItem(-10, -10, 20, 20);
QGraphicsRectItem *itemB = QGraphicsRectItem(0, 0, 20, 20);
QGraphicsRectItem *itemC = QGraphicsRectItem(10, 10, 20, 20);
```

What just happened?

All three items are rectangles with a side length of 20 pixels. The difference between them is the position of their coordinate origin points. `itemA` has its origin in the center of the rectangle, `itemB` has its origin in the top-left corner of the rectangle, and `itemC` has its origin outside the drawn rectangle. In the following diagram, you see the origin points marked as red dots.

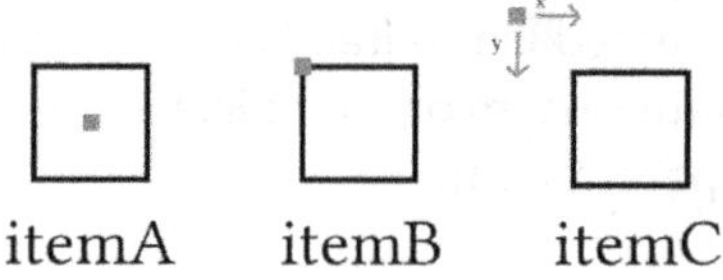

So what's the deal with these origin points? On the one hand, the origin point is used to create a relation between the item's coordinate system and the scene's coordinate system. As you will see later in more detail, if you set the position of the item on the scene, the position on the scene is the origin of the item. You can say scene *(x, y) = item(0, 0)*. On the other hand, the origin point is used as a center point for all transformations you can use with items, such as scaling, rotating, or adding a freely definable transformation matrix of `QTransform` type. As an additional feature, you always have the option to combine a new transformation with the already applied ones or to replace the old transformation(s) with a new one.

Time for action – rotating an item

As an example, let's rotate `itemB` and `itemC` by 45 degrees counter-clockwise. For `itemB`, the function call would look like this:

```
itemB->setRotation(-45);
```

The `setRotation()` function accepts `qreal` as the argument value, so you can set very precise values. The function interprets the number as degrees for a clockwise rotation around the *z* coordinate. If you set a negative value, a counter-clockwise rotation is performed. Even if it does not make much sense, you can rotate an item by 450 degrees, which would result in a rotation of 90 degrees. Here is what the two items would look like after the rotation by 45 degrees counter-clockwise:

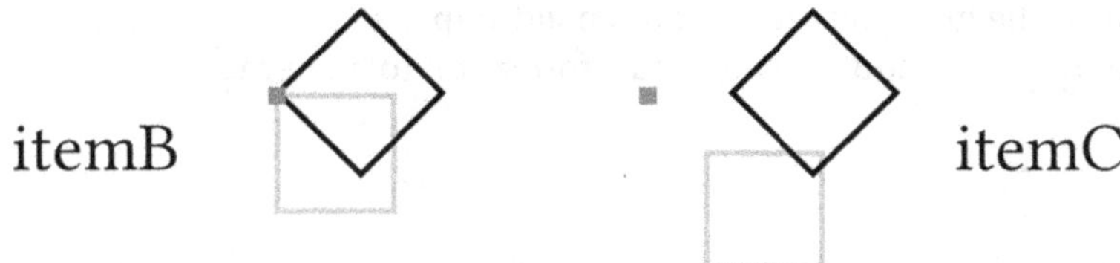

What just happened?

As you can see, the rotation has its center in the item's origin point. Now you could run into the problem that you want to rotate the rectangle of `itemC` around its center point. In such a situation, you can use `setTransformOriginPoint()`. For the described problem, the relevant code would look like this:

```
QGraphicsRectItem *itemC = QGraphicsRectItem(10, 10, 20, 20);
itemC->setTransformOriginPoint(20, 20);
itemC->rotate(-45);
```

Let us take this opportunity to recapitulate the item's coordinate system. The item's origin point is in (0, 0). In the constructor of QGraphicsRectItem, you define that the rectangle should have its top-left corner at (10, 10). And since you gave the rectangle a width and a height of 20 pixels, its bottom-right corner is at (30, 30). This makes (20, 20) the center of the rectangle. After setting the transformation's origin point to (20, 20), you rotate the item around that point 45 degrees counter-clockwise. You will see the result in the following image, where the transformation's origin point is marked with a cross.

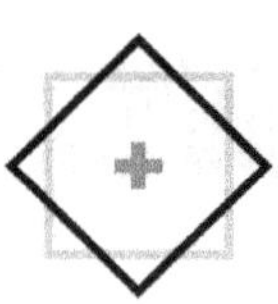

Even if you "change" the item's origin point by such a transformation, this does not affect the item's position on the scene. First, the scene positions the untransformed item with respect to its origin point and only then are all transformations applied to the item.

Have a go hero – applying multiple transformations

To understand the concept of transformations and their origin point, go ahead and try it yourself. Apply `rotate()` and `scale()` sequentially to an item. Also, change the point of origin and see how the item will react. As a second step, use `QTransform` in conjunction with `setTransform()` to add a custom transformation to an item.

Scenes

Let us take a look at how we can improvise the scene.

Adding items to the scene

At this point, you should have a basic understanding of items. The next question is what to do with them. As described earlier, you put the items on a `QGraphicsScene` method. This is done by calling `addItem(QGraphicsItem *item)`. Did you notice the type of the argument? It's a pointer to a `QGraphicsItem` method. Since all items on the scene must inherit `QGraphicsItem`, you can use this function with any item, be it a `QGraphicsRectItem` item or any custom item. If you have a look at the documentation of `QGraphicsScene`, you will notice that all functions returning items or dealing with them expect pointers to a `QGraphicsItem` item. This universal usability is a huge advantage of the object-orientated approach in Graphics View.

If you have a pointer of the type `QGraphicsItem` pointing to an instance of a `QGraphicsRectItem` and you want to use a function of `QGraphicsRectItem`, use `qgraphicsitem_cast<>()` to cast the pointer. This is because it is safer and faster than using `static_cast<>()` or `dynamic_cast<>()`.

```
QGraphicsItem *item = new QGraphicsRectItem(0, 0, 5, 5);
QGraphicsRectItem *rectItem =
qgraphicsitem_cast<QGraphicsRectItem*>(item);
if (rectItem)
  rectItem->setRect(0, 0, 10, 15);
```

Please note that if you want to use `qgraphicsitem_cast<>()` with your own custom item, you have to make sure that `QGraphicsItem::type()` is reimplemented and that it returns a unique type for a particular item. To ensure a unique type, use `QGraphicsItem::UserType + x` as a return value where you count up `x` for every custom item you create.

Time for action – adding an item to a scene

Let's have a first try and add an item to the scene:

```
QGraphicsScene scene;
QGraphicsRectItem *rectItem = new QGraphicsRectItem(0,0,50,50);
scene.addItem(rectItem);
```

What just happened?

Nothing complicated here. You create a scene, create an item of type `QGraphicsRectItem`, define the geometry of the item's rectangle, and then set the item to the scene by calling `addItem()`. Pretty straightforward. But what you do not see here is what this implies for the scene. The scene is now responsible for the added item! First of all, the ownership of the item is transferred to the scene. For you, this means that you do not have to worry about freeing the item's memory because deleting the scene also deletes all items associated with the scene. Now remember what we said about the destructor of a custom item: it must be virtual! `QGraphicsScene` operates with pointers to `QGraphicsItem`. Thus, when it deletes the assigned items, it does that by calling `delete` on the base class pointer. If you have not declared the destructor of the derived class virtual, it will not be executed, which may cause memory leaks. Therefore, form habit of declaring the destructor virtual.

Transferring the ownership of the item to the scene also means that an item can only be added to one single scene. If the item was previously already added to another scene, it gets removed from there before it will be added to the new scene. The following code will demonstrate that:

```
QGraphicsScene firstScene;
QGraphicsScene secondScene;
QGraphicsRectItem *item = new QGraphicsRectItem;
firstScene.addItem(item);
qDebug() << firstScene.items().count(); // 1
secondScene.addItem(item);
qDebug() << firstScene.items().count(); // 0
```

After creating two scenes and one item, we add the item `item` to the scene `firstScene`. Then, with the debug message, we print out the number of associated items with that `firstScene` scene. For this, we call `items()` on the scene, which returns a `QList` list with pointers to all items of the scene. Calling `count()` on that list tells us the size of the list, which is equivalent to the number of added items. As you can see after adding the item on `secondScene`, the `firstScene` item count returns `0`. Before `item` was added to `secondScene`, it was first removed from `firstScene`.

> If you want to remove an item from a scene without setting it directly to another scene or without deleting it, you can call `removeItem()`, which takes a pointer for the item that should be removed. Be aware, however, that now it is your responsibility to delete the item in order to free the allocated memory!

Interacting with items on the scene

When it takes ownership of an item, the scene also has to take care of a lot of other stuff. The scene has to make sure that events get delivered to the right items. If you click on a scene (to be precise, you click on a view that propagates the event to the scene), the scene receives the mouse press event and it then becomes the scene's responsibility to determine which item was meant by the click. In order to be able to do that, the scene always needs to know where all the items are. Therefore, the scene keeps track of the items in a Binary Space Partitioning tree.

You can benefit from this knowledge too! If you want to know which item is shown at a certain position, call `itemAt()` with `QPointF` as an argument. You will receive the topmost item at that position. If you want all items that are located at this position, say in cases where multiple items are on top of each other, call an overloaded function of `items()` (which takes a `QPointF` pointer as an argument). It will return a list of all items that the bounding rectangle contains that point. The `items()` function also accepts `QRectF`, `QPolygonF`, and `QPainterPath` as arguments if you need all visible items of an area. With the second argument of the type `Qt::ItemSelectionMode`, you can alter the mode for how the items in the area will be determined. The following table shows the different modes:

Mode	**Meaning**
`Qt::ContainsItemShape`	The item's shape must be completely inside the selection area.
`Qt::IntersectsItemShape`	Similar to `Qt::ContainsItemShape` but also returns items whose shapes intersect with the selection area.
`Qt::ContainsItemBoundingRect`	The item's bounding rectangle must be completely inside the selection area.
`Qt::IntersectsItemBoundingRect`	Similar to `Qt::ContainsItemBoundingRect` but also returns items whose bounding rectangles intersect with the selection area.

The scene's responsibility for delivering events does not only apply to mouse events; it also applies to key events and all other sorts of events. The events that are passed to the items are subclasses of `QGraphicsSceneEvent`. Thus, an item does not get a `QMouseEvent` event like widgets; it gets a `QGraphicsSceneMouseEvent` event. In general, these scene events behave like normal events, but instead of say a `globalPos()` function you have `scenePos()`.

The scene also handles the selection of items. To be selectable, an item must have the `QGraphicsItem::ItemIsSelectable` flag turned on. You can do that by calling `QGraphicsItem::setFlag()` with the flag and `true` as arguments. Besides that, there are different ways to select items. There is the item's `QGraphicsItem::setSelected()` function, which takes a `bool` value to toggle the selection state on or off, or you can call `QGraphicsScene::setSelectionArea()` on the scene, which takes a `QPainterPath` parameter as argument, in which case all items get selected. With the mouse, you can click on an item to select or deselect it or—if the view's rubber-band selection mode is enabled—you can select multiple items with that rubber band.

> For activating the rubber band selection for the view, call `setDragMode(QGraphicsView::RubberBandDrag)` on the view. Then you can press the left mouse button and, while holding it down, move the mouse to define the selection area. The selection rectangle is then defined by the point of the first mouse press and the current mouse position.

With the scene's `QGraphicsScene::selectedItems()` function, you can query the actual selected items. The function returns a `QList` list holding `QGraphicsItem` pointers to selected items. For example, calling `QList::count()` on that list would give you the number of selected items. To clear the selection, call `QGraphicsScene::clearSelection()`. To query the selection state of an item, use `QGraphicsItem::isSelected()`, which returns `true` if the item is selected and `false` otherwise. If you write a customized `paint` function, do not forget to alter the item's appearance to indicate that it is selected. Otherwise, the user cannot know this. The determination inside the paint function is done by `QStyle::State_Selected`, as shown earlier.

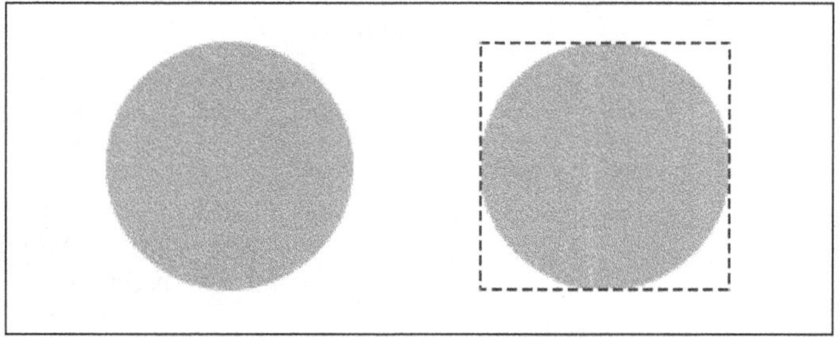

The standard items show a dashed rectangle around a selected item.

The item's handling of focus is done in a similar way. To be focusable an item must have the `QGraphicsItem::ItemIsFocusable` flag enabled. Then, the item can be focused by a mouse click, through the item's `QGraphicsItem::setFocus()` function, or through the scene's `QGraphicsScene::setFocusItem()` function, which expects a pointer to the item you like to focus as a parameter. To determine if an item has focus, you again have two possibilities. One is that you can call `QGraphicsItem::hasFocus()` on an item, which returns `true` if the item has focus or `false` otherwise. Alternatively, you can get the actual focused item by calling the scene's `QGraphicsScene::focusItem()` method. On the other hand, if you call the item's `QGraphicsItem::focusItem()` function, the focused item is returned if the item itself or any descendant item has focus; otherwise, `0` is returned. To remove focus, call `clearFocus()` on the focused item or click somewhere in the scene's background or on an item that cannot get focus.

If you want a click on the scene's background not to cause the focused item to lose its focus, set the scene's `stickyFocus` property to `true`.

Rendering

It is also the scene's responsibility to render itself with all the assigned items.

Time for action – rendering the scene's content to an image

Let's try to render a scene to an image. In order to do that, we take the following code snippet from our first example where we tried to put items on a scene:

```
QGraphicsScene scene;
QGraphicsRectItem *rectItem = new QGraphicsRectItem();
rectItem->setRect(0,0,50,50);
rectItem->setBrush(Qt::green);
rectItem->setPen(QColor(255,0,0));
scene.addItem(rectItem);
```

The only change we make here is that we set a brush resulting in a green-filled rectangle with a red border, which was defined through `setBrush()` and `setPen()`. You can also define the thickness of the stroke by passing a `QPen` object with the corresponding arguments. To render the scene, you only need to call `render()`, which takes a pointer to a `QPainter` pointer. This way, the scene can render its contents to any paint device the painter is pointing to. For us, a simple PNG file will do the job.

```
QRect rect = scene.sceneRect().toAlignedRect();
QImage image(rect.size(), QImage::Format_ARGB32);
image.fill(Qt::transparent);
QPainter painter(&image);
scene.render(&painter);
image.save("scene.png", "PNG");
```

Result of the rendering

What just happened?

First you determined the rectangle of the scene with `sceneRect()`. Since this returns a `QRectF` parameter and `QImage` can only handle `QRect`, you transformed it on-the-fly by calling `toAlignedRect()`. The difference between the `toRect()` function and `toAlignedRect()` is that the former rounds to the nearest integer, which may result in a smaller rectangle whereas the latter expands to the smallest possible rectangle containing the original `QRectF` parameter. Then, you created a `QImage` file with the size of the aligned scene's rectangle. Because the image is created with uninitialized data, you need to call `fill()` with `Qt::transparent` to receive a transparent image. You can assign any color you like as an argument both a value of `Qt::GlobalColor` enumeration and an ordinary `QColor` object; `QColor(0, 0, 255)` would result in a blue background. Next, you create a `QPainter` object which points to the image. This painter object is now used in the scene's `render()` function to draw the scene. After that, all you have to do is to save the image to a place of your choice. The file name (which can also contain an absolute path such as `/path/to/image.png`) is given by the first argument whereas the second argument determines the format of the image. Here, we set the file name to `scene.png` and choose the PNG format. Since we haven't specified a path, the image will be saved in the application's current directory.

Have a go hero – rendering only specific parts of a scene

This example draws the whole scene. Of course, you can also render only specific parts of the scene by using the other arguments of `render()`. We will not go into this here but you may want to try it as an exercise.

Coordinate system of the scene

What is left is a look at the coordinate system of the scene. Like the items, the scene lives in its own coordinate system with the origin at (0, 0). Now when you add an item via `addItem()`, the item is positioned at the scene's (0, 0) coordinate. If you want to move the item to another position on the scene, call `setPos()` on the item.

```
QGraphicsScene scene;
QGraphicsRectItem *item = QGraphicsRectItem(0, 0, 10, 10);
scene.addItem(item);
item.setPos(50,50);
```

After creating the scene and the item, you add the item to the scene by calling `addItem()`. At this stage, the scene's origin and the item's origin are stacked on top of each other at (0, 0). By calling `setPos()`, you move the item 50 pixels right and down. Now the item's origin is at (50, 50) in scene coordinates. If you need to know the position of the bottom-right corner of the item's rectangle in scene coordinates, you have to do a quick calculation. In the item's coordinate system, the bottom right corner is at (10, 10). The item's origin point is (0, 0) in the item's coordinate system, which corresponds to the point (50, 50) in the scene's coordinate system. So you just have to take (50, 50) and add (10,10) to get (60, 60) as the scene's coordinates for the bottom-right corner of the item. This is an easy calculation, but it quickly gets complicated when you rotate, scale, and/or shear the item. Because of this, you should use one of the convenience functions provided by `QGraphicsItem`:

Function	Description
`mapToScene(const QPoint &point)`	Maps the point `point` that is in the item's coordinate system to the corresponding point in the scene's coordinate system.
`mapFromScene(const QPoint &point)`	Maps the point `point` that is in the scene's coordinate system to the corresponding point in the item's coordinate system. This function is the reverse function to `mapToScene()`.
`mapToParent(const QPoint &point)`	Maps the point `point` that is in the item's coordinate system to the corresponding point in the coordinate system of the item's parent. If the item does not have a parent, this function behaves like `mapToScene()`; thus, it returns the corresponding point in the scene's coordinate system.
`mapFromParent(const QPoint &point)`	Maps the point `point` that is in the coordinate system of the item's parent to the corresponding point in the item's own coordinate system. This function is the reverse function to `mapToParent()`.
`mapToItem(const QGraphicsItem *item, const QPointF &point)`	Maps the point `point` that is in the item's own coordinate system to the corresponding point in the coordinate system of the item `item`.
`mapFromItem(const QGraphicsItem *item, const QPointF &point)`	Maps the point `point` which is in the coordinate system of the item `item` to the corresponding point in the item's own coordinate system. This function is the reverse function to `mapToItem()`.

What is great about these functions is that they are not only available for `QPointF`. The same functions are also available for `QRectF`, `QPolygonF`, and `QPainterPath`. Not to mention that these are of course convenience functions: If you call these functions with two numbers of the type `qreal`, the numbers get interpreted as the *x* and *y* coordinates of a `QPointF` pointer; if you call the functions with four numbers, the numbers get interpreted as the *x* and *y* coordinates and the width and the height of a `QRectF` parameter.

Since the positioning of the items is done by the items themselves, it is possible that an item independently moves around. Do not worry; the scene will get notified about any item position change. And not only the scene! Remember the parent-child relationship of items and that parents delete their child items when they get destroyed themselves? It's the same with `setPos()`. If you move a parent, all child items get moved as well. This can be very useful if you have a bunch of items that should stay together. Instead of moving all items by themselves, you only have to move one item. Since transformations that you apply on a parent also affect the children, this might not be the best solution for grouping together equal items that should be independently transformable but also transformable altogether. The solution for such a case is `QGraphicsItemGroup`. It behaves like a parent in a parent-child relationship. The `QGraphicsItemGroup` is an invisible parent item so that you can alter the child items separately through their transformation functions or all together by invoking the transformation functions of `QGraphicsItemGroup`.

Time for action – transforming parent items and child items

Have a look at the following code:

```
QGraphicsScene scene;
QGraphicsRectItem *rectA = new QGraphicsRectItem(0,0,45,45);
QGraphicsRectItem *rectB = new QGraphicsRectItem(0,0,45,45);
QGraphicsRectItem *rectC = new QGraphicsRectItem(0,0,45,45);
QGraphicsRectItem *rectD = new QGraphicsRectItem(0,0,45,45);
rectB->moveBy(50,0);
rectC->moveBy(0,50);
rectD->moveBy(50,50);
QGraphicsItemGroup *group = new QGraphicsItemGroup;
group->addToGroup(rectA);
group->addToGroup(rectB);
group->addToGroup(rectC);
rectD->setGroup(group);
group->setRotation(70);
rectA->setRotation(-25);
rectB->setRotation(-25);
rectC->setRotation(-25);
rectD->setRotation(-25);
scene.addItem(group);
```

What just happened?

After creating a scene, we create four rectangle items that are arranged in a 2 x 2 matrix. This is done with the calls of the `moveBy()` function, which interprets the first argument as a shift to the right or left when negative and the second argument as a shift to the bottom or top when negative. Then we create a new `QGraphicsItemGroup` item which, since it subclasses `QGraphicsItem`, is a regular item and can be used as such. By calling `addToGroup()`, we add the items that we want to position inside that group. If you'd like to remove an item from the group later on, simply call `removeFromGroup()` and pass the respective item. The `rectD` parameter is added to the group in a different way. By calling `setGroup()` on `rectD`, it gets assigned to `group`; this behavior is comparable to `setParent()`. If you want to check whether an item is assigned to a group, just call `group()` on it. It will return a pointer to the group or `0` if the item is not in a group. After adding the group to the scene, and thus also the items, we rotate the whole group by 70 degrees clockwise. Afterward, all items are separately rotated 25 degrees counter-clockwise around their top left corner. This will result in the following appearance:

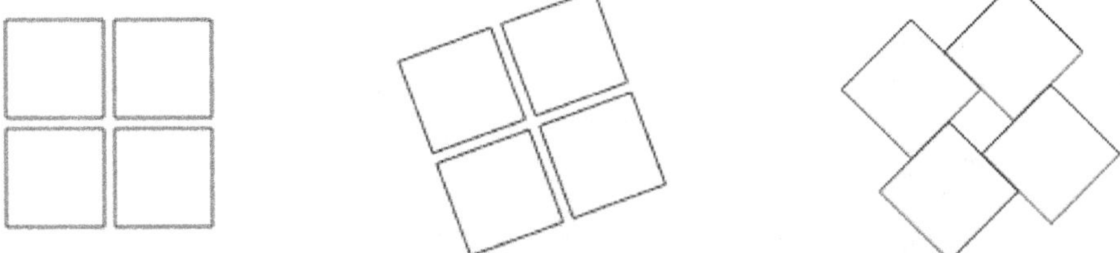

Here you see the initial state after moving the items, then after rotating the group by 70 degrees, and then after rotating each item by -25 degrees

If we were to rotate the items more, they would overlap each other. But which item would overlap which? This is defined by the item's *z* value; you can define the value by using `QGraphicsItem::setZValue()` otherwise it is `0`. Based on that, the items get stacked. Items with a higher *z* value are displayed on top of items with lower *z* values. If items have the same *z* value, the order of insertion decides the placement: items added later overlap those added earlier. Also, negative values are possible.

Have a go hero – playing with the z value

Take the item group from the example as a starting point and apply various transformations to it as well as different *z* values for the item. You will be astonished at what crazy geometrical figures you can create with these four items. Coding really is fun!

For the sake of completeness, a word on the scene's bounding rectangle is required (set through `setSceneRect()`). Just as the offset of an item's bounding rectangle affects its position on the scene, the offset of the scene's bounding rectangle affects the scene's position on the view. More importantly, however, the bounding rectangle is used for various internal computations, such as the calculation of the view's scroll bar value and position. Even if you do not have to set the scene's bounding rectangle, it is recommended that you do. This applies especially when your scene holds a lot of items. If you do not set a bounding rectangle, the scene calculates this itself by going through all the items, retrieving their positions and their bounding rectangles as well as their transformations to figure out the maximum occupied space. This calculation is done by the function `itemsBoundingRect()`. As you may imagine, this becomes increasingly resource-intensive the more items a scene has. Furthermore, if you do not set the scene's rectangle, the scene checks on each item's update if the item is still in the scene's rectangle. Otherwise, it enlarges the rectangle to hold the item inside the bounding rectangle. The downside to is that it will never adjust by shirking; it will only enlarge. Thus, when you move an item to the outside and then to the inside again, you will mess up the scroll bars.

> If you do not want to calculate the size of your scene yourself, you can add all items to the scene and then call `setSceneRect()` with `itemsBoundingRect()` as an argument. With this, you stop the scene from checking and updating the maximum bounding rectangle on item updates.

View

With `QGraphicsView`, we are back in the world of widgets. Since `QGraphicsView` inherits `QWidget`, you can use the view like any other widget and place it into layouts for creating neat graphical user interfaces. For the Graphics View architecture, `QGraphicsView` provides an inspection window on a scene. With the view, you can display the whole scene or only part of it, and by using a transformation matrix you can manipulate the scene's coordinate system. Internally, the view uses `QGraphicsScene::render()` to visualize the scene. By default, the view uses a `QWidget` element as a painting device. Since `QGraphicsView` inherits `QAbstractScrollArea`, the widget is set as its viewport. Therefore, when the rendered scene exceeds the view's geometry, scroll bars are automatically shown.

> Instead of using the default `QWidget` element as the viewport widget, you can set your own widget by calling `setViewport()` with the custom one as an argument. The view will then take ownership of the assigned widget, which is accessible by `viewport()`. This also gives you the opportunity to use OpenGL for rendering. Simply call `setViewport(new QGLWidget)`.

Time for action – putting it all together!

Before we go on, however, and after talking a lot about items and scenes, let's see how the view, the scene, and the items all work together:

```
#include <QApplication>
#include <QGraphicsView>
#include <QGraphicsRectItem>
int main(int argc, char *argv[]) {
  QApplication app(argc, argv);
  QGraphicsScene scene;
  scene.addEllipse(QRectF(0, 0, 100, 100), QColor(0, 0, 0));
  scene.addLine(0, 50, 100, 50, QColor(0, 0, 255));
  QGraphicsRectItem *item = scene.addRect(0, 0, 25, 25, Qt::NoPen,
                                          Qt::red);
  item->setPos(scene.sceneRect().center() - item->rect().center());
  QGraphicsView view;
  view.setScene(&scene);
  view.show();
  return app.exec();
}
```

Build and run this example and you will see following image in the middle of the view:

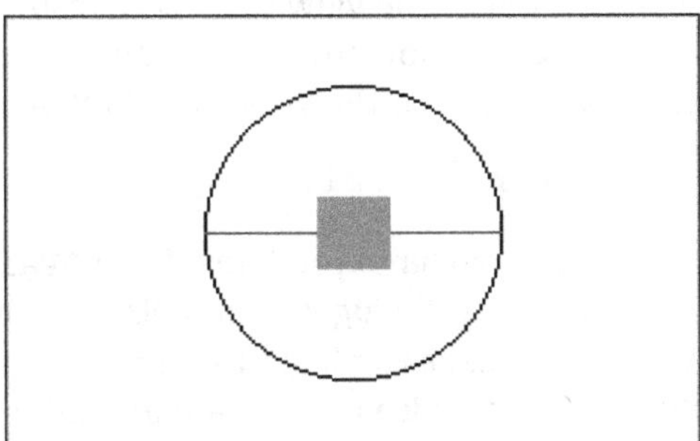

What just happened?

What have we done here? On top, we included the needed headers and then wrote a normal main function and created a `QApplication` elment. Its event loop is started in the return statement on the bottom. In between, we created a scene and added the first item to it by calling `addEllipse()`. This function is one of the many convenience functions of Qt and is, in our case, equivalent to the following code:

```
QGraphicsEllipseItem *item = new QGraphicsEllipseItem;
item->setRect(0, 0, 100, 100);
```

```
item->setPen(QColor(0, 0, 0));
scene.addItem(item);
```

We thus have put a circle with a radius of 50 pixels in the scene. The origins of the circle and of the scene are stacked on top of each other. Next, by calling `addLine()`, we add a blue line that goes through the center point of the circle, parallel to the scene's bottom line. The first two arguments are the *x* and *y* coordinates of the line's starting point and the second two arguments the *x* and *y* coordinates of the end point. With `addRect()`, we add a square with a 25-pixel side at the top-left corner of the scene. This time, however, we fetch the pointer, which is then returned by these functions. This is because we want to move the rectangle to the center of the scene. In order to do that, we use `setPos()` and need to do some arithmetic. Why? Because of the relationship between the scene's and the item's coordinate systems. By simply calling `item->setPos(scene.sceneRect().center())`, the origin of the item (which is (0, 0) in the item's coordinates and thus the rectangle's top left corner) would be in the middle of the scene, not the red square itself. Thus we need to shift the rectangle back by half of its width and height. This is done by subtracting its center point from the scene's center point. As you probably have already guessed, `QRectF::center()` returns the center point of a rectangle as a `QPointF` pointer. Lastly, we create a view and declare that it should display the scene by calling `setScene()` with the scene as an argument. Then we show the view. That's all you need to do to show a scene with items.

Two things you will probably notice if you have a look at the result are that the drawing looks pixelated and that it stays in the center of the view when you resize the view. The solution for the first problem you should already know from what you learned in the previous chapter. You have to turn on antialiasing. For the view, you do that with this line of code

```
view.setRenderHint(QPainter::Antialiasing);
```

With `setRenderHint()`, you can set all hints you know from `QPainter` to the view. Before the view renders the scene on its viewport widget, it initializes the internally used `QPainter` element with these hints. With the antialiasing flag turned on, the painting is done much more smoothly. Unfortunately, the line is also painted antialiased (even though we do not want this since now the line looks washy). To prevent the line from getting drawn antialiased, you have to override the `paint()` function of the item and explicitly turn off antialiasing. However, you might want to have a line with aliasing somewhere, so there is another small and easy solution for that problem without the need for reimplementing the `paint` function. All you have to do is to shift the position by half of the pen's width. For that, write the following code:

```
QGraphicsLineItem *line = scene.addLine(0, 50, 100, 50,
                                        QColor (0, 0, 255));
const qreal shift = line->pen().widthF() / 2.0;
line->moveBy(-shift, -shift);
```

By calling `pen()`, you get the pen that is used to draw the line. Then you determine its width by calling `widthF()` and dividing it by 2. Then just move the line whereby the `moveBy()` function behaves as if we had called the following:

```
line->setPosition(item.pos() - QPointF(shift, shift))
```

To be pixel-perfect, you might need to alter the length of the line.

The second "problem" was that the scene is always visualized in the center of the view, which is the default behavior of the view. You can change this setting with `setAlignment()`, which accepts `Qt::Alignment` flags as arguments. So, calling `view.setAlignment(Qt::AlignBottom | Qt::AlignRight);` would result in the scene staying in the lower-right corner of the view.

Showing specific areas of the scene

As soon as the scene's bounding rectangle exceeds the viewport's size, the view will show scroll bars. Besides using them with the mouse to navigate to a specific item or point on the scene, you can also access them by code. Since the view inherits `QAbstractScrollArea`, you can use all its functions for accessing the scroll bars. `horizontalScrollBar()` and `verticalScrollBar()` return a pointer to `QScrollBar`, and thus you can query their range with `minimum()` and `maximum()`. By invoking `value()` and `setValue()`, you get and can set the current value, which results in scrolling the scene.

But normally, you do not need to control free scrolling inside the view from your source code. The normal task would be to scroll to a specific item. In order to do that, you do not need to do any calculations yourself; the view offers a pretty simple way to do that for you: `centerOn()`. With `centerOn()`, the view ensures that the item, which you have passed as an argument, is centered on the view unless it is too close to the scene's border or even outside. Then, the view tries to move it as far as possible on the center. The `centerOn()` function does not only take a `QGraphicsItem` item as argument; you can also center on a `QPointF` pointer or as a convenience on an *x* and *y* coordinate.

If you do not care where an item is shown, you can simply call `ensureVisible()` with the item as an argument. Then the view scrolls the scene as little as possible so that the item's center remains or becomes visible. As a second and third argument, you can define a horizontal and vertical margin, which are both the minimum space between the item's bounding rectangle and the view's border. Both values have 50 pixels as their default value. Beside a `QGraphicsItem` item, you can also ensure the visibility of a `QRectF` element (of course, there is also the convenience function taking four `qreal` elements).

If you like to ensure the entire visibility of an item (since `ensureVisible(item)` only takes the item's center into account) use `ensureVisible(item->boundingRect())`. Alternatively, you can use `ensureVisible(item)`, but then you have to set the margins at least to the item's half width or half height respectively.

`centerOn()` and `ensureVisible()` only scroll the scene but do not change its transformation state. If you absolutely want to ensure the visibility of an item or a rectangle that exceeds the size of the view, you have to transform the scene as well. With this task, again the view will help you. By calling `fitInView()` with `QGraphicsItem` or a `QRectF` element as argument, the view will scroll and scale the scene so that it fits in the viewport size. As a second argument, you can control how the scaling is done. You have the following options:

Value	Description
`Qt::IgnoreAspectRatio`	The scaling is done absolutely freely regardless of the item's or rectangle's aspect ratio.
`Qt::KeepAspectRatio`	The item's or rectangle's aspect ratio is taken into account while trying to expand as far as possible while respecting the viewport's size.
`Qt::KeepAspectRatioByExpanding`	The item's or rectangle's aspect ratio is taken into account, but the view tries to fill the whole viewport's size with the smallest overlap.

The `fitInView()` function does not only scale larger items down to fit the viewport, it also enlarges items to fill the whole viewport. The following picture illustrates the different scaling options for an item that is enlarged:

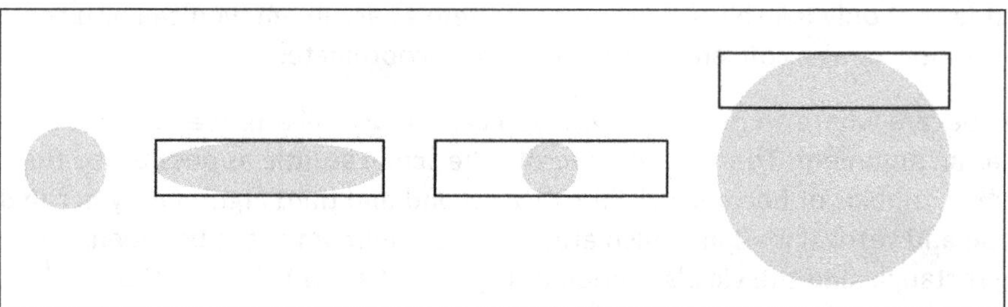

The circle on the left is the original item. Then, from left to right it is `Qt::IgnoreAspectRatio`, `Qt::KeepAspectRatio`, and `Qt::KeepAspectRatioByExpanding`.

Transforming the scene

In the view, you can transform the scene as you like. Besides the normal convenience functions, such as `rotate()`, `scale()`, `shear()`, and `translate()`, you can also apply a free definable `QTransform` parameter via `setTransform()`, where you also can decide if the transformation should be combined with existing ones or if it should replace them. As an example of probably the most used transformation on a view, let us have a look how you can scale and move the scene inside the view.

Time for action – creating an item where transformations can easily be seen

First we set up a playground. To do this, we subclass a `QGraphicsRectItem` item and customize its paint function as follows:

```
void ScaleItem::paint(QPainter *painter, const
QStyleOptionGraphicsItem *option, QWidget *widget) {
  Q_UNUSED(option)
  Q_UNUSED(widget)
  const QPen oldPen = painter->pen();

  const QRectF r = rect();
  const QColor fillColor = Qt::red;
  const qreal square = r.width() / 10.0;
  painter->fillRect(QRectF(0, 0, square, square), fillColor);
  painter->fillRect(QRectF(r.width() - square, 0, square, square),
                    fillColor);
  painter->fillRect(QRectF(0,r.height() - square, square, square),
                    fillColor);
  painter->fillRect(QRectF(r.width() - square, r.height() - square,
                    square, square), fillColor);

  painter->setPen(Qt::black);
  painter->drawRect(r);
  painter->drawLine(r.topLeft(), r.bottomRight());
  painter->drawLine(r.topRight(), r.bottomLeft());
  const qreal padding = r.width() / 4;
  painter->drawRect(r.adjusted(padding, padding, -padding,
                     - padding));

  painter->setPen(oldPen);
}
```

What just happened?

By using the `Q_UNUSED` macro, we simply suppress compiler warnings about unused variables. The macro expands to `(void)x;`, which does nothing. Then we cache the current pen for putting it back at the end of the function. This gives `painter` back unchanged. Of course, we could have called `save()` and `restore()` on the painter, but these functions save a lot of other properties we do not want to change, so simply saving and restoring the pen is much faster. Next, we draw four red rectangles at the corners of the bounding rectangle (`r`) by calling `fillRect()`, which does not change the painter state. Then we set a 1-pixel thick and solid black pen—because this changes the pen's state, we have saved the old pen—and draw the bounding rectangle, the diagonals, and a centered rectangle, which is a quarter of the size of the bounding rectangle. This will give us the following item, which shows the transformations better than with a black-filled rectangle:

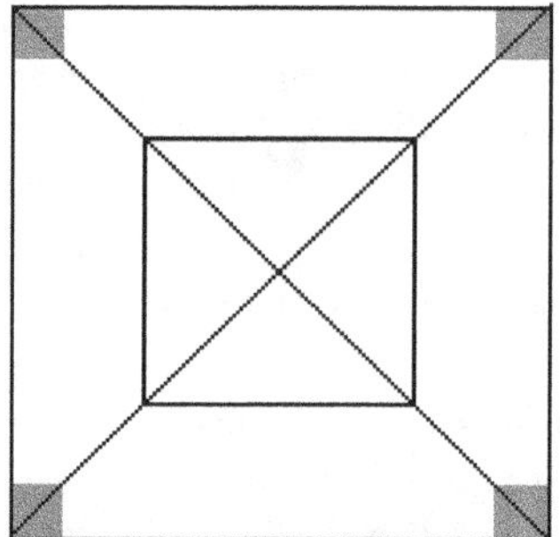

Time for action – implementing the ability to scale the scene

Let's do the scaling first. We add the item to a scene and put that scene on a custom view we have subclassed from `QGraphicsView`. In our customized view, we only need to reimplement `wheelEvent()` as we want to scale the view by using the mouse's scroll wheel.

```
void MyView::wheelEvent(QWheelEvent *event) {
  const qreal factor = 1.1;
  if (event->angleDelta().y() > 0)
    scale(factor, factor);
  else
    scale(1/factor, 1/factor);
}
```

What just happened?

The `factor` parameter for the zooming can be freely defined. You can also create a getter and setter method for it. For us, 1.1 will do the work. With `event->angleDelta()`, you get the distance of the mouse's wheel rotation as a `QPoint` pointer. Since we only care about vertical scrolling, just the *y* axis is relevant for us. In our example, we also do not care about how far the wheel was turned because, normally, every step is delivered separately to `wheelEvent()`. But if you should need it, it's in eighths of a degree, and since a mouse works in general steps of 15 degrees, the value should be 120 or -120, depending on whether you move the wheel forward or backward. On a forward wheel move, if `y()` is greater than zero, we zoom in by using the built-in `scale()` function. It takes the scale factor for the *x* and the *y* coordinates. Otherwise, if the wheel was moved backwards, we zoom out. That's all there is to it. When you try this example, you will notice that, while zooming, the view zooms in and out on the center of the view, which is the default behavior for the view. You can change this behavior with `setTransformationAnchor()`. `QGraphicsView::AnchorViewCenter` is, as described, the default behavior. With `QGraphicsView::NoAnchor`, the zoom center is in the top-left corner of the view, and the value you probably want to use is `QGraphicsView::AnchorUnderMouse`. With that option, the point under the mouse builds the center of the zooming and thus stays at the same position inside the view.

Time for action – implementing the ability to move the scene

Next it would be good to move the scene around without the need of using the scroll bars. Let us add the functionality for pressing and holding the left mouse button. First, we add two private members to the view: the `m_pressed` parameter of type `bool` and the `m_lastMousePos` element of type `QPoint`. Then, we reimplement the `mousePressEvent()` and `mouseReleaseEvent()` functions as follows:

```
void MyView::mousePressEvent(QMouseEvent *event) {
  if (Qt::LeftButton == event->button()) {
    m_pressed = true;
    m_lastMousePos = event->pos();
  }
  QGraphicsView::mousePressEvent(event);
}

void MyView::mouseReleaseEvent(QMouseEvent *event) {
  if (Qt::LeftButton == event->button())
    m_pressed = false;
  QGraphicsView::mouseReleaseEvent(event);
}
```

What just happened?

Within `mousePressEvent()`, we check whether the left mouse button was pressed. If it was `true`, we then set `m_pressed` to `true` and save the current mouse position in `m_lastMousePos`. Then we pass the event to the base class event handler. Within `mouseReleaseEvent()`, we set `m_pressed` to `false` if it was the left button; then we pass the event to the base class implementation. We do not need to alter `m_pressPoint` here. With `mouseMoveEvent()`, we can then react on the value of those two variables:

```
void MyView::mouseMoveEvent(QMouseEvent *event) {
  if (!m_pressed)
    return QGraphicsView::mouseMoveEvent(event);

  QPoint diff = m_lastMousePos - event->pos();
  if (QScrollBar *hbar = horizontalScrollBar())
    hbar->setValue(hbar->value() + diff.x());
  if (QScrollBar *vbar = verticalScrollBar())
    vbar->setValue(vbar->value() + diff.y());
  m_lastMousePos = event->pos();
  return QGraphicsView::mouseMoveEvent(event);
}
```

If `m_pressed` is `false`—this means the left button wasn't pressed and held—we will be exiting the function while passing the event to the base class implementation. This is, by the way, important for getting unhandled events propagated to the scene correctly. If the button has been pressed, we first calculate the difference (`diff`) between the point where the mouse was pressed and the current position. Thus we know how far the mouse was moved. Now we simply move the scroll bars by that value. For the horizontal scroll bar, the pointer to it is received by calling `horizontalScrollBar()`. The encapsulation in an `if` clause is just a paranoid safety check to ensure that the pointer is not null. Normally, this should never happen. Through that pointer, we set a new value by adding the old value, received by `value()`, to the moved distance, `diff.x()`. We then do the same for the vertical scroll bar. Last, we save the current mouse position to `m_lastMousePos`. That's all. Now you can move the scene around while holding the left mouse button down. The downside of this method is that the left mouse click does not reach the scene and, therefore, features such as item selection do not work. If you need that or a similar functionality on the scene, check for a keyboard modifier too. For example, if the *Shift* key must also be pressed to move the scene, additionally check the events `modifiers()` for whether `Qt::ShiftModifier` is set to activate the mouse-moving functionality:

```
void MyView::mousePressEvent(QMouseEvent *event) {
  if (Qt::LeftButton == event->button()
    && (event->modifiers() & Qt::ShiftModifier)) {
    m_pressed = true;
      //...
```

Time for action – taking the zoom level into account

As a last detail, I would like to mention that you can draw an item differently depending on its scale. To do that, the level of detail can be used. You use the passed pointer to `QStyleOptionGraphicsItem` of the item's `paint` function and call `levelOfDetailFromTransform()` with the painter's world transformation. We change the paint function of the `ScaleItem` item to the following:

```
const qreal detail = option->levelOfDetailFromTransform(
  painter->worldTransform());
const QColor fillColor = (detail >= 5) ? Qt::yellow : Qt::red;
```

What just happened?

The `detail` parameter now contains the maximum width of unity square, which was mapped to the painter coordinate system via the painter's world transformation matrix. Based on that value, we set the fill color of the border rectangles to yellow or red. The expression `detail >= 5` will become `true` if the rectangle is displayed at least five times as large as in a normal state. The level of detail is helpful when you want to draw more detail on an item only if it is visible. By using the level of detail, you can control when a possibly resource-intensive drawing should be performed. It makes sense, for example, to make difficult drawings only when you can see them.

When you zoom into the scene, the diagonal lines as well as the rectangle lines get zoomed. But you may want to leave the stroke the same regardless of the zoom level. Here Qt also has an easy approach to offer. In the paint function of the item we used earlier for exemplifying the zoom functionality, locate the following line of code:

```
painter->setPen(Qt::black);
```

Replace it with the following lines:

```
QPen p(Qt::black);
p.setCosmetic(true);
painter->setPen(p);
```

The important part is to make the painter cosmetic. Now, regardless of the zoom or any other transformation, the pen's width stays the same. This can be very helpful for drawing outlined shapes.

Questions you should keep in mind

Whenever you are going to use the Graphics View architecture, ask yourself these questions: Which standard items are suited for my specific needs? Am I reinventing the wheel over and over again? Do I need `QGraphicsTextItem` or is `QGraphicsSimpleTextItem` good enough? Do I need the items to inherit `QObject` or will plain items not suffice? (We will cover this topic in the next section.) Could I group items together for the sake of cleaner and leaner code? Is the parent-child relationship sufficient or do I need to use a `QGraphicsItemGroup` element?

Now you really know most of the functions of the Graphics View framework. With this knowledge, you can already do a lot of cool stuff. But for a game, it is still too static. We will change that next!

The jumping elephant or how to animate the scene

By now, you should have a good understanding about the items, the scene, and the view. With your knowledge of how to create items, standard and custom ones, of how to position them on the scene, and of how to set up the view to show the scene, you can make pretty awesome things. You even can zoom and move the scene with the mouse. That's surely good, but for a game, one crucial point is still missing: you have to animate the items. Instead of going through all possibilities for how to animate a scene, let us develop a simple jump-and-run game where we recap parts of the previous topics and learn how to animate items on a screen. So let's meet Benjamin, the elephant:

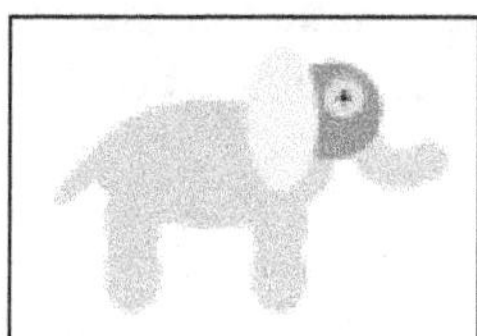

The game play

The goal of the game is for Benjamin to collect the coins that are placed all over the game field. Besides walking right and left, Benjamin can, of course, also jump. In the following screenshot, you see what this minimalistic game should look like in the end:

The player item

Let's now look at how we can mobilize Benjamin.

Time for action – creating an item for Benjamin

First we need a custom item class for Benjamin. We call the class `Player` and choose `QGraphicsPixmapItem` as the base class because Benjamin is a PNG image. In the item's `Player` class, we further create a property of integer type and call it `m_direction`. Its value signifies in which direction Benjamin walks—left or right—or if he stands still. Of course, we use a getter and setter function for this property. Since the header file is simple, let's have a look at the implementation right away (you will find the whole source code at the end of this book):

```
Player::Player(QGraphicsItem *parent)
  : QGraphicsPixmapItem(parent), m_direction(0) {
    setPixmap(QPixmap(":/elephant"));
    setTransformOriginPoint(boundingRect().center());
}
```

In the constructor, we set `m_direction` to `0`, which means that Benjamin isn't moving at all. If `m_direction` is `1`, Benjamin moves right, and if the value is `-1`, he moves left. In the body of the constructor, we set the image for the item by calling `setPixmap()`. The image of Benjamin is stored in the Qt Resource System; thus, we access it through `QPixmap(":/elephant")` with `elephant` as the given alias for the actual image of Benjamin. Last, we set the point of origin for all transformations we are going to apply to the center of the item. This equals the center of the image.

```
int Player::direction() const {
  return m_direction;
}
```

The `direction()` function is a standard getter function for `m_direction` returning its value. The next function of this class is much more important:

```
void Player::addDirection(int direction) {
  direction = qBound(-1, direction, 1);
  m_direction += direction;
  if (0 == m_direction)
    return;

  if (-1 == m_direction)
    setTransform(QTransform(-1, 0, 0, 1, boundingRect().width(), 0));
  else
    setTransform(QTransform());
}
```

What just happened?

With `addDirection()`, one "sets" the direction of Benjamin's movement. "Set" is put in quotes because you do not set `m_direction` to the passed value; instead, you add the passed value to `m_direction`. This is done in the second line after we have ensured the correctness of `m_direction`. For that, we use `qBound()`, which returns a value that is bound by the first and last argument. The argument in the middle is the actual value that we want to get bound. So the possible values for `m_direction` are restricted to -1, 0, and 1. If the property `direction` is 0, the player item does not move and the function exits.

If you haven't already done so earlier, you might wonder by now why not simply set the value? Why that addition? Well, it is because of how we will use this function: Benjamin is moved by the left and right arrow key. If the right key is pressed, 1 is added; if it gets released, -1 is added. Think of it as an impulse to the right (1) and to the left (-1). The first accelerates the player and the second slows him down. The same applies for the left key, but only the other way around. As we do not allow multiple acceleration, we limit the value of `m_direction` to 1 and -1. The addition of the value rather than setting it is now necessary because of the following situation: A user presses and holds the right key, and the value of `m_direction` is therefore 1. Now, without releasing the right key, he also presses and holds the left key. Therefore, the value of `m_direction` is getting decreased by one; the value is now 0 and Benjamin stops. But remember, both keys are still being pressed. What happens when the left key is released? How would you know in this situation in which direction Benjamin should move? To achieve that, you would have to find out an additional bit of information: whether the right key is still pressed down or not. That seems too much trouble and overhead. In our implementation, when the left key is released, 1 is added and the value of `m_direction` becomes 1, making Benjamin move right. Voilà! All without any concern about what the state of the other button might be.

Lastly, we check in which direction Benjamin is moving. If he is moving left, we need to flip his image so that Benjamin looks to the left, the direction in which he is moving. Therefore, we apply a `QTransform` matrix, which flips the image vertically. If he is moving towards the right, we restore the normal state by assigning an empty `QTransform` object, which is an identity matrix.

So we now have our item of class `Player` for the game's character, which shows the image of Benjamin. The item also stores the current moving direction, and based on that information, the image is flipped vertically if needed.

The playing field

To understand the following code, it might be good to know the composition of the environment in which our elephant will be walking and jumping. Overall, we have a view fixed in size holding a scene which is exactly as big as the view. We do not take size changes into account since they would complicate the example too much, and when you develop a game for a mobile device, you know the available size up front.

All animations inside the playing field are done by moving the items, not the scene. So we have to distinguish between the view's, or rather the scene's width and the width of the elephant's virtual "world" in which he can move. The width of this virtual world is defined by `m_fieldWidth` and has no (direct) correlation with the scene. Within the range of `m_fieldWidth`, which is 500 pixels in the example, Benjamin or the graphics item can be moved from the minimum *x* coordinate, defined by `m_minX`, to the maximum *x* coordinate, defined by `m_maxX`. We keep track of his actual *x* position with the variable `m_realPos`. Next, the minimum *y* coordinate the item is allowed to have is defined by `m_groundLevel`. For `m_maxX` and `m_groundLevel`, we have to take into account that the position of the item is determined by its top-left corner. Lastly, what is left is the view, which has a fixed size defined by the scene's bounding rectangle size, which is not as wide as `m_fieldWidth`. So the scene (and the view) follows the elephant while he walks through his virtual world of the length `m_fieldWidth`. Have a look at the picture to see the variables in their graphical representation:

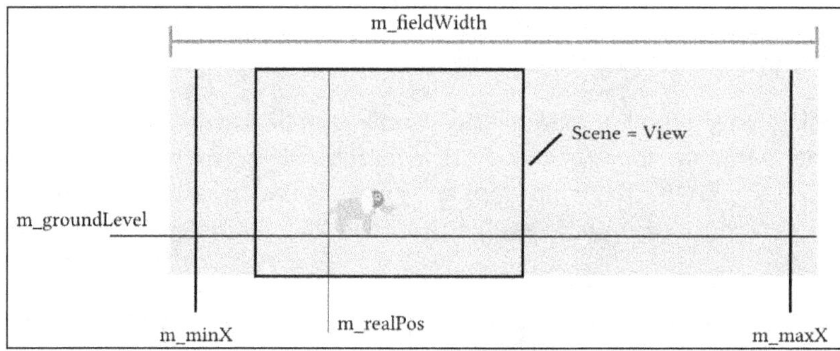

The scene

Since we will have to do some work on the scene, we subclass `QGraphicsScene` and name the new class `MyScene`. There we implement one part of the game logic. This is convenient since `QGraphicsScene` inherits `QObject` and thus we can use Qt's signal and slot mechanism. Also, for the next code of the scene, we only go through the implementation of the functions. For more information on the header, have a look at the sources bundled with this book.

Time for action – making Benjamin move

The first thing we want to do is to make our elephant movable. In order to achieve that, we use a `QTimer` parameter called `m_timer`, which is a private member of `MyScene`. In the constructor we set up the timer with the following code:

```
m_timer.setInterval(30);
connect(&m_timer, &QTimer::timeout, this, &MyScene::movePlayer);
```

First we define that the timer emits a timeout signal every 30 milliseconds. Then we connect that signal to the scene's slot called `movePlayer()`, but we do not start the timer yet. This is done by the arrow keys in a way we have already discussed when the `m_direction` variable of the class `Player` was introduced. Here is the implementation of what was described there:

```
void MyScene::keyPressEvent(QKeyEvent *event) {
  if (event->isAutoRepeat())
    return;

  switch (event->key()) {
    case Qt::Key_Right:
      m_player->addDirection(1);
      checkTimer();
      break;
    case Qt::Key_Left:
      m_player->addDirection(-1);
      checkTimer();
      break;
    //...
    default:
      break;
  }
}
```

As a small side note, whenever code snippets in the following code passages are irrelevant for the actual detail, I am going to skip the code but will indicate missing code with `//...` so that you know it is not the entire code. We will cover the skipped parts later when it is more appropriate.

What just happened?

In the key press event handler, we first check if the key event was triggered because of an auto repeat. If this is the case, we exit the function because we only want to react on the first real key press event. We also do not call the base class implementation of that event handler since no item on the scene needs to get a key press event. If you do have items that could and should receive events, do not forget to forward them while reimplementing event handlers at the scene.

If you press and hold a key down, Qt will continuously deliver the key press event. To determine if it was the first real key press or an auto-generated event, use `QKeyEvent::isAutoRepeat()`. It returns `true` if the event was automatically generated. There is no easy way to turn off the auto repeat since it is platform-dependent and you have to use the platform API for that.

As soon as we know that the event was not delivered by an auto repeat, we react to the different key presses. If the left key was pressed, we decrease the direction property of the player item by one; if the right key was pressed, we increase it by one. The `m_player` element is our instance of the player item. After calling `addDirection()`, we call `checkTimer()` in both cases:

```
void MyScene::checkTimer() {
  if (0 == m_player->direction())
    m_timer.stop();
  else if (!m_timer.isActive())
    m_timer.start();
}
```

This function first checks whether the player moves. If not, the timer is stopped because nothing has to be updated when our elephant stands still. Otherwise, the timer gets started, but only if it isn't already running. This we check by calling `isActive()` on the timer.

When the user presses the right key, for example at the beginning of the game, `checkTimer()` will start `m_timer`. Since its time out signal was connected to `movePlayer()`, the slot will be called every 30 milliseconds till the key is released. Since the `move()` function is a bit longer, let's go through it step-by-step:

```
void MyScene::movePlayer() {
  const int direction = m_player->direction();
  if (0 == direction)
    return;
```

First, we cache the player's current direction in a local variable to avoid multiple calls of `direction()`. Then we check whether the player is moving at all. If they aren't, we exit the function because there is nothing to animate.

```
  const int dx = direction * m_velocity;
  qreal newPos = m_realPos + dx;
  newPos = qBound(m_minX, newPos, m_maxX);
  if (newPos == m_realPos)
    return;
  m_realPos = newPos;
```

Next we calculate the shift the player item should get and store it in `dx`. The distance the player should move every 30 milliseconds is defined by the member variable `m_velocity`, expressed in pixels. You can create setter and getter functions for that variable if you like. For us, the default value of 4 pixels will do the job. Multiplied by the direction (which could only be 1 or -1 at this point), we get a shift of the player by 4 pixels to the right or to the left. Based on this shift, we calculate the new *x* position of the player and store it in `newPos`. Next, we check whether that new position is inside the range of `m_minX` and `m_maxX`, two member variables that are already calculated and set up properly at this point. Next, if the new position is not equal to the actual position, which is stored in `m_realPos`, we proceed by assigning the new position as the current one. Otherwise, we exit the function since there is nothing to move.

```
const int leftBorder = 150;
const int rightBorder = 350 - m_player->boundingRect().width();
```

The next question to tackle is whether the view should always move when the elephant is moving, which means that the elephant would always stay say in the middle of the view. No, he shouldn't stay at a specific point inside the view. Rather, the view should be fixed when the elephant is moving. Only if he reaches the borders should the view follow. The "non-movable" center is defined by `leftBorder` and `rightBorder`, which are related to the item's position; thus we must subtract the item's width from the `rightBorder` element. If we don't take the item's width into account, the right side of a player with a width of more than 150 pixels will disappear before the scrolling takes place. Please note that the values for `leftBorder` and `rightBorder` are randomly chosen. You can alter them as you like. Here we decided to set the border at 150 pixels. Of course, you can create a setter and getter for these parameters too:

```
if (direction > 0) {
  if (m_realPos > m_fieldWidth - (width() - rightBorder)) {
    m_player->moveBy(dx, 0);
  } else {
    if (m_realPos - m_skippedMoving < rightBorder) {
      m_player->moveBy(dx, 0);
    } else {
      m_skippedMoving += dx;
    }
  }
} else {
  if (m_realPos < leftBorder && m_realPos >= m_minX) {
    m_player->moveBy(dx, 0);
  } else {
    if (m_realPos - m_skippedMoving > leftBorder) {
      m_player->moveBy(dx, 0);
    } else {
```

```
                m_skippedMoving = qMax(0, m_skippedMoving + dx);
            }
        }
    }
    //...
}
```

Ok, so what have we done here? Here we have calculated whether only the elephant moves or the view as well so that the elephant does not walk out of the screen. The `if` clause applies when the elephant is moving towards the right. For a better understanding, let's begin at the end of this scope. There is a situation where we do not move the elephant but simply add the shift `dx` to a variable named `m_skippedMoving`. What does that mean? It means that the virtual "world" is moving but the elephant inside the view is not. This is the case when the elephant moves too far to the borders. In other words, you move the view with the elephant above the virtual world by `dx` to the left. Let's take a look at the following figure:

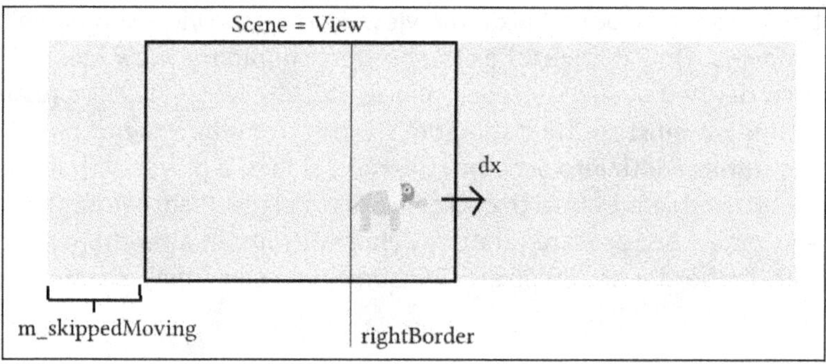

The `m_skippedMoving` element is the difference between the view's *x* coordinate and the virtual world's *x* coordinate. So the `if` clause `m_realPos - m_skippedMoving < rightBorder` reads: *If the position of the elephant in "view coordinates", calculated by* `m_realPos - m_skippedMoving`*, is smaller than* `rightBorder`*, then move the elephant by calling* `moveBy()` *since he is allowed to walk till* `rightBorder`. `m_realPos - m_skippedMoving` *is the same as* `m_player->pos().x() + dx`.

Lastly, let's turn to the first clause: `m_realPos > m_fieldWidth - (width() - rightBorder)`. This returns `true` when the actual position is behind the `rightBorder` element but the fictional world is moved to its maximum left. Then we also have to move the elephant so that he can reach `m_maxX`. The expression `width() - rightBorder` calculates the width between `rightBorder` and the scene's right border.

The same considerations and calculations apply for moving to the left, the other branch.

So far, we have accomplished two things. First, with a `QTimer` object, we trigger a slot that moves an item; thus, we have animated the scene. Second, we have determined the elephant's position in the virtual world. You might wonder why we have done this. To be able to do parallax scrolling!

Parallax scrolling

Parallax scrolling is a trick to add an illusion of depth to the background of the game. This illusion occurs when the background has different layers which move at different speeds. The nearest background must move faster than the ones farther away. In our case, we have these four backgrounds ordered from the most distant to the nearest:

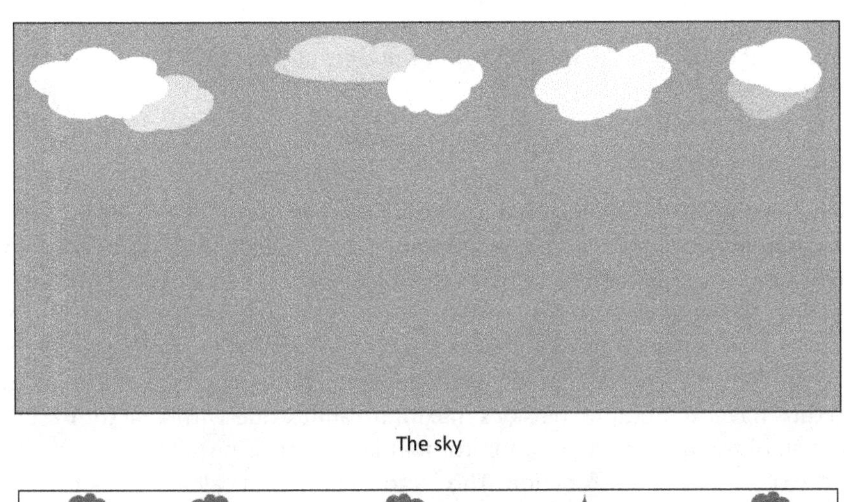

The sky

The trees

The grass

The ground

Time for action – moving the background

Now the question is how to move them at different speeds. The solution is quite simple: the slowest one, the sky, is the smallest image. The fastest background, the ground and the grass, are the largest images. Now when we have a look at the end of the `movePlayer()` function's slot we see this:

```
qreal ff = qMin(1.0, m_skippedMoving/(m_fieldWidth - width()));
m_sky->setPos(-(m_sky->boundingRect().width() - width()) * ff, 0);
m_grass->setPos(-(m_grass->boundingRect().width() - width()) *
  ff, m_grass->y());
m_trees->setPos(-(m_trees->boundingRect().width() - width()) *
  ff, m_trees->y());
m_ground->setPos(-(m_ground->boundingRect().width() - width()) *
  ff, m_ground->y());
```

What just happened?

What are we doing here? At the beginning, the sky's left border is the same as the view's left border, both at point (0, 0). At the end, when Benjamin has walked to the maximum right, the sky's right border should be the same as the view's right border. So the distance we have to move the sky over time is the sky's width (`m_sky->boundingRect().width()`) minus the width of the view (`width()`). The shift of the sky depends on the position of the player: If he is far to the left, the sky isn't shifted, if the player is far to the right, the sky is maximally shifted. We thus have to multiply the sky's maximum shift value with a factor based on the current position of the player. The relation to the player's position is the reason why this is handled in the `movePlayer()` function. The factor we have to calculate has to be between 0 and 1. So we get the minimum shift (0 * shift, which equals 0) and the maximum shift (1 * shift, which equals shift). This factor we name `ff`. The calculation reads: *If we subtract the width of the view (*`width()`*) from the virtual field's width* `m_fieldWidth`*, we have the area where the player isn't moved by (*`m_player->moveBy()`*) because in that range only the background should move.*

How often the moving of the player was skipped is saved in `m_skippedMoving`. So by dividing `m_skippedMoving` through `m_fieldWidth - width()`, we get the needed factor. It is 0 when the player is to the far left and 1 if they are to the far right. Then we simply have to multiply `ff` with the maximum shift of the sky. To avoid the backgrounds from being moved too far, we ensure through `qMin()` that the factor is always lesser than, or equal to, 1.0.

The same calculation is used for the other background items. The calculation also explains why a smaller image is moving slower. It's because the overlap of the smaller image is less than that of the larger one. And since the backgrounds are moved in the same time period, the larger has to move faster.

Have a go hero – adding new background layers

Try to add additional background layers to the game following the preceding example. As an idea, you can add a barn behind the trees or let an airplane fly through the sky.

QObject and items

The `QGraphicsItem` item and all standard items introduced so far don't inherit `QObject` and thus can't have slots or emit signals; they also don't benefit from the `QObject` property system. But we can make them use `QObject`!

Time for action – using properties, signals, and slots with items

So let's alter the `Player` class to use `QObject`:

```
class Player : public QObject, public QGraphicsPixmapItem {
  Q_OBJECT
```

All you have to do is to add `QObject` as a base class and add the `Q_OBJECT` macro. Now you can use signals and slots with items too. Be aware that `QObject` must be the first base class of an item.

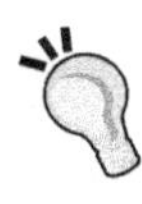

> If you want an item that inherits from `QObject` and `QGraphicsItem`, you can directly inherit `QGraphicsObject`. Moreover, this class defines and emits some useful signals such as `xChanged()` when the *x* coordinate of the item has changed or `scaleChanged()` when the item is scaled.

> A word of warning: Only use `QObject` with items if you really need its capabilities. `QObject` adds a lot of overhead to the item, which will have a noticeable impact on performance when you have many items. So use it wisely and not only because you can.

Let us go back to our player item. After adding `QObject`, we define a property called `m_jumpFactor` with a getter, a setter, and a change signal. We need that property to make Benjamin jump, as we will see later on. In the header file, we define the property as follows:

```
Q_PROPERTY(qreal jumpFactor READ jumpFactor WRITE setjumpFactor
                            NOTIFY jumpFactorChanged)
```

The getter function `jumpFactor()` simply returns the private member `m_jumpFactor`, which is used to store the actual position. The implementation of the setter looks like this:

```
void Player::setjumpFactor(const qreal pos) {
  if (pos == m_jumpFactor)
    return;
  m_jumpFactor = pos;
  emit jumpFactorChanged(m_jumpFactor);
}
```

It is important to check if `pos` would change the current value of `m_jumpFactor`. If this is not the case, exit the function because, otherwise, a change signal will be emitted even if nothing has changed. Otherwise, we set `m_jumpFactor` to `pos` and emit the signal that informs about the chance.

Property animations

The new `jumpFactor` property we use immediately with a `QPropertyAnimation` element, a second way to animate items.

Time for action – using animations to move items smoothly

In order to use it, we add a new private member called `m_animation` of type `QPropertyAnimation` and initialize it in the constructor of `Player`:

```
m_animation = new QPropertyAnimation(this);
m_animation->setTargetObject(this);
m_animation->setPropertyName("jumpFactor");
m_animation->setStartValue(0);
m_animation->setKeyValueAt(0.5, 1);
m_animation->setEndValue(0);
m_animation->setDuration(800);
m_animation->setEasingCurve(QEasingCurve::OutInQuad);
```

What just happened?

For the instance of `QPropertyAnimation` created here, we define the item as parent; thus, the animation will get deleted when the scene deletes the item and we don't have to worry about freeing the used memory. Then we define the target of the animation—our `Player` class—and the property that should be animated—`jumpFactor`, in this case. Then we define the start and the end value of that property, and in addition to that we also define a value in between by setting `setKeyValueAt()`. The first argument of type `qreal` defines time inside the animation, where 0 is the beginning and 1 the end, and the second argument defines the value that the animation should have at this time. So your `jumpFactor` element will get animated from 0 to 1 and back to 0 in 800 milliseconds. This was defined by `setDuration()`. Finally, we define how the interpolation between the start and end value should be done and call `setEasingCurve()` with `QEasingCurve::OutInQuad` as an argument. Qt defines up to 41 different easing curves for linear, quadratic, cubic, quartic, quintic, sinusoidal, exponential, circular, elastic, back easing, and bounce functions. These are too many to describe here. Instead, have a look at the documentation. Simply search for `QEasingCurve::Type`. In our case, `QEasingCurve::OutInQuad` makes sure that the jump speed of Benjamin looks like an actual jump: fast in the beginning, slow at the top, and fast at the end again. We start this animation with the jump function:

```
void Player::jump() {
  if (QAbstractAnimation::Stopped == m_animation->state())
    m_animation->start();
}
```

We only start the animation by calling `start()` when the animation isn't running. Therefore, we check the animation's state to see if it is stopped. Other states could be `Paused` or `Running`. We want this jump action to be activated whenever the player presses the Space key on their keyboard. Therefore, we expand the switch statement inside the key press event handler by using this code:

```
case Qt::Key_Space:
  m_player->jump();
  break;
```

Now the property gets animated but Benjamin will still not jump yet. Therefore, we connect the `jumpFactorChange()` signal to a slot of the scene that handles the jump:

```
void MyScene::jumpPlayer(qreal factor) {
  const qreal y = (m_groundLevel - m_player->boundingRect().height())
    - factor * m_jumpHeight;
  m_player->setPos(m_player->pos().x(), y);
  //...
}
```

Inside that function, we calculate the *y* coordinate of the player item to respect the ground level defined by `m_groundLevel`. This is done by subtracting the item's height from the ground level's value since the item's origin point is the top-left corner. Then we subtract the maximum jump height, defined by `m_jumpHeight`, which is multiplied by the actual jump factor. Since the factor is in range from 0 to 1, the new *y* coordinate stays inside the allowed jump height. Then we alter the player item's *y* position by calling `setPos()`, leaving the *x* coordinate the same. Et voilà, Benjamin is jumping!

Have a go hero – letting the scene handle Benjamin's jump

Of course, we could have done the property animation inside the scene's class without the need to extend `Player` by `QObject`. But this should be an example of how to do it. So try to put the logic of making Benjamin jump to the scene's class. This is, however, more consistent as we already move Benjamin left and right there. Or, also consistent, do it the other way around; move Benjamin's movement to the left and right also to the `Player` class.

Time for action – keeping multiple animations in sync

If you have a look at how the coins (their class being called `Coin`) are created, you see similar structures. They inherit from `QObject` and `QGraphicsEllipseItem` and define two properties: opacity of type `qreal` and `rect` of type `QRect`. This is done only by the following code:

```
Q_PROPERTY(qreal opacity READ opacity WRITE setOpacity)
Q_PROPERTY(QRectF rect READ rect WRITE setRect)
```

No function or slot was added because we simply used built-in functions of `QGraphicsItem` and "redeclared" them as properties. Then, these two properties are animated by two `QPropertyAnimation` objects. One fades the coin out, while the other scales the coin in. To ensure that both animations get started at the same time, we use `QParallelAnimationGroup` as follows:

```
QPropertyAnimation *fadeAnimation = /* set up */
QPropertyAnimation *scaleAnimation = /* set up */
```

```
QParallelAnimationGroup *group = new QParallelAnimationGroup(this);
group->addAnimation(fadeAnimation);
group->addAnimation(scaleAnimation);
group->start();
```

What just happened?

After setting up each property animation, we add them to the group animation by calling `addAnimation()` on the group while passing a pointer to the animation we would like to add. Then, when we start the group, `QParallelAnimationGroup` makes sure that all assigned animations start at the same time.

The animations are set up for when the coin explodes. You may want to have a look at the `explode()` function of Coin in the sources. A coin should explode when Benjamin touches the coin.

If you want to play animations one after the other you can use `QSequentialAnimationGroup`.

Item collision detection

Whether the player item collides with a coin is checked by the scene's `checkColliding()` function, which is called after the player item has moved (`movePlayer()`) or after Benjamin jumped (`jumpPlayer()`).

Time for action – making the coins explode

The implementation of `checkColliding()` looks like this:

```
QList<QGraphicsItem*> items =  collidingItems(m_player);
for (int i = 0, total = items.count(); i < total; ++i) {
  if (Coin *c = qgraphicsitem_cast<Coin*>(items.at(i)))
    c->explode();
}
```

What just happened?

First we call the scene's `QGraphicsScene::collidingItems()` function, which takes the item for which colliding items should be detected as a first argument. With the second, optional argument, you could define how the collision should be detected. The type of that argument is `Qt::ItemSelectionMode`, which was explained earlier. In our case, a list of all the items that collide with `m_player` will be returned. So we loop through that list and check whether the current item is a `Coin` object. This is done by trying to cast the pointer to `Coin`. If it is successful, we explode the coin by calling `explode()`. Calling the `explode()` function multiple times is no problem since it will not allow more than one explosion. This is important since `checkColliding()` will be called after each movement of the player. So the first time the player hits a coin, the coin will explode, but this takes time. During this explosion, the player will most likely be moved again and thus collides with the coin once more. In such a case, `explode()` may be called for a second, third, xth time.

The `collidingItems()` function will always return the background items as well since the player item is above all of them most of the time. To avoid the continuous check if they actually are coins, we use a trick. In the used `BackgroundItem` class for the background items, implement the `QGraphicsItem` item's virtual `shape()` function as follows:

```
QPainterPath BackgroundItem::shape() const {
  return QPainterPath();
}
```

Since the collision detection is done with the item's shape, the background items can't collide with any other item since their shape is permanently empty. `QPainterPath` itself is a class holding information about graphical shapes. For more information—since we do not need anything special for our game—have a look at the documentation. The class is pretty straightforward.

Had we done the jumping logic inside `Player`, we could have implemented the item collision detection from within the item itself. `QGraphicsItem` also offers a `collidingItems()` function that checks against colliding items with itself. So `scene->collidingItems(item)` is equivalent to `item->collidingItems()`.

If you are only interested in whether a item collides with another item, you can call `collidesWithItem()` on the item passing the other item as an argument.

Setting up the playing field

The last function we have to discuss is the scene's `initPlayField()` function where all is set up. Here we initialize the sky, trees, ground, and player item. Since there is nothing special, we skip that and look directly at how the coins get initialized:

```
const int xrange = (m_maxX - m_minX) * 0.94;
m_coins = new QGraphicsRectItem(0,0,m_fieldWidth, m_jumpHeight);
m_coins->setPen(Qt::NoPen);
for (int i = 0; i < 25; ++i) {
  Coin *c = new Coin(m_coins);
  c->setPos(m_minX + qrand()%xrange, qrand()%m_jumpHeight);
}
addItem(m_coins);
m_coins->setPos(0, m_groundLevel - m_jumpHeight);
```

In total, we are adding 25 coins. First we calculate the width between `m_minX` and `m_maxX`. That is the space where Benjamin can move. To make it a little bit smaller, we only take 94 percent of that width. Then we set up an invisible item with the size of the virtual world called `m_coins`. This item should be the parent to all coins. Then, in the `for` loop we create a coin and randomly set its *x* and *y* position, ensuring that Benjamin can reach them by calculating the modulo of the available width and of the maximal jump height. After all 25 coins are added, we place the parent item holding all coins on the scene. Since most coins are outside the actual view's rectangle, we also need to move the coins while Benjamin is moving. Therefore, `m_coins` must behave like any other background. For this, we simply add the following code:

```
m_coins->setPos(-(m_coins->boundingRect().width() - width()) * ff,
                 m_coins->y());
```

We add the preceding code to the `movePlayer()` function where we also move the sky by the same pattern.

Have a go hero – extending the game

That is it. This is our little game. Of course, there is much room to improve and extend it. For example, you can add some barricades Benjamin has to jump over. Then, you would have to check if the player item collides with such a barricade item when moving forward, and if so, refuse movement. You have learned all the necessary techniques you need for that task, so try to implement some additional features to deepen your knowledge.

A third way of animation

Besides QTimer and QPropertyAnimation, there is a third way to animate the scene. The scene provides a slot called advance(). If you call that slot, the scene will forward that call to all items it holds by calling advance() on each one. The scene does that twice. First, all item advance() functions are called with 0 as an argument. This means that the items are about to advance. Then in the second round, all items are called passing 1 to the item's advance() function. In that phase each item should advance, whatever that means; maybe moving, maybe a color change, and so on. The scene's slot advance is typically called by a QTimeLine element; with this, you can define how many times during a specific period of time the timeline should be triggered.

```
QTimeLine *timeLine = new QTimeLine(5000, this);
timeLine->setFrameRange(0, 10);
```

This timeline will emit the signal frameChanged() every 5 seconds for 10 times. All you have to do is to connect that signal to the scene's advance() slot and the scene will advance 10 times during 50 seconds. However, since all items receive two calls for each advance, this may not be the best animation solution for scenes with a lot of items where only a few should advance.

Widgets inside Graphics View

In order to show a neat feature of Graphics View, have a look at the following code snippet, which adds a widget to the scene:

```
QSpinBox *box = new QSpinBox;
QGraphicsProxyWidget *proxyItem = new QGraphicsProxyWidget;
proxyItem->setWidget(box);
QGraphicsScene scene;
scene.addItem(proxyItem);
proxyItem->setScale(2);
proxyItem->setRotation(45);
```

First we create a QSpinBox and a QGraphicsProxyWidget element, which act as containers for widgets and indirectly inherit QGraphicsItem. Then we add the spin box to the the proxy widget by calling addWidget(). The ownership of the spin box isn't transferred, but when QGraphicsProxyWidget gets deleted, it calls delete on all assigned widgets. We thus do not have to worry about that ourselves. The widget you add should be parentless and must not be shown elsewhere. After setting the widget to the proxy, you can treat the proxy widget like any other item. Next, we add it to the scene and apply a transformation for demonstration. As a result we get this:

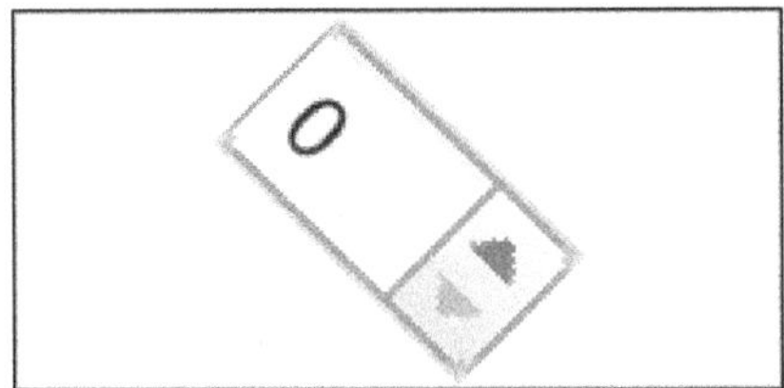

A rotated and scaled spin box on a scene

Since it is a regular item, you can even animate it, for example, with a property animation. Nevertheless, be aware that, originally, Graphics View wasn't designed for holding widgets. So when you add a lot of widgets to the scene, you will quickly notice performance issues, but in most situations it should be fast enough.

If you want to arrange some widgets in a layout, you can use `QGraphicsAnchorLayout`, `QGraphicsGridLayout`, or `QGraphicsLinearLayout`. Create all widgets, create a layout of your choice, add the widgets to that layout, and set the layout to a `QGraphicsWidget` element, which is the base class for all widgets and is easily spoken the `QWidget` equivalent for Graphics View by calling `setLayout()`:

```
QGraphicsScene scene;
QGraphicsProxyWidget *edit = scene.addWidget(
  new QLineEdit("Some Text"));
QGraphicsProxyWidget *button = scene.addWidget(
  new QPushButton("Click me!"));
QGraphicsLinearLayout *layout = new QGraphicsLinearLayout;
layout->addItem(edit);
layout->addItem(button);
QGraphicsWidget *graphicsWidget = new QGraphicsWidget;
graphicsWidget->setLayout(layout);
scene.addItem(graphicsWidget);
```

The scene's `addWidget()` function is a convenience function and behaves in the first usage for `QLineEdit`, as shown in the following code snippet:

```
QGraphicsProxyWidget *proxy = new QGraphicsProxyWidget(0);
proxy->setWidget(new QLineEdit("Some Text"));
scene.addItem(proxy);
```

The item with the layout will look like this:

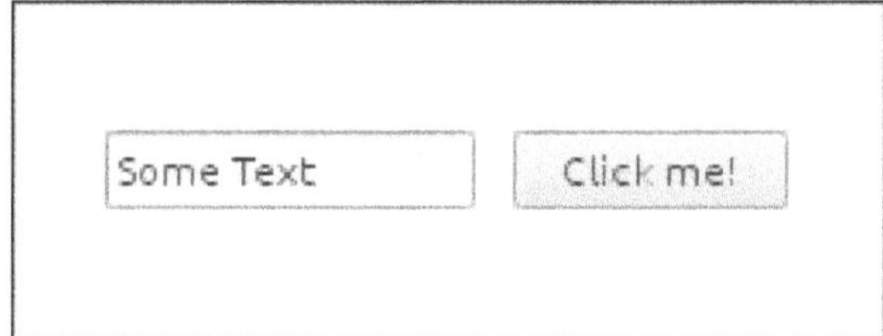

Optimization

Let us now take a look at some of the optimizations we can perform to speed up the scene.

A binary space partition tree

The scene constantly keeps record of the position of the item in its internal binary space partition tree. Thus, on every move of an item, the scene has to update the tree, an operation that can become quite time-and memory-consuming. This is especially true of scenes with a large number of animated items. On the other hand, the tree enables you to find an item (for example, with `items()` or `itemAt()`) incredibly fast even if you have thousands of items.

So when you do not need any positional information about the items—this also includes collision detection—you can disable the index function by calling `setItemIndexMethod(QGraphicsScene::NoIndex)`. Be aware, however, that a call to `items()` or `itemAt()` results in a loop through all items in order to do the collision detection, which can cause performance problems for scenes with many items. If you cannot relinquish the tree in total, you still can adjust the depth of the tree with `setBspTreeDepth()`, taking the depth as an argument. By default, the scene will guess a reasonable value after it takes several parameters, such as the size and the number of items, into account.

Caching the item's paint function

If you have items with a time-consuming paint function, you can change the item's cache mode. By default, no rendering is cached. With `setCacheMode()`, you can set the mode to either `ItemCoordinateCache` or to `DeviceCoordinateCache`. The former renders the the item in a cache of a given `QSize` element. The size of that cache can be controlled with the second argument of `setCacheMode()`. So the quality depends on how much space you assign. The cache is then used for every subsequent paint call. The cache is even used for applying transformations. If the quality deteriorates too much, just adjust the resolution by calling `setCacheMode()` again, but with a larger `QSize` element. `DeviceCoordinateCache`, on the other hand, does not cache the item on an item base but rather on a device level. This is therefore optimal for items that do not get transformed all the time, because every new transformation will cause a new caching. Moving the item, however, does not end in a new cache. If you use this cache mode, you do not have to define a resolution with the second argument. The caching is always performed at maximum quality.

Optimizing the view

Since we are talking about the item's paint function, let's touch on something related. At the beginning, when we discussed the item's appearance and made a black rectangle item, I told you to return the painter as you get. If you have followed this advice, you can call `setOptimizationFlag(DontSavePainterState, true)` on the view. By default, the view ensures that the painter state is saved before calling the item's paint function and that the state gets restored afterward. This will end up saving and restoring the painter state say 50 times if you have a scene with 50 items. If you prevent automatic saving and restoring, keep in mind that now the standard items will alter the painter state. So if you use both standard and custom items, either stay with the default behavior or set `DontSavePainterState`, but then set up the pen and brush with a default value in each item's paint function.

Another flag that can be used with `setOptimizationFlag()` is `DontAdjustForAntialiasing`. By default, the view adjusts the painting area of each item by 2 pixels in all directions. This is useful because when one paints antialiased, one easily draws outside the bounding rectangle. Enable that optimization if you do not paint antialiased or if you are sure your painting will stay inside the bounding rectangle. If you enable this flag and spot painting artifacts on the view, you haven't respected the item's bounding rectangle!

As a further optimization, you can define how the view should update its viewport when the scene changes. You can set the different modes with `setViewportUpdateMode()`. By default (`QGraphicsView::MinimalViewportUpdate`), the view tries to determinate only those areas which need an update and repaints only these. However, sometimes it is more time-consuming to find all the areas that need a redraw than to just paint the entire viewport. This applies if you have many small updates. Then, `QGraphicsView::FullViewportUpdate` is the better choice since it simply repaints the whole viewport. A kind of combination of the last two modes is `QGraphicsView::BoundingRectViewportUpdate`. In this mode, Qt detects all areas that need a redraw and then it redraws a rectangle of the viewport that covers all areas affected by the change. If the optimal update mode changes over time, you can tell Qt to determine the best mode by using `QGraphicsView::SmartViewportUpdate`. The view then tries to find the best update mode.

As a last optimization, you can take advantage of OpenGL. Instead of using the default viewport based on `QWidget`, advise Graphics View to use an OpenGL widget. This way, you can use all the power that comes with OpenGL.

```
GraphicsView view;
view.setViewport(new QGLWidget(&view));
```

Unfortunately, you have to do a little more than just putting in this line, but that goes beyond the topic and scope of this chapter. You can, however, find more information about OpenGL and Graphics View in Qt's documentation example under "Boxes" as well as in Rødal's Qt Quarterly article–issue 26–which can be found online at `http://doc.qt.digia.com/qq/qq26-openglcanvas.html`.

A general note on optimization: Unfortunately I can't say that you have to do this or that to optimize Graphics View as it highly depends on your system and view/scene. What I can tell you, however, is how to proceed. Once you have finished your game based on Graphics View, measure the performance of your game using a profiler. Make an optimization you think may pay or simply guess and then profile your game again. If the results are better, keep the change; otherwise, reject it. This sounds simple and is the only way optimization can be done. There are no hidden tricks or deeper knowledge. With time, however, your forecasting will get better.

Pop quiz – mastering Graphics View

After studying this chapter, you should be able to answer these questions as they are important when it comes to designing the components of a game based on Graphics View:

Q1. What standard items does Qt offer?

Q2. How is the coordinate system of an item related to the coordinate system of the scene? Next, how is the coordinate system of the scene related to the coordinate system of the view?

Q3. How can one extend items to use properties as well as signals and slots?

Q4. How can one create realistic movements with the help of animations?

Q5. How can Graphics View's performance be improved?

Summary

In the first part of this chapter, you have learned how the Graphics View architecture works. First, we had a look at the items. There you learned how to create your own items by using `QPainter` and which kinds of standard item Qt has to offer. Later on, we also discussed how to transform these items and what the point of origin for that transformation has to do with it. Next we went through the coordinate system of the items, the scene, and the view. We also saw how these three parts work together, for example. how to put items on a scene. Lastly, we learned how to scale and move the scene inside the view. At the same time, you read about advanced topics, such as taking the zoom level into account when painting an item.

In the second part you, deepened your knowledge about items, about the scene, and about the view. While developing the game, you became familiar with different approaches on how to animate items, and you were taught how to detect collisions. As an advanced topic, you were introduced to parallax scrolling.

After having completed the entire chapter, you should now know almost everything about Graphics View. You are able to create complete custom items, you can alter or extend standard items, and with the information about the level of detail you even have the power to alter an item's appearance, depending on its zoom level. You can transform items and the scene, and you can animate items and, thus, the entire scene.

Furthermore, as you have seen while developing the game, your skills are good enough to develop a jump-and-run game with parallax scrolling as it is used in highly professional games. To keep your game fluid and highly responsive, finally we saw some tricks on how to get the most out of Graphics View.

In order to build a bridge to the world of widgets, you also learned how to incorporate items based on `QWidget` into Graphics View. With that knowledge, you can create modern, widget-based user interfaces.

7
Networking

In this chapter, you will be taught how to communicate with the Internet servers and with sockets in general. First, we will have a look at `QNetworkAccessManager`*, which makes sending network requests and receiving replies really easy. Building on this basic knowledge, we are then going to use Google's Distance API to get information about the distance between two locations and how long it would take to get from one to the other. This technique and the respective knowledge can also be used to include Facebook or Twitter in your application via their respective APIs. Then, we will have a look at Qt's Bearer API, which provides information on a device's connectivity state. In the last section, you will learn how to use sockets to create your own server and clients using TCP or UDP as the network protocol.*

QNetworkAccessManager

The easiest way to access files on the Internet is to use Qt's Network Access API. This API is centered on `QNetworkAccessManager`, which handles the complete communication between your game and the Internet.

When we now develop and test a network-enabled application, it is recommended that you use a private, local network if feasible. This way, it is possible to debug both ends of the connection and errors will not expose sensitive data. If you are not familiar with setting up a web server locally on your machine, there are luckily a number of all-in-one installers that are freely available. These will automatically configure Apache2, MySQL (or MariaDB), PHP, and many more on your system. On Windows, for example, you could use XAMPP (`http://www.apachefriends.org`) or the Uniform Server (`http://www.uniformserver.com`); on Apple computers, there is MAMP (`http://www.mamp.info`); and on Linux you normally don't have to do anything since there is already a localhost. If not, open your preferred package manager, search for a package called `Apache2` or a similar one, and install it. Alternatively, have a look at your distribution's documentation.

Before you install Apache on your machine, think about using a virtual machine such as VirtualBox (`http://www.virtualbox.org`) for this task. This way, you keep your machine clean and you can easily try different settings for your test server. With multiple virtual machines, you can even test the interaction between different instances of your game. If you are on Unix, Docker (`http://www.docker.com`) might be worth having a look at.

Downloading files over HTTP

For this, first try to set up a local server and create a file called `version.txt` in the root directory of the installed server. This file should contain a small piece of text such as "I am a file on localhost" or something similar. To test whether the server and the file are correctly setup, start a web browser and open `http://localhost/version.txt`. You should then see the file's content. Of course, if you have access to a domain, you can also use that. Just alter the URL used in the example correspondingly. If this fails, it may be the case that your server does not allow you to display text files. Instead of getting lost in the server's configuration, just rename the file to `version.html`. This should do the trick!

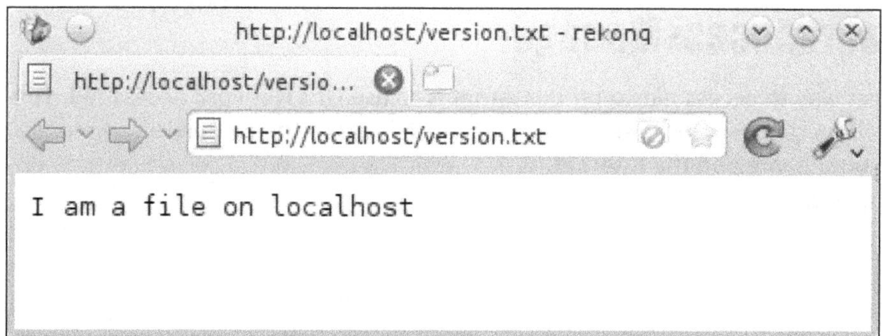

Result of requesting http://localhost/version.txt on a browser

As you might have guessed, because of the file name a real-life scenario could be to check whether there is an updated version of your game or application on the server. To get the content of a file, only five lines of code are needed.

Time for action – downloading a file

First, create an instance of `QNetworkAccessManager`:

```
QNetworkAccessManager *m_nam = new QNetworkAccessManager(this);
```

Since `QNetworkAccessManager` inherits `QObject`, it takes a pointer to `QObject`, which is used as a parent. Thus, you do not have to take care of deleting the manager later on. Furthermore, one single instance of `QNetworkAccessManager` is enough for an entire application. So, either pass a pointer to the network access manager in your game or, for ease of use, create a singleton pattern and access the manager through that.

A singleton pattern ensures that a class is instantiated only once. The pattern is useful for accessing application-wide configurations or—as in our case—an instance of `QNetworkAccessManager`. On the wiki pages for `http://www.qtcentre.org` and `http://www.qt-project.org`, you will find examples for different singleton patterns. A simple template-based approach would look like this (as a header file):

```
template <class T>
class Singleton
{
public:
  static T& Instance()
  {
    static T _instance;
    return _instance;
  }
private:
  Singleton();
  ~Singleton();
  Singleton(const Singleton &);
  Singleton& operator=(const Singleton &);
};
```

In the source code, you will include that header file and acquire a singleton of a class called `MyClass` with:

```
MyClass *singleton = &Singleton<MyClass>::Instance();
```

If you are using Qt Quick—it will be explained in *Chapter 9, Qt Quick Basics*—with `QQuickView`, you can directly use the view's instance of `QNetworkAccessManager`:

```
QQuickView *view = new QQuickView;
QNetworkAccessManager *m_nam
  = view->engine()->networkAccessManager();
```

Secondly, we connect the manager's `finished()` signal to a slot of our choice; for example, in our class, we have a slot called `downloadFinished()`:

```
connect(m_nam, SIGNAL(finished(QNetworkReply*)), this,
  SLOT(downloadFinished(QNetworkReply*)));
```

Thirdly, we actually request the `version.txt` file from localhost:

```
m_nam->get(QNetworkRequest(QUrl("http://localhost/version.txt")));
```

With `get()`, a request to get the contents of the file, specified by the URL, is posted. The function expects `QNetworkRequest`, which defines all the information needed to send a request over the network. The main information for such a request is naturally the URL of the file. This is the reason why `QNetworkRequest` takes `QUrl` as an argument in its constructor. You can also set the URL with `setUrl()` to a request. If you wish to define some additional headers, you can either use `setHeader()` for the most common header or use `setRawHeader()` to be fully flexible. If you want to set, for example, a custom user agent to the request, the call will look like:

```
QNetworkRequest request;
request.setUrl(QUrl("http://localhost/version.txt"));
request.setHeader(QNetworkRequest::UserAgentHeader, "MyGame");
m_nam->get(request);
```

The `setHeader()` function takes two arguments, the first is a value of the `QNetworkRequest::KnownHeaders` enumeration, which holds the most common—self-explanatory—headers such as `LastModifiedHeader` or `ContentTypeHeader`, and the second is the actual value. You could also write the header using `setRawHeader()`:

```
request.setRawHeader("User-Agent", "MyGame");
```

When you use `setRawHeader()`, you have to write the header field names yourself. Besides this, it behaves like `setHeader()`. A list of all the available headers for the HTTP protocol Version 1.1 can be found in section 14 of RFC 2616 (`http://www.w3.org/Protocols/rfc2616/rfc2616-sec14.html#sec14`).

Back to our example: with the `get()` function, we requested the `version.txt` file from the localhost. All we have to do from now on is to wait for the server to reply. As soon as the server's reply is finished, the `downloadFinished()` slot will be called that was defined by the preceding connection statement. As an argument, a reply of the `QNetworkReply` type is transferred to the slot, and we can read the reply's data and set it to `m_edit`, an instance of `QPlainTextEdit`, with:

```
void FileDownload::downloadFinished(QNetworkReply *reply) {
  const QByteArray content = reply->readAll();
  m_edit->setPlainText(content);
  reply->deleteLater();
}
```

Since `QNetworkReply` inherits `QIODevice`, there are also other possibilities to read the contents of the reply including `QDataStream` or `QTextStream` to either read and interpret binary data or textual data. Here, as the fourth command, `QIODevice::readAll()` is used to get the full content of the requested file in `QByteArray`. The responsibility for the transferred pointer to the corresponding `QNetworkReply` lies with us, so we need to delete it at the end of the slot. This would be the fifth line of code that is needed to download a file with Qt. However, be careful and do not call delete on the reply directly. Always use `deleteLater()`, as the documentation suggests!

The full source code can be found in the **FileDownload** example bundled with this book. If you start the small demo application and click on the **Load File** button you should see:

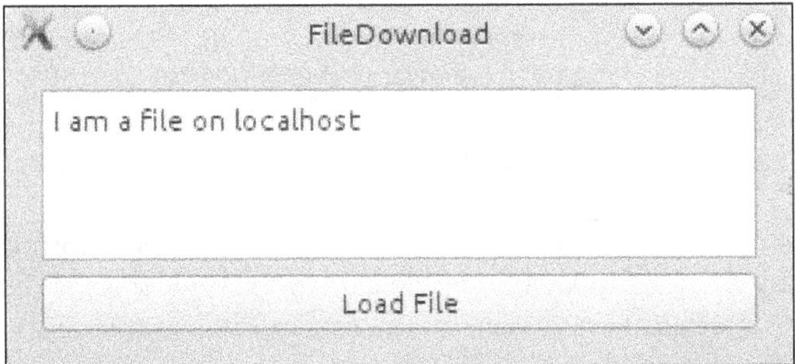

Have a go hero – extending the basic file downloader

If you haven't set up a localhost, just alter the URL in the source code to download another file. Of course, having to alter the source code in order to download another file is far from an ideal approach. So, try to extend the dialog by adding a line edit in which you can specify the URL you want to download. Also, you can offer a file dialog to choose the location to where the downloaded file will be saved.

Error handling

If you do not see the content of the file, something went wrong. Just as in real life, this can often happen. So, we need to make sure that there is a good error handling mechanism in such cases to inform the user about what is going on.

Time for action – displaying a proper error message

Fortunately, QNetworkReply offers several possibilities to do this. In the slot called downloadFinished(), we first want to check whether an error occurred:

```
if (reply->error() != QNetworkReply::NoError) {/* error occurred */}
```

The QNetworkReply::error() function returns the error that occurred while handling the request. The error is encoded as a value of the QNetworkReply::NetworkError type. The two most common errors are probably these:

Error code	Meaning
ContentNotFoundError	This error indicates that the URL of the request could not be found. It is similar to the HTTP error code 404.
ContentAccessDenied	This error indicates that you do not have the permission to access the requested file. It is similar to the HTTP error code 401.

You can look up the other 23 error codes in the documentation. But normally, you do not need to know exactly what went wrong. You only need to know whether everything worked out—QNetworkReply::NoError would be the return value in this case—or if something went wrong.

Since QNetworkReply::NoError has the value 0, you can shorten the test phrase to check whether an error occurred to be:

```
if (reply->error()) {
  // an error occurred
}
```

To provide the user with a meaningful error description, you can use QIODevice::errorString(). The text is already set up with the corresponding error message and we only have to display it:

```
if (reply->error()) {
  const QString error = reply->errorString();
  m_edit->setPlainText(error);
  return;
}
```

In our example, assuming we made an error in the URL and wrote `versions.txt` by mistake, the application would look like this:

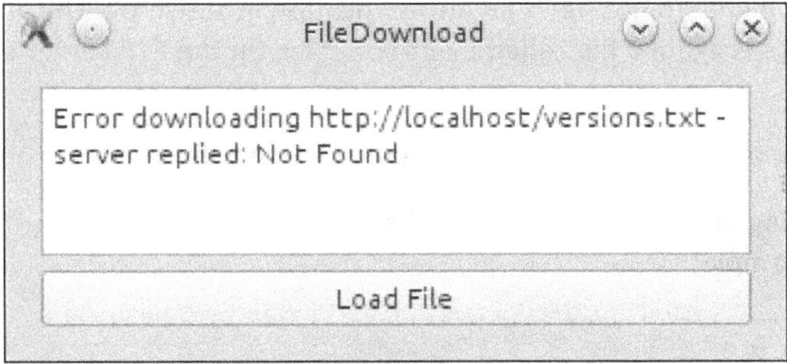

If the request was an HTTP request and the status code is of interest, it could be retrieved by `QNetworkReply::attribute()`:

```
reply->attribute(QNetworkRequest::HttpStatusCodeAttribute)
```

Since it returns `QVariant`, you can either use `QVariant::toInt()` to get the code as an integer or `QVariant::toString()` to get the number as `QString`. Beside the HTTP status code, you can query a lot of other information through `attribute()`. Have a look at the description of the `QNetworkRequest::Attribute` enumeration in the documentation. There, you will also find `QNetworkRequest::HttpReasonPhraseAttribute`, which holds a human-readable reason phrase for the HTTP status code. For example, "Not Found" if an HTTP error 404 has occurred. The value of this attribute is used to set the error text for `QIODevice::errorString()`. So, you can either use the default error description provided by `errorString()` or compose your own by interpreting the reply's attributes.

If a download failed and you want to resume it or if you only want to download a specific part of a file, you can use the `Range` header:

```
QNetworkRequest req(QUrl("..."));
req.setRawHeader("Range", "bytes=300-500");
QNetworkReply *reply = m_nam->get(req);
```

In this example, only the bytes from `300` to `500` would be downloaded. However, the server must support this.

Downloading files over FTP

Downloading a file over FTP is as simple as downloading files over HTTP. If it is an anonymous FTP server for which you do not need an authentication, just use the URL like we did before. Assuming that there is again a file called `version.txt` on the FTP server on the localhost, type:

```
m_nam->get(QNetworkRequest(QUrl("ftp://localhost/version.txt")));
```

That is all, everything else stays the same. If the FTP server requires an authentication, you'll get an error, for example:

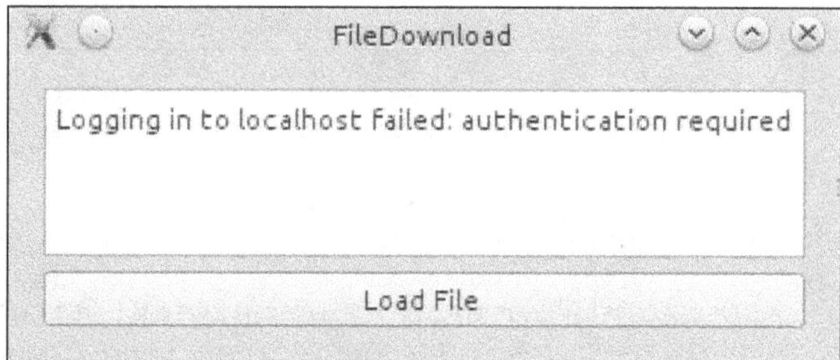

Setting the username and password to access an FTP server is likewise easy: either write it in the URL, or use the `setUserName()` and `setPassword()` functions of `QUrl`. If the server does not use a standard port, you can set the port explicitly with `QUrl::setPort()`.

> To upload a file to an FTP server, use `QNetworkAccessManager::put()`, which takes `QNetworkRequest` as its first argument, calling a URL that defines the name of the new file on the server, and the actual data as its second argument, which should be uploaded. For small uploads, you can pass the content as `QByteArray`. For larger content, it's better to use a pointer to `QIODevice`. Make sure that the device is open and stays available until the upload is done.

Downloading files in parallel

A very important note on `QNetworkAccessManager`: it works asynchronously. This means that you can post a network request without blocking the main event loop, and this is what keeps the GUI responsive. If you post more than one request, they are put on the manager's queue. Depending on the protocol used, they get processed in parallel. If you are sending HTTP requests, normally up to six requests will be handled at a time. This will not block the application. Therefore, there is really no need to encapsulate `QNetworkAccessManager` in a thread; however, unfortunately, this unnecessary approach is frequently recommended all over the Internet. `QNetworkAccessManager` already threads internally. Really, don't move `QNetworkAccessManager` to a thread unless you know exactly what you are doing.

If you send multiple requests, the slot connected to the manager's `finished()` signal is called in an arbitrary order depending on how quickly a request gets a reply from the server. This is why you need to know to which request a reply belongs. This is one reason why every `QNetworkReply` carries its related `QNetworkRequest`. It can be accessed through `QNetworkReply::request()`.

Even if the determination of the replies and their purpose may work for a small application in a single slot, it will quickly get large and confusing if you send a lot of requests. This problem is aggravated by the fact that all replies are delivered to only one slot. Since most probably there are different types of replies that need different treatments, it would be better to bundle them in specific slots that are specialized for a given task. Fortunately, this can be achieved very easily. `QNetworkAccessManager::get()` returns a pointer to `QNetworkReply`, which will get all information about the request that you post with `get()`. By using this pointer, you can then connect specific slots to the reply's signals.

For example, if you have several URLs and you want to save all linked images from these sites to your hard drive, then you request all web pages via `QNetworkAccessManager::get()` and connect their replies to a slot specialized for parsing the received HTML. If links to the images are found, this slot will request them again with `get()`. However, this time the replies to these requests will be connected to a second slot, which is designed for saving the images to the disk. Thus, you can separate the two tasks: parsing HTML and saving data to a local drive.

The most important signals of `QNetworkReply` are discussed next.

The finished signal

The `finished()` signal is an equivalent of the `QNetworkAccessManager::finished()` signal that we used earlier. It is triggered as soon as a reply is returned—successfully or not. After this signal is emitted, neither the reply's data nor its metadata will be altered anymore. With this signal, you are now able to connect a reply to a specific slot. This way, you can realize the scenario the scenario on saving images that was outlined in the previous section.

However, one problem remains: if you post simultaneous requests, you do not know which one has finished and thus called the connected slot. Unlike `QNetworkAccessManager::finished()`, `QNetworkReply::finished()` does not pass a pointer to `QNetworkReply`; this would actually be a pointer to itself in this case. A quick solution to solve this problem is to use `sender()`. It returns a pointer to the `QObject` instance that has called the slot. Since we know that it was `QNetworkReply`, we can write:

```
QNetworkReply *reply = qobject_cast<QNetworkReply*>
  (sender());
if (!reply)
  return;
```

This was done by casting `sender()` to a pointer of the `QNetworkReply` type.

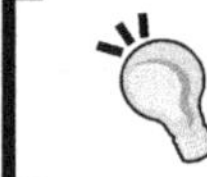

[Whenever you're casting classes that inherit `QObject`, use `qobject_cast`. Unlike `dynamic_cast`, it does not use RTTI and works across the dynamic library boundaries.]

Although we can be pretty confident that the cast will work, do not forget to check whether the pointer is valid. If it is a null pointer, exit the slot.

Time for action – writing the OOP conform code using QSignalMapper

A more elegant way that does not rely on `sender()` would be to use `QSignalMapper` and a local hash, in which all replies that are connected to that slot are stored. So, whenever you call `QNetworkAccessManager::get()`, store the returned pointer in a member variable of the `QHash<int, QNetworkReply*>` type and set up the mapper. Let's assume that we have the following member variables and that they are set up properly:

```
QNetworkAccessManager *m_nam;
QSignalMapper *m_mapper;
QHash<int, QNetworkReply*> m_replies;
```

Then, you connect the `finished()` signal of a reply this way:

```
QNetworkReply *reply = m_nam->get(QNetworkRequest(QUrl(/*...*/)));
connect(reply, SIGNAL(finished()), m_mapper, SLOT(map()));
int id = /* unique id, not already used in m_replies*/;
m_replies.insert(id, reply);
m_mapper->setMapping(reply, id);
```

What just happened?

First, we posted the request and fetched the pointer to `QNetworkReply` with reply. Then, we connected the reply's finished signal to the mapper's slot `map()`. Next, we found a unique ID, which must not already be in use in the `m_replies` variable. You can use random numbers generated with `qrand()` and fetch numbers as long as they are not unique. To determine whether a key is already in use, call `QHash::contains()`. It takes the key as an argument against which it should be checked. Or even simpler, count up another private member variable. Once we have a unique ID, we insert the pointer to `QNetworkReply` in the hash using the ID as a key. Last, with `setMapping()`, we set up the mapper's mapping: the ID's value corresponds to the actual reply.

In a prominent place, most likely the constructor of the class, we already have connected the mappers `map()` signal to a custom slot. For example:

```
connect(m_mapper, SIGNAL(mapped(int)), this,
  SLOT(downloadFinished(int)));
```

When the `downloadFinished()` slot is called, we can get the corresponding reply with:

```
void SomeClass::downloadFinished(int id) {
  QNetworkReply *reply = m_replies.take(id);
  // do some stuff with reply here
  reply->deleteLater();
}
```

`QSignalMapper` also allows you to map with `QString` as an identifier instead of an integer as used in the preceding code. So, you could rewrite the example and use the URL to identify the corresponding `QNetworkReply`, at least as long as the URLs are unique.

The error signal

If you download files sequentially, you can swap the error handling out. Instead of dealing with errors in the slot connected to the `finished()` signal, you can use the reply's `error()` signal, which passes the error of the `QNetworkReply::NetworkError` type to the slot. After the `error()` signal has been emitted, the `finished()` signal will most likely also be emitted shortly.

The readyRead signal

Until now, we have used the slot connected to the `finished()` signal to get the reply's content. This works perfectly if you deal with small files. However, this approach is unsuitable when dealing with large files, as they would unnecessarily bind too many resources. For larger files, it is better to read and save the transferred data as soon as it is available. We are informed by `QIODevice::readyRead()` whenever new data is available to be read. So, for large files you should use the following code:

```
connect(reply, SIGNAL(readyRead()), this, SLOT(readContent()));
file.open(QIODevice::WriteOnly);
```

This will help you connect the reply's `readyRead()` signal to a slot, set up `QFile`, and open it. In the connected slot, type in the following snippet:

```
const QByteArray ba = reply->readAll();
file.write(ba);
file.flush();
```

Now, you can fetch the content, which has been transferred so far, and save it to the (already opened) file. This way, the resources needed are minimized. Don't forget to close the file after the `finished()` signal is emitted.

In this context, it would be helpful if you knew upfront the size of the file you want to download. Therefore, we can use `QNetworkAccessManager::head()`. It behaves like the `get()` function, but does not transfer the content of the file. Only the headers are transferred. And if we are lucky, the server sends the "Content-Length" header, which holds the file size in bytes. To get that information, we type:

```
reply->head(QNetworkRequest::ContentLengthHeader).toInt();
```

With this information, we can also check upfront whether there is enough space left on the disk.

The downloadProgress method

Especially when a big file is downloaded, the user usually wants to know how much data has already been downloaded and approximately how long it will take for the download to finish.

Time for action – showing the download progress

In order to achieve this, we can use the reply's `downloadProgress()` signal. As the first argument, it passes the information on how many bytes have already been received and as the second argument, how many bytes there are in total. This gives us the possibility to indicate the progress of the download with `QProgressBar`. As the passed arguments are of the `qint64` type, we can't use them directly with `QProgressBar`, as it only accepts `int`. So, in the connected slot, we first calculate the percentage of the download progress:

```
void SomeClass::downloadProgress(qint64 bytesReceived,
  qint64 bytesTotal) {
  qreal progress = (bytesTotal < 1) ? 1.0
                 : bytesReceived * 100.0 / bytesTotal;
  progressBar->setValue(progress * progressBar->maximum());
}
```

What just happened?

With the percentage, we set the new value for the progress bar where `progressBar` is the pointer to this bar. However, what value will `progressBar->maximum()` have and where do we set the range for the progress bar? What is nice is that you do not have to set it for every new download. It is only done once, for example, in the constructor of the class containing the bar. As range values, I would recommend:

```
progressBar->setRange(0, 2048);
```

The reason is that if you take, for example, a range of 0 to 100 and the progress bar is 500 pixels wide, the bar would jump 5 pixels forward for every value change. This will look ugly. To get a smooth progression where the bar expands by 1 pixel at a time, a range of 0 to 99.999.999 would surely work, but would be highly inefficient. This is because the current value of the bar would change a lot without any graphical depiction. So, the best value for the range would be 0 to the actual bar's width in pixels. Unfortunately, the width of the bar can change depending on the actual widget width, and frequently querying the actual size of the bar every time the value changes is also not a good solution. Why `2048`, then? The idea behind this value is the resolution of the screen. Full HD monitors normally have a width of 1920 pixels, thus taking 2^11 (2048) ensures that the progress bar runs smoothly, even if it is fully expanded. So, 2048 isn't the perfect number but is a fairly good compromise. If you are targeting smaller devices, choose a smaller, more appropriate number.

To be able to calculate the remaining time for the download to finish, you have to start a timer. In this case, use `QElapsedTimer`. After posting the request with `QNetworkAccessManager::get()`, start the timer by calling `QElapsedTimer::start()`. Assuming that the timer is called `m_timer`, the calculation will be:

```
qint64 total = m_timer.elapsed() / progress;
qint64 remaining = (total - m_timer.elapsed()) / 1000;
```

`QElapsedTimer::elapsed()` returns the milliseconds that are counted from the moment when the timer is started. This value divided by the progress equals the estimated total download time. If you subtract the elapsed time and divide the result by 1,000, you'll get the remaining time in seconds.

Using a proxy

If you like to use a proxy, you first have to set up `QNetworkProxy`. You have to define the type of the proxy with `setType()`. As arguments, you will most likely want to pass `QNetworkProxy::Socks5Proxy` or `QNetworkProxy::HttpProxy`. Then, set up the hostname with `setHostName()`, the username with `setUserName()`, and the password with `setPassword()`. The last two properties are, of course, only needed if the proxy requires an authentication. Once the proxy is set up, you can set it to the access manager via `QNetworkAccessManager::setProxy()`. Now, all new requests will use this proxy.

Connecting to Google, Facebook, Twitter, and co.

Since we discussed `QNetworkAccessManager`, you now have the knowledge you need to integrate Facebook, Twitter, or similar sites into your application. They all use the HTTP protocol and simple requests in order to retrieve data from them. For Facebook, you have to use the so-called Graph API. It describes which interfaces are available and what options they offer. If you want to search for users who are called "Helena", you have to request `https://graph.facebook.com/search?q=helena&type=user`. Of course, you can do this with `QNetworkManager`. You will find more information about the possible requests to Facebook at `http://developers.facebook.com/docs/graph-api`.

If you wish to display tweets in your game, you have to use Twitter's REST or Search API. Assuming that you know the ID of a tweet you would like to display, then you can get it through `https://api.twitter.com/1.1/statuses/show.json?id=12345`, where `12345` is the actual ID for the tweet. If you would like to find tweets mentioning `#Helena`, you would write `https://api.twitter.com/1.1/search/tweets.json?q=%23Helena`. You can find more information about the parameters and the other possibilities of Twitter's API at `https://dev.twitter.com/docs/api`.

Since both Facebook and Twitter need an authentication to use their APIs, we will have a look at Google instead. Let's use Google's Distance Matrix API in order to get information about how long it would take for us to get from one city to another. The technical documentation for the API we are going to use can be found at `https://developers.google.com/maps/documentation/distancematrix`.

Time for action – using Google's Distance Matrix API

The GUI for this example is kept simple—the source code is attached with the book. It consists of two line edits (`ui->from` and `ui->to`) that allow you to enter the origin and destination of the journey. It also provides you with a combo box (`ui->vehicle`) that allows you to choose a mode of transportation—whether you want to drive a car, ride a bicycle, or walk—a push button (`ui->search`) to start the request, and a text edit or (`ui->result`) to show the results. The result will look like this:

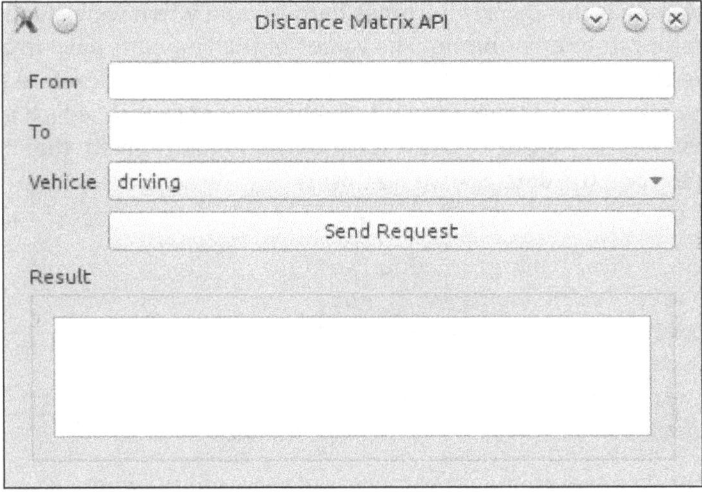

`MainWindow`—a subclass of `QMainWindow`—is the application's main class that holds two private members: `m_nam`, which is a pointer to `QNetworkAccessManager`, and `m_reply`, which is a pointer to `QNetworkReply`.

Time for action – constructing the query

Whenever the button is pressed, the `sendRequest()` slot is called:

```
void MainWindow::sendRequest()
{
  if (m_reply != 0 && m_reply->isRunning())
    m_reply->abort();
  ui->result->clear();
```

In this slot, we first check whether there is an old request, which was stored in `m_reply`, and if it is still running. If that is `true`, we abort the old request as we are about to schedule a new one. Then, we also wipe out the result of the last request by calling `QPlainTextEdit::clear()` on the text edit.

Next, we will construct the URL for the request. We can do this by composing the string by hand where we add the query parameters to the base URL similar to:

```
url = baseUrl + "?origin=" + ui->from->text() + "&...";
```

Besides the problem that this quickly becomes hard to read when we include multiple parameters, it is also rather error-prone. The values of the line edits have to be encoded to fit the criteria for a valid URL. For every user value, we therefore have to call `QUrl::toPercentEncoding()` explicitly. A much better approach, which is easier to read and less error-prone, is to use `QUrlQuery`. It circumvents the problem that may result from you forgetting to encode the data. So, we do this:

```
QUrlQuery query;
query.addQueryItem("sensor", "false");
query.addQueryItem("language", "en");
query.addQueryItem("units", "metric");
query.addQueryItem("origins", ui->from->text());
query.addQueryItem("destinations", ui->to->text());
query.addQueryItem("mode", ui->vehicle->currentText());
```

The usage is pretty clear: we create an instance and then add the query parameters with `addQueryItem()`. The first argument is taken as the key and the second as the value resulting in a string such as "key=value". The value will be automatically encoded when we use `QUrlQuery` in conjunction with `QUrl`. Other benefits of using `QUrlQuery` are that we can check whether we have already set a key with `hasQueryItem()`, taking the key as an argument, or removed a previous set key by calling `removeQueryItem()`.

In a real situation, we would, of course, wrap all the preceding literals in `QStringLiteral`, but this is omitted here in favor of a better reading. So, let's review which parameters we have set. The `sensor` key is set to `false` as we are not using a GPS device to locate our position. The `language` key is set to `English`, and for units, we favor metric over imperial. Then, the search-related parameters are set. The `origins` key holds the places we want to start from. As its value, the text of the `ui->from` line edit is chosen. If you want to query multiple starting positions, you just have to combine them using |. Equivalent to the origins, we set up the value for destinations. Last, we pass the value of the combo box to mode, which defines whether we want to go by a car, bicycle, or whether we want to walk, as shown in the following code:

```
  QUrl url
    = ("http://maps.googleapis.com/maps/api/distancematrix/json");
  url.setQuery(query);
  m_reply = m_nam->get(QNetworkRequest(url));
}
```

Next, we create `QUrl` that contains the address to which the query should be posted. By including "json" at the end, we define that the server should transfer its reply using the JSON format. Google also provides the option for us to get the result as XML. To achieve this, simply replace "json" with "xml". However, since the APIs of Facebook and Twitter return JSON, we will use this format.

Then, we set the previous constructed `query` to the URL by calling `QUrl::setQuery()`. This automatically encodes the values so we do not have to worry about that. Last, we post the request by calling the `get()` function and store the returned `QNetworkReply` in `m_reply`.

Time for action – parsing the server's reply

In the constructor, we have connected the manager's `finish()` signal to the `finished()` slot of the `MainWindow` class. It will thus be called after the request has been posted:

```
void MainWindow::finished(QNetworkReply *reply)
{
  if (m_reply != reply) {
    reply->deleteLater();
    return;
  }
```

First, we check whether the reply that was passed is the one that we have requested through `m_nam`. If this is not the case, we delete `reply` and exit the function. This can happen if a reply was aborted by the `sendRequest()` slot:

```
m_reply = 0;
if (reply->error()) {
  ui->result->setPlainText(reply->errorString());
  reply->deleteLater();
  return;
}
```

Since we are now sure that it is our request, we set `m_reply` to null because we have handled it and do not need this information anymore. Next we check whether an error occurred, and if it did, we put the reply's error string in the text edit, delete reply, and exit the function:

```
const QByteArray content = reply->readAll();
QJsonDocument doc = QJsonDocument::fromJson(content);
if (doc.isNull() || !doc.isObject()) {
  ui->result->setPlainText("Error while reading the JSON file.");
  reply->deleteLater();
  return;
}
```

With `readAll()`, we get the content of the server's reply. Since the transferred data is not large, we do not need to use partial reading with `readyRead()`. The content is then converted to `QJsonDocument` using the `QJsonDocument::fromJson()` static function, which takes `QByteArray` as an argument and parses its data. If the document is null, the server's reply wasn't valid, and then, we show an error message on the text edit, delete the reply, and exit the function. We do the same if the document does not contain an object, as the API call should respond with a single object, as shown:

```
QJsonObject obj = doc.object();
QVariantList origins = obj.value("origin_addresses")
                       .toArray().toVariantList();
QVariantList destinations = obj.value("destination_addresses")
                            .toArray().toVariantList();
```

Since we now made sure that there is an object, we store it in `obj`. Furthermore, due to the API, we also know that the object holds the `origin_addresses` and `destination_addresses` keys. Both values are arrays that hold the requested origins and destinations. From this point on, we will skip any tests if the values exist and are valid since we trust the API. The object also holds a key called `status`, whose' value can be used to check whether the query may have failed and if yes, why? The last two lines of the source code store the origins and destinations in two variant lists. With `obj.value("origin_addresses")`, we get `QJsonValue` that holds the value of the pair specified by the `origin_addresses` key. `QJsonValue::toArray()` converts this value to `QJsonArray`, which then is converted to `QVariantList` using `QJsonArray::toVariantList()`. The returned JSON file for a search requesting the distance from Warsaw or Erlangen to Birmingham will look like:

```
{
  "destination_addresses" : [ "Birmingham, West Midlands, UK" ],
  "origin_addresses" : [ "Warsaw, Poland", "Erlangen, Germany" ],
  "rows" : [ ... ],
  "status" : "OK"
}
```

The `rows` key holds the actual results as an array. The first object in this array belongs to the first origin, the second object to the second origin, and so on. Each object holds a key named `elements`, whose' value is also an array of objects that belong to the corresponding destinations:

```
"rows" : [
    {
      "elements" : [{...}, {...}]
    },
    {
      "elements" : [{...}, {...}]
    }
  ],
```

Each JSON object for an origin-destination pair (`{...}` in the preceding example) consists of two pairs with the distance and duration keys. Both the values of these keys are arrays that hold the `text` and `value` keys, where `text` is a human-readable phrase for `value`. The object for the Warsaw-Birmingham search looks as shown in the following snippet:

```
{
  "distance" : {
    "text" : "1,835 km",
    "value" : 1834751
  },
  "duration" : {
    "text" : "16 hours 37 mins",
    "value" : 59848
  },
  "status" : "OK"
}
```

As you can see, the value of `value` for distance is the distance expressed in meters—since we have used `units=metric` in the request—and the value of `text` is value transformed into kilometers with the post fix "km". The same applies to duration. Here, value is expressed in seconds and text is value converted into hours and minutes.

Now that we know how the returned JSON is structured, we display the value of each origin-destination pair in the text edit. Therefore, we loop through each possible pairing using `QVariantLists`:

```
for (int i = 0; i < origins.count(); ++i) {
  for (int j = 0; j < destinations.count(); ++j) {
```

This scope will be reached for each combination. Think of the transferred result as a table where the origins are rows and the destinations are columns:

```
QString output;
output += QString("From:").leftJustified(10, ' ')
          + origins.at(i).toString() + "\n";
output += QString("To:").leftJustified(10, ' ')
          + destinations.at(j).toString() + "\n";
```

We cache the constructed text in a local variable called output. First, we add the string "From:" and the current origin to output. To make it look at least a little bit nicer, we call `leftJustified()`. It causes "From:" to be filled with spaces until the size of the entire string is `10`. The output will then be aligned. The value of the current origin is normally accessed through `QList::at()`, and since it is `QVariantList`, we need to convert the returned `QVariant` to `QString`. Thus, we call `toString()`. The same is done for the destination, which results in the following as the value for output:

```
From:      Warsaw, Poland
To:        Birmingham, West Midlands, UK
```

Next, we will read duration and distance from the corresponding `QJsonObject` from where we call `data`:

```
QJsonObject data = obj.value("rows").toArray().at(i).toObject()
                   .value("elements").toArray().at(j).toObject();
```

Starting at the reply's root object, we fetch the value of rows and convert it to an array (`obj.value("rows").toArray()`). Then, we fetch the value of the current row (`.at(i)`), convert it to a JSON object, and fetch its elements key (`.toObject().value("elements")`). Since this value is also an array—the columns of the row—we convert it to an array, fetch the current column (`.toArray().at(j)`), and convert it to an object. This is the object that contains the distance and duration for an origin-destination pair in the cell (`i;j`). Beside these two keys, the object also holds a key called `status`. Its value indicates whether the search was successful (`OK`), whether the origin or destination could not be found (`NOT_FOUND`), or whether the search could not find a route between the origin and destination (`ZERO_RESULTS`):

```
QString status = data.value("status").toString();
```

We store the value of status in a local variable that is also named status:

```
if (status == "OK") {
  output += QString("Distance:").leftJustified(10, ' ') +
    data.value("distance").toObject().value("text").toString()
    + "\n";
  output += QString("Duration:").leftJustified(10, ' ') +
    data.value("duration").toObject().value("text").toString()
    + "\n";
}
```

If all goes well, we then add `distance` and `duration` to the output and also align the labels as we did before using `leftJustified()`. For distance, we want to show the phrased result. Therefore, we first get the JSON value of the distance key (`data.value("distance")`), convert it to an object, and request the value for the text key (`.toObject().value("text")`). Lastly, we convert `QJsonValue` to `QString` using `toString()`. The same applies for duration:

```
else if (status == "NOT_FOUND") {
  output += "Origin and/or destination of this
    pairing could not be geocoded.\n";
} else if (status == "ZERO_RESULTS") {
  output += "No route could be found.\n";
} else {
```

```
        output += "Unknown error.\n";
    }
```

If the API returns errors, we set an appropriate error text as output:

```
            output += QString("\n").fill('=', 35) + "\n\n";
            ui->result->moveCursor(QTextCursor::End);
            ui->result->insertPlainText(output);
          }
        }
        reply->deleteLater();
    }
```

Finally, we add a line consisting of 35 equals signs (`fill('=', 35)`) to separate the result in one cell from the other cells. The output is then placed at the end of the text edit. This is done by moving the cursor to the end of the edit, by calling `moveCursor(QTextCursor::End)`, and inserting output into the edit with `insertPlainText(output)`.

When the loops finish, we must not forget to delete the reply. The actual result then looks as follows:

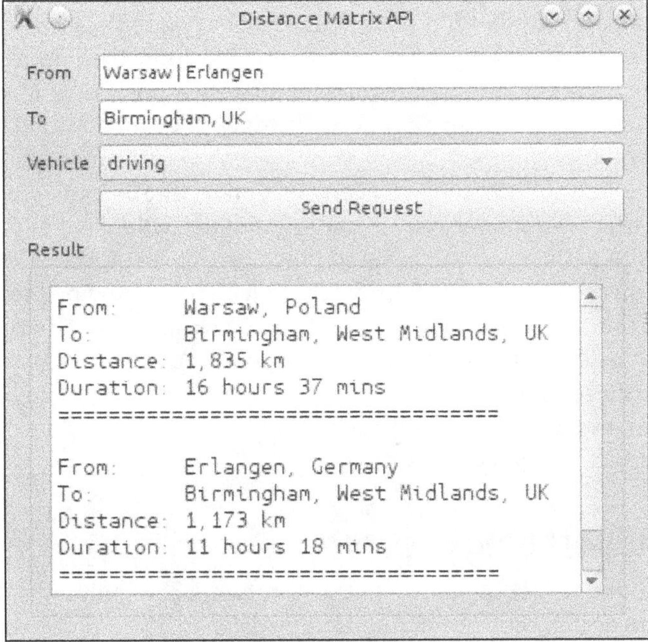

Have a go hero – choosing XML as the reply's format

To hone your XML skills, you can use `http://maps.googleapis.com/maps/api/distancematrix/xml` as a URL to which you send the requests. Then, you can parse the XML file as we did with JSON and display the retrieved data likewise.

Controlling the connectivity state

As a matter of fact, you can only use `QNetworkAccessManager` if you have an active connection to the Internet. Since you cannot theoretically know the connectivity state, you have to check this at the runtime of the application. With the help of the Bearer API, you can check whether the computer, mobile device, or tablet is online and you can even start a new connection—if the operating system supports it.

The Bearer API mainly consists of four classes. `QNetworkConfigurationManager` is the base and starting point. It holds all network configurations available on the system. Furthermore, it provides information about the network capabilities, for example, whether you can start and stop interfaces. The network configurations found by it are stored as `QNetworkConfiguration` classes. `QNetworkConfiguration` holds all information about an access point but not about a network interface, as an interface can provide multiple access points. This class also provides only the information about network configurations. You can't configure an access point or a network interface through `QNetworkConfiguration`. The network configuration is up to the operating system, and therefore, `QNetworkConfiguration` is a read-only class. With `QNetworkConfiguration`, however, you can determine whether the type of connection is an Ethernet, WLAN, or 2G connection. This may influence what kind of data and, more importantly, what size of data you are going to download. With `QNetworkSession`, you can then start or stop system network interfaces, which are defined by the configurations. This way, you gain control over an access point. `QNetworkSession` also provides session management that is useful when a system's access point is used by more than one application. The session ensures that the underlying interface only gets terminated after the last session has been closed. Lastly, `QNetworkInterface` provides classic information such as the hardware address or interface name.

QNetworkConfigurationManager

`QNetworkConfigurationManager` manages all network configurations that are available on a system. You can access these configurations by calling `allConfigurations()`. Of course, you have to create an instance of the manager first:

```
QNetworkConfigurationManager manager;
QList<QNetworkConfiguration> cfgs = manager.allConfigurations();
```

The configurations are returned as a list. The default behavior of `allConfigurations()` is to return all possible configurations. However, you can also retrieve a filtered list. If you pass `QNetworkConfiguration::Active` as an argument, the list only contains configurations that have at least one active session. If you create a new session based on such a configuration, it will be active and connected. By passing `QNetworkConfiguration::Discovered` as an argument, you will get a list with configurations that can be used to immediately start a session. Note, however, that at this point, you cannot be sure whether the underlying interface can be started. The last important argument is `QNetworkConfiguration::Defined`. With this argument, `allConfigurations()` returns a list of configurations that are known to the system but are not usable right now. This may be a previously used WLAN hotspot, which is currently out of range.

You will be notified whenever the configurations change. If a new configuration becomes available, the manager emits the `configurationAdded()` signal. This may happen, for example, if mobile data transmission becomes available or if the user turns his/her device's WLAN adapter on. If a configuration is removed, for example, if the WLAN adapter is turned off, `configurationRemoved()` is emitted. Lastly, when a configuration gets changed, you will be notified by the `configurationChanged()` signal. All three signals pass a constant reference to the configuration about what was added, removed, or changed. The configuration passed by the `configurationRemoved()` signal is, of course, invalid. It still contains, the name and identifier of the removed configuration.

To find out whether any network interface of the system is active, call `isOnline()`. If you want to be notified about a mode change, track the `onlineStateChanged()` signal.

> Since a WLAN scan takes a certain amount of time, `allConfigurations()` may not return all the available configurations. To ensure that configurations are completely populated, call `updateConfigurations()` first. Due to the long time it may take to gather all of the information about the system's network configurations, this call is asynchronous. Wait for the `updateCompleted()` signal and only then, call `allConfigurations()`.

`QNetworkConfigurationManager` also informs you about the Bearer API's capabilities. The `capabilities()` function returns a flag of the `QNetworkConfigurationManager::Capabilities` type and describes the available possibilities that are platform-specific. The values you may be most interested in are as follows:

Value	Meaning
CanStartAndStopInterfaces	This means that you can start and stop access points.
ApplicationLevelRoaming	This indicates that the system will inform you if a more suitable access point is available, and that you can actively change the access point if you think there is a better one available.
DataStatistics	With this capability, QNetworkSession contains information about the transmitted and received data.

QNetworkConfiguration

QNetworkConfiguration holds, as mentioned earlier, information about an access point. With name(), you get the user-visible name for a configuration, and with identifier() you get a unique, system-specific identifier. If you develop games for mobile devices, it may be of advantage to you to know which type of connection is being used. This might influence the data that you request; for example, the quality and thus, the size of a video. With bearerType(), the type of bearer used by a configuration is returned. The returned enumeration values are rather self-explanatory: BearerEthernet, BearerWLAN, Bearer2G, BearerCDMA2000, BearerWCDMA, BearerHSPA, BearerBluetooth, BearerWiMAX, and so on. You can look up the full-value list in the documentation for QNetworkConfiguration::BearerType.

With purpose(), you get the purpose of the configuration, for example, whether it is suitable to access a private network (QNetworkConfiguration::PrivatePurpose) or to access a public network (QNetworkConfiguration::PublicPurpose). The state of the configuration, if it is defined, discovered or active, as previously described, can be accessed through state().

QNetworkSession

To start a network interface or to tell the system to keep an interface connected for as long as you need it, you have to start a session:

```
QNetworkConfigurationManager manager;
QNetworkConfiguration cfg = manager.defaultConfiguration();
QNetworkSession *session = new QNetworkSession(cfg, this);
session->open();
```

A session is based on a configuration. When there is more than one session and you are not sure which one to use, use `QNetworkConfigurationManager::defaultConfiguration()`. It returns the system's default configuration. Based on this, you can create an instance of `QNetworkSession`. The first argument, the configuration, is required. The second is optional but is recommended since it sets a parent and we do not have to take care of the deletion. You may want to check whether the configuration is valid (`QNetworkConfiguration::isValid()`) first. Calling `open()` will start the session and connect the interface if needed and supported. Since `open()` can take some time, the call is asynchronous. So, either listen to the `opened()` signal, which is emitted as soon as the session is open, or to the `error()` signal if an error happened. The error is of the `QNetworkSession::SessionError` type. Alternatively, instead of checking the `opened()` signal, you can also watch the `stateChanged()` signal. The possible states for a session can be: `Invalid`, `NotAvailable`, `Connecting`, `Connected`, `Closing`, `Disconnected`, and `Roaming`. If you want to make `open()` synchronous, call `waitForOpened()` right after calling `open()`. It will block the event loop till the session is open. This function will return `true` on success and `false` otherwise. To limit the waiting time, you can define a time-out. Just pass the milliseconds that you are willing to wait as an argument to `waitForOpened()`. To check whether a session is open, use `isOpen()`.

To close the session, call `close()`. If no session is left on the interface, it will be shot down. To force an interface to disconnect, call `stop()`. This call will invalidate all the sessions that are based on that interface.

You may receive the `preferredConfigurationChanged()` signal, which indicates that the preferred configuration, that is, for example, the preferred access point, has changed. This may be the case if a WLAN network is now in range and you do not have to use 2G anymore. The new configuration is passed as the first argument and the second one indicates whether changing the new access point will also alter the IP address. Besides checking for the signal, you can also inquire whether roaming is available for a configuration by calling `QNetworkConfiguration::isRoamingAvailable()`. If roaming is available, you have to decide to either reject the offer by calling `ignore()` or to accept it by calling `migrate()`. If you accept roaming, it will emit `newConfigurationActivated()` when the session is roamed. After you have checked the new connection, you can either accept the new access point or reject it. The latter means that you will return to the previous access point. If you accept the new access point, the previous one will be terminated.

QNetworkInterface

To get the interface that is used by a session, call `QNetworkSession::interface()`. It will return the `QNetworkInterface` object, which describes the interface. With `hardwareAddress()`, you get the low-level hardware address of the interface that is normally the MAC address. The name of the interface can be obtained by `name()`, which is a string such as "eth0" or "wlan0". A list of IP addresses as well as their netmasks and broadcast addresses registered with the interface is returned by `addressEntries()`. Furthermore, information about whether the interface is a loopback or whether it supports multicasting can be queried with `flags()`. The returned bitmask is a combination of these values: `IsUp`, `IsRunning`, `CanBroadcast`, `IsLoopBack`, `IsPointToPoint`, and `CanMulticast`.

Communicating between games

After having discussed Qt's high-level network classes such as `QNetworkAccessManager` and `QNetworkConfigurationManager`, we will now have a look at a lower-level network classes and see how Qt supports you when it comes to implementing TCP or UDP servers and clients. This becomes relevant when you plan to extend your game by including a multiplayer mode. For such a task, Qt offers `QTcpSocket`, `QUdpSocket`, and `QTcpServer`.

Time for action – realizing a simple chat program

To get familiar with `QTcpServer` and `QTcpSocket`, let's develop a simple chat program. This example will teach you the basic knowledge of network handling in Qt so that you can use this skill later to connect two or more copies of a game. At the end of this exercise, we want to see something like this:

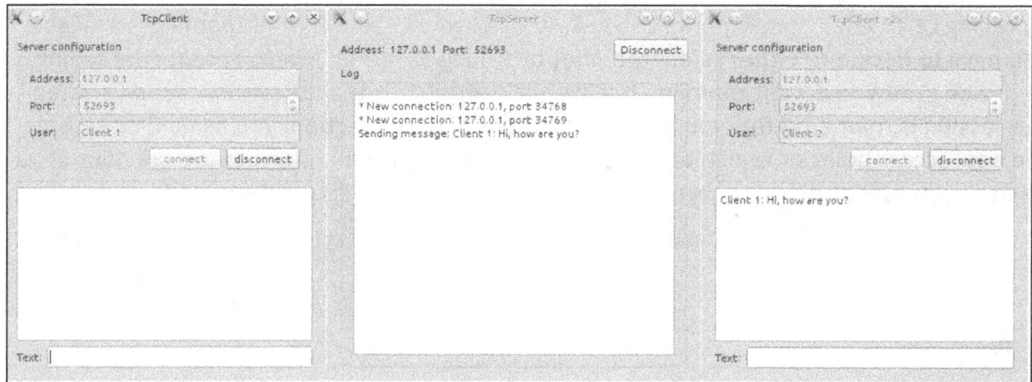

On both the left-hand side and the right-hand side of the preceding figure, you can see a client, whereas the server is in the middle. We'll start by taking a closer look at the server.

The server – QTcpServer

As a protocol for communication, we will use **Transmission Control Protocol** (**TCP**). You may know this network protocol from the two most popular Internet protocols: HTTP and FTP. Both use TCP for their communication and so do the globally used protocols for e-mail traffic: SMTP, POP3, and IMAP. The main advantage of TCP, however, is its reliability and connection-based architecture. Data transferred by TCP is guaranteed to be complete, ordered, and without any duplicates. The protocol is furthermore stream orientated, which allows us to use `QDataStream` or `QTextStream`. A downside to TCP is its speed. This is because the missing data has to be retransmitted until the receiver fully receives it. By default, this causes a retransmission of all the data that was transmitted after the missing part. So, you should only choose TCP as a protocol if speed is not your top priority, but rather the completeness and correctness of the transmitted data. This applies if you send unique nonrepetitive data.

Time for action – setting up the server

A look at the server's GUI shows us that it principally consists of `QPlainTextEdit` (`ui->log`) that is used to display system messages and a button (`ui->disconnectClients`), which allows us to disconnect all the current connected clients. On top, next to the button, the server's address and port are displayed (`ui->address` and `ui->port`). After setting up the user interface in the constructor of the server's class `TcpServer`, we initiate the internally used `QTcpServer`, which is stored in the `m_server` private member variable:

```
if (!m_server->listen(QHostAddress::LocalHost, 52693)) {
  ui->log->setPlainText("Failure while starting server: "
                        + m_server->errorString());
  return;
}
connect(m_server, SIGNAL(newConnection()),
        this, SLOT(newConnection()));
```

What just happened?

With `QTcpServer::listen()`, we defined that the server should listen to the localhost and the `52693` port for new incoming connections. The value used here, `QHostAddress::LocalHost` of the `QHostAddress::SpecialAddress` enumeration, will resolve to `127.0.0.1`. If you instead pass `QHostAddress::Any`, the server will listen to all IPv4 interfaces as well as to IPv6 interfaces. If you only want to listen to a specific address, just pass this address as `QHostAddress`:

```
m_server->listen(QHostAddress("127.0.0.1"), 0);
```

This will behave like the one in the preceding code only in that the server will now listen to a port that will be chosen automatically. On success, `listen()` will return as `true`. So, if something goes wrong in the example it will show an error message on the text edit and exit the function. To compose the error message, we are using `QTcpServer::errorString()`, which holds a human-readable error phrase.

To handle the error in your game's code, the error string is not suitable. In any case where you need to know the exact error, use `QTcpServer::serverError()`, which returns the enumeration value of `QAbstractSocket::SocketError`. Based on this, you know exactly what went wrong, for example, `QAbstractSocket::HostNotFoundError`. If `listen()` was successful, we connect the server's `newConnection()` signal to the class's `newConnection()` slot. The signal will be emitted every time a new connection is available:

```
ui->address->setText(m_server->serverAddress().toString());
ui->port->setText(QString::number(m_server->serverPort()));
```

Lastly, we show the server's address a port number that can be accessed through `serverAddress()` and `serverPort()`. This information is needed by the clients so that they are able to connect to the server.

Time for action – reacting on a new pending connection

As soon as a client tries to connect to the server, the `newConnection()` slot will be called:

```
void TcpServer::newConnection() {
  while (m_server->hasPendingConnections()) {
    QTcpSocket *con = m_server->nextPendingConnection();
    m_clients << con;
    ui->disconnectClients->setEnabled(true);
    connect(con, SIGNAL(disconnected()), this,
      SLOT(removeConnection()));
    connect(con, SIGNAL(readyRead()), this, SLOT(newMessage()));
    ui->log->insertPlainText(
      QString("* New connection: %1, port %2\n")
      .arg(con->peerAddress().toString())
      .arg(QString::number(con->peerPort())));
  }
}
```

What just happened?

Since more than one connection may be pending, we use `hasPendingConnections()` to determine whether there is at least one more pending connection. Each one is then handled inside the `while` loop. To get a pending connection of the `QTcpSocket` type, we call `nextPendingConnection()` and add this connection to a private list called `m_clients`, which holds all active connections. In the next line, as there is now at least one connection, we enable the button that allows all connections to be closed. Therefore, the slot connected to the button's `click()` signal will call `QTcpSocket::close()` on each single connection. When a connection is closed, its socket emits a `disconnected()` signal. We connect this signal to our `removeConnection()` slot. With the last connection, we react to the socket's `readyRead()` signal, which indicates that new data is available. In such a situation, our `newMessage()` slot is called. Lastly, we print a system message that a new connection has been established. The address and port of the connecting client and peer can be retrieved by the socket's `peerAddress()` and `peerPort()` functions.

> If a new connection can't be accepted, the `acceptError()` signal is emitted instead of `newConnection()`. It passes the reason for the failure of the `QAbstractSocket::SocketError` type as an argument. If you want to temporarily decline new connections, call `pauseAccepting()` on `QTcpServer`. To resume accepting new connections, call `resumeAccepting()`.

Time for action – forwarding a new message

When a connected client sends a new chat message, the underlying socket—since it inherits `QIODevice`—emits `readyRead()`, and thus, our `newMessage()` slot will be called.

Before we have a look at this slot, there is something important that you need to keep in mind. Even though TCP is ordered and without any duplicates, this does not mean that all the data is delivered in one big chunk. So, before processing the received data, we need to make sure that we get the entire message. Unfortunately, there is neither an easy way to detect whether all data was transmitted nor a globally usable method for such a task. Therefore, it is up to you to solve this problem, as it depends on the use case. Two common solutions, however, are to either send magic tokens to indicate the start and the end of a message, for example, single characters or XML tags, or you can send the size of the message upfront. The second solution is shown in the Qt documentation where the length is put in a `quint16` in front of the message. We, on the other hand, will look at an approach that uses a simple magic token to handle the messages correctly. As a delimiter, we use the "End of Transmission Block" character–ASCII code 23–to indicate the end of a message.

Since the processing of received data is quite complex, we will go through the code step by step this time:

```
void TcpServer::newMessage()
{
  if (QTcpSocket *con = qobject_cast<QTcpSocket*>(sender())) {
    m_receivedData[con].append(con->readAll());
```

To determine which socket called the slot, we use `sender()`. If the cast to `QTcpSocket` is successful, we enter the `if` scope and read the transferred—potentially fragmentary—message with `readAll()`.

Please note that `sender()` is used for simplicity. If you write real-life code, it is better to use `QSignalMapper`.

The `read` data is then concatenated with the previously received data that is stored in the `QHash` private member called `m_receivedData`, where the socket is used as a key:

```
    if (!m_receivedData[con].contains(QChar(23)))
      return;
```

Here we check whether the received data contains our special token, the "End of Transmission Block". Otherwise, we exit and wait for the further data to arrive, which then gets appended to the string. As soon as we have at least one special token, we proceed by splitting the data into single messages:

```
    QStringList messages = m_receivedData[con].split(QChar(23));
    m_receivedData[con] = messages.takeLast();
```

The received data contains exactly one single message for which the "End of Transmission Block" token is the last character, and thus, the messages list has two elements: the first one with the actual message and the last one without any content. This way, `m_receivedData[con]` is reset. What if `QChar(23)` is not the last character of the received text? Then, the last element is the beginning of the next, which is not yet complete, message. So, we store that message in `m_receivedData[con]`. This guarantees that no data will be lost:

```
    foreach (QString message, messages) {
      ui->log->insertPlainText("Sending message: " + message + "\n");
```

Since we do not know how many messages we will get with the last read from the socket, we need to go through the list of messages. For every message, we display a short notice on the server's log and then send it to the other clients:

```
      message.append(QChar(23));
      foreach (QTcpSocket *socket, m_clients) {
```

```
            if (socket == con)
              continue;
            if (socket->state() == QAbstractSocket::ConnectedState)
              socket->write(message.toLocal8Bit());
          }
        }
      }
    }
```

Before sending the message, we append `QChar(23)` to indicate the end of the message, of course, and then send it to all the connected clients, except the one who sent it in the first place, by simply calling write on the socket. Since the socket inherits `QIODevice`, you can use most of the functions that you know from `QFile`.

Have a go hero – using QSignalMapper

As discussed earlier, using `sender()` is a convenient, but not an object-orientated, approach. Thus, try to use `QSignalMapper` instead to determine which socket called the slot. To achieve this, you have to connect the socket's `readyRead()` signal to a mapper and the slot directly. All the signal-mapper-related code will go into the `newConnection()` slot.

The same applies to the connection to the `removeConnection()` slot. Let's have a look at it next.

Time for action – detecting a disconnect

When a client terminates the connection, we have to delete the socket from the local `m_clients` list. Therefore, we have to connected the socket's `disconnected()` signal to:

```
void TcpServer::removeConnection()
{
  if (QTcpSocket *con = qobject_cast<QTcpSocket*>(sender())) {
    ui->log->insertPlainText(
      QString("* Connection removed: %1, port %2\n")
      .arg(con->peerAddress().toString())
      .arg(QString::number(con->peerPort())));
    m_clients.removeOne(con);
    con->deleteLater();
    ui->disconnectClients->setEnabled(!m_clients.isEmpty());
  }
}
```

What just happened?

After getting the socket that emitted the call through `sender()`, we post the information that a socket is being removed. Then, we remove the socket from `m_clients` and call `deleteLater()` on it. Do not use delete. Lastly, if no client is left, the disconnect button is disabled.

This is the first part. Now let's have a look at the client.

The client

The graphical user interface of the client (`TcpClient`) is pretty simple. It has three input fields to define the server's address (`ui->address`), the server's port (`ui->port`), and a username (`ui->user`). Of course, there is also a button to connect to (`ui->connect`) and disconnect from (`ui->disconnect`) the server. Finally, the GUI has a text edit that holds the received messages (`ui->chat`) and a line edit (`ui->text`) to send messages.

Time for action – setting up the client

When the user has provided the server's address and port and has chosen a username, he/she can connect to the server:

```
void TcpClient::on_connect_clicked()
{
  //...
  if (m_socket->state() != QAbstractSocket::ConnectedState) {
    m_socket->connectToHost(ui->address->text(), ui->port->value());
    ui->chat->insertPlainText("== Connecting...\n");
  }
  //...
}
```

What just happened?

The private member variable m_socket holds an instance of QTcpSocket. If this socket is already connected, nothing happens. Otherwise, the socket is connected to the given address and port by calling connectToHost(). Besides the obligatory server address and port number, you can pass a third argument to define the mode in which the socket will be opened. For possible values, you can use OpenMode just like we did for QIODevice. Since this call is asynchronous, we print a notification to the chat, so that the user is informed that the application is currently trying to connect to the server. When the connection is established, the socket sends the connected() signal that prints "Connected to server" on the chat to indicate that we have connected to a slot. Besides the messages in the chat, we also updated the GUI by, for example, disabling the connect button, but this is all basic stuff. You won't have any trouble understanding this if you have had a look at the sources. So, these details are left out here.

Of course, something could go wrong when trying to connect to a server, but luckily, we are informed about a failure as well through the error() signal passing a description of error in the form of QAbstractSocket::SocketError. The most frequent errors will probably be QAbstractSocket::ConnectionRefusedError if the peer refused the connection or QAbstractSocket::HostNotFoundError if the host address could not be found. If the connection, however, was successfully established, it should be closed later on. You can either call abort() to immediately close the socket, whereas disconnectFromHost() will wait until all pending data has been written.

Time for action – receiving text messages

In the constructor, we have connected the socket's readyRead() signal to a local slot. So, whenever the server sends a message through QTcpSocket::write(), we read the data and display it in the chat window:

```
m_receivedData.append(m_socket->readAll());
if (!m_receivedData.contains(QChar(23)))
  return;

QStringList messages = m_receivedData.split(QChar(23));
m_receivedData = messages.takeLast();
foreach (const QString &message, messages) {
  ui->chat->insertPlainText(message + "\n");
}
```

As you already know, `QTcpSocket` inherits `QIODevice`, so we use `QIODevice::readAll()` to get the entire text that was sent. Next, we store the received data and determine whether the message was transmitted completely. This approach is the same as we used previously for the server. Lastly, in the `for` loop, we add the messages to the chat window.

Time for action – sending text messages

What is left is now is to describe how to send a chat massage. On hitting return inside the line edit, a local slot will be called that checks whether there is actual text to send and whether `m_socket` is still connected:

```
QString message = m_user + ": " + ui->text->text();
m_socket->write(message.toLocal8Bit());
ui->text->clear();
```

If so, a message is composed that contains the self-given username, a colon, and the text of the line edit. To send this string to the peer, the `QTcpSocket::write()` server is called. Since `write()` only accepts const `char*` or `QByteArray`, we use `QString::toLocal8Bit()` to get `QByteArray` that we can send over the socket.

That's all. It's like writing and reading from a file. For the complete example, have a look at the sources bundled with this book and run the server and several clients.

Have a go hero – extending the chat with a user list

This example has shown us how to send a simple text. If you now go on and define a schema for how the communication should work, you can use it as a base for more complex communication. For instance, if you want to enable the client to receive a list of all other clients (and their usernames), you need to define that the server will return such a list if it gets a message such as `rq:allClients` from a client. Therefore, you have to parse all messages received by the server before forwarding them to all the connected clients. Go ahead and try to implement such a requirement yourself. By now, it is possible that multiple users have chosen the same username. With the new functionality of getting a user list, you can prevent this from happening. Therefore, you have to send the username to the server that keeps track of them.

Improvements

The example we explained uses a nonblocking, asynchronous approach. For example, after asynchronous calls such as `connectToHost()`, we do not block the thread until we get a result, but instead, we connect to the socket's signals to proceed. On the Internet as well as Qt's documentation, on the other hand, you will find dozens of examples explaining the blocking and the synchronous approaches. You will easily spot them by their use of `waitFor...()` functions. These functions block the current thread until a function such as `connectToHost()` has a result—the time `connected()` or `error()` will be emitted. The corresponding blocking function to `connectToHost()` is `waitForConnected()`. The other blocking functions that can be used are `waitForReadyRead()`, which waits until new data is available on a socket for reading; `waitForBytesWritten()`, which waits until the data has been written to the socket; and `waitForDisconnected()`, which waits until the connection has been closed.

Look out; even if Qt offers these `waitFor...()` functions, do not use them! The synchronous approach is not the smartest one since it will freeze your game's GUI. A frozen GUI is the worst thing that can happen in your game and it will annoy every user. So, when working inside the GUI thread, you are better to react to the `QIODevice::readyRead()`, `QIODevice::bytesWritten()`, `QAbstractSocket::connected()`, and `QAbstractSocket::disconnected()` corresponding signals.

`QAbstractSocket` is the base class of `QTcpSocket` as well as of `QUdpSocket`.

Following the asynchronous approach shown, the application will only become unresponsive while both reading and writing to the socket as well as during determining whether a message is complete. The optimum, however, would be to move the entire socket handling to an extra thread. Then, the GUI thread would only get signals, passing the new messages, and to send, it would simply pass `QString` to the worker thread. This way, you will get a super fluent velvet GUI.

Using UDP

In contrast to TCP, UDP is unreliable and connectionless. Neither the order of packets, nor their delivery is guaranteed. UDP, however, is very fast. So, if you have frequent data, which does not necessarily need to be received by the peer, use UDP. This data could, for example, be real-time positions of a player that get updated frequently or live video/audio streaming. Since `QUdpSocket` is mostly the same as `QTcpSocket`—both inherit `QAbstractSocket`—there is not much to explain. The main difference between them is that TCP is stream-orientated, whereas UDP is datagram-orientated. This means that the data is sent in small packages, containing among the actual content, the sender's as well as the receiver's IP address and port number. Due to the lack of `QUdpServer`, you have to use `QAbstractSocket::bind()` instead of `QTcpServer::listen()`. Like `listen()`, `bind()` takes the addresses and ports that are allowed to send datagrams as arguments. Whenever a new package arrives, the `QIODevice::readyRead()` signal is emitted. To read the data, use the `readDatagram()` function, which takes four parameters. The first one of the `char*` type is used to write the data in, the second specifies the amount of bytes to be written, and the last two parameters of the `QHostAddress*` and `quint16*` types are used to store the sender's IP address and port number. Sending data works likewise: `writeDatagram()` sends the first argument's data of the `char*` type to the host, which is defined by the third (address) and fourth (port number) argument. With the second parameter, you can limit the amount of data to be sent.

Time for action – sending a text via UDP

As an example, let's assume that we have two sockets of the `QUpSocket` type. We will call the first one `socketA` and the other `socketB`. Both are bound to the localhost, `socketA` to the `52000` port and `socketB` to the `52001` port. So, if we want to send the string "Hello!" from `socketA` to `socketB`, we have to write in the application that is holding `socketA`:

```
socketA->writeDatagram(QByteArray("Hello!"),
  QHostAddress("127.0.0.1"), 52001);
```

Here, we have used the convenient function of `writeDatagram()`, which takes `QByteArray` instead of const `char*` and `qint64`. The class that holds `socketB` must have the socket's `readyRead()` signal connected to a slot. This slot will then be called because of our `writeDatagram()` call, assuming that the datagram is not lost! In the slots, we read the datagram and the sender's address and port number with:

```
while (socketB->hasPendingDatagrams()) {
  QByteArray datagram;
  datagram.resize(socketB->pendingDatagramSize())
  QHostAddress sender;
  quint16 senderPort;
```

```
    socketB->readDatagram(datagram.data(), datagram.size(),
                          &sender, &senderPort);
    // do something with datagram, sender and port.
}
```

As long as there are pending datagrams—this is checked by `hasPendingDatagrams()`, which returns `true` as long as there are pending datagrams—we read them. This is done by creating `QByteArray`, which is used to store the transferred datagram. To be able to hold the entire transmitted data, it is resized to the length of the pending datagram. This information is retrieved by `pendingDatagramSize()`. Next we create `QHostAddress` and `quint16` so that `readDatagram()` can store the sender's address and port number in these variables. Now, all is set up to call `readDatagram()` so that we get the datagram.

Have a go hero – connecting players of the Benjamin game

With this introductory knowledge, you can go ahead and try some stuff by yourself. For example, you can take the game Benjamin the elephant and send Benjamin's current position from one client to another. This way, you can either clone the screen from one client to the other or both clients can play the game and additionally can see where the elephant of the other player currently is. For such a task, you would use UDP, as it is important that the position is updated very fast while it isn't a disaster when one position gets lost.

Pop quiz – test your knowledge

Q1. Which three (main) classes do you need to download a file?

Q2. How can you download only the first 100 bytes of a file?

Q3. If you need to extend a URL by parameters with special characters, you need to escape them with `QUrl::toPercentEncoding()`. Which other, more convenient, option does Qt offer?

Q4. How do you delete `QNetworkReply` received from `QNetworkAccessManager`?

Q5. What is the type hierarchy of `QTcpSocket` and `QUdpSocket` and what's the big advantage of this hierarchy?

Q6. The `readDatagram()` function belongs to `QTcpSocket` or `QUdpSocket`?

Summary

In the first part of this chapter, you familiarized yourself with `QNetworkAccessManager`. This class is at the heart of your code whenever you want to download or upload files to the Internet. After having gone through the different signals that you can use to fetch errors, to get notified about new data or to show the progress, you should now know everything you need on that topic.

The example about the Distance Matrix API depended your knowledge of `QNetworkAccessManager`, and it shows you a real-life application case for it. Dealing with JSON as the server's reply format was a recapitulation of *Chapter 4, Qt Core Essentials*, but was highly needed since Facebook or Twitter only use JSON to format their network replies.

In the last section, you learned how to set up your own TCP server and clients. This enables you to connect different instances of a game to provide the multiplayer functionality. Alternatively, you were taught how to use UDP.

Please keep in mind that we only scratched the surface of this topic due to its complexity. Covering it fully would have exceeded this beginner's guide. For a real game, which uses a network, you should learn more about Qt's possibilities for establishing a secure connection via SSL or some other mechanism.

In the next chapter, you'll learn how to extend your game with a scripting engine. This allows you to, for example, easily change various aspects of your game without the need for recompiling it.

8
Scripting

In this chapter, you will learn how to bring scripting facilities to your programs. You will gain knowledge of how to use a language based on JavaScript to implement the logic and details of your game without having to rebuild the main game engine. Although the environment we are going to focus on blends best with Qt applications, if you don't like JavaScript you will be given suggestions about other languages that you can use to make your games scriptable.

Why script?

You might ask yourself, why should I use any scripting language if I can implement everything I need in C++? There are a number of benefits to providing a scripting environment to your games. Most modern games really consist of two parts. One of them is the main game engine that implements the core of the game (data structures, processing algorithms, and the rendering layer) and exposes an API to the other component, which provides details, behavior patterns, and action flows for the game. This other component is usually written in a scripting language. The main benefit of this is that story designers can work independently from the engine developers and they don't have to rebuild the whole game just to modify some of its parameters or check whether the new quest fits well into the existing story. This makes the development much quicker compared to the monolithic approach. Another benefit is that this development opens the game to modding—skilled end users can extend or modify the game to provide some added value to the game. It's also a way to make additional money on the game by implementing extensions on it on top of the existing scripting API without having to redeploy the complete game binary to every player or to expose new scripting endpoints to boost the creativity of the modders even more. Finally, you can reuse the same game driver for other games and just replace the scripts to obtain a totally different product.

Qt provides two implementations of a JavaScript-based scripting environment. In this chapter, we will be focusing on Qt Script. In the docs, you can see that the module is marked as "deprecated"; however, it currently provides a richer API (albeit with slower execution) than the other implementation. After we describe Qt Script, we will have a brief look at the other implementation as well. We will not discuss the details of the JavaScript language itself, as there are many good books and websites available out there where you can learn JavaScript. Besides, the JavaScript syntax is very similar to that of C, and you shouldn't have any problems understanding the scripts that we use in this chapter even if you haven't seen any JavaScript code before.

The basics of Qt Script

To use Qt Script in your programs, you have to enable the script module for your projects by adding the `QT += script` line to the project file.

Evaluating JavaScript expressions

C++ compilers do not understand JavaScript. Therefore, to execute any script, you need to have a running interpreter that will parse the script and evaluate it. In Qt, this is done with the `QScriptEngine` class. This is a Qt Script runtime that handles the execution of script code and manages all the resources related to scripts. It provides the `evaluate()` method, which can be used to execute JavaScript expressions. Let's look at a "Hello World" program in Qt Script:

```
#include <QCoreApplication>
#include <QScriptEngine>

int main(int argc, char **argv) {
  QCoreApplication app(argc, argv);
  QScriptEngine engine;
  engine.evaluate("print('Hello World!')");
  return 0;
}
```

This program is very simple. First, it creates an application object that is required for the script environment to function properly, and then it just instantiates `QScriptEngine` and invokes evaluate to execute the script source given to it as a parameter. After building and running the program, you will see a well-known `Hello World!` printed to the console.

If you don't get any output, then this probably means that the script didn't get executed properly, possibly because of an error in the script's source code. To verify that, we can extend our simple program to check whether there were any problems with the execution of the script. For this, we can query the engine state with `hasUncaughtExceptions()`:

```
#include <QCoreApplication>
#include <QScriptEngine>
#include <QtDebug>

int main(int argc, char **argv) {
  QCoreApplication app(argc, argv);
  QScriptEngine engine;
  engine.evaluate("print('Hello World!')");
  if(engine.hasUncaughtException()) {
    QScriptValue exception = engine.uncaughtException();
    qDebug() << exception.toString();
  }
  return 0;
}
```

The highlighted code checks whether there is an exception and if yes, it fetches the exception object. You can see that its type is `QScriptValue`. This is a special type that is used to exchange data between the script engine and the C++ world. It is somewhat similar to `QVariant` in the way that it is really a facade for a number of primitive types that the script engine uses internally. One of the types is the type holding errors. We can check whether a script value object is an error using its `isError()` method, but in this case, we don't do that since `uncaughtException()` is meant to return error objects. Instead, we immediately convert the error to a string representation and dump it to the console using `qDebug()`. For example, if you omit the closing single quote in the script source text and run the program, the following message will be displayed:

```
"SyntaxError: Parse error"
```

`QScriptEngine::evaluate()` also returns `QScriptValue`. This object represents the result of the evaluated script. You can make a script calculate some value for you that you can later use in your C++ code. For example, the script can calculate the amount of damage done to a creature when it is hit with a particular weapon. Modifying our code to use the result of the script is very simple. All that is required is to store the value returned by `evaluate()` and then it can be used elsewhere in the code:

```
QScriptValue result = engine.evaluate("(7+8)/2");
if(engine.hasUncaughtException()) {
  // ...
} else {
  qDebug() << result.toString();
}
```

Time for action – creating a Qt Script editor

Let's do a simple exercise and create a graphical editor to write and execute scripts. Start by creating a new GUI project and implement a main window composed of two plain text edit widgets (`ui->codeEditor` and `ui->logWindow`) that are separated using a vertical splitter. One of the edit boxes will be used as an editor to input code and the other will be used as a console to display script results. Then, add a menu and toolbar to the window and create actions to open (`ui->actionOpen`) and save (`ui->actionSave`) the document, create a new document (`ui->actionNew`), execute the script (`ui->actionExecute`), and to quit the application (`ui->actionQuit`). Remember to add them to the menu and toolbar. As a result, you should receive a window similar to the one shown in the following screenshot:

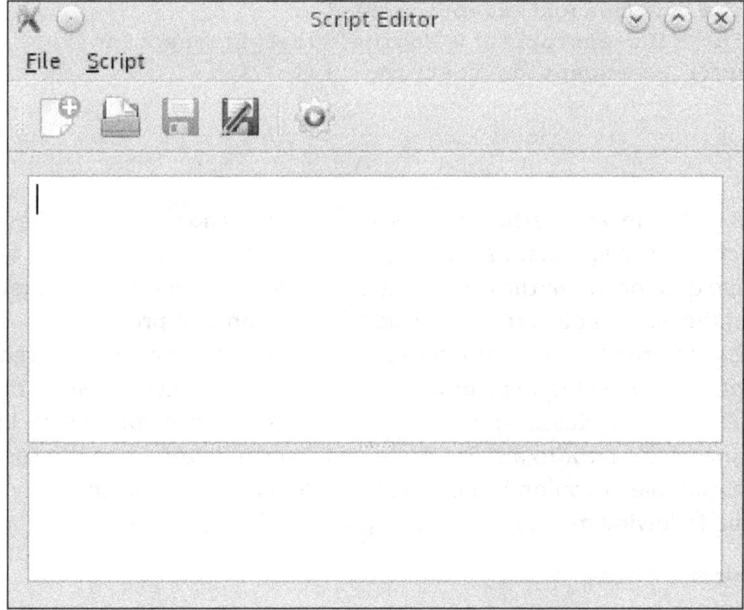

Connect the quit action to the `QApplication::quit()` slot. Then, create an `openDocument()` slot and connect it to the appropriate action. In the slot, use `QFileDialog::getOpenFileName()` to ask the user for a document path as follows:

```
void MainWindow::openDocument() {
  QString filePath = QFileDialog::getOpenFileName
    (this, "Open Document", QDir::homePath(),
    "JavaScript Documents (*.js)");
  if(filePath.isEmpty()) return;
  open(filePath);
}
```

In a similar fashion, implement the **Save** and **Save As** action handlers. Lastly, create the `open(const QString &filePath)` slot, make it read the document, and put its contents into the code editor:

```
void MainWindow::open(const QString &filePath) {
  QFile file(filePath);
  if(!file.open(QFile::ReadOnly|QFile::Text)) {
      QMessageBox::critical(this, "Error", "Can't open file.");
      return;
  }
  setWindowFilePath(filePath);
  ui->codeEditor->setPlainText(QTextStream(&file).readAll());
  ui->logWindow->clear();
}
```

The `windowFilePath` property of `QWidget` can be used to associate a file with a window. You can then use it in actions related to using the file—when saving a document, you can check whether this property is empty and ask the user to provide a filename. Then, you can reset this property when creating a new document or when the user provides a new path for the document.

At this point, you should be able to run the program and use it to create scripts and save and reload them in the editor.

Now, to execute the scripts, add a `QScriptEngine m_engine` member variable to the window class. Create a new slot, call it `run`, and connect it to the execute action. Put the following code in the body of the slot:

```
void Main Window::run() {
   ui->logWindow->clear();
   QScriptValue result
     = m_engine.evaluate(scriptSourceCode, windowFilePath());
   if(m_engine.hasUncaughtException()) {
     QScriptValue exception = m_engine.uncaughtException();
     QTextCursor cursor = ui->logWindow->textCursor();
     QTextCharFormat errFormat;
     errFormat.setForeground(Qt::red);
     cursor.insertText(
       QString("Exception at line %1:")
       .arg(m_engine.uncaughtExceptionLineNumber()),
       errFormat
     );
     cursor.insertText(exception.toString(), errFormat);
```

```
        QStringList trace = m_engine.uncaughtExceptionBacktrace();
        errFormat.setForeground(Qt::darkRed);
        for(int i = 0; i < trace.size(); ++i) {
          const QString & traceFrame = trace.at(i);
          cursor.insertBlock();
          cursor.insertText(QString("#%1: %2")
            .arg(i).arg(traceFrame), errFormat);
        }
      } else {
        QTextCursor cursor = ui->logWindow->textCursor();
        QTextCharFormat resultFormat;
        resultFormat.setForeground(Qt::blue);
        cursor.insertText(result.toString(), resultFormat);
      }
    }
```

Build and run the program. To do so, enter the following script in the editor:

```
function factorial(n) {
  if( n < 0 ) return undefined
  if( n == 0 ) return 1
  return n*factorial(n-1)
}

factorial(7)
```

Save the script in a file called `factorial.js` and then run it. You should get an output as shown in the following screenshot:

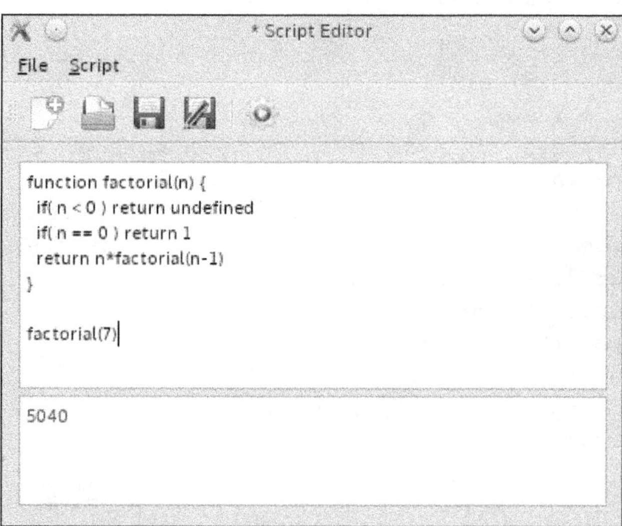

Next, replace the script with the following one:

```
function factorial(n) {
  return N
}

factorial(7)
```

Running the script should yield the following result:

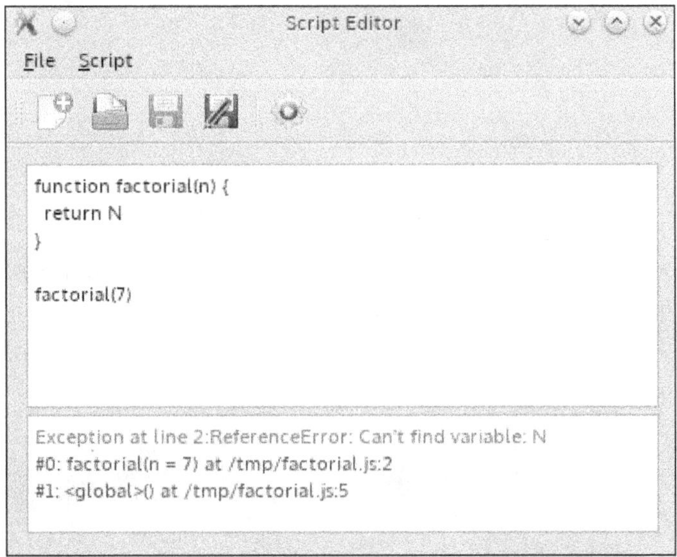

What just happened?

The `run()` method clears the log window and evaluates the script using the method that we learned earlier in this chapter. If the evaluation is successful, it prints the result in the log window, which is what we see in the first screenshot shown in the previous section.

In the second attempt, we made an error in the script using a nonexistent variable. Evaluating such code results in an exception. In addition to reporting the actual error, we also use `uncaughtExceptionLineNumber()` to report the line that caused the problem. Next, we call the engine's `uncaughtExceptionBacktrace()` method, which returns a list of strings containing the backtrace (a stack of function calls) of the problem, which we also print on the console.

Let's try another script. The following code defines the local variable `fun`, which is assigned an anonymous function that returns a number:

```
var fun = function() { return 42 }
```

You can then call `fun()` like a regular function as follows:

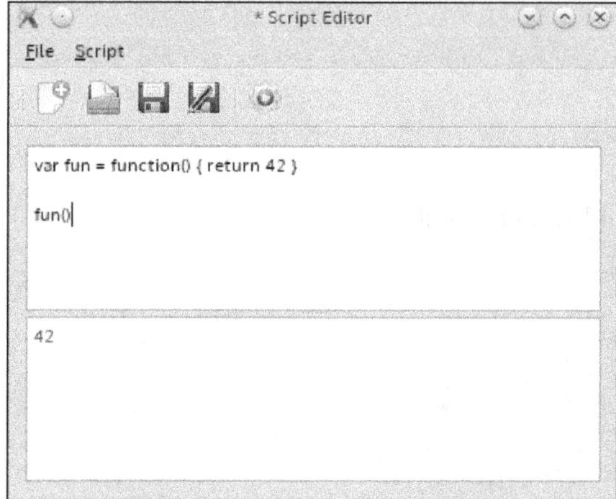

Now, let's look at what happens if we delete the definition of `fun` from the script, but still keep the invocation:

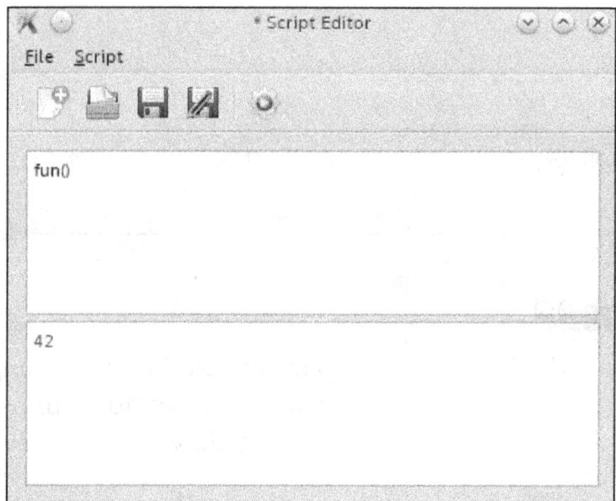

We still get the same result even though we didn't define what fun means! This is because the `QScriptEngine` object keeps its state across `evaluate()` invocations. If you define a variable in a script, it is kept in the current context of the engine. The next time `evaluate()` is called, it executes the script in the same context as before; therefore, all variables defined earlier are still valid. Sometimes, this is a desired behavior; however, a malicious script can wreck the context, which can cause trouble for subsequent evaluations in the engine. Therefore, it is usually better to make sure that the engine is left in a clean state after a script is done with the execution.

Time for action – sandboxed script evaluation

The next task for us is to modify our script editor so that it cleans up after the execution of each script. As was said, each script is executed in the current context of the engine, so the task of solving the problem boils down to making sure that each script executes in a separate context. Incorporate the following code in the `run()` method:

```
void MainWindow::run() {
    ui->logWindow->clear();
    QString scriptSourceCode = ui->codeEditor->toPlainText();
    m_engine.pushContext();
  QScriptValue result = m_engine.evaluate
   (scriptSourceCode, windowFilePath());
    if(m_engine.hasUncaughtException()) {
        // …
    }
    m_engine.popContext();
}
```

Run the program and repeat the last test to see that `fun` no longer persists across executions.

What just happened?

When a function is called, a new execution context is pushed to the top of the stack. When the engine tries to resolve an object, it first looks for the object in the topmost context (which is the context of the function call). If it is not found, the engine looks into the next context on the stack and then the next until it finds the object or reaches the bottom of the stack. When the function returns, the context is popped from the stack and all variables defined there are destroyed. You can see how this works using the following script:

```
var foo = 7
function bar() { return foo }
bar()
```

When `bar` is called, a new context is added to the stack. The script requests for the `foo` object, which is not present in the current context, so the engine looks into the surrounding context and finds a definition of `foo`. In our code, we follow this behavior by explicitly creating a new context using `pushContext()` and then removing it with `popContext()`.

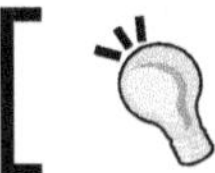

[You can retrieve the current context object with `currentContext()`.]

The context has two important objects associated with it: the `activation` object and the `this` object. The former defines an object where all local variables are stored as the object's properties. If you set any properties on the object before invoking a script, they will be directly available to the script:

```
QScriptContext *context = engine.pushContext();
QScriptValue activationObject = context->activationObject();
activationObject.setProperty("foo", "bar");
engine.evaluate("print(foo)");
```

The `this` object works in a similar fashion—it determines the object to be used when the script refers to an object called `this`. Any properties defined in C++ are accessible from the script and the other way round:

```
QScriptContext *context = engine.pushContext();
QScriptValue thisObject = context->thisObject();
thisObject.setProperty("foo", "bar");
engine.evaluate("print(this.foo)");
```

Integrating Qt and Qt Script

So far, we were only evaluating some standalone scripts that could make use of the features built in JavaScript. Now, it is time to learn to use data from your programs in the scripts.

This is done by exposing different kinds of entities to and from scripts.

Exposing objects

The simplest way to expose data to Qt Script is to take advantage of Qt's meta-object system. Qt Script is able to inspect `QObject` instances and detect their properties and methods. To use them in scripts, the object has to be visible to the script execution context. The easiest way to make this happen is to add it to the engine's global object or to some context's activation object. As you remember, all data between the script engine and C++ is exchanged using the `QScriptValue` class, so first we have to obtain a script value handle for the C++ object:

```
QScriptEngine engine;
QPushButton *button = new QPushButton("Button");
// ...
QScriptValue scriptButton = engine.newQObject(button);
engine.globalObject().setProperty("pushButton", scriptButton);
```

`QScriptEngine::newQObject()` creates a script wrapper for an existing `QObject` instance. We then set the wrapper as a property of the global object called `pushButton`. This makes the button available in the global context of the engine as a JavaScript object. All the properties defined with `Q_PROPERTY` are available as properties of the object and every slot is accessible as a method of that object. Using this approach, you can share an existing object between the C++ and JavaScript worlds:

```
int main(int argc, char **argv) {
  QApplication app(argc, argv);
  QScriptEngine engine;
  QPushButton button;
  engine.globalObject().setProperty
  ("pushButton", engine.newQObject(&button));
  QString script = "pushButton.text = 'My Scripted Button'\n"+
                   "pushButton.checkable = true\n" +
                   "pushButton.setChecked(true)"
  engine.evaluate(script);
  return app.exec();
}
```

There are cases when you want to provide a rich interface for a class to manipulate it from within C++ easily, but to have a strict control over what can be done using scripting, you want to prevent scripters from using some of the properties or methods of the class.

For methods, this is quite easy—just don't make them slots. Remember that you can still use them as slots if you use the `connect()` variant, which takes a function pointer as an argument.

For properties, you can mark a property as accessible or inaccessible from scripts using the `SCRIPTABLE` keyword in the `Q_PROPERTY` declaration. By default, all properties are scriptable, but you can forbid their exposure to scripts by setting `SCRIPTABLE` to `false` as shown in the following example:

```
Q_PROPERTY(QString internalName READ internalName SCRIPTABLE false)
```

Time for action – employing scripting for npc AI

Let's implement a script serving as **artificial intelligence** (**AI**) for a nonplayer character in a simple Dungeons & Dragons game. The engine will periodically execute the script, exposing two objects to it—the creature and the player. The script will be able to query the properties of the player and invoke functions on the creature.

Let's create a new project. We'll start by implementing the C++ class for creatures in our game world. Since both the NPC and player are living entities, we can have a common base class for them. In *Chapter 4, Qt Core Essentials*, we already had a data structure for players, so let's use that as a base by equipping our entities with similar attributes. Implement `LivingEntity` as a subclass of `QObject` with the following properties:

```
Q_PROPERTY(QString name      READ name        NOTIFY nameChanged)
Q_PROPERTY(char direction    READ direction   NOTIFY directionChanged)
Q_PROPERTY(QPoint position   READ position    NOTIFY positionChanged)
Q_PROPERTY(int hp            READ hp          NOTIFY hpChanged)
Q_PROPERTY(int maxHp         READ maxHp       NOTIFY maxHpChanged)
Q_PROPERTY(int dex           READ dex         NOTIFY dexChanged)
Q_PROPERTY(int baseAttack    READ baseAttack  NOTIFY baseAttackChanged)
Q_PROPERTY(int armor         READ armor       NOTIFY armorChanged)
```

You can see that this interface is read only—you cannot modify any of the properties using the `LivingEntity` class. Of course, we still need methods to change those values; so, implement them in the `public` interface of the class:

```
public:
  void setName(const QString &newName);
  void setDirection(char newDirection);
  void setPosition(const QPoint &newPosition);
  void setHp(int newHp);
  void setMaxHp(int newMaxHp);
  void setBaseAttack(int newBaseAttack);
  void setArmor(int newArmor);
  void setDex(int newDex);
```

When you implement these methods, be sure to emit proper signals when you modify property values. Let's add more methods that correspond to the actions that a creature can take:

```
public:
  void attack(LivingEntity *enemy);
  void dodge();
  void wait();
  bool moveForward();
  bool moveBackward();
  void turnLeft();
  void turnRight();
```

The last four methods are simple to implement; for the first three methods, use the following code:

```
void LivingEntity::wait() {  if(hp() < maxHp()) setHp(hp()+1); }
```

```
void LivingEntity::dodge() {
    m_armorBonus += dex();
    emit armorChanged(armor()); // m_baseArmor + m_armorBonus
}
void LivingEntity::attack(LivingEntity *enemy) {
  if (baseAttack() <=0) return;
  int damage = qrand() % baseAttack();
  int enemyArmor = enemy->armor();
  int inflictedDamage = qMax(0, damage-enemyArmor);
  enemy->setHp(qMax(0, enemy->hp() - inflictedDamage));
}
```

Essentially, if the creature chooses to wait, it regains one hit point. If it dodges, this increases its chances to avoid damage when attacked. If it attacks another creature, this inflicts damage based on its own attack and the opponent's defensive score.

The next step is to implement the subclasses of `LivingEntity` so that we can manipulate the objects from Qt Script. To do this, implement the `NPC` class as follows:

```
class NPC : public LivingEntity {
  Q_OBJECT
public:
  NPC(QObject *parent = 0) : LivingEntity(parent) {}
public slots:
  void attack(LivingEntity *enemy) { LivingEntity::attack(enemy); }
  void dodge() { LivingEntity::dodge(); }
  void wait() { LivingEntity::wait(); }
  bool moveForward() { return LivingEntity::moveForward(); }
  bool moveBackward() { return LivingEntity::moveBackward(); }
  void turnLeft() { LivingEntity::turnLeft(); }
  void turnRight() { LivingEntity::turnRight(); }
};
```

What remains is to create a simple game engine to test our work. To do this, start by adding a `reset()` method to `LivingEntity` that will reset the armor bonus before every turn. Then, implement the `GameEngine` class:

```
class GameEngine : public QScriptEngine {
public:
  GameEngine(QObject *parent = 0) : QScriptEngine(parent) {
    m_timerId = 0;
    m_player = new LivingCreature(this);
    m_creature = new NPC(this);
    QScriptValue go = globalObject();
    go.setProperty("player", newQObject(m_player));
    go.setProperty("self", newQObject(m_creature));
  }
```

```
    LivingCreature *player() const {return m_player; }
    LivingCreature *npc() const { return m_creature; }
    void start(const QString &fileName) {
      if(m_timerId) killTimer(m_timerId);
      m_npcProgram = readScriptFromFile(fileName);
      m_timerId = startTimer(1000);
    }
  protected:
    QScriptProgram readScriptFromFile(const QString &fileName) const {
      QFile file(fileName);
      if(!file.open(QFile::ReadOnly|QFile::Text))
        return QScriptProgram();
      return QScriptProgram(file.readAll(), fileName);
    }
    void timerEvent(QTimerEvent *te) {
      if(te->timerId() != m_timerId) return;
      m_creature->reset();
      m_player->reset();
      evaluate(m_npcProgram);
    }
  private:
    LivingEntity *m_player;
    NPC *m_creature;
    QScriptProgram m_npcProgram;
    int m_timerId;
  };
```

Finally, write the main function:

```
int main(int argc, char **argv) {
  QCoreApplication app(argc, argv);
  GameEngine engine;

  engine.player()->setMaxHp(50);
  engine.player()->setHp(50);
  engine.player()->setDex(10);
  engine.player()->setBaseAttack(12);
  engine.player()->setArmor(3);

  engine.npc()->setMaxHp(100);
  engine.npc()->setHp(100);
  engine.npc()->setDex(4);
  engine.npc()->setBaseAttack(2);
  engine.npc()->setArmor(1);

  engine.start(argv[1]);
  return app.exec();
}
```

You can test the application using the following script:

```
print("Player HP:", player.hp)
print("Creature HP:", self.hp)
var val = Math.random() * 100
if(val < 50) {
  print("Attack!")
  self.attack(player)
} else {
  print("Dodge!");
  self.dodge();
}
```

What just happened?

We created two classes of objects: `LivingCreature`, which is the basic API to read data about a creature, and NPC, which provides a richer API. We obtained this effect by redeclaring the existing functions as slots. This is possible even when the methods are not virtual, as when slots are executed using Qt's meta-object system, they are always treated as if they were virtual methods—a declaration in the derived class always shadows the declaration in the parent class. Having the two classes, we exposed their instances to the scripting environment, and we use a timer to call a user-defined script every second. Of course, this is a very simple approach to scripting, which can easily be abused if the user calls multiple action functions in the script, for example, by calling `attack()` many times in one script, the creature can perform multiple strikes on the opponent. Speaking of `attack()`, note that it takes a `LivingCreature` pointer as its parameter. In the script, we fed it with the player object that corresponds to the needed type in C++. The conversion is done by Qt Script automatically. Therefore, you can define methods by taking `QObject` pointers and using them with `QObject` instances that are exposed to scripts. In a similar fashion, you can define functions by taking `QVariant` or `QScriptValue` and passing any value to them in the script. If the script engine is able to convert the given value to the requested type, it will do so.

Have a go hero – extending the Dungeons & Dragons game

Here is a number of ideas that can be used to extend our small game. The first is to add a script execution for the player as well so that it tries to defend against the creature. For that, you'll need to expose the creature's data using the `LivingCreature` API so that it is read only and exposes the player using a read-write interface. There are many ways to obtain it; the easiest is to provide two public `QObject` interfaces that operate on a shared pointer as shown in the following diagram:

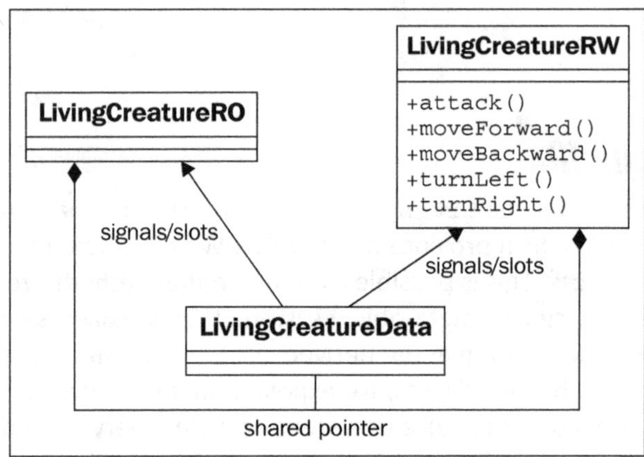

The API already contains methods to move creatures. You can extend the fighting rules to take into consideration the distance between opponents and their relative orientation (for example, striking from behind usually yields more damage than when standing face-to-face with the enemy). You can even introduce ranged combat. Extend the `LivingCreature` interface with the properties and methods that manipulate the creature's inventory. Allow the creature to change its active weapon.

The final modification that you can apply is to prevent cheating, using the mechanism described earlier. Instead of executing an action immediately, mark which action the script has chosen (along with its parameters) and only execute that action after the script finishes executing, for example, like this:

```
void timerEvent(QTimerEvent *te) {
  if(te->timerId() != m_timerId) return;
  m_creature.reset();
  m_player.reset();
  evaluate(m_npcProgram);
  evaluate(m_playerProgram);
  m_creature.executeAction();
  m_player.executeAction();
}
```

Another approach to this would be to assign action points to each creature's every turn and allow the creature to spend them on different actions. If there are not enough points left to execute an action, the script is notified about this and the action fails.

Exposing functions

Until now, we have been exporting objects to scripts and calling their properties and methods. However, there is also a way to call standalone C++ functions from scripts as well as call functions written in JavaScript from within C++ code. Let's have a look at how this works.

Exposing C++ functions to scripts

You can expose a standalone function to Qt Script with the help of the `QScriptEngine::newFunction()` call. It returns `QScriptValue` as any function in JavaScript, is also an object, and can be represented by `QScriptValue`. In C++, if a function accepts three parameters, you have to pass exactly three parameters when calling it. In JavaScript, this is different—you can always pass any number of parameters to a function, and it is the function's responsibility to do a proper argument validation. Therefore, the actual function that is exported should be wrapped in another function that will do what JavaScript expects from it before calling the actual function. The wrapper function needs to have an interface that is compatible with what `newFunction()` expects. It should take two parameters: the script context and the script engine, and it should return `QScriptValue`. The `context` contains all the information regarding the parameters of the function, including their count. Let's try wrapping a function that takes two integers and returns their sum:

```
int sum(int a, int b) { return a+b; }

QScriptValue sum_wrapper(QScriptContext *context,
  QScriptEngine *engine) {
  if(context->argumentCount() != 2) return engine->undefinedValue();
  QScriptValue arg0 = context->argument(0);
  QScriptValue arg1 = context->argument(1);
  if(!arg0.isNumber() || !arg1.isNumber())
  return engine->undefinedValue();
  return sum(arg0.toNumber()+arg1.toNumber());
}
```

Now that we have the wrapper, we can create a function object for it and export it to the scripting environment in exactly the same way as we export regular objects—by making it a property of the script's global object:

```
QScriptValue sumFunction = engine.newFunction(sum_wrapper, 2);
engine.globalObject().setProperty("sum", sumFunction);
```

The second argument to `newFunction()` defines how many arguments the function expects and is retrievable with the function object's length property. This is just for your information, as the caller can pass as many arguments as he/she wants. Try evaluating the following script after exporting the sum function:

```
print("Arguments expected:", sum.length)
print(sum(1,2,3) // sum returns Undefined
```

We can make use of such behavior and extend the functionality of our `sum` function by making it return a sum of all the parameters passed to it:

```
QScriptValue sum_wrapper(QScriptContext *context,
  QScriptEngine *engine) {
  int result = 0;
  for(int i=0; i<context->argumentCount();++i) {
    QScriptValue arg = context->argument(i);
    result = sum(result, arg.toNumber());
  }
  return result;
}
```

Now, you can call the sum with any number of arguments:

```
print(sum());
print(sum(1,2));
print(sum(1,2,3));
```

This brings us to an interesting question: can the function have different functionality depending on how many parameters you pass to it? The answer is positive; you can implement the function in any way you want, with the whole power of C++ at hand. There is a specific case for JavaScript when such behavior makes particular sense. This is when the function is supposed to work as a getter and setter for a property. Getters and setters are functions that are called when the script wants to retrieve or set the value of a property in some object. By attaching getters and setters to objects, you can control where the value is stored (if at all) and how it is retrieved. This opens the possibility of adding properties to the exported Qt objects that have not been declared with the `Q_PROPERTY` macro:

```
class CustomObject : public QObject {
  Q_OBJECT
public:
  CustomObject(QObject *parent = 0) : QObject(parent)
    { m_value = 0; }
  int value() const { return m_value; }
  void setValue(int v) { m_value = v; }
private:
  int m_value;
```

```
};

QScriptValue getSetValue(QScriptContext *, QScriptEngine*);
  // function prototype

int main(int argc, char **argv) {
  QCoreApplication app(argc, argv);
  QScriptEngine engine;
  CustomObject object;
  QScriptValue object_value = engine.newQObject(&object);
  QScriptValue getSetValue_fun = engine.newFunction(getSetValue);
  object_value.setProperty("value", getSetValue_fun,
    QScriptValue::PropertyGetter|QScriptValue::PropertySetter);
  engine.globalObject().setProperty("customObject", object_value);
  engine.evaluate("customObject.value = 42");
  qDebug() << object.value();
  return 0;
}
```

Let's analyze this code; here, we expose an instance of `CustomObject` to the script engine in a standard way. We also set the object's value property to a function, passing an additional value to `setProperty()`, which contains a set of flags that tell the scripting environment how it should treat the property. In this case, we tell it that the passed value should be used as a getter and setter for the property. Let's see how the function itself is implemented:

```
QScriptValue getSetValue(QScriptContext *context,
  QScriptEngine *engine) {
  QScriptValue object = context->thisObject();
  CustomObject *customObject =
    qobject_cast<CustomObject*>(object.toQObject());
  if(!customObject) return engine->undefinedValue();
  if(context->argumentCount() == 1) {
    // property setter
    customObject->setValue(context->argument(0).toNumber());
    return engine->undefinedValue();
  } else {
    // property getter
    return customObject->value();
  }
}
```

First, we ask the function the context for the value representing the object that the function is called on. Then, we extract a `CustomObject` pointer from it using `qobject_cast`. Next, we check the number of arguments to the function call. In the case of a setter, the function is passed one parameter—the value to be set to the property. In such a situation, we use a C++ method of the object to apply that value to the object. Otherwise, (no arguments are passed) the function is used as a getter and we return the value after fetching it with the C++ method.

Exposing script functions to C++

In the same way as C++ functions are exported to Qt Script with the use of `QScriptValue`, JavaScript functions can be imported to C++. You can ask for a script value representing a function like any other property. The following code asks the engine for the `Math.pow()` function, which performs the power operation on its arguments:

```
QScriptValue powFunction =
  engine.globalObject().property("Math").property("pow");
```

Having `QScriptValue` represent a function, you can invoke it using the value's `call()` method and pass any parameters as a list of script values:

```
QScriptValueList arguments = { QScriptValue(2), QScriptValue(10) };
QScriptValue result = powFunction.call(QScriptValue(), arguments);
qDebug() << result.toNumber(); // yields 1024
```

The first parameter to `call()` is the value that is to be used as the `this` object of the function. In this particular case, we pass an empty object since the function is standalone—it does not make any use of its environment. There are situations, however, when you will want to set an existing object here, for example, to allow a function to directly access the existing properties or define new properties of an object.

Let's use the newly learned functionality to improve our Dungeons & Dragons game in order to use a richer set of scripting functionality that is based on JavaScript functions and properties. The script used will contain a set of functions written in JavaScript that are going to be stored in the program and called in various situations. We'll be focusing here only on the scripting part. You will surely be able to fill in the C++ gaps yourself.

Time for action – storing the script

The first task is to read the script, extract the needed functions from it, and store them in a safe place. Then, load the project for the game and add a new class with the following code:

```
class AIScript {
public:
  QScriptProgram read(const QString &fileName);
  bool evaluate(const QScriptProgram &program,
    QScriptEngine *engine);
```

```
    QScriptValue initFunction;
    QScriptValue heartbeatFunction;
    QScriptValue defendFunction;
};
```

The reading method can have the same content as the original `readScriptFromFile` method. The evaluate method looks as follows:

```
bool AIScript::evaluate(const QScriptProgram &program,
  QScriptEngine *engine) {
  QScriptContext *context = engine->pushContext();
  QScriptValue activationObject;
  QScriptValue result = engine->evaluate(program);
  activationObject = context->activationObject();
  if(!result.isError()) {
    initFunction = activationObject.property("init");
    heartbeatFunction = activationObject.property("heartbeat");
    defendFunction = activationObject.property("defend");
  }
  engine->popContext();
  return !result.isError();
}
```

Modify the `GameEngine` class to make use of the new code (remember to add the `m_ai` class member):

```
void start(const QString &fileName) {
  m_ai = AIScript();
  QScriptProgram program = m_ai.read(fileName);
  m_ai.evaluate(program, this);
  qDebug() << m_ai.initFunction.toString();
  qDebug() << m_ai.heartbeatFunction.toString();
  qDebug() << m_ai.defendFunction.toString();
}
```

Run the program by feeding it the following script:

```
function init() {
  print("This is init function")
}

function heartbeat() {
  print("This is heartbeat function")
}

function defend() {
  print("This is defend function")
}
```

What just happened?

The `AIScript` object contains information about the AI for a single entity. The `start()` method now loads a script from the file and evaluates it. The script is expected to define a number of functions that are then retrieved from the activation object and stored in the `AIScript` object.

Time for action – providing an initialization function

The task for this exercise is to make it possible for the AI to initialize itself by invoking the `init()` function. Let's get right down to business. Extend the `AIScript` structure with yet another field:

```
QScriptValue m_thisObject;
```

This object will represent the AI itself. The script will be able to store data or define functions in it. Add the following code to the class as well:

```
void AIScript::initialize(QScriptEngine *engine) {
  m_thisObject = engine->newObject();
  engine->pushContext();
  initFunction.call(m_thisObject);
  engine->popContext();
}
```

Add a call to `initialize()` at the end of `start()`:

```
void start(const QString &fileName) {
  m_ai = AIScript();
  QScriptProgram program = m_ai.read(fileName);
  evaluate(program, this);
  m_ai.initialize(this);
}
```

Now, run the program using the following `init()` function:

```
function init() {
  print("This is init function")
  this.distance = function(p1, p2) {
    // Manhattan distance
    return Math.abs(p1.x-p2.x)+Math.abs(p1.y-p2.y)
  }
  this.actionHistory = []
}
```

What just happened?

In initialize, we prepare the script object with an empty JavaScript object and we call the function stored in `initFunction`, passing the script object as this. The function prints a debug statement and defines two properties in this object—one is a function to calculate the Manhattan distance and the other is an empty array where we will store a history of actions that the AI has taken.

Manhattan distance is a metric to calculate the distance between objects; this is much faster to calculate than the real Euclidean distance. It is based on the assumption that when traversing a large city with a grid of buildings, one can only follow streets that go along those buildings and take 90 degree turns. The Manhattan distance between positions is then the number of crossings one has to walk through to get from the source to the destination. In C++ and Qt, you can compute this distance easily using the `manhattanLength()` method in the `QPoint` class.

Time for action – implementing the heartbeat event

The heart of AI is the heartbeat function that is executed at equal intervals of time to allow the AI to decide about the actions of the object. The script that is executed will have access to the creature that it operates on as well as its environment. It can also use anything that it defines in the `this` object. Now, add a heartbeat function to `AIScript`:

```
void AIScript::heartbeat(QScriptEngine *engine, QObject *personObject,
  QObject *otherObject) {
  QScriptValueList params;
  params << engine->newQObject(personObject);
  m_thisObject.setProperty("enemy", engine->newQObject(otherObject));
  heartbeatFunction.call(m_thisObject, params);
  m_thisObject.setProperty("enemy", QScriptValue::UndefinedValue);
}
```

Bring the timer back, set it to `start()`, and also enable the running heartbeat functionality from within the timer event:

```
void timerEvent(QTimerEvent *te) {
    if(te->timerId() != m_timerId) return;
    m_creature->reset();
    m_player->reset();
    m_ai.heartbeat(this, m_creature, m_player);
}
```

Run the program, giving it the following `heartbeat` function:

```
function heartbeat(person) {
  person.attack(this.enemy)
  this.actionHistory.push("ATTACK")
}
```

What just happened?

In `heartbeat`, we proceed in similar way as with `init`, but here, we pass the creature that the AI works on as a parameter of the function and we set the other entity as the enemy property of the `this` object, which makes it accessible to the function. After the call we remove the enemy property from the this object. The function itself performs an attack on the enemy and pushes an entry to the script object history. Unlike a direct invocation of evaluate when making a function call we don't have to push and pop an execution context as it is done for us automatically during `QScriptValue::call`.

Have a go hero – defending against attacks

You may have noticed that we left out the defend script. Try extending the game by calling a script whenever the subject is attacked by the opponent. In the script, allow the creature to take different defensive stances, such as evading, blocking, or parrying attacks. Make each action have a different influence on the outcome of the strike. Also, apply all the modifications that you made to the original game. Try expanding on the code that was already written by providing additional hooks where scripts are run and adding new actions and objects. How about adding more enemies to the game? What about organizing a contest for the best AI algorithm?

Using signals and slots in scripts

Qt Script also offers the capability to use signals and slots. The slot can be either a C++ method or a JavaScript function. The connection can be made either in C++ or in the script.

First, let's see how to establish a connection within a script. When a `QObject` instance is exposed to a script, the object's signals become the properties of the wrapping object. These properties have a `connect` method that accepts a function object that is to be called when the signal is emitted. The receiver can be a regular slot or a JavaScript function. To connect the `clicked()` signal of an object called `button` to a `clear()` slot of another object called `lineEdit`, you can use the following statement:

```
button.clicked.connect(lineEdit.clear)
```

If the receiver is a standalone function called `clearLineEdit`, the call becomes:

```
button.clicked.connect(clearLineEdit)
```

You can also connect a signal to an anonymous function that was defined directly in the connection statement:

```
button.clicked.connect(function() { lineEdit.clear() })
```

There is additional syntax available where you can define the `this` object for the function:

```
var obj = { "name": "FooBar" }
button.clicked.connect(obj, function() { print(this.name) })
```

If you need to disconnect a signal from within a script, just replace `connect` with `disconnect`:

```
button.clicked.disconnect(clearLineEdit)
```

Emitting signals from within the script is also easy—just call the signal as a function and pass to it any necessary parameters:

```
spinBox.valueChanged(7)
```

To create a signal-slot connection on the C++ side where the receiver is a script function, instead of a regular `connect()` statement, use `qScriptConnect()`. Its first two parameters are identical with the regular call and the two other parameters correspond to a script value that represents an object that is to act as the `this` object and a script value that represents a function to be called:

```
QScriptValue function = engine.evaluate("(function() { })");
qScriptConnect(button, SIGNAL(clicked()), QScriptValue(), function);
```

In this particular example, we pass an invalid object as the third parameter. In such a case, the `this` object will point to the engine's global object.

As for disconnecting signals, of course, there is `qScriptDisconnect()` available.

Have a go hero – triggering defense using signals and slots

As a task for yourself, try modifying the Dungeons & Dragons game so that the defend script function is not called manually by the script engine, but instead is invoked using a signal-slot connection. Have a creature emit the `attacked()` signal when it is attacked, and let the script connect a handler to that signal. Use a variant of connect that defines the `this` object for the connection.

Creating Qt objects in scripts

Using existing objects from scripts sometimes is not enough to get a rich scripting experience. It is also useful to be able to create new Qt objects from within scripts and even return them to C++ so that they can be used by the game engine. There are two ways to approach this problem. Before we describe them, it is important to understand how JavaScript instantiates objects.

JavaScript has no notion of classes. It constructs objects using prototypes—a prototype is an object whose properties are cloned into the new object. The object is constructed by invoking a constructor, which can be any function. When you invoke a function using the keyword new, the engine creates a new empty object, sets its constructor property to the function serving as the constructor, sets the object prototype to the function's prototype, and finally, invokes the function in the context of the new object, making that function act as a factory function for objects with a particular set of properties. Therefore, to construct objects of the type `QLineEdit`, there needs to be a function that can be called as a constructor for objects that behave like Qt's widget to enter a single line of text.

We already know that functions can be stored in `QScriptValue` objects. There are two ways to obtain a function that can act as a constructor for Qt objects. First, we can implement it ourselves:

```
QScriptValue pushbutton_ctor(QScriptContext *context,
  QScriptEngine *engine) {
    QScriptValue parentValue = context->argument(0);
    QWidget *parent = qscriptvalue_cast<QWidget*>(parentValue);
    QPushButton *button = new QPushButton(parent);
    QScriptValue buttonValue = engine->newQObject(button,
      QScriptEngine::AutoOwnership);
    return buttonValue;
}
QScriptValue buttonConstructor = engine.newFunction(pushbutton_ctor);
engine.globalObject().setProperty("QPushButton", buttonConstructor);
```

We did three things here. First, we defined a function that instantiates `QPushButton` with a parent passed as the first argument to the function, wraps the object in `QScriptValue` (with an extra parameter noting that the environment responsible for deleting the object should be determined by the parent object), and that returns `QScriptValue` to the caller. Secondly, we wrapped the function itself into `QScriptValue` as we already did earlier with other functions. Finally, we set the function as a property of the global object of the engine so that it is always accessible.

The second way to obtain a constructor function is to make use of Qt's meta-object system. You can use the following macro to define a constructor function very similar to what we have written manually:

```
Q_SCRIPT_DECLARE_QMETAOBJECT(QPushButton, QWidget*)
```

Next, you can use the `QScriptEngine::scriptValueFromQMetaObject()` template method to get a script value wrapping that function:

```
QScriptValue pushButtonClass =
  engine.scriptValueFromQMetaObject<QPushButton>();
```

Lastly, you can set the obtained script value as a constructor in the script engine just like before. Here is a complete code to make push buttons creatable from within the scripts:

```
#include <QtWidgets>
#include <QScriptEngine>

Q_SCRIPT_DECLARE_QMETAOBJECT(QPushButton, QWidget*)

int main(int argc, char **argv) {
  QApplication app(argc, argv);
  QScriptEngine engine;
  QScriptValue pushButtonClass
  = engine.scriptValueFromQMetaObject<QPushButton>();
  engine.globalObject().setProperty("QPushButton",
    pushButtonClass);
  QString script = "pushButton = new QPushButton\n"
                   "pushButton.text = 'Script Button'\n"
                   "pushButton.show()";
  engine.evaluate(script);
  return app.exec();
}
```

Error recovery and debugging

The only error recovery we've talked about so far is checking whether a script has ended up with an error and executing a script in a dedicated context to prevent polluting the namespace with local variables that are not used anymore. This is already a lot; however, we can do more. First, we can take care of preventing pollution of the global namespace. Pushing and popping the execution context does not prevent a script from modifying the engine's global object, and we should prevent situations when a script, for example, replaces the `Math` object or the print function. The solution is to provide your own global object in place of the original one. There are two easy ways to do this. First, you can use the class called `QScriptValueIterator` to copy all the properties of the global object to a new object:

```
QScriptValue globalObject = engine.globalObject();
QScriptValue newGO = engine.newObject();
QScriptValueIterator iter(globalObject);
while(iter.hasNext()) {
  iter.next(); newGO.setProperty(iter.key(), iter.value());
}
```

Alternatively, you can set the original global object as an internal prototype of the new object:

```
QScriptValue globalObject = engine.globalObject();
QScriptValue newGO = engine.newObject();
newGO.setPrototype(globalObject);
```

Either way, you will then need to replace the original global object with the temporary one:

```
engine.setGlobalObject(newGO);
```

The other big thing to do when talking about error recovery is to provide debugging capabilities for scripts. Luckily, Qt contains a built-in component to debug scripts. If you build your project with the `QT+=scripttools` option, you will gain access to the `QScriptEngineDebugger` class. To start using the debugger with a script engine, you need to attach and bind them:

```
QScriptEngine engine;
QScriptEngineDebugger debugger;
debugger.attachTo(&engine);
```

Whenever an uncaught exception occurs, the debugger will kick in and show its window:

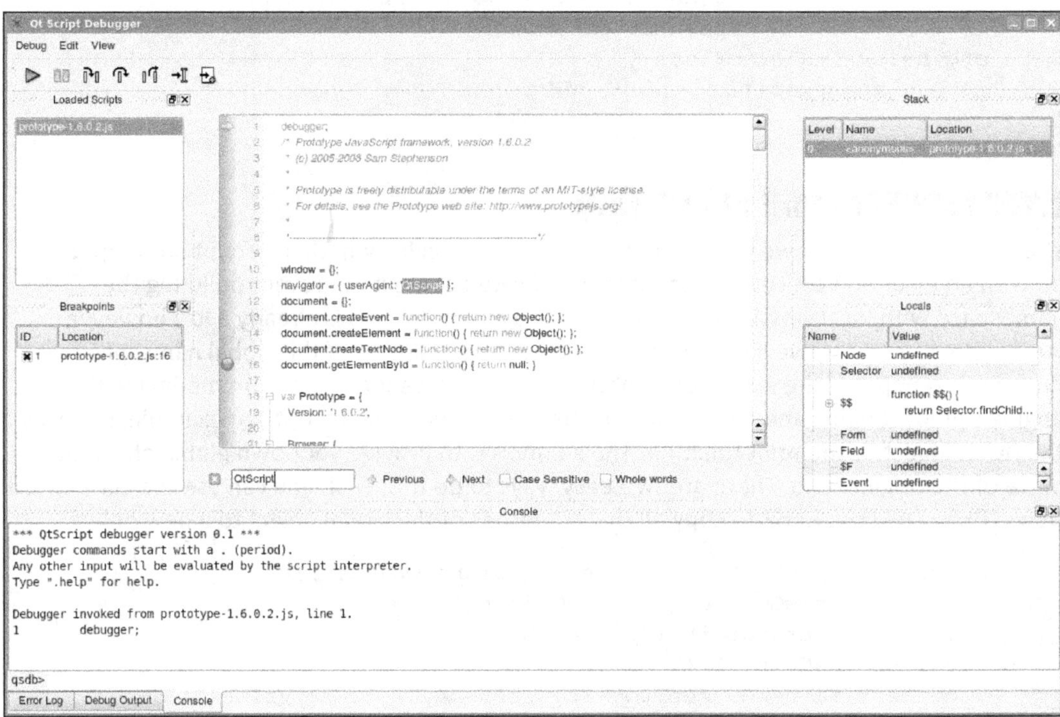

You can then set breakpoints in the script, inspect variables or the call stack, and continue or break the execution. A good idea is to incorporate the debugger in your game so that script designers can use it when developing scripts. Of course, the debugger should not be running with the release version of the game.

Extensions

`QScriptEngine` has the ability to import extensions that provide additional functionality to the scripting environment (for example, a library of utility functions that can be used in different parts of the game without having to redefine them here and there) using the `importExtension()` method. The extension can be implemented in JavaScript by providing a set of files that contain scripts, making the extension or in C++ by subclassing `QScriptExtensionPlugin`. Now, we will focus on the second approach. Here is how a simple C++ extension looks:

```
class SimpleExtension : public QScriptExtensionPlugin {
  Q_OBJECT
  Q_PLUGIN_METADATA(IID "org.qt- project.Qt.QScriptExtensionInterface")
public:
  SimpleExtension(QObject *parent = 0) :
    QScriptExtensionPlugin(parent) {}
  QStringList keys() const Q_DECL_OVERRIDE
    { return QStringList() << "simple"; }
  void initialize(const QString &key, QScriptEngine *engine) {
    QScriptValue simple = engine->newObject();
    simple.setProperty("name", "This is text from Simple extension");
    engine->globalObject().setProperty("Simple", simple);
  }
};
```

The extension defined here is simple—it only attaches one property to the engine's global object, which has a name property returning as a text string. You should put the resulting library in a subdirectory called `Simple` in a script subdirectory of a directory where your application looks for plugins (for example, the application where your application binary is placed). Then, you can import the plugin using `importExtension()`:

```
QScriptEngine engine;
engine.importExtension("Simple");
engine.evaluate("print(Simple.name)")
```

Refer to the *Deploying Plugins* section of the Qt reference manual for more information about where you can put plugins and how you can tell Qt where to look for them.

The other Qt JavaScript environment

As mentioned at the beginning of this chapter, Qt provides two environments to use JavaScript. We already talked about Qt Script; now it is time for us to tell you about its counterpart: `QJSEngine`. The newer JavaScript engine in Qt, which is also used for QML, about which you will learn in the next chapter. It has a different internal architecture than Qt Script, but most of what we have taught you also applies to `QJSEngine`. The main difference is that the root classes are named differently. Have a look at the following table, which shows equivalent classes for the two engines:

QtScript	QJSEngine
`QScriptEngine`	`QJSEngine`
`QScriptValue`	`QJSValue`
`QScriptContext`	-

The `QJSEngine` class is the equivalent of `QScriptEngine`. It also has an `evaluate()` method that is used to evaluate scripts. This method can create objects, wrap `QObject` instances, and use `QJSValue` (the equivalent of `QScriptValue`) to store values used in scripts in a way that they can be accessed from C++. You can also see that there is no equivalent to `QScriptContext` and thus its functionality is not available in the implementation based on `QJSEngine`. Another missing component is the integrated engine debugger. Also, at the time of writing, there is no easy way to export your own classes to the `QJSEngine`-based JavaScript environment to allow the creation of instances of those classes.

Alternatives to JavaScript

Qt Script is an environment that is designed to be part of the Qt world. Since not everyone knows or likes JavaScript, we will present another language that can easily be used to provide scripting environments for games that are created with Qt. Just be aware that this is not going to be an in-depth description of the environment—we will just show you the basics that can provide foundations for your own research.

Python

A popular language used for scripting is Python. There are two variants of Qt bindings that are available for Python: PySide and PyQt. PySide is the official binding that is available under LGPL, but currently, it only work with Qt 4. PyQt is a third-party library that is available under GPL v3 and commercial licenses that have variants for Qt 4 as well as Qt 5. Note that PyQt is not available under LGPL, so for commercial closed-source products you need to obtain a commercial license from Riverbank Computing!

These bindings allow you to use the Qt API from within Python—you can write a complete Qt application using just Python. However, to call Python code from within C++, you will need a regular Python interpreter. Luckily, it is very easy to embed such an interpreter in a C++ application.

First, you will need Python installed along with its development package. For example, for Debian-based systems, it is easiest to simply install the `libpythonX.Y-dev` (or a newer) package, where `X` and `Y` stand for the version of Python:

```
sudo apt-get install libpython3.3-dev
```

Then, you need to tell your program to link it against the library:

```
LIBS += -lpython3.3m
INCLUDEPATH += /usr/include/python3.3m/
```

To call Python code from within a Qt app, the simplest way is to use the following code:

```
#include <Python.h>
#include <QtCore>

int main(int argc, char **argv) {
  QApplication app(argc, argv);
  Py_SetProgramName(argv[0]);
  Py_Initialize();
  const char *script = "print(\"Hello from Python\")"
  PyRun_SimpleString(script);
  Py_Finalize();
  return app.exec();
}
```

This code initializes a Python interpreter, then invokes a script by passing it directly as a string, and finally, it shuts down the interpreter before invoking Qt's event loop. Such code makes sense only for simple scripting. In real life, you'd want to pass some data to the script or fetch the result. For that, we have to write some more code. As the library exposes the C API only, let's write a nice Qt wrapper for it.

Time for action – writing a Qt wrapper for embedding Python

As the first task, we will implement the last program using an object-oriented API. Create a new console project and add the following class to it:

```
#include <Python.h>
#include <QObject>
#include <QString>
```

```
class QtPython : public QObject {
  Q_OBJECT
public:
  QtPython(const char *progName, QObject *parent = 0) :
QObject(parent) {
    if(progName != 0) {
        wchar_t buf[strlen(progName+1)];
        mbstowcs(buf, progName, strlen(progName));
        Py_SetProgramName(buf);
    }
    Py_InitializeEx(0);
  }
  ~QtPython() { Py_Finalize(); }
  void run(const QString &program) {
    PyRun_SimpleString(qPrintable(program));
  }
};
```

Then, add a `main()` function as shown in the following snippet:

```
#include "qtpython.h"

int main(int argc, char **argv) {
  QtPython python(argv[0]);
  python.run("print('Hello from Python')");
  return 0;
}
```

Finally open the `.pro` file and tell Qt to link with the Python library. In case of Linux you can use `pkg-config` by adding two lines to the file:

```
CONFIG += link_pkgconfig
PKGCONFIG += python-3.3m # adjust the version number to suit your
needs
```

You might need to install Python library using a call equivalent to `apt-get install libpython3.4-dev`. For Windows you need to manually pass information to the compiler:

```
INCLUDEPATH += C:\Python33\include
LIBS += -LC:\Python33\include -lpython33
```

What just happened?

We created a class called `QtPython` that wraps the Python C API for us.

Never use a `Q` prefix to call your custom classes, as this prefix is reserved for official Qt classes. This is to make sure that your code will never have a name clash with future code added to Qt. The Qt prefix on the other hand is meant to be used with classes that are extensions to Qt. You probably still shouldn't use it, but the probability of a name clash is much smaller and yields a lesser impact than clashes with an official class. It is best to come up with your own prefix (such as `Qxy`, where `x` and `y` are your initials).

The class constructor creates a Python interpreter and the class destructor destroys it. We use `Py_InitializeEx(0)`, which has the same functionality as `Py_Initialize()`, but it does not apply C signal handlers, as this is not something we would want when embedding Python. Prior to this, we use `Py_SetProgramName()` to inform the interpreter of our context. We also defined a `run()` method, taking `QString` and returning `void`. It uses `qPrintable()`, which is a convenience function that extracts a C string pointer from a `QString` object, which is then fed into `PyRun_SimpleString()`.

Never store the output of `qPrintable()` as it returns an internal pointer to a temporary byte array (this is equivalent to calling `toLocal8Bit().constData()` on a string). It is safe to use directly, but the byte array is destroyed immediately afterwards; thus, if you store the pointer in a variable, the data may not be valid later when you try using that pointer.

The hardest work when using embedded interpreters is to convert values between C++ and the types that the interpreter expects. With Qt Script, the `QScriptValue` type was used for this. We can implement something similar for our Python scripting environment.

Time for action – converting data between C++ and Python

Create a new class and call it `QtPythonValue`. Then, add the following code to it:

```
#include <Python.h>

class QtPythonValue {
public:
  QtPythonValue() { incRef(Py_None);}
```

```
    QtPythonValue(const QtPythonValue &other) { incRef(other.m_value); }
    QtPythonValue& operator=(const QtPythonValue &other) {
      if(m_value == other.m_value) return *this;
      decRef();
      incRef(other.m_value);
      return *this;
    }

    QtPythonValue(int val) {  m_value = PyLong_FromLong(val); }
    QtPythonValue(const QString &str) {
      m_value = PyUnicode_FromString(qPrintable(str));
    }
    ~QtPythonValue() { decRef(); }
    int toInt() const { return PyLong_Check(m_value) ? PyLong_AsLong
                                           (m_value) : 0; }
    QString toString() const {
      return PyUnicode_Check(m_value) ? QString::fromUtf8(PyUnicode_
      AsUTF8(m_value)) : QString();
    }
    bool isNone() const { return m_value == Py_None; }

  private:
    QtPythonValue(PyObject *ptr) { m_value = ptr; }
    void incRef() { if(m_value) Py_INCREF(m_value); }
    void incRef(PyObject *val) { m_value = val; incRef(); }
    void decRef() { if(m_value) Py_DECREF(m_value); }
    PyObject *m_value;
    friend class QtPython;
  };
```

Next, let's modify the `main()` function to test our new code:

```
#include "qtpython.h"
#include "qtpythonvalue.h"
#include <QtDebug>

int main(int argc, char *argv[]) {
    QtPython python(argv[0]);
    QtPythonValue integer = 7, string = QStringLiteral("foobar"),
      none;
    qDebug() << integer.toInt() << string.toString() << none.isNone();
    return 0;
}
```

When you run the program, you will see that the conversion between C++ and Python works correctly in both directions.

What just happened?

The `QtPythonValue` class wraps a `PyObject` pointer (through the `m_value` member), providing a nice interface to convert between what the interpreter expects and our Qt types. Let's see how this is done. First, take a look at the three private methods: two versions of `incRef()` and one `decRef()`. `PyObject` contains an internal reference counter that counts the number of handles on the contained value. When that counter drops to `0`, the object can be destroyed. Our three methods use adequate Python C API calls to increase or decrease the counter in order to prevent memory leaks and keep Python's garbage collector happy.

The second important aspect is that the class defines a private constructor that takes a `PyObject` pointer, effectively creating a wrapper over the given value. The constructor is private; however, the `QtPython` class is declared as a friend of `QtPythonValue`, which means that only `QtPython` and `QtPythonValue` can instantiate values by passing `PyObject` pointers to it. Now, let's have a look at public constructors.

The default constructor creates an object pointing to a `None` value, which is Python's equivalent to the C++ null. The copy constructor and assignment operator are pretty standard, taking care of bookkeeping of the reference counter. Then, we have two constructors—one taking `int` and the other taking a `QString` value. They use appropriate Python C API calls to obtain a `PyObject` representation of the value. Note that these calls already increase the reference count for us, so we don't have to do it ourselves.

The code ends with a destructor that decreases the reference counter and three methods that provide safe conversions from `QtPythonValue` to appropriate Qt/C++ types.

Have a go hero – implementing the remaining conversions

Now, you should be able to implement other constructors and conversions for `QtPythonValue` that operates on the `float`, `bool`, or even on `QDate` and `QTime` types. Try implementing them yourself. If needed, have a look at `https://docs.python.org/3/` to find appropriate calls that you should use. We'll give you a head start by providing a skeleton implementation of how to convert `QVariant` to `QtPythonValue`. This is especially important because Python makes use of two types whose equivalents are not available in C++, namely, tuples and dictionaries. We will need them later, so having a proper implementation is crucial. Here is the code:

```
QtPythonValue::QtPythonValue(const QVariant &variant)
{
  switch(variant.type()) {
    case QVariant::Invalid: incRef(Py_None);
    return;
    case QVariant::String: m_value
```

```
      = PyUnicode_FromString(qPrintable(variant.toString()));
    return;
    case QVariant::Int: m_value = PyLong_FromLong(variant.toInt());
    return;
    case QVariant::LongLong: m_value
      = PyLong_FromLongLong(variant.toLongLong());
    return;
    case QVariant::List: {
      QVariantList list = variant.toList();
      const int listSize = list.size();
      PyObject *tuple = PyTuple_New(listSize);
      for(int i=0;i<listSize;++i) {
        PyTuple_SetItem(tuple, i, QtPythonValue(list.at(i)).m_value);
      }
      m_value = tuple;
      return;
    }
    case QVariant::Map: {
      QVariantMap map = variant.toMap();
      PyObject *dict = PyDict_New();
      for(QVariantMap::const_iterator iter = map.begin();
      iter != map.end(); ++iter) {
        PyDict_SetItemString(dict,
            qPrintable(iter.key()),
            QtPythonValue(iter.value()).m_value
        );
    }
    m_value = dict;
    return;
  }
  default: incRef(Py_None); return;
  }
}
```

The highlighted code shows how to create a tuple (which is a list of arbitrary elements) from `QVariantList` and how to create a dictionary (which is an associative array) from `QVariantMap`. Try adding constructors by taking `QStringList`, `QVariantList`, and `QVariantMap` directly and returning tuples or a dictionary, respectively.

We have written quite a lot of code now, but so far there is no way of binding any data from our programs with Python scripting. Let's change that.

Time for action – calling functions and returning values

The next task is to provide ways to invoke Python functions and return values from scripts. Let's start by providing a richer `run()` API. Implement the following method in the `QtPython` class:

```
QtPythonValue QtPython::run(const QString &program,
  const QtPythonValue &globals, const QtPythonValue &locals)
{
  PyObject *retVal = PyRun_String(qPrintable(program),
    Py_file_input, globals.m_value, locals.m_value);
  return QtPythonValue(retVal);
}
```

We'll also need a functionality to import Python modules. Add the following methods to the class:

```
QtPythonValue QtPython::import(const QString &name) const {
  return QtPythonValue(PyImport_ImportModule(qPrintable(name)));
}

QtPythonValue QtPython::addModule(const QString &name) const {
  PyObject *retVal = PyImport_AddModule(qPrintable(name));
  Py_INCREF(retVal);
  return QtPythonValue(retVal);
}

QtPythonValue QtPython::dictionary(const QtPythonValue &module) const
{
  PyObject *retVal = PyModule_GetDict(module.m_value);
  Py_INCREF(retVal);
  return QtPythonValue(retVal);
}
```

The last piece of the code is to extend `QtPythonValue` with this code:

```
bool QtPythonValue::isCallable() const {
  return PyCallable_Check(m_value);
}

QtPythonValue QtPythonValue::attribute(const QString &name) const {
  return QtPythonValue(PyObject_GetAttrString(m_value,
  qPrintable(name)));
}
```

```
bool QtPythonValue::setAttribute(const QString &name, const
QtPythonValue &value) {
  int retVal = PyObject_SetAttrString(m_value, qPrintable(name),
    value.m_value);
  return retVal != -1;
}

QtPythonValue QtPythonValue::call(const QVariantList &arguments) const
{
  return QtPythonValue(PyObject_CallObject
    (m_value, QtPythonValue(arguments).m_value));
}

QtPythonValue QtPythonValue::call(const QStringList &arguments) const
{
  return QtPythonValue(PyObject_CallObject
    (m_value, QtPythonValue(arguments).m_value));
}
```

Finally, you can modify `main()` to test the new functionality:

```
int main(int argc, char *argv[]) {
  QtPython python(argv[0]);

  QtPythonValue mainModule = python.addModule("__main__");
  QtPythonValue dict = python.dictionary(mainModule);
  python.run("foo = (1, 2, 3)", dict, dict);
  python.run("print(foo)", dict, dict);

  QtPythonValue module = python.import("os");
  QtPythonValue chdir = module.attribute("chdir");
  chdir.call(QStringList() << "/home");
  QtPythonValue func = module.attribute("getcwd");
  qDebug() << func.call(QVariantList()).toString();

  return 0;
}
```

You can replace `/home` with a directory of your choice. Then, you can run the program.

What just happened?

We did two tests in the last program. First, we used the new `run()` method, passing to it the code that is to be executed and two dictionaries that define the current execution context—the first dictionary contains global symbols and the second contains local symbols. The dictionaries come from Python's `__main__` module (which among other things, defines the `print` function). The `run()` method may modify the contents of the two dictionaries—the first call defines the tuple called `foo` and the second call prints it to the standard output.

The second test calls a function from an imported module; in this case, we call two functions from the `os` module—the first function, `chdir`, changes the current working directory and the other called `getcwd` returns the current working directory. The convention is that we should pass a tuple to `call()`, where we pass the needed parameters. The first function takes a string as a parameter, therefore, we pass a `QStringList` object, assuming that there is a `QtPythonValue` constructor that converts `QStringList` to a tuple (you need to implement it if you haven't done it already). Since the second function does not take any parameters, we pass an empty tuple to the call. In the same way, you can provide your own modules and call functions from them, query the results, inspect dictionaries, and so on. This is a pretty good start for an embedded Python interpreter. Remember that a proper component should have some error checking code to avoid crashing the whole application.

You can extend the functionality of the interpreter in many ways. You can even use PyQt5 to use Qt bindings in scripts, combining Qt/C++ code with Qt/Python code.

Have a go hero – wrapping Qt objects into Python objects

At this point, you should be experienced enough to try and implement a wrapper for the `QObject` instances to expose signals and slots to Python scripting. If you decide to pursue the goal, `https://docs.python.org/3/` will be your best friend, especially the section about extending Python with C++. Remember that `QMetaObject` provides information about the properties and methods of Qt objects and `QMetaObject::invokeMethod()` allows you to execute a method by its name. This is not an easy task, so don't be hard on yourself if you are not able to complete it. You can always return to it once you gain more experience in using Qt and Python.

Before you head on to the next chapter, try testing your knowledge about scripting in Qt.

Pop quiz – scripting

Q1. Which is the method that you can use to execute JavaScript statements?

1. `QScriptEngine::run()`
2. `QScriptEngine::evaluate()`
3. `QScriptProgram::execute()`

Q2. What is the name of the class that serves as a bridge to exchange data between Qt Script and C++?

1. `QScriptContext`
2. `QScriptValue`
3. `QVariant`

Q3. What is the name of the class that serves as a bridge that is used to exchange data between Python and C++?

1. `PyValue`
2. `PyObject`
3. `QVariant`

Q4. How do execution contexts work?

1. They mark some variables as "executable" to prevent rogue code from being executed.
2. They allow executing scripts in parallel, improving their speed.
3. They contain all the variables defined within a function invocation so that a set of variables visible from within a script can be modified without affecting the global environment (called sandboxing).

Summary

In this chapter, you learned that providing a scripting environment to your games opens up new possibilities. Implementing a functionality using scripting languages is usually faster than doing the full write-compile-test cycle with C++ and you can even use the skills and creativity of your users who have no understanding of the internals of your game engine to make your games better and more feature-rich. You were shown how to use Qt Script, which blends the C++ and JavaScript worlds together by exposing Qt objects to JavaScript and making cross-language signal-slot connections. If you're not a JavaScript fan, you learned the basics of scripting with Python. There are other scripting languages available (for example Lua) and many of them can be used together with Qt. Using the experience gained in this chapter, you should even be able to bring other scripting environments to your programs, as most embeddable interpreters offer similar approaches to that of Python.

In the next chapter, you will be introduced to an environment very much like Qt Script in the way that it is heavily based on JavaScript. However, the purpose of using it is completely different—we will be using it to bleed edge-fancy graphics. Welcome to the world of Qt Quick.

9

Qt Quick Basics

In this chapter, you are going to be introduced to a technology called Qt Quick that allows us to implement resolution-independent user interfaces with lots of eye-candy, animations, and effects that can be combined with regular Qt code that implements the logic of the application. You will learn the basics of the QML declarative language that forms the foundation of Qt Quick. Using this language, you can define fancy graphics and animations, make use of particle engines, and structure your code using finite state machines. Pure QML code can be complemented with JavaScript or C++ logic in a manner similar to what you have learned in the previous chapter. By the end of this chapter, you should have enough knowledge to quickly implement fantastic 2D games with custom graphics, moving elements, and lots of visual special effects.

Fluid user interfaces

So far, we have been looking at graphical user interfaces as a set of panels embedded one into another. This is well-reflected in the world of desktop utility programs composed of windows and subwindows containing mostly static content scattered throughout a large desktop area where the user can use a mouse pointer to move windows around or adjust their size. However, this design doesn't correspond well with modern user interfaces that often try to minimize the area they occupy (because of either a small display size like with embedded and mobile devices or to avoid obscuring the main display panel like in games), at the same time providing rich content with a lot of moving or dynamically resizing items. Such user interfaces are often called "fluid" to signify that they are not formed as a number of separate different screens, but rather contain dynamic content and layout where one screen fluently transforms into another. Part of Qt 5 is the Qt Quick (Qt User Interface Creation Kit) module, which provides a runtime to create rich applications with fluid user interfaces. It builds upon a two-dimensional hardware accelerated canvas that contains a hierarchy of interconnected items.

Declarative UI programming

Although it is technically possible to use Qt Quick by writing C++ code, the module is accompanied by a dedicated programming language called **QML** (**Qt Modeling Language**). QML is an easy to read and understand declarative language that describes the world as a hierarchy of components that interact and relate to one another. It uses a JSON-like syntax and allows us to use imperative JavaScript expressions as well as dynamic property bindings. So, what is a declarative language, anyway?

Declarative programming is one of the programming paradigms that dictates that the program describes the logic of the computation without specifying how this result should be obtained. In contrast to imperative programming, where the logic is expressed as a list of explicit steps forming an algorithm that directly modifies the intermediate program state, a declarative approach focuses on what the ultimate result of the operation should be.

We use QML by creating one or more QML documents where we define hierarchies of objects. Each document is composed of two sections.

You can follow every example we explain in Qt Creator by creating a new Qt Quick UI project and placing the presented code in the QML file created for you. The details about using this project type will be described in a later section of this chapter.

If you can't see a **Qt Quick UI** project in the Creator's wizard, you have to enable a plugin called `QmlProjectManager` by choosing the **About Plugins** entry from the Creator's **Help** menu, then scrolling down to the **QtQuick** section, and making sure the **QmlProjectManager** entry is checked. If it is not, check it and restart Creator:

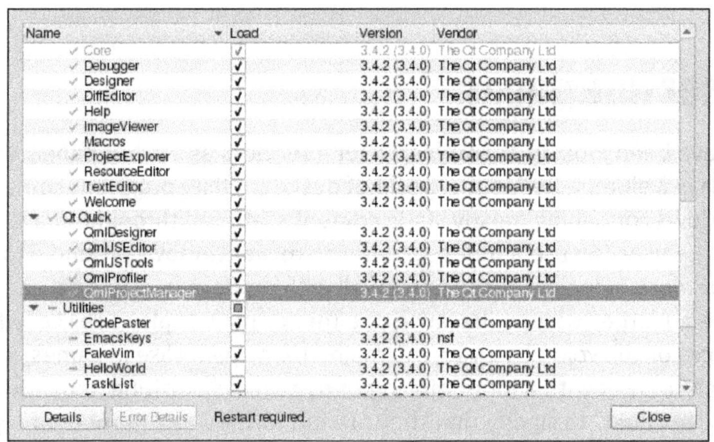

The first section contains a series of `import` statements that define the range of components that can be used in a particular document. In its simplest form, each statement consists of the `import` keyword followed by the module URI (name) and the module version to import. The following statement imports the `QtQuick` module in version 2.1:

```
import QtQuick 2.1
```

The second section contains a definition of a hierarchy of objects. Each object declaration consists of two parts. First, you have to specify the type of the object and then follow it with the detailed definition enclosed in braces. Since the detailed definition can be empty, the simplest object declaration is similar to the following:

```
Item { }
```

This declares an instance of the `Item` element, which is the most basic Qt Quick element and represents an abstract item of the user interface without any visual appearance.

Element properties

Each element type in QML defines a number of properties. Values for these properties can be set as part of the detailed definition of an object. The `Item` type brings a number of properties for specifying the geometry of an item:

```
Item {
  x: 10
  y: 20
  width: 400
  height: 300
}
```

`Item` is a very interesting and useful element, but since it is totally transparent, we will now focus on its descendant type that draws a filled rectangle. This type is called `Rectangle`. It has a number of additional properties, among them, the `color` property for specifying the fill color of the rectangle. To define a red square, we could write the following code:

```
Rectangle {
  color: "red"
  width: 400
  height: 400
}
```

The problem with this code is that if we ever decide to change the size of the square, we will have to update values for the two properties separately. However, we can use the power of the declarative approach and specify one of the properties as a relation to the other properties:

```
Rectangle {
  color: "red"
```

```
    width: 400
    height: width
}
```

This is called **property binding**. It differs from a regular value assignment and binds the value of height to the value of width. Whenever width changes, height will reflect that change in its own value.

Note that the order of statements in the definition does not matter as you declare relations between properties. The following declaration is semantically identical to the previous one:

```
Rectangle {
    height: width
    color: "red"
    width: 400
}
```

You can bind a property not only to a value of another property, but also to any JavaScript statement that returns a value. For example, we can declare rectangle color to be dependent on the proportions between the width and the height of the element by using a ternary conditional expression operator:

```
Rectangle {
    width: 600
    height: 400
    color: width > height ? "red" : "blue"
}
```

Whenever `width` or `height` of the object changes, the statement bound to the `color` property will be re-evaluated and if `width` of the rectangle is larger than its `height`, the rectangle will become `red`; otherwise, it will be `blue`.

Property binding statements can also contain function calls. We can extend the `color` declaration to use a different color if the rectangle is a square by using a custom function:

```
Rectangle {
    width: 600
    height: 400
    color: colorFromSize()

    function colorFromSize() {
        if(width == height) return "green"
        if(width > height) return "red"
        return "blue"
    }
}
```

QML does its best to determine when the function value may change, but it is not omnipotent. For our last function, it can easily determine that the function result depends on the values of the `width` and `height` properties, so it will re-evaluate the binding if either of the two values change. However, in some cases, it can't know that a function might return a different value next time it is called, and in such situations, the statement will not be re-evaluated. Consider the following function:

```
function colorByTime() {
  var d = new Date()
  var minutes = d.getMinutes()
  if(minutes < 15) return "red"
  if(minutes < 30) return "green"
  if(minutes < 45) return "blue"
  return "purple"
}
```

Binding the `color` property to the result of that function will not work properly. QML will only call this function once when the object is initialized, and it will never call it again. This is because it has no way of knowing that the value of this function depends on the current time. Later, we will see how to overcome this with a bit of imperative code and a timer.

Group properties

The `Rectangle` element allows us to define not only the fill color but also the outline size and color. This is done by using the `border.width` and `border.color` properties. You can see they have a common prefix followed by a dot. This means these properties are subproperties of a property group `border`. There are two ways to bind values to these properties. The first approach is to use the dot notation:

```
Rectangle {
  color: "red"
  width: 400
  height: 300
  border.width: 4
  border.color: "black"
}
```

An alternative approach, which is especially useful if you want to set a large number of subproperties in a single group, is to use brackets to enclose definitions in a group:

```
Rectangle {
  color: "red"
  width: 400
  height: 300
  border {
```

```
    width: 4
    color: "black"
  }
}
```

Object hierarchies

We said that QML is about defining object hierarchies. You do this in the simplest way possible–by putting one object declaration into another object's declaration. To create a button-like object containing a rounded frame with some text inside, we'll combine a `Rectangle` item with a `Text` item:

```
Rectangle {
  border { width: 2; color: "black" }
  radius: 5
  color: "transparent"
  width: 50; height: 30

  Text {
    text: "Button Text"
  }
}
```

You can use a semicolon instead of newlines to separate statements in QML in order to have a more compact object definition at the cost of decreased readability.

Running this code produces a result similar to the following diagram:

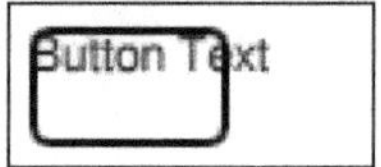

As we can see, it does not look good–the frame is not big enough to hold the text and so it flows outside the frame. Moreover, the text is positioned incorrectly.

Unlike widgets where a child widget is clipped to its parent's geometry, Qt Quick items can be positioned outside their parents.

Since we didn't specify the *x* and *y* coordinates of the text, they are set to their default value, which is `0`. As a result, the text is pinned to the top-left corner of the frame and flows outside the right edge of the frame.

To correct this behavior, we can bind the width of the frame to the width of the text. To do this in the property binding for the rectangle width, we have to specify that we want to use the width of the text object. QML provides a pseudo-property called `id` to allow the programmer to name objects. Let's provide an ID for the `Text` element and bind the width of the outside object to the width of the text, and also do the same for the height. At the same time, let's reposition the text a little to provide padding for the four pixels between the frame and the text itself:

```
Rectangle {
  border { width: 2; color: "black" }
  radius: 5
  color: "transparent"
  width: buttonText.width+8; height: buttonText.height+8

  Text {
    id: buttonText
    text: "Button Text"
    x:4; y: 4
  }
}
```

As you can see in the following image, such code works, but it is still problematic:

If you set empty text to the internal element, the rectangle width and height will drop to `8`, which does not look good. It will also look bad if the text is very long:

This text is so long that the button really doesn't look good

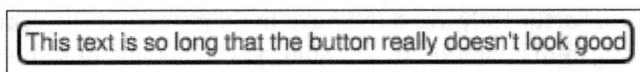

Let's complicate matters even more and add an icon to the button by adding another child element to the rectangle. Qt Quick provides an `Image` type to display images, so let's use it to position our icon on the left side of the text:

```
Rectangle {
  id: button
  border { width: 2; color: "black" }
  radius: 5
  color: "transparent"
  width: 4 + buttonIcon.width + 4 + buttonText.width + 4
  height: Math.max(buttonIcon.height, buttonText.height) + 8
```

```
    Image {
      id: buttonIcon
      source: "edit-undo.png"
      x: 4; y: button.height/2-height/2
    }
    Text {
      id: buttonText
      text: "Button Text"
      x: 4+buttonIcon.width+4
      y: button.height/2-height/2
    }
}
```

In this code, we used the `Math.max` function available in JavaScript to calculate the height of the button, and we modified definitions of the *y* properties of the internal objects to center them vertically in the button. The source property of `Image` contains the URL of a file containing the image to be shown in the item.

> The URL can point not only to a local file, but also to a remote HTTP resource. In such an event, if the remote machine is reachable, the file will be fetched from the remote server automatically.

The result of the code can be seen in the following image:

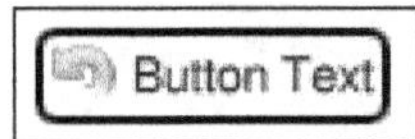

Calculating the positions of each internal element as well as the size of the button frame is becoming complicated. Fortunately, we don't have to do it since Qt Quick provides a much better way of managing item geometry by attaching certain points of some objects to points of another object. These points are called anchor lines. The following anchor lines are available to each Qt Quick item:

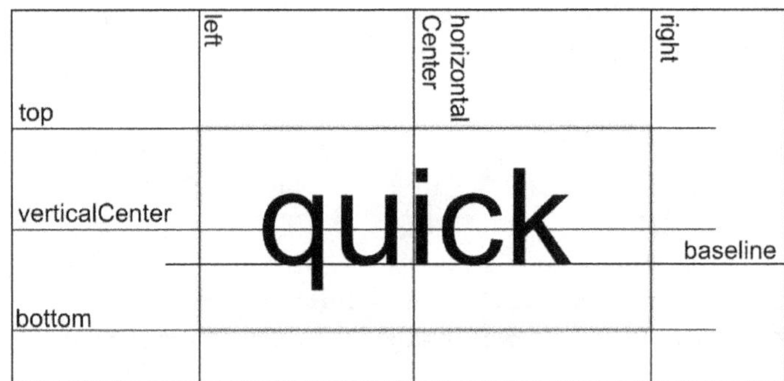

You can establish bindings between anchor lines to manage relative positioning of items. Each anchor line is represented by two properties–one that can be bound to something and another to bind from. Anchors to bind to are regular properties of the object. They can serve as binding arguments for properties defined in an anchors property group. Therefore, to bind the "left" anchor of the current object to the "right" anchor of the object `otherObject`, one would write:

```
anchors.left: otherObject.right
```

In addition to specifying an arbitrary number of anchor bindings, we can also set margins for each of the anchors (or for all of them at once) to offset the two bound anchor lines. Using anchors, we can simplify the previous button definition:

```
Rectangle {
  border { width: 2; color: "black" }
  radius: 5
  color: "transparent"
  width: 4 + buttonIcon.width + 4 + buttonText.width + 4
  height: Math.max(buttonIcon.height, buttonText.height) + 8

  Image {
    id: buttonIcon
    source: "edit-undo.png"
    anchors {
      left: parent.left;
      leftMargin: 4;
      verticalCenter: parent.verticalCenter
    }
  }
  Text {
    id: butonText
    text: "Button Text"
    anchors {
      left: buttonIcon.right;
      leftMargin: 4;
      verticalCenter: parent.verticalCenter
    }
  }
}
```

You can see the `button` ID is not used anymore. Instead, we use parent, which is a property that always points to the item's parent.

Time for action – creating a button component

As an exercise, let's try to use what you've learned so far to create a more complete and better working button component. The button is to have a rounded shape with a nice background and should hold definable text and an icon. The button should look good for different texts and icons.

Start by creating a new project in Qt Creator. Choose **Qt Quick UI** as the project type. When asked for the component set, choose the lowest available version of Qt Quick:

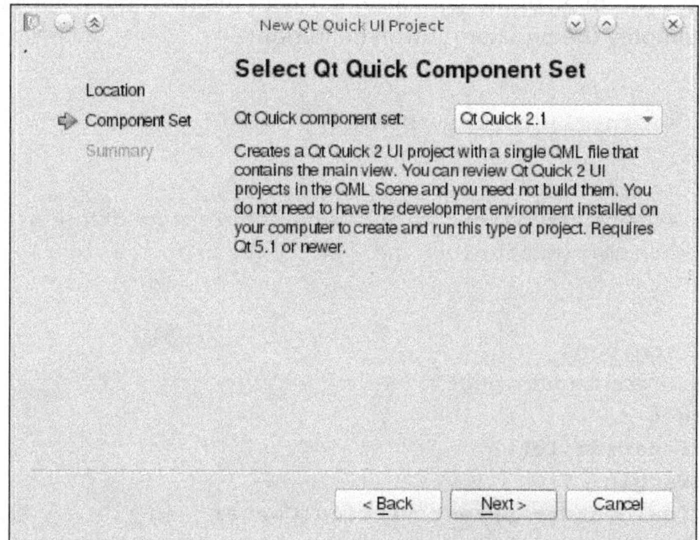

At this point, you should end up with a project containing two files–one with a QML project extension, which is your project management file, and the other with the QML extension, which is your main user interface file. You can see that both files contain QML definitions. That is because Qt Creator manages Qt Quick projects using QML itself (you'll notice it imports the `QmlProject` module).

The QML document that was created for us contains a "Hello World" example code, which we can use as a starting point in our Qt Quick experiments. If you go to the **Projects** pane and look at the **Run Configuration** for the project, you will notice that it uses something called QML Scene to run your project. This configuration invokes an external application called `qmlscene` that is able to load and display an arbitrary QML document. If you run the example code, you should see a white window with some text centered in it. If you click anywhere in the window, the application will close.

Let's start by creating the button frame. Replace the `Text` item with a `Rectangle` item. You can see that the text is centered in the window by using a `centerIn` anchor binding that we didn't mention before. This is one of two special anchors that are provided for convenience to avoid having to write too much code. Using `centerIn` is equivalent to setting both `horizontalCenter` and `verticalCenter`. The other convenience binding is `fill`, which makes one item occupy the whole area of another item (similar to setting the left, right, top, and bottom anchors to their respective anchor lines in the destination item).

Let's give a basic look and feel to the button panel by setting some of its basic properties. This time, instead of setting a solid color for the button, we will declare the background to be a linear gradient. Replace the `Text` definition with the following code:

```
Rectangle {
  id: button
  anchors.centerIn: parent
  border { width: 1; color: "black" }
  radius: 5
  width: 100; height: 30
  gradient: Gradient {
    GradientStop { position: 0; color: "#eeeeee" }
    GradientStop { position: 1; color: "#777777" }
  }
}
```

After running the project, you should see a result similar to the following image:

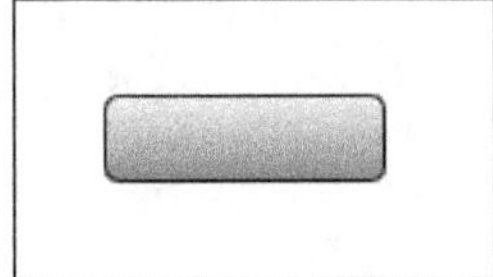

What just happened?

We bound a `Gradient` element to the gradient property and defined two `GradientStop` elements as its children, where we specified two colors to blend between. `Gradient` does not inherit from `Item` and thus is not a visual Qt Quick element. Instead, it is just an object that serves as a data holder for the gradient definition.

The `Item` type has a property called `children` that contains a list of visual children (`Item` instances) of an item and another property called `resources`, which contains a list of non-visual objects (such as `Gradient` or `GradientStop`) for an item. Normally, you don't need to use these properties when adding visual or non-visual objects to an item as the item will automatically assign child objects to appropriate properties. Note that in our code, the `Gradient` object is not a child object of the `Rectangle`; it is just assigned to its `gradient` property.

Time for action – adding button content

The next step is to add text and an icon to the button. We will do this by using another item type called `Row`, as shown:

```
Rectangle {
  id: button
  // …
  gradient: Gradient {
    GradientStop { position: 0; color: "#eeeeee" }
    GradientStop { position: 1; color: "#777777" }
  }
  width: buttonContent.width+8
  height: buttonContent.height+8

  Row {
    id: buttonContent
    anchors.centerIn: parent
    spacing: 4

    Image {
        id: buttonIcon
        source: "edit-undo.png"
    }
    Text {
        id: buttonText
        text: "ButtonText"
    }
  }
}
```

You'll get the following output:

What just happened?

`Row` is one out of four positioner types (the others being `Column`, `Grid`, and `Flow`) that spreads its children in a horizontal row. It makes it possible to position a series of items without using anchors. `Row` has a spacing property that dictates how much space to leave between items.

Time for action – sizing the button properly

Our current panel definition still doesn't behave well when it comes to sizing the button. If the button content is very small (for example, the icon doesn't exist or the text is very short), the button will not look good. Typically, push buttons enforce a minimum size–if the content is smaller than a specified size, the button will be expanded to the minimum size allowed. Another problem is that the user might want to override the width or height of the item. In such cases, the content of the button should not overflow past the border of the button. Let's fix these two issues by replacing the `width` and `height` property bindings with the following code:

```
clip: true
implicitWidth: Math.max(buttonContent.implicitWidth+8, 80)
implicitHeight: buttonContent.implicitHeight+8
```

What just happened?

The `implicitWidth` and `implicitHeight` properties can contain the desired size the item wants to have. It's a direct equivalent of `sizeHint()` from the widget world. By using these two properties instead of `width` and `height` (which are bound to `implicitWidth` and `implicitHeight` by default), we allow the user of our component to override those implicit values. When this happens and the user does not set the width or height big enough to contain the icon and text of the button, we prevent the content from crossing the boundaries of the parent item by setting the `clip` property to `true`.

Time for action – making the button a reusable component

So far, we have been working on a single button. Adding another button by copying the code, changing the identifiers of all components, and setting different bindings to properties are very tedious tasks. Instead, we can make our button item a real component, that is, a new QML type that can be instantiated on demand as many times as required.

First, position the text cursor right before the bracket opening of the definition of the button and press *Alt* + *Enter* on the keyboard to open the refactoring menu, like in the following screenshot:

```
import QtQuick 2.0

Rectangle {
    width: 360
    height: 360

    Rectangle {
        id: Move Component into Separate File
            Wrap Component in Loader
        signal clicked()

        anchors.centerIn: parent
        border { width: 1; color: "black" }
        radius: 5

        gradient: Gradient {
            GradientStop { position: 0; color: "#eeeeee" }
            GradientStop { position: 1; color: "#777777" }
        }
```

From the menu, choose **Move Component into Separate File**. In the popup, type in a name for the new type (for example, `Button`) and accept the dialog by clicking on the **OK** button:

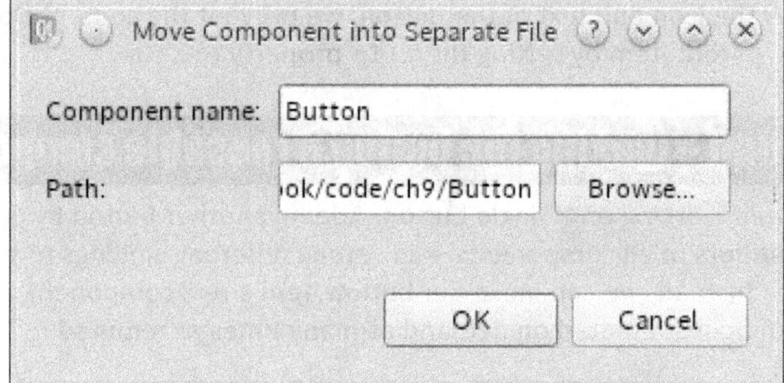

What just happened?

You can see that we have a new file called `Button.qml` in the project, which contains everything the button item used to have. The main file was simplified to something similar the following:

```
import QtQuick 2.0

Rectangle {
  width: 360
  height: 360
  Button {
    id: button
  }
}
```

`Button` has become a component–a definition of a new type of element that can be used the same way as element types imported into QML. Remember that QML component names as well as names of files representing them need to begin with a capital letter! If you name a file "button.qml" instead of "Button.qml", then you will not be able to use "Button" as a component name, and trying to use "button" instead will result in an error message. This works both ways–every QML file starting with a capital letter can be treated as a component definition. We will talk more about components later.

Event handlers

Qt Quick is meant to be used for creating user interfaces that are highly interactive. It offers a number of elements for taking input events from the user.

Mouse input

The simplest of all of them is `MouseArea`. It defines a transparent rectangle that exposes a number of properties and signals related to mouse input. Commonly used signals include clicked, pressed, and released. Let's do a couple of exercises to see how the element can be used.

Time for action – making the button clickable

Thus far, our component only looks like a button. The next task is to make it respond to mouse input. As you may have guessed, this is done by using the `MouseArea` item.

Add a `MouseArea` child item to the button and use anchors to make it fill the whole area of the button. Call the element `buttonMouseArea`. Put the following code in the body of the item:

```
Rectangle {
  id: button
```

```
  // ...
  Row { ... }
  MouseArea {
    id: buttonMouseArea

    anchors.fill:parent
    onClicked: button.clicked()
  }
}
```

In addition to this, set the following declaration in the button object just after its ID is declared:

```
Rectangle {
  id: button

  signal clicked()
  // ...
}
```

To test the modification, add the following code at the end of the button object definition, just before the closing bracket:

```
onClicked: console.log("Clicked!")
```

Then, run the program and click on the button. You'll see your message printed to the Creator's console. Congratulations!

What just happened?

With a signal `clicked()` statement, we declared that the button object emits a signal called clicked. With the `MouseArea` item, we defined a rectangular area (covering the whole button) that reacts to mouse events. Then, we defined `onClicked`, which is a signal handler. For every signal an object has, a script can be bound to a handler named like the signal and prefixed with "on"; hence, for the clicked signal, the handler is called `onClicked` and for `valueChanged` it is called `onValueChanged`. In this particular case, we have two handlers defined–one for the button where we write a simple statement to the console, and the other for the `MouseArea` element where we call the button's signal function effectively emitting that signal.

`MouseArea` has even more features, so now let's try putting them to the right use to make our button more feature-rich.

Time for action – visualizing button states

Currently, there is no visual reaction to clicking on the button. In the real world, the button has some depth and when you push it and look at it from above, its contents seems to shift a little toward the right and downward. Let's mimic this behavior by making use of the pressed property MouseArea has, which denotes whether the mouse button is currently being pressed (note that the pressed property is different from the pressed signal that was mentioned earlier). The content of the button is represented by the Row element, so add the following statements inside its definition:

```
Row {
  id: buttonContent
  // …
  anchors.verticalCenterOffset: buttonMouseArea.pressed ? 1 : 0
  anchors.horizontalCenterOffset: buttonMouseArea.pressed ? 1 : 0
  // …
}
```

We can also make the text change color when the mouse cursor hovers over the button. For this, we have to do two things. First, let's enable receiving hover events on the MouseArea by settings its hoverEnabled property:

```
hoverEnabled: true
```

When this property is set, MouseArea will be setting its containsMouse property to true whenever it detects the mouse cursor over its own area. We can use this value to set the text color:

```
Text {
  id: buttonText
  text: "ButtonText"
  color: buttonMouseArea.containsMouse ? "white" : "black"
}
```

What just happened?

In the last exercise, we learned to use some properties and signals from MouseArea to make the button component more interactive. However, the element is much richer in features. In particular, if hover events are enabled, you can get the current mouse position in the item's local coordinate system through the mouseX and mouseY properties that return values. The cursor position can also be reported by handling the positionChanged signal. Speaking of signals, most MouseArea signals carry a MouseEvent object as their argument. This argument is called mouse and contains useful information about the current state of the mouse, including its position and buttons currently pressed:

```
MouseArea {
  anchors.fill: parent
```

```
    hoverEnabled: true

    onClicked: {
      switch(mouse.button) {
        case Qt.LeftButton:   console.log("Left button clicked");
          break;
        case Qt.MiddleButton: console.log("Middle button clicked");
          break;
        case Qt.RightButton:  console.log("Right button clicked");
          break;
      }
    }
    onPositionChanged: {
      console.log("Position: ["+mouse.x+"; "+mouse.y+"]")
    }
  }
```

Time for action – notifying the environment about button states

We have added some code to make the button look more natural by changing its visual aspects. Now, let's extend the button programming interface so that developers can use more features of the button.

The first thing we can do is make button colors definable by introducing some new properties for the button. Let's put the highlighted code at the beginning of the button component definition:

```
Rectangle {
  id: button
  property color topColor: "#eeeeee"
  property color bottomColor: "#777777"
  property color textColor: "black"
  property color textPressedColor: "white"
  signal clicked()
```

Then, we'll use the new definitions for the background gradient:

```
gradient: Gradient {
  GradientStop { position: 0; color: button.topColor }
  GradientStop { position: 1; color: button.bottomColor }
}
```

Now for the text color:

```
Text {
  id: buttonText
```

```
    text: "ButtonText"
    color: buttonMouseArea.containsMouse ?
      button.textPressedColor : button.textColor
  }
```

Also, please notice that we used the `pressed` property of `MouseArea` to detect whether a mouse button is currently being pressed on the area. We can equip our button with a similar property. Add the following code to the `Button` component:

```
property alias pressed: buttonMouseArea.pressed
```

What just happened?

The first set of changes introduced four new properties defining four colors that we later used in statements defining gradient and text colors for the button. In QML, you can define new properties for objects with the `property` keyword. The keyword should be followed by the property type and property name. QML understands many property types, the most common being int, real, string, font, and color. Property definitions can contain an optional default value for the property preceded with a colon. The situation is different with the pressed property definition. You can see that for the property type, the definition contains the word alias. It is not a property type, but rather an indicator that the property is really an alias to another property–each time the pressed property of the button is accessed, the value of the `buttonMouseArea.pressed` property is returned, and every time the property is changed, it is the mouse area's property that really gets changed. With a regular property declaration, you can provide any valid expression as the default value because the expression is bound to the property. With a property alias, it is different–the value is mandatory and has to be pointing to an existing property of the same or an other object. You can treat property aliases in a similar way as references in C++.

Consider the following two definitions:

```
property int foo: someobject.prop
property alias bar: someobject.prop
```

At first glance, they are similar as they point to the same property and therefore, the values returned for the properties are the same. However, the properties are really very different, which becomes apparent if you try to modify their values:

```
  foo = 7
  bar = 7
```

The first property actually has an expression bound to it, so assigning `7` to `foo` simply releases the binding and assigns the value `7` to the `foo` property, leaving `someobject.prop` with its original value. The second statement, however, acts like a C++ reference; therefore, assigning a new value applies the modification to the someobject.prop property the alias is really pointing to.

Speaking of properties, there is an easy way to react when a property value is modified. For each existing property, there is a handler available that is executed whenever the property value is modified. The handler name is `on` followed by the property name, then followed by the word `Changed`, all in camel case–thus, for a foo property, it becomes `onFooChanged` and for `topColor`, it becomes `onTopColorChanged`. To log the current press state of the button to the console, all we need to do is implement the property change handler for this property:

```
Button {
  // …

  onPressedChanged: {
  console.log("The button is currently "
  +(pressed ? "" : "not ")+"pressed")
}
```

Touch input

As mentioned earlier, `MouseArea` is the simplest of input event elements. Nowadays, more and more devices have touch capabilities and Qt Quick can handle them, as well. Currently, we have three ways of handling touch input.

First of all, we can keep using `MouseArea` as simple touch events are also reported as mouse events; therefore, tapping and sliding a finger on the screen is supported out-of-the-box. The following exercise works on touch-capable devices, as well, when using mouse as input.

Time for action – dragging an item around

Create a new `Qt Quick UI` project. Modify the default code by discarding the existing child items and adding a circle instead:

```
Rectangle {
  id: circle
  width: 60; height: width
  radius: width/2
  color: "red"
}
```

Next, use the `drag` property of `MouseArea` to enable moving the circle by touch (or mouse):

```
MouseArea {
  anchors.fill: parent
  drag.target: circle
}
```

Then, you can start the application and begin moving the circle around.

What just happened?

A circle was created by defining a rectangle with its height equal to width, making it a square and rounding the borders to half the side length. The `drag` property can be used to tell `MouseArea` to manage a given item's position using input events flowing into the area element. We denote the item to be dragged by using the target subproperty. You can use other subproperties to control the axis the item is allowed to move along or constrain the move to a given area. An important thing to remember is that the item being dragged cannot be anchored for the axis on which the drag is requested; otherwise, the item will respect the anchor and not the drag. We didn't anchor our circle item at all since we want it to be draggable along both axes.

The second approach to handling touch input in Qt Quick applications is to use `PinchArea`, which is an item similar to `MouseArea`, but rather than dragging an item around, it allows you to rotate or scale it using two fingers (with a so called "pinch" gesture), as shown. Be aware that `PinchArea` reacts only to touch input, so to test the example you will need a real touch capable device.

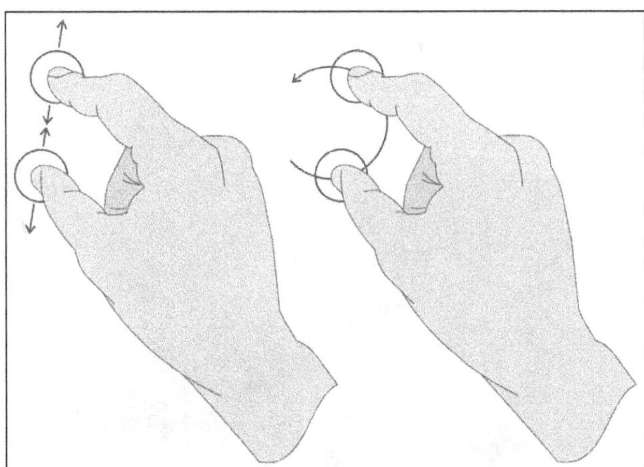

Time for action – rotating and scaling a picture by pinching

Start a new `Qt Quick UI` project. In the QML file, delete everything but the external item. Then, add an image to the UI and make it centered in its parent:

```
Image {
  id: image
  anchors.centerIn: parent
  source: "wilanow.jpg"
}
```

Now, we will add a `PinchArea` element. This kind of item can be used in two ways–either by manually implementing signal handlers `onPinchStarted`, `onPinchUpdated`, and `onPinchFinished` to have total control over the functionality of the gesture or by using a simplified interface similar to the drag property of `MouseArea`. Since the simplified interface does exactly what we want, there is no need to handle pinch events manually. Let's add the following declaration to the file:

```
PinchArea {
  anchors.fill: parent
  pinch {
    target: image
    minimumScale: 0.2; maximumScale: 2.0
    minimumRotation: -90; maximumRotation: 90
  }
}
```

You'll get an output similar to the following screenshot:

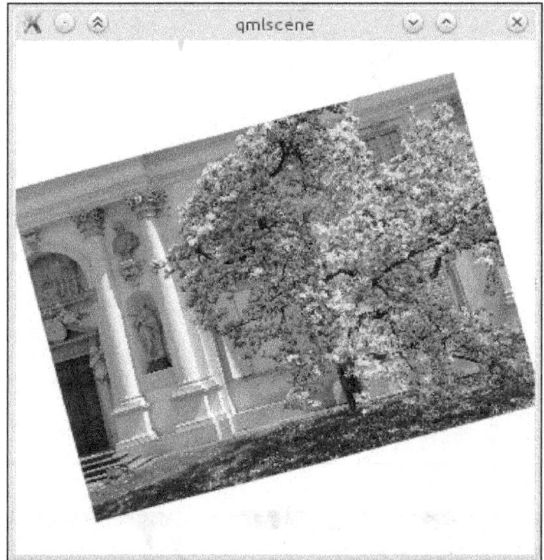

What just happened?

Our simple application loads an image and centers it in the view. Then, there is a `PinchArea` item filling the view area that is told to operate on the image object. We define the range of the scaling and rotating of the item. The rest is left to the `PinchArea` item itself. If you start interacting with the application, you will see the item rotate and scale. What really happens behind the scenes is that `PinchArea` modifies the values of the two properties each Qt Quick item has–`rotation` and `scale`.

PinchArea can also control the dragging of the item with pinch.dragAxis, just like MouseArea does with drag, but for simplicity, we didn't use this part of the API. Feel free to experiment with it in your own code.

Have a go hero – rotating and scaling with a mouse

Of course, you don't have to use PinchArea to rotate or scale an item. Properties controlling those aspects are regular properties that you can read and write at any time. Try replacing PinchArea with MouseArea to obtain a result similar to what we just did by modifying the scale and rotation properties as a result of receiving mouse events–when the user drags the mouse while pressing the left button, the image is scaled and when the user does the same while pressing the right button, the image is rotated. You can control which buttons trigger mouse events by manipulating the acceptedButtons property (setting it to Qt.LeftButton|Qt.RightButton will cause both buttons to trigger events). The button that triggers the event is reported in the event object (which is called mouse) through its button property, and the list of all buttons currently pressed is available in the button property:

```
MouseArea {
  acceptedButtons: Qt.LeftButton|Qt.RightButton
  onPositionChanged: console.log(mouse.button)
}
```

If you manage to do the task, try replacing MouseArea with PinchArea again, but then instead of using the pinch property, handle events manually to obtain the same effect (the event object is called pinch and has a number of properties you can play with).

A third approach to handling touch input is by using the MultiPointTouchArea item. It provides a low-level interface to gestures by reporting each touch point separately. It can be used to create custom high-level gesture handlers similar to PinchArea.

Keyboard input

So far, we've been dealing with pointer input, but user input is not just that–we can also handle keyboard input. This is quite simple and basically boils down to two easy steps.

First, you have to enable receiving keyboard events by stating that a particular item has keyboard focus:

```
focus: true
```

Then, you can start handling events by writing handlers in a similar fashion as for mouse events. However, `Item` doesn't provide its own handler for manipulating keys that is a counterpart for `keyPressEvent` and `keyReleaseEvent` of `QWidget`. Instead, adequate handlers are provided by the `Keys` attached property.

Attached properties are provided by elements that are not used as stand-alone elements but instead provide properties to other objects by getting attached to them. This is a way of adding support for new properties without modifying the API of the original element (it doesn't add new properties through an **is-a** relation, but rather through a **has-a** one). Each object that references an attached property gets its own copy of the attaching object that then handles the extra properties. We will come back to attached properties later in this chapter. For now, you just need to remember that in certain situations, an element can obtain additional properties that are not part of its API.

Let's go back to implementing event handlers for keyboard input. As we said earlier, each Item has a `Keys` attached property that allows us to install our own keyboard handlers. The basic two signals `Keys` adds to `Item` are pressed and released; therefore, we can implement the `onPressed` and `onReleased` handlers that have a `KeyEvent` argument providing similar information as `QKeyEvent` in the widget world. As an example, we can see an item that detects when a spacebar was pressed:

```
Rectangle {
  focus: true
  Keys.onPressed:  { if(event.key == Qt.Key_Space) color = "red"  }
  Keys.onReleased: { if(event.key == Qt.Key_Space) color = "blue" }
}
```

It might become problematic if you want to handle many different keys in the same item as the `onPressed` handler would likely contain a giant switch section with branches for every possible key. Fortunately, `Keys` offers more properties. Most of the commonly used keys (but not letters) have their own handlers that are called when the particular key is pressed. Thus, we can easily implement an item that takes a different color depending on which key was pressed last:

```
Rectangle {
  focus: true
  Keys.onSpacePressed:      color = "purple"
  Keys.onReturnPressed:     color = "navy"
  Keys.onVolumeUpPressed:   color = "blue"
  Keys.onRightPressed:      color = "green"
  Keys.onEscapePressed:     color = "yellow"
  Keys.onTabPressed:        color = "orange"
  Keys.onDigit0Pressed:     color = "red"
}
```

Please note that there is still a single released signal even if a key has its own pressed signal.

Now, consider another example:

```
import QtQuick 2.1
Item {
  property int number: 0
  width: 200; height: width
  focus: true
  Keys.onSpacePressed: number++

  Text { text: number; anchors.centerIn: parent }
}
```

We would expect that when we press and hold the spacebar, we will see the text change from `0` to `1` and stay on that value until we release the key. If you run the example, you will see that instead, the number keeps incrementing as long as you hold down the key. This is because by default, the keys auto-repeat–when you hold the key, the operating system keeps sending a sequence of press-release events for the key (you can verify that by adding the `console.log()` statements to the `Keys.onPressed` and `Keys.onReleased` handlers). To counter this effect, you can either disable key repeats in your system (which will, of course, not work if someone installs your program on his or her own computer) or you can differentiate between auto-repeat and regular events. In Qt Quick, you can do this easily as each key event carries the appropriate information. Simply replace the handler from the last example with the following one:

```
Keys.onSpacePressed: if(!event.isAutoRepeat) number++
```

The event variable we use here is the name of the parameter of the `spacePressed` signal. As we cannot declare our own names for the parameters like we can do in C++, for each signal handler you will have to look up the name of the argument in the documentation, as shown:

- **spacePressed**(KeyEvent *event*)

In standard C++ applications, we usually use the *Tab* key to navigate through focusable items. With games (and fluid user interfaces in general), it is more common to use arrow keys for item navigation. Of course, we can handle this situation by using the `Keys` attached property and adding `Keys.onRightPressed`, `Keys.onTabPressed`, and other signal handlers to each of our items where we want to modify the focus property of the desired item, but it would quickly clutter our code. Qt Quick comes to our help once again by providing a `KeyNavigation` attached property, which is meant to handle this specific situation and allows us to greatly simplify the needed code. Now, we can just specify which item should get into focus when a specific key is triggered:

```
Row {
  spacing: 5
```

```
    Rectangle {
      id: first
      width: 50; height: width
      color: focus ? "blue" : "lightgray"
      focus: true

      KeyNavigation.right: second
    }
    Rectangle {
      id: second
      width: 50; height: width
      color: focus ? "blue" : "lightgray"

      KeyNavigation.right: third
      KeyNavigation.left: first
    }
    Rectangle {
      id: third
      width: 50; height: width
      color: focus ? "blue" : "lightgray"

      KeyNavigation.left: second
    }
  }
```

Notice that we made the first item get into focus in the beginning by explicitly setting the focus property.

Both the `Keys` and `KeyNavigation` attached properties have a way to define the order in which each of the mechanisms receive the events. This is handled by the priority property, which can be set to either `BeforeItem` or `AfterItem`. By default, `Keys` will get the event first (`BeforeItem`), then the internal event handling can take place and finally, `KeyNavigation` will have a chance of handling the event (`AfterItem`). Note that if the key is handled by one of the mechanisms, the event is accepted and the remaining mechanisms will not be able to handle that event.

Have a go hero – practicing key-event propagation

As an exercise, you can expand our last example by building a larger array of items (you can use the `Grid` element to position them) and defining a navigation system that makes use of the `KeyNavigation` attached property. Have some of the items handle events themselves using the `Keys` attached property. See what happens when the same key is handled by both mechanisms. Try influencing the behavior using the priority property.

Apart from the attached properties we described, Qt Quick provides built-in elements for handling keyboard input. The two most basic types are `TextInput` and `TextEdit`, which are QML equivalents of `QLineEdit` and `QTextEdit`. The former are used for single-line text input, while the latter serve as its multi-line counterpart. They both offer cursor handling, undo-redo functionality, and text selections. You can validate text typed into `TextInput` by assigning a validator to the `validator` property. For example, to obtain an item where the user can input a dot-separated IP address, we could use the following declaration:

```
TextInput {
  id: ipAddress
  width: 100
  validator: RegExpValidator {
    regExp: /\d+\.\d+\.\d+\.\d+/
    /* four numbers separated by dots*/
  }
  focus: true
}
```

The regular expression only verifies the format of the address. The user can still insert bogus numbers. You should either do a proper check before using the address or provide a more complex regular expression that will constrain the range of numbers the user can enter.

One thing to remember is that neither `TextInput` nor `TextEdit` has any visual appearance (apart from the text and cursor they contain), so if you want to give the user some visual hint as to where the item is positioned, the easiest solution is to wrap it in a styled rectangle:

```
Rectangle {
  id: textInputFrame
  width: 200
  height: 40
  border { color: "black"; width: 2 }
  radius: 10
  antialiasing: true
  color: "darkGray"
}
TextInput {
  id: textInput
  anchors.fill: textInputFrame
  anchors.margins: 5
  font.pixelSize: height-2
  verticalAlignment: TextInput.AlignVCenter
  clip: true
}
```

Notice the highlighted code–the `clip` property of `textInput`–is enabled such that by default, if the text entered in the box doesn't fit in the item, it will overflow it and remain visible outside the actual item. By enabling clipping, we explicitly say that anything that doesn't fit the item should not be drawn.

Using components in Qt Quick

By now, you should be familiar with the very basics of QML and Qt Quick. Now, we can start combining what you know and fill the gaps with more information to build a functional Qt Quick application. Our target is going to be to display an analog clock.

Time for action – a simple analog clock application

Create a new `Qt Quick UI` project. To create a clock, we will implement a component representing the clock needle and we will use instances of that component in the actual clock element. In addition to this, we will make the clock a reusable component; therefore, we will create it in a separate file and instantiate it from within `main.qml`:

```
import QtQuick 2.0

Clock {
  id: clock
  width:  400
  height: 400
}
```

Then, add the new QML file to the project and call it `Clock.qml`. Let's start by declaring a circular clock plate:

```
import QtQuick 2.0

Item {
  id: clock

  property color color: "lightgray"

  Rectangle {
    id: plate
```

```
        anchors.centerIn: parent
        width: Math.min(clock.width, clock.height)
        height: width
        radius: width/2
        color: clock.color
        border.color: Qt.darker(color)
        border.width: 2
      }
    }
```

If you run the program now, you'll see a plain gray circle hardly resembling a clock plate:

The next step is to add marks dividing the plate into 12 sections. We can do this by putting the following declaration inside the `plate` object:

```
Repeater {
  model: 12

  Item {
    id: hourContainer

    property int hour: index
    height: plate.height/2
    transformOrigin: Item.Bottom
    rotation: index * 30
    x: plate.width/2
    y: 0

    Rectangle {
      width: 2
```

```
        height: (hour % 3 == 0) ? plate.height*0.1
                                : plate.height*0.05
        color: plate.border.color
        antialiasing: true
        anchors.horizontalCenter: parent.horizontalCenter
        anchors.top: parent.top
        anchors.topMargin: 4
      }
    }
  }
```

Running the program should now give the following result, looking much more like a clock plate:

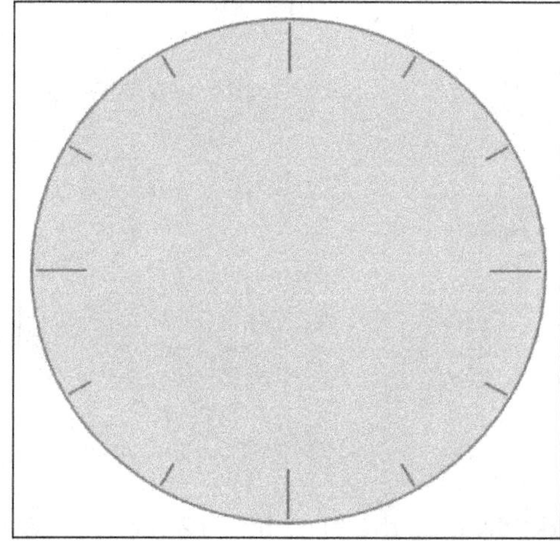

What just happened?

The code we just created introduces a couple of new features. Let's go through them one by one.

First of all, we used a new element called `Repeater`. It does exactly what its name says–it repeats items declared within it using a given model. For each entry in the model, it creates an instance of a component assigned to a property called `delegate` (the property name means that it contains an entity to which the caller delegates some responsibility, such as describing a component to be used as a stencil by the caller). `Item` declared in `Repeater` describes the delegate even though we cannot see it explicitly assigned to a property. This is because `delegate` is a default property of the `Repeater` type, which means anything unassigned to any property explicitly gets implicitly assigned to the default property of the type.

The `Item` type also has a default property called `data`. It holds a list of elements that gets automatically split into two "sublists"–the list of the item's children (which creates the hierarchy of `Item` instances in Qt Quick) and another list called resources, which contains all "child" elements that do not inherit from `Item`. You have direct access to all three lists which means calling `children[2]` will return the third `Item` element declared in the item, and `data[5]` will return the sixth element declared in the `Item` regardless of whether the given element is a visual item (that inherits `Item`) or not.

The model can be a number of things but in our case, it is simply a number denoting how many times the delegate should be repeated. The component to be repeated is a transparent item containing a rectangle. The item has a property declared called `hour` that has something called `index` bound to it. The latter is a property assigned by `Repeater` to each instance of the delegate component. The value it contains is the index of the instance in the `Repeater` object–since we have a model containing twelve elements, `index` will hold values within a range of `0` to `11`. The item can make use of the `index` property to customize instances created by `Repeater`. In this particular case, we use `index` to provide values for a `rotation` property and by multiplying the index by `30`, we get values starting from `0` for the first instance and ending at `330` for the last one.

The `rotation` property brings us to the second most important subject–item transformations. Each item can be transformed in a number of ways, including rotating the item and scaling it in two-dimensional space as we already mentioned earlier. Another property called `transformOrigin` denotes the origin point around which scale and rotation are applied. By default, it points to `Item.Center`, which makes the item scale and rotate around its center, but we can change it to eight other values such as `Item.TopLeft` for the top-left corner or `Item.Right` for the middle of the right edge of the item. In the code we crafted, we rotate each item clockwise around its bottom edge. Each item is positioned horizontally in the middle of the plate using the `plate.width/2` expression and vertically at the top of the plate with the default width of `0` and the height of half the plate's height; thus, each item is a thin vertical line spanning from within the top to the center of the plate. Then, each item is rotated around the center of the plate (each item's bottom edge) by 30 degrees more than a previous item effectively laying items evenly on the plate.

Finally, each item has a gray `Rectangle` attached to the top edge (offset by `4`) and horizontally centered in the transparent parent. Transformations applied to an item influence the item's children similarly to what we have seen in Graphics View; thus, the effective rotation of the rectangle follows that of its parent. The height of the rectangle depends on the value of `hour`, which maps to the index of the item in `Repeater`. Here, you cannot use `index` directly as it is only visible within the top-most item of the delegate. That's why we create a real property called `hour` that can be referenced from within the whole delegate item hierarchy.

> If you want more control over item transformations, then we are happy to inform you that apart from rotation and scale properties, each item can be assigned an array of elements such as `Rotation`, `Scale`, and `Translate` to a property called `transform`, which are applied in order, one at a time. These types have properties for fine-grained control over the transformation. For instance, using `Rotation` you can implement rotation over any of the three axes and around a custom origin point (instead of being limited to nine predefined origin points as when using the `rotation` property of `Item`).

Time for action – adding needles to the clock

The next step is to add the hour, minute, and second needles to the clock. Let's start by creating a new component called `Needle` in a file called `Needle.qml` (remember that component names and files representing them need to start with a capital letter):

```
import QtQuick 2.0

Rectangle {
  id: root

  property int value: 0
  property int granularity: 60
  property alias length: root.height
  width: 2
  height: parent.height/2
  radius: width/2
  antialiasing: true
  anchors.bottom: parent.verticalCenter
  anchors.horizontalCenter: parent.horizontalCenter
  transformOrigin: Item.Bottom
  rotation: 360/granularity * (value % granularity)
}
```

`Needle` is basically a rectangle anchored to the center of its parent by its bottom edge, which is also the item's pivot. It also has `value` and `granularity` properties driving the rotation of the item, where `value` is the current value the needle shows and `granularity` is the number of different values it can display. Also, anti-aliasing for the needle is enabled as we want the tip of the needle nicely rounded. Having such a definition, we can use the component to declare the three needles inside the clock plate object:

```
Needle {
  length: plate.height*0.3
  color: "blue"
```

```
    value: clock.hours; granularity: 12
  }
  Needle {
    length: plate.height*0.4
    color: "darkgreen"
    value: clock.minutes; granularity: 60
  }
  Needle {
    width: 1
    length: plate.height*0.45
    color: "red"
    value: clock.seconds; granularity: 60
  }
```

The three needles make use the of `hours`, `minutes`, and `seconds` properties of clock, so these need to be declared, as well:

```
property int hours: 0
property int minutes: 0
property int seconds: 0
```

By assigning different values to the properties of `Clock` in `main.qml`, you can make the clock show a different time:

```
import QtQuick 2.0

Clock {
  id: clock
  width:  400
  hours: 7
  minutes: 42
  seconds: 17
}
```

You'll get an output as shown:

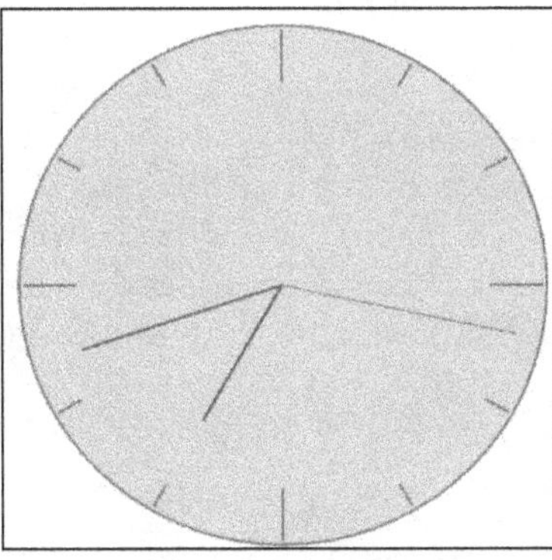

What just happened?

Most `Needle` functionality is declared in the component itself, including geometry and transformations. Then, whenever we want to use the component, we declare an instance of `Needle` and optionally customize the `length` and `color` properties, as well as set its `value` and `granularity` to obtain the exact functionality we need.

Time for action – making the clock functional

The final step in creating a clock is to make it actually show the current time. In JavaScript, we can query the current time using the `Date` object:

```
var currentDate = new Date()
var hours   = currentDate.getHours()
var minutes = currentDate.getMinutes()
var seconds = currentDate.getSeconds()
```

Therefore, the first thing that comes to mind is to use the preceding code to show the current time on the clock:

```
Item {
  id: clock
  property int hours:   currentDate.getHours()
  property int minutes: currentDate.getMinutes()
  property int seconds: currentDate.getSeconds()
  property var currentDate: new Date()
  // ...
}
```

This will indeed show the current time once you start the application, but the clock will not be updating itself as the time passes. This is because `new Date()` returns an object representing one particular moment in time (the date and time at the moment when the object was instantiated). What we need instead is to have the `currentDate` property updated with a new object created as the current time changes. To obtain this effect, we can use a `Timer` element that is an equivalent of `QTimer` in C++ and lets us periodically execute some code. Let's modify the code to use a timer:

```
Item {
  id: clock
  property int hours: currentDate.getHours()
  property int minutes: currentDate.getMinutes()
  property int seconds: currentDate.getSeconds()
  readonly property var currentDate: new Date()
```

```
    property alias running: timer.running
    Timer {
      id: timer
      repeat: true
      interval: 500
      running: true
      onTriggered: clock.currentDate = new Date()
    }
  }
```

What just happened?

Based on the interval property, we can determine that the timer emits a `triggered` signal every 500 ms, causing `currentDate` to be updated with a new `Date` object representing the current time. The clock is also given a `running` property (pointing to its equivalent in the timer) that can control whether updates should be enabled. The timer is set to `repeat`; otherwise, it would trigger just once.

Dynamic objects

To briefly sum up what you have learned so far, we can say that you know how to create hierarchies of objects by declaring their instances and you also know how to program new types in separate files, making definitions available as components to be instantiated in other QML files. You can even use the `Repeater` element to declare a series of objects based on a common stencil.

Using components in detail

We promised to give you more information about components and now is the time to do so. You already know the basics of creating components in separate files. Every QML file beginning with a capital letter is treated as a component definition. This definition can be used directly by other QML files residing in the same directory as the component definition. If you need to access a component definition from a file residing elsewhere, you will have to first import the module containing the component in the file where you want to use it. The definition of a module is very simple–it is just a relative path to the directory containing QML files. The path is constructed using dots as the separator. This means that if you have a file named `Baz.qml` in a directory called `Base/Foo/Bar` and you want to use the `Baz` component from within the `Base/Foo/Ham.qml` file, you will have to put the following import statement in `Ham.qml`:

```
import "Bar"
```

If you want to use the same component from within the `Base/Spam.qml` file, you will have to replace the import statement with:

```
import "Foo.Bar"
```

Importing a module makes all its components available for use. You can then declare objects of types imported from a certain module.

Creating objects on request

The problem with pre-declaring objects directly in a QML file is that you need to know up front how many objects you are going to need. More often than not, you will want to dynamically add and remove objects to your scene, for example, in an alien invasion game where as the player progresses, new alien saucers will be entering the game screen and other saucers will be getting shot down and destroyed. Also, the player's ship will be "producing" new bullets streaking in front of the ship, eventually running out of fuel or otherwise disappearing from the game scene. By putting a good amount of effort into the problem, you would be able to use `Repeater` to obtain this effect, but there is a better tool at hand.

QML offers us another element type called `Component`, which is another way to teach the engine about a new element type by declaring its contents in QML. There are basically two approaches to doing this.

The first approach is to declare a `Component` element instance in the QML file and inline the definition of the new type directly inside the element:

```
Component {
  id: circleComponent
  Item {
    property int diameter: 20
    property alias color: rect.color
    property alias border: rect.border

    implicitWidth: diameter
    implicitHeight: diameter

    Rectangle {
      id: rect
      width: radius; height: radius; radius: diameter/2
      anchors.centerIn: parent
    }
  }
}
```

Such code declares a component called `circleComponent` that defines a circle and exposes its `diameter`, `color`, and `border` properties.

The other approach is to load the component definition from an existing QML file. QML exposes a special global object called `Qt`, which provides a set of interesting methods. One of the methods allows the caller to create a component passing the URL of an existing QML document:

```
var circleComponent = Qt.createComponent("circle.qml")
```

An interesting note is that `createComponent` can not only accept a local file path but also a remote URL, and if it understands the network scheme (for example, `http`), it will download the document automatically. In this case, you have to remember that it takes time to do that, so the component may not be ready immediately after calling `createComponent`. Since the current loading status is kept in the `status` property, you can connect to the `statusChanged` signal to be notified when this happens. A typical code path looks similar to the following:

```
var circleComponent = Qt.createComponent
  ("http://example.com/circle.qml")
if(circleComponent.status === Component.Ready) {
  // use the component
} else {
  circleComponent.statusChanged.connect(function() {
    if(circleComponent.status === Component.Ready) {
       // use the component
    }
  })
}
```

If the component definition is incorrect or the document cannot be retrieved, the status of the object will change to `Error`. In that case, you can make use of the `errorString()` method to see what the actual problem is:

```
if(circleComponent.status === Component.Error) {
  console.warn(circleComponent.errorString())
}
```

Once you are sure the component is ready, you can finally start creating objects from it. For this, the component exposes a method called `createObject`. In its simplest form, it accepts an object that is to become the parent of the newly born instance (similar to widget constructors accepting a pointer to a parent widget) and returns the new object itself so that you can assign it to some variable:

```
var circle = circleComponent.createObject(someItem)
```

Then, you can start setting the object's properties:

```
circle.diameter = 20
circle.color = 'red'
```

A more complex invocation lets us do both these operations (create the object and set its properties) in a single call by passing a second parameter to `createObject`:

```
var circle = circleComponent.createObject(someItem,
  {diameter: 20, color: 'red'})
```

The second parameter is an object (created here using JSON syntax) whose properties are to be applied to the object being created. The advantage of the latter syntax is that all property values are applied to the object as one atomic operation (just like usual when the item is declared in a QML document) instead of a series of separate operations, each of which sets the value for a single property, possibly causing an avalanche of change handler invocations in the object.

After creation, the object becomes a first-class citizen of the scene, acting in the same way as items declared directly in the QML document. The only difference is that a dynamically created object can also be dynamically destructed by calling its `destroy()` method, which is an equivalent of calling `delete` on C++ objects. When speaking of destroying dynamic items, we have to point out that when you assign a result of `createObject` to a variable (like `circle`, in our example) and that variable goes out of scope, the item will not be released and garbage collected as its parent still holds a reference to it, preventing it from being recycled.

We didn't mention this explicitly before, but we have already used inline component definitions earlier in this chapter when we introduced the `Repeater` element. The repeated item defined within the repeater is in fact not a real item, but a component definition that is instantiated as many times as needed by the repeater.

Delaying item creation

Another recurring scenario is that you do know how many elements you are going to need, but the problem is that you cannot determine up front what type of elements they are going to be. At some point during the lifetime of your application, you will learn that information and will be able to instantiate an object. Until you gain the knowledge about the given component, you will need some kind of item placeholder where you will later put the real item. You can, of course, write some code to use the `createObject()` functionality of the component, but this is cumbersome. Fortunately, Qt Quick offers a nicer solution in the form of a `Loader` item. This item type is exactly what we described it to be–a temporary placeholder for a real item that will be loaded on demand from an existing component. You can put `Loader` in place of another item and when you need to create this item, one way is to set the URL of a component to the `source` property:

```
Loader {
  id: ldr
}
ldr.source = "MightySword.qml"You could also directly attach
  a real component to sourceComponent of a Loader:
Component {
  id: swordComponent
  // ...
}
Loader {
  id: ldr
  sourceComponent: shouldBeLoaded ? swordComponent : undefined
}
```

Immediately afterwards, the magic begins and an instance of the component appears in the loader. If the `Loader` object has its size set explicitly (for example, by anchoring or setting the width and height), then the item will be resized to the size of the loader. If an explicit size is not set, then `Loader` will instead be resized to the size of the loaded element once the component is instantiated:

```
Loader {
  anchors {
    left: parent.left; leftMargin: 0.2*parent.width
    right: parent.right;
    verticalCenter: parent.verticalCenter
  }
  height: 250

  source: "Armor.qml"
}
```

In the preceding situation, the loader has its size set explicitly so when its item is created, it will respect the anchors and sizes declared here.

Accessing your item's component functionality

Each item in Qt Quick is an instantiation of some kind of component. Each object has a `Component` attached property that offers two signals informing about important moments of the object's life cycle. The first signal—`completed()`—is triggered after the object has been instantiated. If you provide a handler for the signal, you can perform some late initialization of the object after it has been fully instantiated. There are many use cases for this signal, starting with logging a message to the console:

```
Rectangle {
  Component.onCompleted: console.log("Rectangle created")
}
```

A more advanced use of this signal is to optimize performance by delaying expensive operations until the component is fully constructed:

```
Item {
  id: root

  QtObject {
    id: priv
    property bool complete: false

    function layoutItems() {
      if(!complete) return
      // ...
    }
  }
  onChildrenChanged: priv.layoutItems()
  Component.onCompleted: { priv.complete = true;
    priv.layoutItems(); }
}
```

When items are created, they are added to their parent's `children` property. Thus, as items get created and destroyed, the value of that property is modified, triggering the `childrenChanged` signal. As this happens, we would like to reposition the item's children according to some algorithm. For that, we have an internal `QtObject` instance (representing a `QObject`) called `priv` where we can declare functions and properties that will not be visible outside the component definition. In there, we have a `layoutItems()` function that is called whenever the list of children is updated. This is fine if items are created or destroyed dynamically (for example, using the `Component.createObject()` function). However, as the root object is being constructed, it may have a number of child items declared directly in the document. There is no point in repositioning them over and over again as declarations are instantiated. Only when the list of objects is complete does it make sense to position the items. Therefore, we declare a Boolean property in the private object denoting whether the root item is fully constructed. Until it is, every time `layoutItems()` is called, it will exit immediately without doing any computations. When `Component.onCompleted` is called, we raise the flag and call `layoutItems()`, which computes the geometry of all child items declared statically in the document.

The other signal in the attached `Component` property is `destruction`. It is triggered right after the destruction process for the object starts when the component is still fully constructed. By handling that signal, you can perform actions such as saving the state of the object in persistent storage or otherwise cleaning the object up.

Imperative painting

Declaring graphical items is nice and easy but as programmers, we're more used to writing imperative code, and some things are easier expressed as an algorithm rather than as a description of the final result to be achieved. It is easy to use QML to encode a definition of a primitive shape such as a rectangle in a compact way–all we need is to mark the origin point of the rectangle, its width, height, and optionally, a color. Writing down a declarative definition of a complex shape consisting of many control points positioned in given absolute coordinates, possibly with an outline in some parts of it, maybe accompanied by an image or two, is still possible in language such as QML; however, this will result in a much more verbose and much less readable definition. This is a case where using an imperative approach might prove more effective. HTML (being a declarative language) already exposes a proven imperative interface for drawing different primitives called a `Canvas` that has been used in numerous Web applications. Fortunately, Qt Quick provides us with its own implementation of a `Canvas` interface similar to the one from the Web by letting us instantiate `Canvas` items. Such items can be used to draw straight and curved lines, simple and complex shapes, and graphs and graphic images. It can also add text, colors, shadows, gradients, and patterns. It can even perform low-level pixel operations. Finally, the output may be saved as an image file or serialized to a URL usable as source for an `Image` item. There are many tutorials and papers available out there on using an HTML canvas and they can usually be easily applied to a Qt Quick canvas, as well (the reference manual even includes a list of aspects you need to pay attention to when porting HTML canvas applications to a Qt Quick canvas), so here we will just give you the very basics of imperative drawing in Qt Quick.

Consider a game where the player's health is measured by the condition of his heart–the slower the beat, the more healthy the player is. We will use this kind of visualization as our exercise in practicing painting using the `Canvas` element.

Time for action – preparing Canvas for heartbeat visualization

Let's start with simple things by creating a Quick UI project based on the latest version of Qt Quick. Rename the QML file Creator made for us to `HeartBeat.qml`. Open the `qmlproject` file that was created with the project and change the `mainFile` property of the `Project` object to `HeartBeat.qml`. Then, you can close the `qmlproject` document and return to `HeartBeat.qml`. There, you can replace the original content with the following:

```
import QtQuick 2.2

Canvas {
  id: canvas

  implicitWidth: 600
  implicitHeight: 300
```

```
    onPaint: {
      var ctx = canvas.getContext("2d")
      ctx.clearRect(0, 0, canvas.width, canvas.height)
    }
  }
```

When you run the project, you will see... a blank window.

What just happened?

In the preceding code, we created a basic boilerplate code for using a canvas. First, we renamed the existing file to what we want our component to be called, and then we informed Creator that this document is to be executed when we run the project using `qmlscene`.

Then, we created a `Canvas` instance with an implicit width and height set. There, we created a handler for the `paint` signal that is emitted whenever the canvas needs to be redrawn. The code placed there retrieves a context for the canvas, which can be thought of as an equivalent to the `QPainter` instance we used when drawing on Qt widgets. We inform the canvas that we want its 2D context, which gives us a way to draw in two dimensions. A 2D context is the only context currently present for the `Canvas` element, but you still have to identify it explicitly–similar to in HTML. Having the context ready, we tell it to clear the whole area of the canvas. This is different to the widget world in which when the `paintEvent` handler was called, the widget was already cleared for us and everything had to be redrawn from scratch. With `Canvas`, it is different; the previous content is kept by default so that you can draw over it if you want. Since we want to start with a clean sheet, we call `clearRect()` on the context.

Time for action – drawing a heartbeat

We will extend our component now and implement its main functionality–drawing a heartbeat-like diagram.

Add the following property declarations to `canvas`:

```
property int lineWidth: 2
property var points: []
property real arg: -Math.PI
```

Below, add a declaration for a timer that will drive the whole component:

```
Timer {
  interval: 10
  repeat: true
  running: true
  onTriggered: {
    arg += Math.PI/180
    while(arg >= Math.PI) arg -= 2*Math.PI
  }
}
```

Then, define the handler for when the value of `arg` is modified:

```
onArgChanged: {
  points.push(func(arg))
  points = points.slice(-canvas.width)
  canvas.requestPaint()
}
```

Then, implement `func`:

```
function func(argument) {
  var a=(2*Math.PI/10); var b=4*Math.PI/5
  return Math.sin(20*argument) * (
      Math.exp(-Math.pow(argument/a, 2)) +
      Math.exp(-Math.pow((argument-b)/a,2)) +
      Math.exp(-Math.pow((argument+b)/a,2))
  )
}
```

Finally, modify `onPaint`:

```
onPaint: {
  var ctx = canvas.getContext("2d")
  ctx.reset()
  ctx.clearRect(0, 0, canvas.width, canvas.height)
  var pointsToDraw = points.slice(-canvas.width)
  ctx.translate(0, canvas.height/2)
  ctx.beginPath()
  ctx.moveTo(0, -pointsToDraw[0]*canvas.height/2)
  for(var i=1; i<pointsToDraw.length; i++)
    ctx.lineTo(i, -pointsToDraw[i]*canvas.height/2)
  ctx.lineWidth = canvas.lineWidth
  ctx.stroke()
}
```

Then, you can run the code and see a heart beat-like diagram appear on the canvas:

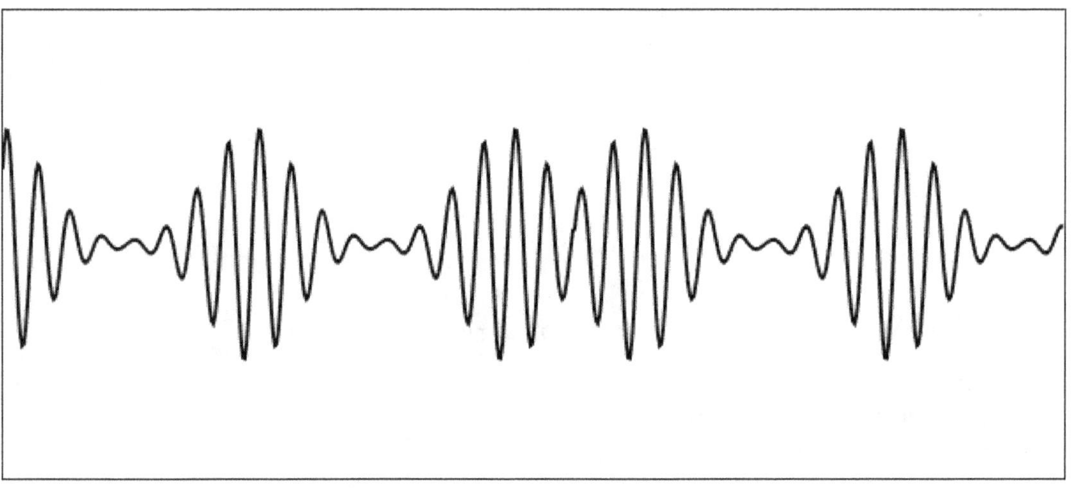

What just happened?

We added two kinds of properties to the element. By introducing `lineWidth`, we can manipulate the width of the line that visualizes the heartbeat. The `points` and `arg` variables are two helper variables that store an array of points already calculated and the function argument that was last evaluated. The function we are going to use is a periodic function that extends from `-Π` to `+Π`; thus, we initialize `arg` to `-Math.PI` and we store an empty array in points.

Then, we added a timer that ticks in regular intervals, incrementing `arg` by 1° until it reaches `+Π`, in which case it is reset to the initial value.

Changes to `arg` are intercepted in the handler we implemented next. In there, we push a new item to the array of points. The value is calculated by the function `func`, which is quite complicated, but it is sufficient to say that it returns a value from within a range of `-1` to `+1`. The array of points is then compacted using `Array.slice()` so that at most, the last canvas.width items remain in the array. This is so we can plot one point for each pixel of the width of the canvas and we don't have to store any more data than required. At the end of the function, we invoke `requestPaint()`, which is an equivalent of `QWidget::update()` and schedules a call to paint.

That, in turn, calls our onPaint. There, after retrieving the context, we reset the canvas to its initial state and then calculate an array of points that is to be drawn again by using slice(). Then, we prepare the canvas by translating and scaling it in the vertical axis so that the origin is moved to half of the height of the canvas (that's the reason for calling reset() at the beginning of the procedure–to revert this transformation). After that, beginPath() is called to inform the context that we are starting to build a new path. Then, the path is built segment by segment by appending lines. Each value is multiplied by canvas.height/2 so that values from the point array are scaled to the size of the item. The value is negated as the vertical axis of the canvas grows to the bottom and we want positive values to be above the origin line. After that, we set the width of the pen and draw the path by calling stroke().

Time for action – making the diagram more colorful

The diagram serves its purpose, but it looks a bit dull. Add some shine to it by defining three new color properties in the canvas object–color, topColor, bottomColor–and setting their default values to black, red, and blue, respectively.

Since points and arg should not really be public properties that anyone can change behind our backs, we'll correct it now. Declare a child element of the canvas of QtObject and set its ID to priv. Move declarations of points and arg inside that object. Move the onArgChanged handler there, as well:

```
QtObject {
  id: priv
  property var points: []
  property real arg: -Math.PI

  onArgChanged: {
    points.push(func(arg))
    points = points.slice(-canvas.width)
    canvas.requestPaint()
  }
}
```

Then, search through the whole code and prefix all occurrences of arg and points outside the newly declared object with priv, so that each of their invocations lead to the priv object.

Then, let's make use of the three colors we defined by extending onPaint:

```
onPaint: {
    ...
    // fill:
    ctx.beginPath()
    ctx.moveTo(0, 0)
```

```
        var i
        for(i=0; i<pointsToDraw.length; i++)
            ctx.lineTo(i, -pointsToDraw[i]*canvas.height/2)
        ctx.lineTo(i, 0)
        var gradient = ctx.createLinearGradient(0,
          -canvas.height/2, 0, canvas.height/2)
        gradient.addColorStop(0.1, canvas.topColor)
        gradient.addColorStop(0.5, Qt.rgba(1, 1, 1, 0))
        gradient.addColorStop(0.9, canvas.bottomColor)
        ctx.fillStyle = gradient
        ctx.fill()

        // stroke:
        ctx.beginPath()
        ctx.moveTo(0, -pointsToDraw[0]*canvas.height/2)
        for(var i=1; i<pointsToDraw.length; i++)
            ctx.lineTo(i, -pointsToDraw[i]*canvas.height/2)
        ctx.lineWidth = canvas.lineWidth
        ctx.strokeStyle = canvas.color
        ctx.stroke()
    }
```

Upon running the preceding code snippet, you get the following output:

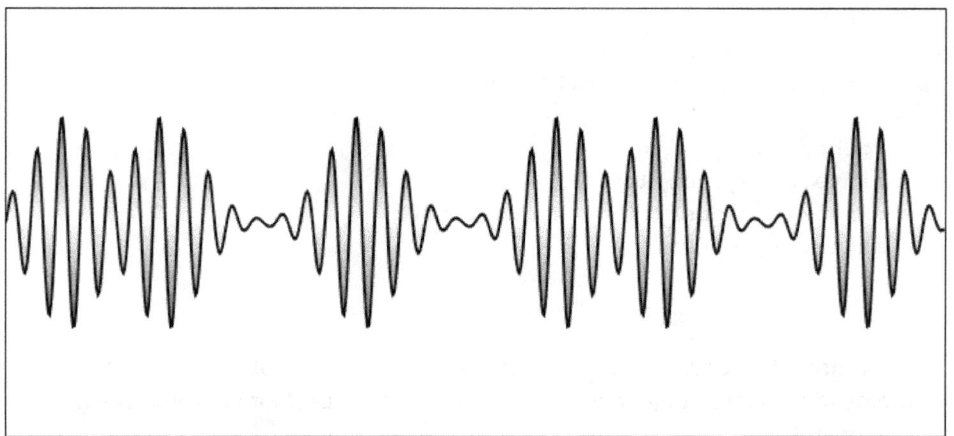

What just happened?

By moving the two properties inside the `priv` object, we have effectively hidden them from the external world as child objects of an object (such as `priv` being a child of `canvas`) are not accessible from outside the QML document that defines the object. This ensures that neither `points` nor `arg` can be modified from outside the `HeartBeat.qml` document.

The modifications to `onPaint` that we implemented are creating another path and using that path to fill an area using a gradient. The path is very similar to the original one, but it contains two additional points that are the first and last point drawn projected onto the horizontal axis. This makes sure the gradient fills the area properly. Please note that the canvas uses imperative code for drawing; therefore, the order of drawing the fill and the stroke matters–the fill has to be drawn first so that it doesn't obscure the stroke.

Qt Quick and C++

Thus far, we have been using standard Qt Quick items or creating new ones by compositing existing element types in QML. But there is a lot more you can do if you interface QML and C++ using the technologies Qt has to offer. Essentially, QML runtime does not differ much in its design from Qt Script, which you read about in the previous chapter of this book. In the following paragraphs, you will learn how to gain access to objects living in one of the environments from within the other one, as well as how to extend QML with new modules and elements.

Until now, all the example projects we did in this chapter were written with just QML and because of that, the project type we were choosing was Qt Quick UI, which let us quickly see the Qt Quick scene we modeled by interpreting it with the `qmlscene` tool. Now, we will want to add C++ to the equation and since C++ is a compiled language, we will need to do some proper compilation to get things working. Therefore, we will be using the **Qt Quick Application** template.

Creating QML objects from C++

When you start a new project of such a type in Qt Creator, after you answer the question about the component set you would like to use (choose any of the Qt Quick 2.*x* options for a regular Qt Quick application), you will receive some boilerplate code–a `main.cpp` file containing the C++ part and `main.qml`, which contains the scene definition. Let's have a look at the latter first:

```
import QtQuick 2.3
import QtQuick.Window 2.2

Window {
  visible: true
  width: 360
  height: 360

  MouseArea {
    anchors.fill: parent
    onClicked: {
      Qt.quit();
```

```
        }
      }

      Text {
        text: qsTr("Hello World")
        anchors.centerIn: parent
      }
    }
```

The code is a little bit different than before; just look at the highlighted parts. Instead of an `Item` root object, we now have a Window together with an `import` statement for a `QtQuick.Window` module. To understand why this is the case, we will have to understand the C++ code which invokes this QML document:

```
#include <QGuiApplication>
#include <QQmlApplicationEngine>

int main(int argc, char *argv[])
{
  QGuiApplication app(argc, argv);

  QQmlApplicationEngine engine;
  engine.load(QUrl(QStringLiteral("qrc:/main.qml")));

  return app.exec();
}
```

The source code is pretty simple. First, we instantiate an application object, just like for any other type of application. As we are not using Qt widgets, `QGuiApplication` is used instead of `QApplication`. The last line of the main function is also obvious–the application's event loop is started. Between those two lines, we can see an instance of `QQmlApplicationEngine` being created and fed with the URL of our QML document.

QML is driven by an engine implemented in `QQmlEngine` that is somewhat similar to `QScriptEngine`. `QQmlApplicationEngine` is a subclass of `QQmlEngine`, which provides a simple way of loading an application from a single QML file. This class does not create a root window to display our Qt Quick scene (QML applications don't have to necessarily be Qt Quick applications; they don't have to deal with the user interface at all), so it is the responsibility of the application to create a window if it wants to show a Qt Quick scene in it.

An alternative fit for loading Qt Quick-based user interfaces would be to use `QQuickView` or its less convenient superclass–`QQuickWindow`, which inherit `QWindow` and are able to render Qt Quick scenes.

You could then replace the main.cpp contents with the following code:

```
#include <QGuiApplication>
#include <QQuickView>

int main(int argc, char *argv[])
{
  QGuiApplication app(argc, argv);

  QQuickView view;
  view.setSource(QUrl::fromLocalFile(QStringLiteral("main.qml")));
  view.show();

  return app.exec();
}
```

Since QQuickView inherits QWindow, we can see that a window will be created to encompass the Qt Quick scene defined in main.qml. In such an event, you could replace the Window declaration with an Item similar to what we have seen in the earlier examples.

If you want to combine a Qt Quick scene with a Qt widgets-based user interface, you can use QQuickWidget present in the QtQuickWidgets module (add QT += quickwidgets to the project file to activate the module), which is similar to QQuickView and has a similar API, but instead of rendering the scene to a separate window, it renders it to a widget you can then put alongside other widgets.

The last way of creating QML objects is to use QQmlComponent. Contrary to the previous approaches, which had a QQmlEngine instance embedded in the object creating the QML object, we have to use a separate engine with the component method.

QQmlComponent is a wrapper around a QML component definition similar to the Component element on the QML side. It can create instances of that component with the create() method using a given QQmlEngine instance:

```
QQmlEngine *engine = new QQmlEngine;
QQmlComponent component(engine,
  QUrl::fromLocalFile(QStringLiteral("main.qml")));
QObject *object = component.create();
```

The object created is `QObject`, since that is the base class for all objects in QML. If the object represents a Qt Quick user interface, you can cast it to `QQuickItem` and use its methods to access Item's functionality:

```
QQuickItem *item = qobject_cast<QQuickItem*>(object);
Q_CHECK_PTR(item);
  // assert to check if qobject_cast returned a valid pointer
item->setOpacity(0.5);
```

`QQmlComponent` is the most "classic" way of instantiating QML objects. You can even use it to create additional objects in existing views:

```
QQuickView *view;
// ...
QQmlComponent component(view->engine(),
  QUrl::fromLocalFile("foobar.qml"));
component.create();
```

A variation on using `QQmlComponent` is to create an object in the QML engine asynchronously using the `QQmlIncubator` object. When creating complex objects, it takes time for them to instantiate and at times, it is desired to not block the control flow for too long by waiting for the operation to complete. In such cases, an incubator object can be used to schedule instantiation and continue the flow of the program. We can query the state of the incubator and when the object is constructed, we will be able to access it. The following code demonstrates how to use the incubator to instantiate an object and process pending events while waiting for the operation to complete:

```
QQmlComponent component(engine,
  QUrl::fromLocalFile("ComplexObject.qml"));
QQmlIncubator incubator;
component.create(incubator);
while(!incubator.isError() && !incubator.isReady())
  QCoreApplication::processEvents();
QObject *object = incubator.isReady() ? incubator.object() : 0;
```

Pulling QML objects to C++

In our terminology, pulling QML objects to C++ means that by using C++ code, we would like to gain access to objects living in the QML engine (for example, those declared in some QML file). Before we do that, it is important that we stress that in general, it is bad practice to try and pull objects from the QML engine. There are a few reasons for that, but we would like to stress just two of them.

First, if we assume the most common case, which is that the QML part of our application deals with a user interface in Qt Quick for the logic written in C++, then accessing QtQuick objects from C++ breaks the separation between logic and the presentation layer, which is one of the major principles in GUI programming. The second reason is that QML documents (and Qt Quick ones in particular) are often made by different people (designers) than those who implement the application logic (programmers). The user interface is prone to dynamic changes, relayouting up to a complete revamp. Heavy modifications of QML documents, such as adding or removing items from the design, would then have to be followed by adjusting the application logic to cope with those changes. This in turn needs recompilation of the whole application, which is cumbersome. In addition, if we allow a single application to have multiple user interfaces (skins), it might happen that because they are so different, it is impossible to decide upon a single set of common entities with hardcoded names that could be fetched from C++ and manipulated. Even if you managed to do that, such an application could crash easily if the rules were not strictly followed by designers.

That said, we have to admit that there are cases when it does make sense to pull objects from QML to C++, and that is why we decided to familiarize you with the way to do it. One of the situations where such an approach is desired is when QML serves us as a way to quickly define a hierarchy of objects with properties of different objects linked through more or less complex expressions, allowing them to answer to changes taking place in the hierarchy.

For example, if you create a `Qt Quick UI` project, among the files generated, you will find a `qmlproject` file containing the project definition expressed in QML itself, such as this one:

```
import QmlProject 1.1

Project {
  mainFile: "main.qml"

  importPaths: [ "plugins" ]

  QmlFiles {
    files: [ "Clock.qml", "Needle.qml" ]
  }
  JavaScriptFiles {
    directory: "."
  }
  ImageFiles {
    directory: "."
   }
}
```

It contains project contents specified as a set of file selectors and additional properties such as the main project file or a list of directories of where to look for QML modules. It is very easy to specify such a project description in QML and after doing so and by getting a handle on the `Project` instance from C++, one can read the required information directly from the object and its properties as needed.

`Project` is considered a root object of this document. There are five ways to get access to a root object, based on how the document was actually loaded into the engine:

- `QQmlApplicationEngine::rootObjects()` if using `QQmlApplicationEngine`
- `QQuickView::rootObject()` if using `QQuickView`
- `QQuickWidget::rootObject()` if using `QQuickWidget`
- `QQmlComponent::create()` if using `QQmlComponent`
- `QQmlIncubator::object()` if using `QQmlComponent` with `QQmlIncubator`

As we noted earlier, after retrieving an object, you can downcast it to a proper type using `qobject_cast`. Alternatively, you can start using the object through the generic `QObject` interface–accessing properties with `property()` and `setProperty()`, running functions through `QMetaObject::invokeMethod()`, and connecting to signals as usual.

The use case provided is a valid and fair situation when you want to pull a view root object or a manually created object from the QML world into C++. Now, we are going to show you how to do the same for an object from an arbitrary depth of the object tree.

QML documents define object trees. We can ask Qt to traverse a `QObject` tree and return a single object or a list of objects in the tree matching specified criteria. The same approach can be implemented for QML object trees. There are two criteria that can be used when searching. First, we can search for objects inheriting from a given class. Then, we can search for objects matching a given value of the `objectName` property defined in `QObject`. To search the tree for objects, one uses a `findChild` template method.

Consider a Qt Quick document defining a number of items:

```
import QtQuick 2.0

Item {
  width: 400; height: 400
  Rectangle {
    id: rect
    objectName: "redRectangle"
    color: "red"
    anchors.centerIn: parent
    width: height; height: parent.height*2/3
  }
```

```
    Rectangle {
      id: circle
      objectName: "blueCircle"
      color: "blue"
      anchors.centerIn: parent
      radius: width/2; width: height; height: parent.height*1/3
    }
  }
```

After gaining access to the root object using one of the methods described earlier, we can query the object tree for any of the colored shape items using the `objectName` values:

```
QObject *root = view->rootObject();
QObject *rect = root->findChild<QObject*>("redRectangle");
QObject *circle = root->findChild<QObject*>("blueCircle");
if(circle && rect)
    circle->setProperty("width", rect->property("width").toInt());
```

The `findChild()` method requires us to pass a class pointer as the template argument. Without knowing what class actually implements a given type, it is safest to simply pass `QObject*` as, once again, we know all QML objects inherit this. It is more important what gets passed as the function argument value–it is the name of the object we want returned. Notice it is not `id` of the object, but the value of the `objectName` property. When the results get assigned to the variables, we verify whether items have been successfully found and if that is the case, the generic `QObject` API is used to set the width of the circle to that of the rectangle.

Let us stress this again: if you have to use this approach, limit it to the minimum. And always verify whether the returned item exists (is a non-null pointer); the QML document might change between subsequent compilations of the program, and items and their names existing in one version of the document might cease to exist in the next version.

Pushing C++ objects to QML

A much better approach is to cross the boundary in the other direction–by exporting objects from C++ to QML. This allows C++ developers to decide what API is available for the script. The choice of which API to use is left to QML developers. Separation between the application logic and the user interface is maintained.

In the previous chapter, you learned to use Qt Script. We told you how to expose existing `QObject` instances to scripting through the use of the script engine's global object. We also discussed execution contexts, which provide layers of object visibility while calling functions. As already mentioned, QML has many similarities to that framework and in QML, a very similar approach is used to expose objects to the engine.

QML engines also use contexts to provide data scopes for the language. You can set properties on a context to make certain names resolve to given objects:

```
QQmlContext *context = new QQmlContext(engine);
QObject *object = new MyObject(...);
context->setContextProperty("foo", object);
```

From this moment, `object` is visible within `context` under the name `foo`.

Contexts can form hierarchies. On the top of the hierarchy resides a root context of the engine. Context properties are resolved from the bottom up, meaning that redefining a name in a child context shadows the name defined in the parent context. Let's see an example:

```
QQmlContext *parentContext = new QQmlContext(engine);
QQmlContext *childContext1 = new QQmlContext(parentContext);
QQmlContext *childContext2 = new QQmlContext(parentContext);
QQmlContext *childContext3 = new QQmlContext(parentContext);
QObject *objectA = new A, *objectB = new B, *object C = new C;
parentContext->setContextProperty("foo", objectA);
childContext1->setContextProperty("foo", objectB);
childContext2->setContextProperty("foo", objectC);
```

We created instances of classes `A`, `B`, and `C` and assigned them to a `foo` property of different contexts forming a hierarchy of five contexts. Why five? When passing a `QQmlEngine` to a constructor of `QQmlContext`, the context created becomes a child of the engine's root context. Therefore, we have four contexts we created ourselves and an additional context that always exists in the engine:

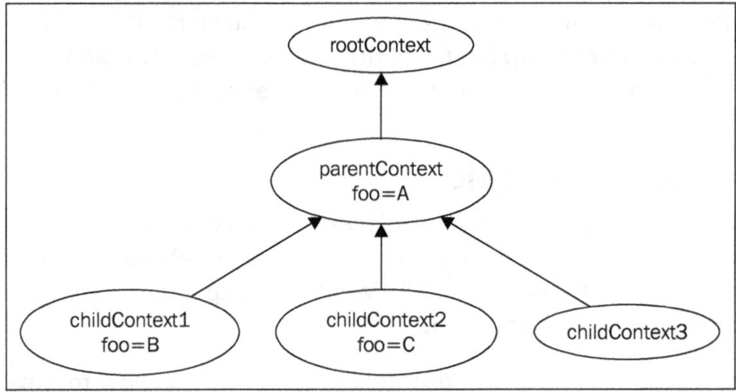

Now, if we call foo from within `childContext1`, we will access object `B`, and when we call `foo` from `childContext2`, we will access `C`. If we call it from `childContext3`, then, since `foo` is not defined there, the call will propagate to `parentContext` and hence `A` will be accessed. In `rootContext`, the context foo will not be available at all.

In most cases, we will not be creating contexts ourselves and thus, the most common situation is when we will have control over just the root context since it always exists and is easily accessible. Therefore, this context will usually be used to register C++ objects. As the root engine context is an ancestor of all other contexts, an object registered there will be visible from any QML document.

So what can we do with an exported object using QML? The object itself is accessible using the identifier given to it with the `setContextProperty()`. The identifier can be treated as the ID pseudo-property declared on objects in QML documents. Features that can be accessed from QML depend on the kind of object exported.

You can export two kinds of object. First, you can export a `QVariant` value that is then converted to an equivalent QML entity. The following table lists the most commonly used basic types:

Qt type	**QML basic type**
`bool`	`bool`
`unsigned int, int`	`int`
`double`	`double`
`float, qreal`	`real`
`QString`	`string`
`QUrl`	`url`
`QColor`	`color`
`QFont`	`font`
`QDate`	`date`
`QPoint, QPointF`	`point`
`QSize, QSizeF`	`size`
`QRect, QRectF`	`rect`

It allows us to export a wide range of objects:

```
int temperature = 17;
double humidity = 0.648;
QDate today = QDate::currentDate();
engine->rootContext()->setContextProperty("temperature",
  temperature);
engine->rootContext()->setContextProperty("humidity", humidity);
engine->rootContext()->setContextProperty("today",
  Qt.formatDate(today, ""));
```

And use them easily in QtQuick:

```
import QtQuick 2.0

Rectangle {
  id: root
  width: 400; height: width; radius: width/10
  color: "navy"
  border { width: 2; color: Qt.darker(root.color) }

  Grid {
    id: grid
    anchors.centerIn: parent
    columns: 2; spacing: 5
    Text { color: "white"; font.pixelSize: 20; text: "Temperature:" }
    Text { color: "white"; font.pixelSize: 20; text: temperature+"°C"}
    Text { color: "white"; font.pixelSize: 20; text: "Humidity:" }
    Text { color: "white"; font.pixelSize: 20; text: humidity*100+"%"}
  }
  Text {
    anchors {
      horizontalCenter: grid.horizontalCenter;
      bottom: grid.top; bottomMargin: 5
    }
    font.pixelSize: 24; color: "white"
    text: "Weather for "+Qt.formatDate(today)
  }
}
```

This will give us the following output:

In addition to the basic types, the QML engine provides automatic type conversions between special `QVariant` cases and JavaScript types–`QVariantList` is converted to JavaScript array and `QVariantMap` to a JavaScript object. This allows for an even more versatile approach. We can group all the weather information within a single JavaScript object by taking advantage of the `QVariantMap` conversion:

```
QVariantMap weather;
weather["temperature"] = 17;
weather["humidity"] = 0.648;
weather["today"] = QDate::currentDate();
engine->rootContext()->setContextProperty("weather", weather);
```

As a result, we get better encapsulation on the QML side:

```
Grid {
  // ...
  Text { color: "white"; font.pixelSize: 20; text: "Temperature:" }
  Text { color: "white"; font.pixelSize: 20; text:
    weather.temperature+"°C" }
  Text { color: "white"; font.pixelSize: 20; text: "Humidity:" }
  Text { color: "white"; font.pixelSize: 20; text:
    weather.humidity*100+"%"}
}
Text {
  // ...
  text: "Weather for "+Qt.formatDate(weather.today)
}
```

That's all fine and dandy in a world where weather conditions never change. In real life, however, one needs a way to handle situations where the data changes. We could, of course, re-export the map every time any of the values changed, but that would be very tedious.

Fortunately, the second kind of object that can be exported to QML comes to our rescue. Apart from `QVariant`, the engine can accept `QObject` instances as context property values. When exporting such an instance to QML, all the object's properties are exposed and all its slots become callable functions in the declarative environment. Handlers are made available for all the object's signals.

Time for action – self-updating car dashboard

In the next exercise, we will implement a car dashboard that can be used in a racing game and will show a number of parameters such as current speed and motor revolutions per minute. The final result will look similar to the following image:

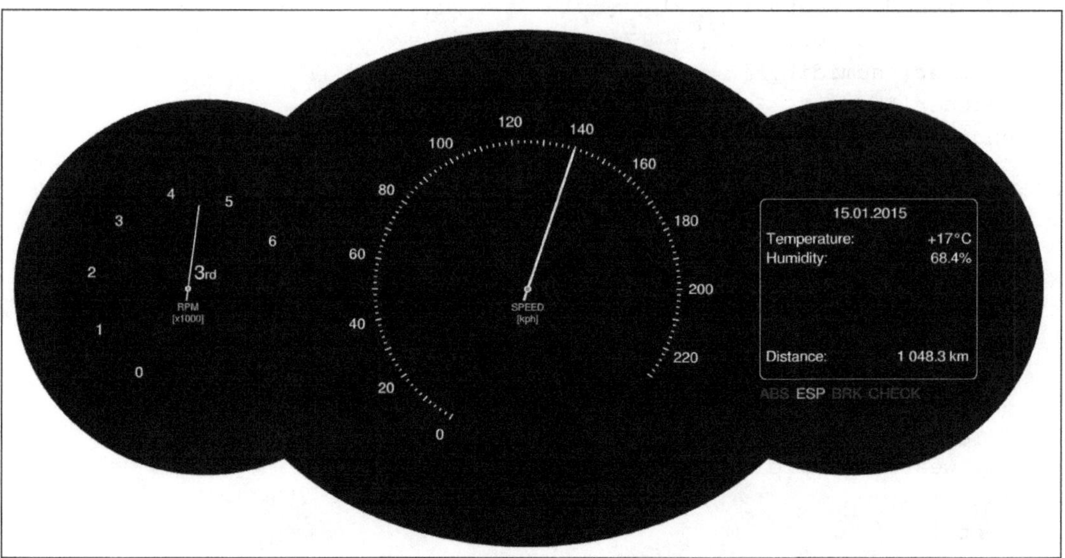

We will start with the C++ part. Set up a new Qt Quick Application. Choose the most recent Qt Quick version for the Qt Quick component set. This will generate a main function for you that instantiates `QGuiApplication` and `QQmlApplicationEngine` and sets them up to load a QML document.

Use the **File** menu to create **New file or Project** and create a new C++ class. Call it `CarInfo` and choose `QWidget` as its base class. Why not `QObject`, you may ask? This is because our class will also be a widget, which will be used for modifying values of different parameters so that we may observe how they influence what the Qt Quick scene displays. In the class header, declare the following properties:

```
Q_PROPERTY(int rpm READ rpm NOTIFY rpmChanged)
Q_PROPERTY(int gear READ gear NOTIFY gearChanged)
Q_PROPERTY(int speed READ speed NOTIFY speedChanged)
Q_PROPERTY(QDate today READ today NOTIFY todayChanged)
Q_PROPERTY(double distance READ distance NOTIFY distanceChanged)
```

The properties are read-only and the `NOTIFY` clause defines signals emitted when respective property values change. Go ahead and implement the appropriate functions for each property. Apart from the getter, also implement a setter as a public slot. Here is an example for a property controlling the speed of the car:

```
int CarInfo::speed() const { return m_speed; }
void CarInfo::setSpeed(int newSpeed) {
  if(m_speed == newSpeed) return;
  m_speed = newSpeed;
  emit speedChanged(m_speed);
}
```

You should be able to follow the example for the remaining properties on your own.

Since we want to use the widget to tweak property values, design the user interface for it using a Qt Designer Form. It can something look like this:

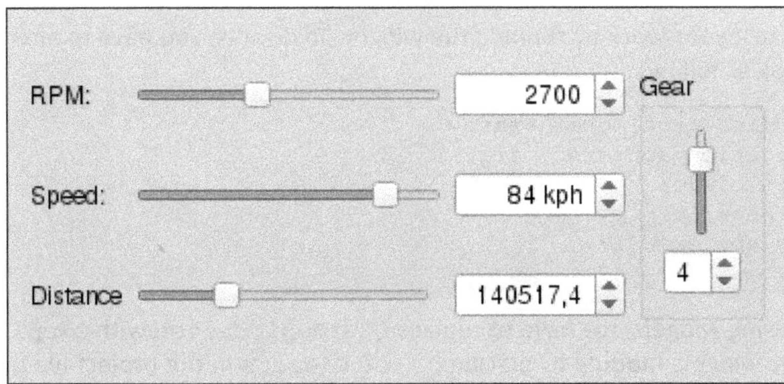

Make appropriate signal-slot connections in the widget so that modifying any of the widgets for a given parameter or using the setter slot directly updates all the widgets for that parameter.

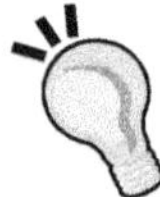

Instead of adding member variables to the `CarInfo` class for properties such as `speed`, `rpm`, `distance`, or `gear` you can operate directly on the widgets placed on the `ui` form so that, for example, a getter for the `distance` property will look like:

```
qreal CarInfo::distance() const
{ return ui->distanceBox->value(); }
```

The setter would then be modified to:

```
void CarInfo::setDistance(qreal newDistance)
{ ui->distanceBox->setValue(newDistance); }
```

You will then need to add `connect()` statements to the constructor to be sure that signals are propagated from the ui form:

```
connect(ui->distanceBox,
SIGNAL(valueChanged(double)), this, SIGNAL(distanceC
hanged(double)));
```

Next, you can test your work by running the widget. To do this, you have to alter the main function to look as follows:

```
int main(int argc, char **argv) {
  QApplication app(argc, argv);
  CarInfo cinfo;
  cinfo.show();
  return app.exec();
};
```

Since we are using widgets, we have to replace `QGuiApplication` with `QApplication` and enable the widgets module by placing `QT += widgets` in the project file (remember to run `qmake` from the project's context menu afterwards). Make sure everything works as expected (that is, that moving sliders and changing spinbox values reflect the changes to widget properties) before moving on to the next step.

We are now going to add `QtQuick` to the equation, so let's start by updating our main function to display our scene. Introduce the highlighted changes to the code:

```
int main(int argc, char **argv) {
  QApplication app(argc, argv);
  CarInfo cinfo;
  QQuickView view;
  view.engine()->rootContext()->setContextProperty
    ("carData", &cinfo);
  view.setSource("qrc:/main.qml");
  view.show();
  cinfo.show();
  return app.exec();
};
```

The modifications create a view for our scene, export the `CarInfo` instance to the global context of the QML engine, and load and display the scene from a file located in a resource.

It is important to first export all the objects and only then load the scene. This is because we want all the names to be already resolvable when the scene is being initialized so that they can be used right away. If we reversed the order of calls, we would get a number of warnings on the console about the identities being undefined.

Finally, we can focus on the QML part. Look at the picture of the result we want to be shown at the beginning of the exercise. For the black background, we used a bitmap image created in a graphical editor (you can find the file in the materials for this book), but you can obtain a similar effect by composing three black rounded rectangles directly in `QtQuick`–the two outer parts are perfect circles and the inner module is a horizontally stretched ellipse.

If you decide to use our background file (or make your own prettier image), you can put the following code into `main.qml`:

```
import QtQuick 2.3

Image {
  source: "dashboard.png"
  Item {
    id: leftContainer
    anchors.centerIn: parent
    anchors.horizontalCenterOffset: -550
    width: 400; height: width
  }
  Item {
    id: middleContainer
    anchors.centerIn: parent
    width: 700; height: width
  }
  Item {
    id: rightContainer
    anchors.centerIn: parent
    anchors.horizontalCenterOffset: 525
    width: 400; height: width
  }
}
```

What we do here is make the image our root item and create three items to serve as containers for different elements of the dashboard. The containers are all centered in the parent and we use a `horizontalCenterOffset` property to move the two outer items sideways. The values of the offset, as well as the widths, are calculated by trial and error to look good (note that all three containers are perfect squares). If instead of using our file, you settle for creating the three parts yourself using Qt Quick items, the containers will simply be anchored to the centers of the three black items.

The dials look complicated, but in reality, they are very easy to implement and you have already learned everything you need to design them.

Let's start with the needle. Create a new QML document and call it `Needle.qml`. Open the file and place the following content:

```
import QtQuick 2.0

Item {
  id: root
  property int length: parent.width*0.4
  property color color: "white"
  property color middleColor: "red"
  property int size: 2

  Rectangle {     // needle
    width: root.size
    height: length+20
    color: root.color
    anchors.horizontalCenter: parent.horizontalCenter
    anchors.bottom: parent.bottom
    anchors.bottomMargin: -20
    antialiasing: true
  }
  Rectangle {     // fixing
    anchors.centerIn: parent
    width: 8+root.size; height: width; radius: width/2
    color: root.color
    Rectangle {  // middle dot
      anchors { fill: parent; margins: parent.width*0.25 }
      color: root.middleColor
    }
  }
}
```

The document defines an item with four attributes–the length of the needle (defaults to 80% of the dial's radius), the color of the needle, `middleColor`, which stands for the color of the needle's fixing, and the size, which defines how wide the needle is. The code is self-explanatory. The item itself does not have any dimensions and onlys acts as an anchor for visual elements–the needle itself is a thin rectangle oriented vertically with a fixing 20 units from the end. The fixing is a circle of the same color as the needle with a smaller circle in the middle that uses a different fill color. The smaller radius of the inner circle is obtained by filling the outer circle with a 25% margin from each side.

As for the dials, we will put their code inline in the main file since we just have two of them and they differ a bit, so the overhead of creating a separate component with a well-designed set of properties would outweigh the benefits of having nicely encapsulated objects.

If you think about what needs to be done to have the dial displayed and working, it seems the hardest thing is to layout the numbers nicely on the circle, so let's start with that. Here is an implementation of a function for calculating the position along a circle circumference, based on the radius of the circle and angle (in degrees) where an item should be positioned:

```
function calculatePosition(angle, radius) {
  if( radius === undefined) radius = width/2*0.8
  var a = angle * Math.PI/180 // convert degrees to radians
  var px = width/2 + radius * Math.cos(a)
  var py = width/2 + radius * Math.sin(a)
  return Qt.point(px, py)
}
```

The function converts degrees to radians and returns the desired point. The function expects a width property to be available that helps to calculate the center of the circle and in case a radius was not given, serves as a means to calculate a feasible value for it.

With such a function available, we can use the already familiar `Repeater` element to position items where we want them. Let's put the function in `middleContainer` and declare the dial for car speed:

```
Item {
  id: middleContainer
  // ...
  function calculatePosition(angle, radius) { /* ... */ }
  Repeater {
    model: 24/2
    Item {
      property point pt:
      middleContainer.calculatePosition(120+index*12*2)
```

```
        x: pt.x; y: pt.y
        Label {
          anchors.centerIn: parent
          text: index*20
        }
      }
    }
    Needle {
      anchors.centerIn: parent
      length: parent.width*0.35
      size: 4
      rotation: 210+(carData.speed*12/10)
      color: "yellow"
    }
  }
```

You might have noticed we used an element called `Label`. We created it to avoid having to set the same property values for all the texts we use in the user interface:

```
import QtQuick 2.0

Text {
  color: "white"
  font.pixelSize: 24
}
```

The dial consists of a repeater that will create 12 elements. Each element is an item positioned using the earlier described function. The item has a label anchored to it that displays the given speed. We use `120+index*12*2` as the angle expression as we want "0" to be positioned at 120 degrees and each following item positioned 24 degrees further.

The needle is given rotation based on the value read from the `carData` object. Since the angular distance between consecutive 20 kph labels is 24 degrees, the distance for one kph is 1.2 and thus we multiply `carData.speed` by that factor. Item rotation is calculated with 0 degrees "pointing right"; therefore, we add 90 to the initial 120 degree offset of the first label to obtain starting coordinates matching those of the label system.

As you can see in the image, the speed dial contains small lines every 2 kph, with those divisible by 10 kph longer than others. We can use another `Repeater` to declare such ticks:

```
Repeater {
  model: 120-4
```

```
  Item {
    property point pt: middleContainer.calculatePosition(
      120+index*1.2*2, middleContainer.width*0.35
    )
    x: pt.x; y: pt.y
    Rectangle {
      width: 2
      height: index % 5 ? 5 : 10
        color: "white"
        rotation: 210+index*1.2*2
        anchors.centerIn: parent
        antialiasing: true
    }
  }
}
```

Finally, we can put a label for the dial:

```
Text {
    anchors.centerIn: parent
    anchors.verticalCenterOffset: 40
    text: "SPEED\n[kph]"
    horizontalAlignment: Text.AlignHCenter
    color: "#aaa"
    font.pixelSize: 16
}
```

Make sure the label is declared before the dial needle, or give the needle a higher *z* value so that the label doesn't overpaint the needle.

Next, repeat the process on your own for the left container by creating an RPM dial reading values from `carData.rpm`. The dial also displays the current gear of the car's engine. Place the following code inside the `leftContainer` object definition:

```
Item {
  id: gearContainer
  anchors.centerIn: parent
  anchors.horizontalCenterOffset: 10
  anchors.verticalCenterOffset: -10

  Text {
    id: gear
    property int value: carData.gear
    property var gears: [
      "R", "N",
```

```
        "1<sup>st</sup>", "2<sup>nd</sup>", "3<sup>rd</sup>",
        "4<sup>th</sup>", "5<sup>th</sup>"
      ]
      text: gears[value+1]
      anchors.left: parent.left
      anchors.bottom: parent.bottom
      color: "yellow"
      font.pixelSize: 32
      textFormat: Text.RichText
    }
  }
```

The only part needing explanation is highlighted. It defines an array of gear labels starting with reverse, going through neutral, and then through five forward gears. The array is then indexed with the current gear and the text for that value is applied to the label. Notice that the value is incremented by 1, which means the 0th index of the array will be used when `carData.gear` is set to `1`.

We will not show how to implement the right container. You can do that easily yourself now with the use of the `Grid` positioner to lay out the labels and their values. To display the series of controls on the bottom of the right container (with texts `ABS`, `ESP`, `BRK`, and `CHECK`), you can use `Row` of `Label` instances.

Now, start the program and begin moving the sliders on the widget. See how the Qt Quick scene follows the changes.

What just happened?

We have created a very simple `QObject` instance and exposed it as our "data model" to QML. The object has a number of properties that can receive different values. Changing a value results in emitting a signal, which in turn notifies the QML engine and causes bindings containing those properties to be reevaluated? As a result, our user interface gets updated.

The data interface between the QML and C++ worlds that we created is very simple and has a small number of properties. But as the amount of data we want to expose grows, the object can become cluttered. Of course, we can counter that effect by dividing it into multiple smaller objects each having separate responsibilities and then exporting all those objects to QML, but that is not always desirable. In our case, we can see that rpm and gear are properties of the engine sub-system so we could move them to a separate object; however, in reality, their values are tightly coupled with the speed of the car and to calculate the speed, we will need to know the values of those two parameters. But the speed also depends on other factors such as the slope of the road, so putting the speed into the engine sub-system object just doesn't seem right. Fortunately, there is a nice solution for that problem.

Time for action – grouping engine properties

QML has a concept called grouped properties. These are properties of an object that contain a group of "sub-properties." You already know a number of them–the border property of the `Rectangle` element or the anchors property of the `Item` element, for example. Let's see how to define such properties for our exposed object.

Create a new `QObject`-derived class and call it `CarInfoEngine`. Move the property definitions of rpm and gear to that new `class.Add` the following property declaration to `CarInfo`:

```
Q_PROPERTY(Object* engine READ engine NOTIFY engineChanged)
```

Implement the getter and the private field:

```
    QObject* engine() const { return m_engine; }
private:
    CarInfoEngine *m_engine;
```

We are not going to use the signal right now; however, we had to declare it otherwise QML would complain we were binding expressions that depend on properties that are non-notifiable:

```
signals:
    void engineChanged();
```

Initialize `m_engine` in the constructor of `CarInfo`:

```
m_engine = new CarInfoEngine(this);
```

Next, update the code of `CarInfo` to modify properties of `m_engine` whenever respective sliders on the widget are moved. Provide a link the other way, as well–if the property value is changed, update the user interface accordingly.

Update the QML document and replace `carData.gear` with `carData.engine.gear`. Do the same for `carData.rpm` and `carData.engine.rpm`. You should end up with something along the lines of:

```
Item {
  id: leftContainer
  // ...

  Item {
    id: gearContainer
    Text {
      id: gear
```

```
            property int value: carData.engine.gear
            // ...
          }
        }
        Needle {
          anchors.centerIn: parent
          length: parent.width*0.35
          rotation: 210+(carInfo.engine.rpm*35)
        }
    }
```

What just happened?

Essentially, what we did is expose a property in `CarInfo` that is itself an object that exposes a set of properties. This object of the type `CarInfoEngine` is bound to the `CarInfo` instance it refers to.

Extending QML

Thus far, what we did was exposing to QML single objects created and initialized in C++. But we can do much more–the framework allows us to define new QML types. These can either be generic `QObject` derived QML elements or items specialized for Qt Quick. In this section, you will learn to do both.

Registering classes as QML elements

We will start with something simple–exposing the `CarInfo` type to QML so that instead of instantiating it in C++ and then exposing it in QML, we can directly declare the element in QML and still allow the changes made to the widget to be reflected in the scene.

To make a certain class (derived from `QObject`) instantiable in QML, all that is required is to register that class with the declarative engine using the `qmlRegisterType` template function. This function takes the class as its template parameter along a number of function arguments: the module `uri`, the major and minor version numbers, and the name of the QML type we are registering. The following call would register the class `FooClass` as the QML type `Foo`, available after importing `foo.bar.baz` in Version 1.0:

```
qmlRegisterType<FooClass>("foo.bar.baz", 1, 0, "Foo");
```

You can place this invocation anywhere in your C++ code; just make sure this is before you try to load a QML document that might contain declarations of `Foo` objects. A typical place to put the function call is in the program's main function:

```
#include <QGuiApplication>
#include <QQuickView>
#include <QtQml>

int main(int argc, char **argv) {
  QGuiApplication app(argc, argv);
  QQuickView view;
  qmlRegisterType<FooClass>("foo.bar.baz", 1, 0, "Foo");
  view.setSource(QUrl("main.qml"));
  view.show();
  return app.exec();
}
```

Afterwards, you can start declaring objects of the type `Foo` in your documents. Just remember you have to import the respective module first:

```
import QtQuick 2.0
import foo.bar.baz 1.0

Item {
  Foo {
    id: foo
  }
}
```

Time for action – making CarInfo instantiable from QML

First, we will update the QML document to create an instance of `CarInfo` present in the CarInfo 1.0 module:

```
import QtQuick 2.0
import CarInfo 1.0

Image {
  source: "dashboard.png"

  CarInfo {
    id: carData
    visible: true // make the widget visible
  }
  // ...
}
```

As for registering `CarInfo`, it might be tempting to simply call `qmlRegisterType` on `CarInfo` and congratulate ourselves for a job well done:

```
int main(int argc, char **argv) {
  QGuiApplication app(argc, argv);
  QQuickView view;
  qmlRegisterType<CarInfo>("CarInfo", 1, 0, "CarInfo");
  view.setSource(QUrl("qrc://main.qml"));
  view.show();
  return app.exec();
}
```

In general this would work (yes, it is as simple as that). However, at the time of writing, trying to instantiate any widget in a QML document as the child of some `QtQuick` item will lead to a crash (maybe at the time you are reading this text the issue will have already been resolved). To avoid this, we need to make sure that what we instantiate is not a widget. For that, we will use a proxy object that will forward our calls to the actual widget. Therefore, create a new class called `CarInfoProxy` derived from `QObject` and make it have the same properties as `CarInfo`, for example:

```
class CarInfoProxy : public QObject {
  Q_OBJECT
  Q_PROPERTY(QObject *engine READ engine NOTIFY engineChanged)
  Q_PROPERTY(int speed READ speed WRITE setSpeed NOTIFY speedChanged)
  // ...
```

Declare one more property that will let us show and hide the widget on demand:

```
  Q_PROPERTY(bool visible READ visible WRITE
    setVisible NOTIFY visibleChanged)
```

Then, we can place the widget as a member variable of the proxy so that it is created and destroyed alongside its proxy:

```
private:
  CarInfo m_car;
```

Next, implement the missing interface. For simplicity, we are showing you code for some of the properties. The others are similar so you can fill in the gaps on your own:

```
public:
  CarInfoProxy(QObject *parent = 0) : QObject(parent) {
    connect(&m_car, SIGNAL(engineChanged()), this,
      SIGNAL(engineChanged()));
    connect(&m_car, SIGNAL(speedChanged(int)), this,
      SIGNAL(speedChanged(int)));
```

```
    }
    QObject *engine() const { return m_car.engine(); }
    bool visible() const { return m_car.isVisible(); }
    void setVisible(bool v) {
      if(v == visible()) return;
      m_car.setVisible(v);
      emit visibleChanged(v);
    }
    int speed() const { return m_car.speed(); }
    void setSpeed(int v) { m_car.setSpeed(v); }
  signals:
    void engineChanged();
    void visibleChanged(bool);
    void speedChanged(int);
};
```

You can see that we reuse the `CarInfoEngine` instance from the widget instead of duplicating it in the proxy class. Finally, we can register `CarInfoProxy` as `CarInfo`:

```
qmlRegisterType<CarInfoProxy>("CarInfo", 1, 0, "CarInfo");
```

If you run the code now, you will see it works–`CarInfo` has become a regular QML element. Because of this, its properties can be set and modified directly in the document, right? If you try setting the speed or the distance, it will work just fine. However, as soon as you try setting any of the properties grouped in the engine property, QML runtime will start complaining with a message similar to the following one:

```
Cannot assign to non-existent property "gear"
             engine.gear: 3
                    ^
```

This is because the runtime does not understand the engine property–we declared it as `QObject` and yet we are using a property this class doesn't have. To avoid this issue, we have to teach the runtime about `CarInfoEngine`.

First, let's update the property declaration macro to use `CarInfoEngine` instead of `QObject`:

```
Q_PROPERTY(CarInfoEngine* engine READ engine NOTIFY engineChanged)
```

And the getter function itself, as well:

```
CarInfoEngine* engine() const { return m_engine; }
```

Then, we should teach the runtime about the type:

```
QString msg = QStringLiteral("Objects of
  type CarInfoEngine cannot be created");
qmlRegisterUncreatableType<CarInfoEngine>
  ("CarInfo", 1, 0, "CarInfoEngine", msg);
```

What just happened?

In this exercise, we let the QML runtime know about two new elements. One of them is `CarInfo`, which is a proxy to our widget class. We told the engine this is a full-featured class that is instantiable from QML. The other class, `CarInfoEngine`, also became known to QML; however, the difference is that every attempt to declare an object of this type in QML fails with a given warning message. There are other functions available for registering types in QML but they are rarely used, so we will not be describing them here. If you are curious about them, type in qmlRegister in the Index tab of Creator's **Help** pane.

Custom Qt Quick items

It is nice to be able to create new QML element types that can be used to provide dynamic data engines or some other type of non-visual objects; however, this chapter is about Qt Quick so it is time now to learn how to provide new types of items to Qt Quick.

The first question you should ask yourself is whether you really need a new type of item. Maybe you can achieve the same goal with already existing elements? Very often you can use vector or bitmap images to use custom shapes in your applications, or you can use Canvas to quickly draw the graphics you need directly in QML.

If you decide that you do require custom items, you will be doing that by implementing subclasses of `QQuickItem`, which is the base class for all items in Qt Quick. After creating the new type, you will always have to register it with QML using `qmlRegisterType`.

OpenGL items

To provide very fast rendering of its scene, Qt Quick uses a mechanism called scene-graph. The graph consists of a number of nodes of well-known types, each describing a primitive shape to be drawn. The framework makes use of knowledge of each of the primitives allowed and their parameters to find the most performance-wise optimal order in which items can be rendered. Rendering itself is done using OpenGL, and all the shapes are defined in terms of OpenGL calls.

Providing new items for Qt Quick boils down to delivering a set of nodes that define the shape using terminology the graph understands. This is done by subclassing `QQuickItem` and implementing the pure virtual `updatePaintNode()` method, which is supposed to return a node that will tell the scene-graph how to render the item. The node will most likely be a describing a geometry (shape) with a material (color, texture) applied.

Time for action – creating a regular polygon item

Let's learn about the scene-graph by delivering an item class for rendering convex regular polygons. We will draw the polygon using the OpenGL drawing mode called "triangle fan." It draws a set of triangles that all have a common vertex. Subsequent triangles are defined by the shared vertex, the vertex from the previous triangle, and the next vertex specified. Have a look at the diagram to see how to draw a hexagon as a triangle fan using 8 vertices as control points:

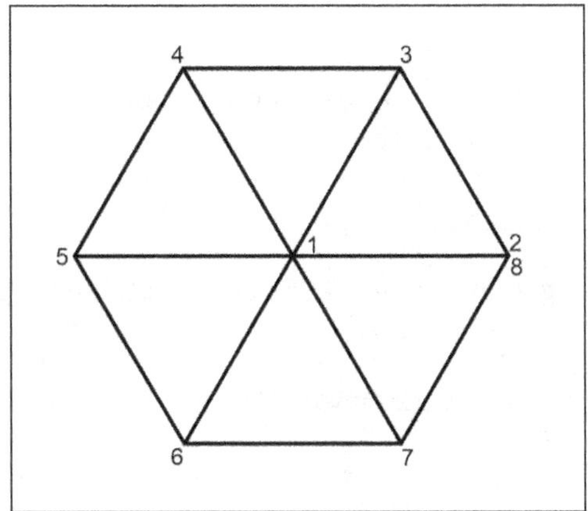

The same method applies for any regular polygon. The first vertex defined is always the shared vertex occupying the center of the shape. The remaining points are positioned on the circumference of a bounding circle of the shape at equal angular distances. The angle is easily calculated by dividing the full angle by the number of sides. For a hexagon, this yields 60 degrees.

Let's get down to business and the subclass `QQuickItem`. We will give it a very simple interface:

```
class RegularPolygon : public QQuickItem {
  Q_OBJECT
  Q_PROPERTY(int sides READ sides WRITE
    setSides NOTIFY sidesChanged)
  Q_PROPERTY(QColor color READ color WRITE
    setColor NOTIFY colorChanged)
public:
```

```
    RegularPolygon(QQuickItem *parent = 0);

    int sides() const { return m_sideCount; }
    void setSides (int s);

    QColor color() const { return m_color; }
    void setColor(const QColor &c);

    QSGNode *updatePaintNode(QSGNode *,
      UpdatePaintNodeData *);

  signals:
    void sidesChanged(int);
    void colorChanged(QColor);
  private:
    int m_sideCount;
    QColor m_color;
  };
```

Our polygon is defined by the number of sides and fill color. We also get everything we inherited from `QQuickItem`, including the width and height of the item. Besides the obvious getters and setters for the properties, we define just one method–`updatePaintNode()`, which is responsible for building the scene-graph.

Before we deal with updating graph nodes, let's deal with the easy parts first. Implement the constructor as follows:

```
RegularPolygon::RegularPolygon(QQuickItem *parent) :
  QQuickItem(parent) {
  setFlag(ItemHasContents, true);
  m_sideCount = 6;
}
```

We make our polygon a hexagon by default. We also set a flag, `ItemHasContents`, which tells the scene-graph that the item is not fully transparent and should ask us how the item should be painted by calling `updatePaintNode()`. This is an early optimization to avoid having to prepare the whole infrastructure if the item would not be painting anything anyway.

The setters are also quite easy to grasp:

```
void RegularPolygon::setSides(int s) {
  s = qMax(3, s);
  if(s == sides()) return;
  m_sideCount = v;
  emit sidesChanged(v);
```

```
    update();
}

void RegularPolygon::setColor(const QColor &c) {
    if(color() == c) return;
    m_color = c;
    emit colorChanged(c);
    update();
}
```

A polygon has to have at least three sides; thus, we enforce this as a minimum, sanitizing the input value with `qMax`. After we change any of the properties that might influence the look of the item, we call `update()` to let Qt Quick know that the item needs to be rerendered. Let's tackle `updatePaintNode()` now. We'll disassemble it into smaller pieces so that it is easier for you to understand how the function works:

```
QSGNode *RegularPolygon::updatePaintNode(QSGNode *oldNode,
                                QQuickItem::UpdatePaintNodeData *) {
```

When the function is called, it might receive a node it returned during a previous call. Be aware the graph is free to delete all the nodes when it feels like it, so you should never rely on the node being there even if you returned a valid node during the previous run of the function:

```
    QSGGeometryNode *node = 0;
    QSGGeometry *geometry = 0;
    QSGFlatColorMaterial *material = 0;
```

The node we are going to return is a geometry node that contains information about the geometry and the material of the shape being drawn. We will be filling those variables as we go through the method:

```
    if (!oldNode) {
      node = new QSGGeometryNode;
      geometry = new QSGGeometry(QSGGeometry::
        defaultAttributes_Point2D(), m_sideCount+2);
      geometry->setDrawingMode(GL_TRIANGLE_FAN);
      node->setGeometry(geometry);
      node->setFlag(QSGNode::OwnsGeometry);
```

As we already mentioned, the function is called with the previously returned node as the argument but we should be prepared for the node not being there and we should create it. Thus, if that is the case, we create a new `QSGGeometryNode` and a new `QSGGeometry` for it. The geometry constructor takes a so-called attribute set as its parameter, which defines a layout for data in the geometry. Most common layouts have been predefined:

Attribute set	Usage	First attribute	Second attribute
`Point2D`	`Solid colored shape`	`float x, y`	`-`
`ColoredPoint2D`	`Per-vertex color`	`float x, y`	`uchar red, green, blue, alpha`
`TexturedPoint2D`	`Per-vertex texture coordinate`	`float x, y`	`float tx, float ty`

We will be defining the geometry in terms of 2D points without any additional information attached to each point; therefore, we pass `QSGGeometry::defaultAttributes_Point2D()` to construct the layout we need. As you can see in the preceding table for that layout, each attribute consists of two floating point values denoting the *x* and *y* coordinates of a point.

The second argument of the `QSGGeometry` constructor informs us about the number of vertices we will be using. The constructor will allocate as much memory as is needed to store the required number of vertices using the given attribute layout. After the geometry container is ready, we pass its ownership to the geometry node so that when the geometry node is destroyed, the memory for the geometry is freed as well. At this moment, we also mark that we are going to be rendering in the `GL_TRIANGLE_FAN` mode:

```
        material = new QSGFlatColorMaterial;
        material->setColor(m_color);
        node->setMaterial(material);
        node->setFlag(QSGNode::OwnsMaterial);
```

The process is repeated for the material. We use `QSGFlatColorMaterial` as the whole shape is going to have one color that is set from `m_color`. Qt provides a number of predefined material types. For example, if we wanted to give each vertex a separate color, we would have used `QSGVertexColorMaterial` together with the `ColoredPoint2D` attribute layout:

```
    } else {
      node = static_cast<QSGGeometryNode *>(oldNode);
      geometry = node->geometry();
      geometry->allocate(m_sideCount+2);
```

This piece of code deals with a situation in which `oldNode` did contain a valid pointer to a node that was already initialized. In this case, we only need to make sure the geometry can hold as many vertices as we need in case the number of sides changed since the last time the function was executed:

```
material = static_cast<QSGFlatColorMaterial*>(node->material());
if(material->color() != m_color) {
```

```
        material->setColor(m_color);
        node->markDirty(QSGNode::DirtyMaterial);
    }
    }
```

This is repeated for the material. If the color differs, we reset it and tell the geometry node that the material needs to be updated by marking the `DirtyMaterial` flag:

```
        QRectF bounds = boundingRect();
        QSGGeometry::Point2D *vertices = geometry->vertexDataAsPoint2D();

        // first vertex is the shared one (middle)
        QPointF center = bounds.center();

        vertices[0].set(center.x(), center.y());

        // vertices are distributed along circumference of a circle

        const qreal angleStep = 360.0/m_sideCount;
        const qreal radius = qMin(width(), height())/2;

        for (int i = 0; i < m_sideCount; ++i) {
          qreal rads = angleStep*i*M_PI/180;
          qreal x = center.x()+radius*std::cos(rads);
          qreal y = center.y()+radius*std::sin(rads);
          vertices[1+i].set(x, y);
        }
        vertices[1+m_sideCount] = vertices[1];
```

Finally, we can set vertex data. First, we ask the geometry object to prepare a mapping for us from the allocated memory to a `QSGGeometry::Point2D` structure, which can be used to conveniently set data for each vertex. Then, actual calculations are performed using the equation for calculating points on a circle. The radius of the circle is taken as the smaller part of the width and height of the item so that the shape is centered in the item. As you can see on the diagram at the beginning of the exercise, the last point in the array has the same coordinates as the second point in the array to close the fan into a regular polygon:

```
        node->markDirty(QSGNode::DirtyGeometry);
        return node;
    }
```

At the very end, we mark the geometry as changed and return the node to the caller.

What just happened?

Rendering in Qt Quick can happen in a thread different than the main thread. By implementing `updatePaintNode()`, we performed synchronization between the GUI thread and the rendering thread. The function executing the main thread is blocked. Due to this reason, it is crucial that it executes as quickly as possible and doesn't do any unnecessary calculations as this directly influences performance. This is also the only place in your code where you can safely call functions from your item (such as reading properties) as well as interact with the scene-graph (creating and updating the nodes). Try not emitting any signals nor creating any objects from within this method as they will have affinity to the rendering thread rather than the GUI thread.

Having said that, you can now register your class with QML and test it with the following QML document:

```
RegularPolygon {
  id: poly
  vertices: 5
  color: "blue"
}
```

This should give you a nice blue pentagon. If the shape looks aliased, you can enforce anti-aliasing on the window:

```
int main(int argc, char **argv) {
  QGuiApplication app(argc, argv);
  QQuickView view;
  QSurfaceFormat format = view.format();
  format.setSamples(16); // enable multisampling
  view.setFormat(format);
  qmlRegisterType<RegularPolygon>("RegularPolygon", 1, 0,
                                  "RegularPolygon");
  view.setSource(QUrl("qrc://main.qml"));
  view.setResizeMode(QQuickView::SizeRootObjectToView);
  view.show();
  return app.exec();
}
```

Have a go hero – creating a supporting border for RegularPolygon

What is returned by `updatePaintNode()` might not just be a single `QSGGeometryNode` but also a larger tree of `QSGNode` items. Each node can have any number of child nodes. By returning a node that has two geometry nodes as children, you can draw two separate shapes in the item:

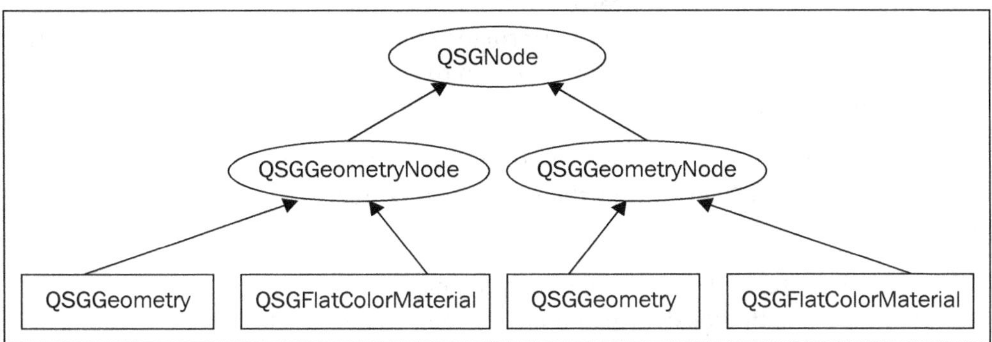

As a challenge, extend `RegularPolygon` to draw not only the internal filled part of the polygon but also an edge that can be of a different color. You can draw the edge using the `GL_QUAD_STRIP` drawing mode. Coordinates of the points are easy to calculate–the points closer to the middle of the shape are the same points that form the shape itself. The remaining points also lie on a circumference of a circle that is slightly larger (by the width of the border). Therefore, you can use the same equations to calculate them. The `GL_QUAD_STRIP` mode renders quadrilaterals with every two vertices specified after the first four, composing a connected quadrilateral. The following diagram should give you a clear idea of what we are after:

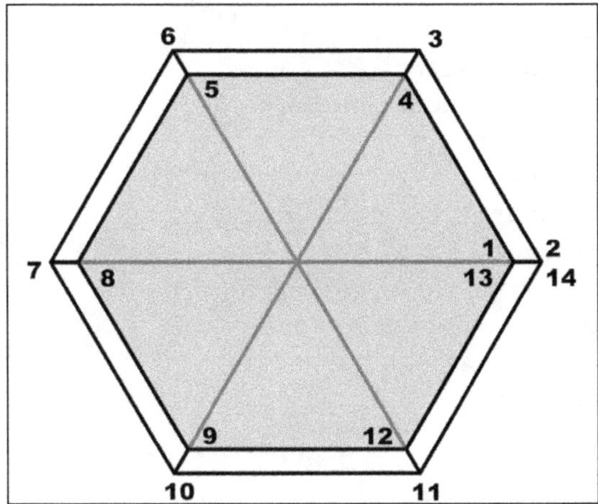

Painted items

Implementing items in OpenGL is quite difficult–you need to come up with an algorithm of using OpenGL primitives to draw the shape you want, and then you also need to be skilled enough with OpenGL to build a proper scene graph node tree for your item. But there is another way–you can create items by painting them with `QPainter`. This comes at a cost of performance as behind the scenes, the painter draws on an indirect surface (a frame buffer object or an image) that is then converted to OpenGL texture and rendered on a quad by the scene-graph. Even considering that performance hit, it is often much simpler to draw the item using a rich and convenient drawing API than to spend hours doing the equivalent in OpenGL or by using Canvas.

To use that approach, we will not be subclassing `QQuickItem` directly but rather `QQuickPaintedItem`, which gives us the infrastructure needed to use the painter for drawing items.

Basically, all we have to do, then, is implement the pure virtual `paint()` method that renders the item using the received painter. Let's see this put into practice and combine it with the skills we gained earlier.

Time for action – creating an item for drawing outlined text

The goal of the current exercise is to be able to make the following QML code work:

```
import QtQuick 2.3
import OutlineTextItem 1.0

Rectangle {
  width: 800; height: 400
  OutlineTextItem {
    anchors.centerIn: parent
    text: "This is outlined text"
    fontFamily: "Arial"
    fontPixelSize: 64
    color: "#33ff0000"
    antialiasing: true
    border {
      color: "blue"
      width: 2
      style: Qt.DotLine
    }
  }
}
```

And produce the following result:

This is outlined text

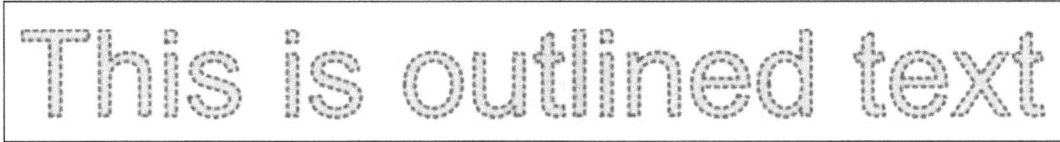

Start with an empty Qt project with the `core`, `gui`, and `quick` modules activated. Create a new class and call it `OutlineTextItemBorder`. Delete the implementation file as we are going to put all code into the header file. Place the following code into the class definition:

```
class OutlineTextItemBorder : public QObject {
  Q_OBJECT
  Q_PROPERTY(int width MEMBER m_width NOTIFY widthChanged)
  Q_PROPERTY(QColor color MEMBER m_color NOTIFY colorChanged)
  Q_PROPERTY(int style MEMBER m_style NOTIFY styleChanged)
public:
  OutlineTextItemBorder(QObject *parent) : QObject(parent),
    m_width(0), m_color(Qt::transparent),
    m_style(Qt::SolidLine) {}

  int width() const { return m_width; }
  QColor color() const { return m_color; }
  Qt::PenStyle style() const { return (Qt::PenStyle)m_style; }
  QPen pen() const {
   QPen p;
   p.setColor(m_color);
   p.setWidth(m_width);
   p.setStyle((Qt::PenStyle)m_style);
   return p;
  }
signals:
  void widthChanged(int);
  void colorChanged(QColor);
  void styleChanged(int);
private:
  int m_width;
  QColor m_color;
  int m_style;
};
```

You can see that `Q_PROPERTY` macros don't have the `READ` and `WRITE` keywords we've been using thus far. This is because we are taking a shortcut right now and we let `moc` produce code that will operate on the property by directly accessing the given class member. Normally, we would recommend against such an approach as without getters, the only way to access the properties is through the generic `property()` and `setProperty()` calls. However, in this case, we are not going to be exposing this class to the public in C++ so we won't need the setters, and we implement the getters ourselves, anyway. The nice thing about the `MEMBER` keyword is that if we also provide the `NOTIFY` signal, the generated code will emit that signal when the value of the property changes, which will make property bindings in QML work as expected. The rest of the class is pretty simple–we are, in fact, providing a class for defining a pen that is going to be used for stroking text, so implementing a method that returns the actual pen seems like a good idea.

The class will provide a grouped property for our main item class. Create a class called `OutlineTextItem` and derive it from `QQuickPaintedItem`, as follows:

```
class OutlineTextItem : public QQuickPaintedItem {
  Q_OBJECT
  Q_PROPERTY(OutlineTextItemBorder* border READ
    border NOTIFY borderChanged)
  Q_PROPERTY(QString text MEMBER m_text NOTIFY textChanged)
  Q_PROPERTY(QColor color MEMBER m_color NOTIFY colorChanged)
  Q_PROPERTY(QString fontFamily MEMBER m_ffamily
    NOTIFY fontFamilyChanged)
  Q_PROPERTY(int fontPixelSize MEMBER m_fsize NOTIFY
    fontPixelSizeChanged)
public:
  OutlineTextItem(QQuickItem *parent = 0);
  void paint(QPainter *painter);
  OutlineTextItemBorder* border() const { return m_border; }
  QPainterPath shape(const QPainterPath &path) const;
private slots:
  void updateItem();
signals:
  void textChanged(QString);
  void colorChanged(QColor);
  void borderChanged();
  void fontFamilyChanged(QString);
  void fontPixelSizeChanged(int);
private:
  OutlineTextItemBorder* m_border;
  QPainterPath m_path;
  QRectF m_br;
  QString m_text;
```

```
    QColor m_color;
    QString m_ffamily;
    int m_fsize;
};
```

The interface defines properties for the text to be drawn, in addition to its color, font, and the grouped property for the outline data. Again, we use `MEMBER` to avoid having to manually implement getters and setters. Unfortunately, this makes our constructor code more complicated as we still need a way to run some code when any of the properties are modified. Implement the constructor using the following code:

```
OutlineTextItem::OutlineTextItem(QQuickItem *parent) :
  QQuickPaintedItem(parent) {
    m_border = new OutlineTextItemBorder(this);
    connect(this, SIGNAL(textChanged(QString)), SLOT(updateItem()));
connect(this, SIGNAL(colorChanged(QColor)), SLOT(updateItem()));
connect(this, SIGNAL(fontFamilyChanged(QString)), SLOT(updateItem()));
connect(this, SIGNAL(fontPixelSizeChanged(int)), SLOT(updateItem()));
connect(m_border, SIGNAL(widthChanged(int)), SLOT(updateItem()));
connect(m_border, SIGNAL(colorChanged(QColor)), SLOT(updateItem()));
connect(m_border, SIGNAL(styleChanged(int)), SLOT(updateItem()));
updateItem();
}
```

We basically connect all the property change signals from both the object and its grouped property object to the same slot that is going to update the data for the item if any of its components are modified. We also call the same slot directly to prepare the initial state of the item. The slot can be implemented like this:

```
void OutlineTextItem::updateItem() {
  QFont font(m_ffamily, m_fsize);
  m_path = QPainterPath();
  m_path.addText(0, 0 , font, m_text);
  m_br = shape(m_path).controlPointRect();
  setImplicitWidth(m_br.width());
  setImplicitHeight(m_br.height());
  update();
}
```

At the beginning, the function resets a painter path object that serves as a backend for drawing outlined text and initializes it with the text drawn using the font set. Then, the slot calculates the bounding rect for the path using a function `shape()` that we will shortly see. Finally, it sets the calculated size as the size hint for the item and asks the item to repaint itself with the `update()` call:

```
QPainterPath OutlineTextItem::shape(const QPainterPath &path) const
{
  QPainterPathStroker ps;
  if(m_border->width() > 0 && m_border->style() != Qt::NoPen) {
    ps.setWidth(m_border->width());
  } else {
    ps.setWidth(0.0000001); // workaround a bug in Qt
  }
  QPainterPath p = ps.createStroke(path);
  p.addPath(path);
  return p;
}
```

The `shape()` function returns a new painter path that includes both the original path and its outline created with the `QPainterPathStroker` object. This is so that the width of the stroke is correctly taken into account when calculating the bounding rectangle. We use `controlPointRect()` to calculate the bounding rectangle as it is much faster than `boundingRect()` and returns an area greater or equal to the one `boundingRect()` would, which is okay for us.

What remains is to implement the `paint()` routine itself:

```
void OutlineTextItem::paint(QPainter *painter) {
  if(m_text.isEmpty()) return;
  painter->setPen(m_border->pen());
  painter->setBrush(m_color);
  painter->setRenderHint(QPainter::Antialiasing, true);
  painter->translate(-m_br.topLeft());
  painter->drawPath(m_path);
}
```

The code is really simple–we bail out early if there is nothing to draw. Otherwise, we set up the painter using the pen and color obtained from the item's properties. We enable anti-aliasing and calibrate the painter coordinates with that of the bounding rectangle of the item. Finally, we draw the path on the painter.

What just happened?

During this exercise, we made use of the powerful API of Qt's graphical engine to complement an existing set of Qt Quick items with a simple functionality. This is otherwise very hard to achieve using predefined Qt Quick elements and even harder to implement using OpenGL. We agreed to take a small performance hit in exchange for having to write just about a hundred lines of code to have a fully working solution. Remember to register the class with QML if you want to use it in your code:

```
qmlRegisterUncreatableType<OutlineTextItemBorder>(
  "OutlineTextItem", 1, 0, "OutlineTextItemBorder",
  "Can't create items of OutlineTetItemBorder type"
);
qmlRegisterType<OutlineTextItem>(
  "OutlineTextItem", 1, 0, "OutlineTextItem"
);
```

Summary

In this chapter, you have been familiarized with a declarative language called QML. The language is used to drive Qt Quick–a framework for highly dynamic and interactive content. You learned the basics of Qt Quick–how to create documents with a number of element types and how to create your own in QML or in C++. You also learned how to bind expressions to properties to automatically re-evaluate them. But so far, despite us talking about "fluid" and "dynamic" interfaces, you haven't seen much of that. Do not worry; in the next chapter, we will focus on animations in Qt Quick, as well as fancy graphics and applying what you learned in this chapter for creating nice looking and interesting games. So, read on!

10
Qt Quick

In the previous chapter, we introduced you to the basics of Qt Quick and QML. By now, you should be fluent enough with the syntax and understand the basic concepts of how Qt Quick works. In this chapter, we will show you how to make your games stand out from the crowd by introducing different kinds of animations that make your applications feel more like the real world. You will also learn to treat Qt Quick objects as separate entities programmable using state machines. A large section of this chapter is devoted to making your games prettier by using OpenGL effects and particle systems. Another significant part of this chapter will introduce how to implement a number of important gaming concepts using Qt Quick. All this is going to be shown with the building of a simple 2D action game using the presented concepts.

Bringing life into static user interfaces

What we have described so far can be called anything but "fluid." Let's change that now by learning how to add some dynamics into the user interfaces we create. Thus far, books cannot contain moving pictures, so most things we describe here you will have to test yourself by running the provided Qt Quick code.

Animating elements

Qt Quick provides a very extensive framework for creating animations. By that, we don't mean only moving items around. We define an animation as *changing an arbitrary value over time*. So, what can we animate? Of course, we can animate item geometry. But we can also animate rotation, scale, other numeric values, and even colors. But let's not stop here. Qt Quick also lets you animate the parent-child hierarchy of items or anchor assignments. Almost anything that can be represented by an item property can be animated.

Moreover, the changes are rarely linear—if you kick a ball in the air, it first gains height quickly because its initial speed was large. However, the ball is a physical object being pulled down by the Earth's gravity, which slows the climb down until the ball stops and then starts falling down, accelerating until it hits the ground. Depending on the properties of both the ground and ball, the object can bounce off the surface into the air again with less momentum, repeating the spring-like motion until eventually it fades away, leaving the ball on the ground. Qt Quick lets you model all that using easing curves that can be assigned to animations.

Generic animations

Qt Quick provides a number of animation types derived from a generic `Animation` element that you will never use directly. The type exists only to provide an API common to different animation types.

Let's take a closer look at the animation framework by looking at a family of animation types derived from the most common animation type—`PropertyAnimation`. As the name implies, they provide the means to animate values of object properties. Despite the fact that you can use the `PropertyAnimation` element directly, it is usually more convenient to use one of its subclasses that are specialized in dealing with peculiarities of different data types.

The most basic property animation type is `NumberAnimation`, which lets you animate all kinds of numeric values of both integral and real numbers. The simplest way of using it is to declare an animation, tell it to animate a specific property in a specific object, and then set the length of the animation and the starting and ending value for the property:

```
import QtQuick 2.0

Item {
  id: root
  width: 600; height: width
  Rectangle {
    id: rect
    color: "red"; width: 50; height: width
  }
```

```
    NumberAnimation {
      target: rect
      property: "x"
      from: 0; to: 550
      duration: 3000
      running: true
    }
}
```

Time for action – scene for an action game

Create a new Qt Quick UI project. In the project directory, make a subdirectory called `images` and from the game project that we have created using Graphics View copy `grass.png`, `sky.png`, and `trees.png`. Then, put the following code into the QML document:

```
import QtQuick 2.1

Image {
  id: root
  property int dayLength: 60000 // 1 minute
  source: "images/sky.png"

  Item {
    id: sun
    x: 140
    y: root.height-170
    Rectangle {
      id: sunVisual
      width: 40
      height: width
      radius: width/2
      color: "yellow"
      anchors.centerIn: parent
    }
  }
  Image {
    source: "images/trees.png"
    x: -200
    anchors.bottom: parent.bottom
  }
  Image {
    source: "images/grass.png"
    anchors.bottom: parent.bottom
  }
}
```

When you run the project now, you will see a screen similar to this one:

What just happened?

We set up a very simple scene consisting of three images stacked up to form a landscape. Between the background layer (the sky) and the foreground (trees), we placed a yellow circle representing the sun. Since we are going to be moving the sun around in a moment, we anchored the center of the object to an empty item without physical dimensions so that we can set the sun's position relative to its center. We also equipped the scene with a `dayLength` property, which is going to hold information about the length of one day of game time. By default, we set it to 60 seconds so that things happen really fast and we can see the animation's progress without waiting. After all things are set correctly, the length of the day can be balanced to fit our needs.

The graphical design lets us easily manipulate the sun while keeping it behind the tree line. Notice how the stacking order is implicitly determined by the order of elements in the document.

Time for action – animating the sun's horizontal movement

The everyday cruise of the sun in the sky starts in the east and continues west to hide beneath the horizon in the evening. Let's try to replicate this horizontal movement by adding animation to our `sun` object.

Open the QML document of our last project. Inside the `root` item add the following declaration:

```
NumberAnimation {
  target: sun
  property: "x"
  from: 0
  to: root.width
  duration: dayLength
  running: true
}
```

Running the program with such modifications will produce a run with a horizontal movement of the sun. The following image is a composition of a number of frames of the run:

What just happened?

We introduced a `NumberAnimation` element that is set to animate the `x` property of the `sun` object. The animation starts at `0` and lasts until `x` reaches the `root` item's width (which is the right edge of the scene). The movement lasts for `dayLength` miliseconds. The `running` property of the animation is set to `true` to enable the animation. Since we didn't specify otherwise, the motion is linear.

You might be thinking that the animation runs in the wrong direction—"west" is on the left and "east" is on the right, yes? That's true, however, only if the observer faces north. If that were the case for our scene, we wouldn't be seeing the sun at all—at noon, it crosses the south direction.

Composing animations

The animation we made in the last section looks okay but is not very realistic. The sun should rise in the morning, reach its peak sometime before noon, and then sometime later start setting toward the evening, when it should cross the horizon and hide beneath the landscape.

To achieve such an effect, we could add two more animations for the `y` property of the sun. The first animation would start right at the beginning and decrease the vertical position of the sun (remember that the vertical geometry axis points down, so decreasing the vertical position means the object goes up). The animation would be complete at one third of the day length. We would then need a way to wait for some time and then start a second animation that would pull the object down toward the ground. Starting and stopping the animation is easy—we can either call the `start()` and `stop()` functions on the animation item or directly alter the value of the `running` property. Each `Animation` object emits `started()` and `stopped()` signals. The delay can be implemented by using a timer. We could provide a signal handler for the stopped signal of the first animation to trigger a timer to start the other one like this:

```
NumberAnimation {
  id: sunGoesUpAnim
  // …
  onStopped: sunGoesDownAnimTimer.start()
}
Timer {
  id: sunGoesDownAnimTimer
  interval: dayLength/3
  onTriggered: sunGoesDownAnim.start()
}
```

Even ignoring any side problems this would bring (for example, how to stop the animation without starting the second one), such an approach couldn't be called "declarative," could it?

Fortunately, similar to what we had in C++, Qt Quick lets us form animation groups that run either parallel to each other or in sequence. There are the `SequentialAnimation` and `ParallelAnimation` types where you can declare any number of child animation elements forming the group. To run two animations in parallel, we could declare the following hierarchy of elements:

```
ParallelAnimation {
  id: parallelAnimationGroup

  NumberAnimation {
    target: obj1; property: "prop1"
    from: 0; to: 100
```

```
    duration: 1500
  }
  NumberAnimation {
    target: obj2; property: "prop2"
    from: 150; to: 0
    duration: 1500
  }
  running: true
}
```

The same technique can be used to synchronize a larger group of animations, even if each component has a different duration:

```
SequentialAnimation {
  id: sequentialAnimationGroup

  ParallelAnimation {
    id: parallelAnimationGroup

    NumberAnimation {
      id: A1
      target: obj2; property: "prop2"
      from: 150; to: 0
      duration: 1000
    }
    NumberAnimation {
      id: A2
      target: obj1; property: "prop1"
      from: 0; to: 100
      duration: 2000
    }
  }
  PropertyAnimation {
    id: A3
    target: obj1; property: "prop1"
    from: 100; to: 300
    duration: 1500
  }
  running: true
}
```

The group presented in the snippet consists of three animations. The first two animations are executed together as they form a parallel subgroup. One member of the group runs twice as long as the other. Only after the whole subgroup completes is the third animation started. This can be visualized using a UML activity diagram where the size of each activity is proportional to the duration of that activity:

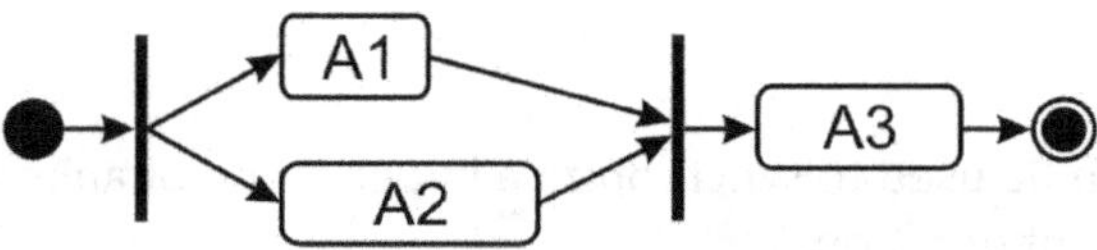

Time for action – making the sun rise and set

Let's add vertical movement (animation of the `y` property) to our sun by adding a sequence of animations to the QML document. As our new animations are going to be running in parallel to the horizontal animation, we could enclose animations for both directions within a single `ParallelAnimation` group. It would work, but in our opinion this would unnecessarily clutter the document. Another way of specifying parallel animations is to declare them as separate hierarchies of elements, making each animation independent of the other, and that is what we are going to do here.

Open our document from the last exercise and right under the previous animation, place the following code:

```
SequentialAnimation {
  NumberAnimation {
    target: sun
    property: "y"
    from: root.height+sunVisual.height
    to: root.height-270
    duration: dayLength/3
  }
  PauseAnimation { duration: dayLength/3 }
  NumberAnimation {
    target: sun
    property: "y"
    from: root.height-270
    to: root.height+sunVisual.height
    duration: dayLength/3
  }
running: true
}
```

Running the program will result in the light source rising in the morning and setting in the evening. However, the trajectory of the move seems somewhat awkward.

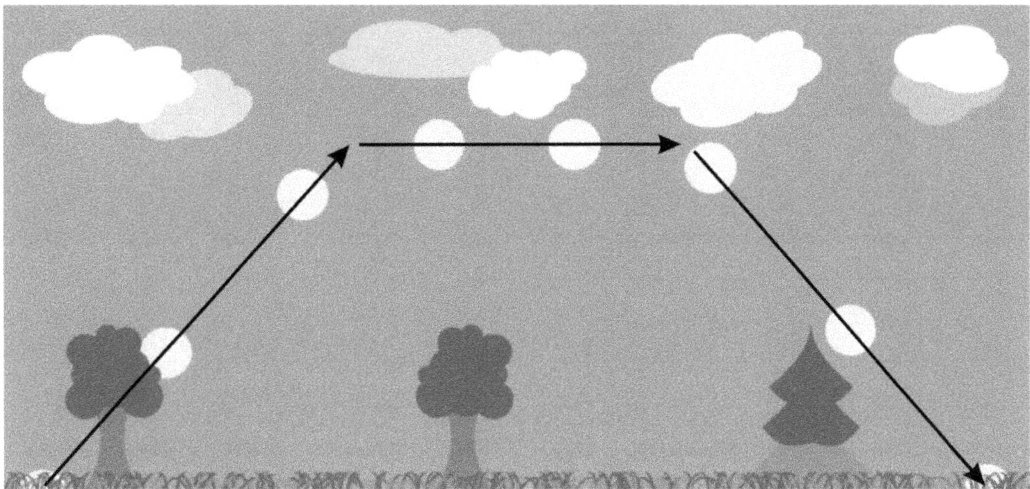

What just happened?

We declared a sequential animation group consisting of three animations, each taking 1/3 of the day length. The first member of the group makes the sun go up. The second member, which is an instance of a new element type—`PauseAnimation`—introduces a delay equal to its duration. This in turn lets the third component start its work in the afternoon to pull the sun down toward the horizon.

The problem with such a declaration is that the sun moves in a horribly angular way, as can be seen in the image.

Non-linear animations

The reason for the described problem is that our animations are linear. As we noted in the beginning of this chapter, linear animations rarely occur in nature, which usually makes their use yield a very unrealistic result.

We also said earlier that Qt Quick allows us to use easing curves to perform animations along non-linear paths. There are a large number of curves offered. Here is a diagram listing available non-linear easing curves:

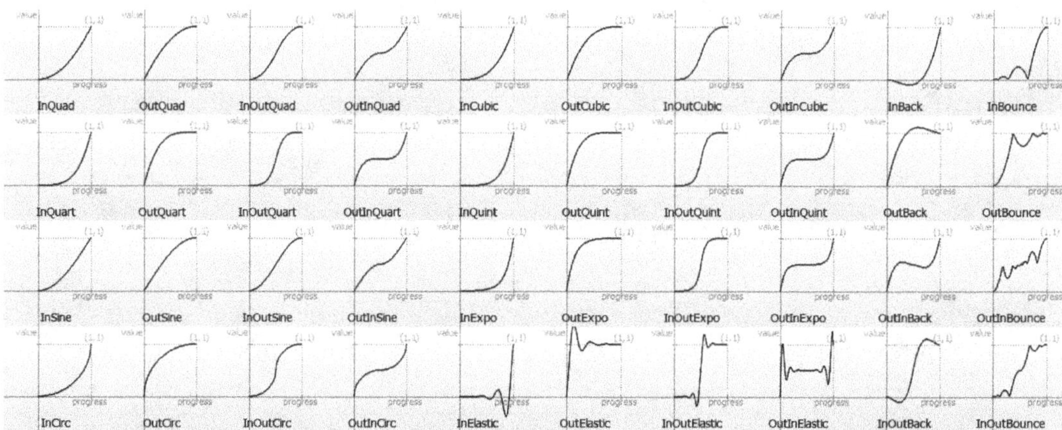

You can use any of the curves on an element of the type `PropertyAnimation` or one derived from it (for example, `NumberAnimation`). This is done by using the `easing` property group, where you can set the `type` of the curve. Different curve types may further be tweaked by setting a number of properties in the `easing` property group, such as `amplitude` (for bounce and elastic curves), `overshoot` (for back curves), or `period` (for elastic curves).

Declaring an animation along an `InOutBounce` path is very easy:

```
NumberAnimation {
  target: obj; property: prop;
  from: startValue; to: endValue;
  easing.type: Easing.InOutBounce
}
```

Time for action – improving the path of the sun

The task at hand is going to be to improve the animation of the sun so that it behaves in a more realistic way. We will do this by adjusting the animations so that the object moves over a curved path.

In our QML document, replace the previous vertical animation with the following one:

```
SequentialAnimation {
  NumberAnimation {
```

```
      target: sun
      property: "y"
      from: root.height+sunVisual.height
      to: root.height-270
      duration: dayLength/2
      easing.type: Easing.OutCubic
    }
    NumberAnimation {
      target: sun
      property: "y"
      to: root.height+sunVisual.height
      duration: dayLength/2
      easing.type: Easing.InCubic
    }

    running: true
  }
```

What just happened?

The sequence of three animations (two linear ones and a pause) was replaced by another sequence of two animations that follow a path determined by a cubic function. This makes our sun rise pretty fast and then slow down to an amount almost unnoticeable near the moment when the sun approaches noon. When the first animation is finished, the second one reverses the motion, making the sun descend very slowly and then increase its velocity as dusk approaches. As a result, the further the sun is away from the ground, the slower it seems to move. At the same time, the horizontal animation remains linear as the speed of Earth in its motion around the Sun is practically constant. When we combine the horizontal and vertical animations, we get a path that looks very similar to what we can observe in the real world.

Property value sources

From a QML perspective, animation and element types derived from it are something called *property value source*. This means they can be attached to a property and generate values for it. What is important is that it allows us to use animations using a much simpler syntax. Instead of explicitly declaring the target and property of an animation, one can attach the animation to a named property of the parent object.

To do this, instead of specifying `target` and `property` for `Animation`, use the `on` keyword followed by the name of a property name for which the animation is to be a value source. For example, to animate the `rotation` property of an object with a `NumberAnimation` object, the following code can be used:

```
NumberAnimation on rotation {
  from: 0
  to: 360
  duration: 500
}
```

It is valid to specify more than one property value source for the same property of an object.

Time for action – adjusting the sun's color

If you look at the sun at dusk or dawn, you will see that it is not yellow, but rather becomes red the closer it is to the horizon. Let's teach our object representing the sun to do the same by providing a property value source for it.

Open the QML document, find the declaration for the `sunVisual` object, and extend it with the highlighted part:

```
Rectangle {
  id: sunVisual
  // ...
  SequentialAnimation on color {
    ColorAnimation {
      from: "red"
      to: "yellow"
      duration: 0.2*dayLength/2
    }
    PauseAnimation { duration: 2*0.8*dayLength/2 }
    ColorAnimation {
      to: "red"
      duration: 0.2*dayLength/2
    }
    running: true
  }
}
```

What just happened?

An animation was attached to the `color` property of our rectangle modeling the visual aspects of the sun. The animation consists of three parts. First, we perform a transition from red to yellow using the `ColorAnimation` object. This is an `Animation` subtype dedicated to modifying colors. Since the rectangle color is not a number, using the `NumberAnimation` object would not have worked as the type cannot interpolate color values. Therefore, we either have to use the `PropertyAnimation` or `ColorAnimation` object. The duration for the animation is set to 20 percent of half the day length so that the yellow color is obtained very quickly. The second component is a `PauseAnimation` object to provide a delay before the third component is executed, which gradually changes the color back to red. For the last component, we do not provide a value for the `from` property. This causes the animation to be initiated with the value of the property current to the time when the animation is executed (in this case, the sun should be yellow).

Notice that we only had to specify the property name for the top-level animation. This particular element is what serves as the property value source, and all descendant animation objects "inherit" the target property from that property value source.

Time for action – furnishing sun animation

The animation of the sun looks almost perfect right now. We can still improve it, though. If you look into the sky in the early morning and then again at noon, you will notice that the sun appears much bigger during sunrise or sunset compared to its size in zenith. We can simulate that effect by scaling the object.

In our scene document, add another sequential animation that operates on the `scale` property of the sun:

```
SequentialAnimation on scale {
  NumberAnimation {
    from: 1.6; to: 0.8
    duration: dayLength/2
    easing.type: Easing.OutCubic
  }
  NumberAnimation {
    from: 0.8; to: 1.6
    duration: dayLength/2
    easing.type: Easing.InCubic
  }
}
```

What just happened?

In this section, we just followed the path set for an earlier declaration—the vertical movement of the stellar body influences its perceived size; therefore, it seems like a good decision to bind the two animations together. Notice that instead of specifying a new property value source for the scale, we might have modified the original animation and made the scale animation parallel to that operate on the `y` property:

```
SequentialAnimation {
  ParallelAnimation {
    NumberAnimation {
      target: sun
      property: "y"
      from: root.height+sunVisual.height
      to: root.height-270
      duration: dayLength/2
```

```
        easing.type: Easing.OutCubic
      }
      NumberAnimation {
        target: sun
        property: "scale"
        from: 1.6; to: 0.8
        duration: dayLength/2
        easing.type: Easing.OutCubic
      }
    // ...
```

Have a go hero – animating the sun's rays

By now, you should be an animation expert. If you want to try your skills, here is a task for you. The following code can be applied to the sun object and will display very simple red rays emitted from the sun:

```
Item {
  id: sunRays
  property int count: 10
  width: sunVisual.width
  height: width
  anchors.centerIn: parent
  z: -1
  Repeater {
    model: sunRays.count
    Rectangle {
      color: "red"
      rotation: index*360/sunRays.count
      anchors.fill: parent
    }
  }
}
```

The goal is to animate the rays so that the overall effect looks good and fits the tune like style of the scene. Try different animations—rotations, size changes, and colors. Apply them to different elements—all rays at once (for example, using the `sunRays` identifier) or only particular rectangles generated by the repeater.

Behaviors

In the previous chapter, we implemented a dashboard for a racing game where we had a number of clocks with needles. We could set values for each clock (for example, car speed) and a respective needle would immediately set itself to the given value. But such an approach is unrealistic—in the real world, changes of a value happen over time. In our example, the car accelerates from 10 mph to 50 mph by going through 11 mph, 12 mph and so on, until after some time it reaches the desired value. We call this the *behavior* of a value—it is essentially a model that tells how the parameter reaches its destined value. Defining such models is a perfect use case for declarative programming. Fortunately, QML exposes a `Behavior` element that lets us model behaviors of property changes in Qt Quick.

The `Behavior` elements let us associate an animation with a given property so that, every time the property value is to be changed, it is done by running the given animation instead of by making an immediate change to the property value:

```
import QtQuick 2.0

Item {
  width: 600; height: width
  Item {
    id: empty
    x: parent.width/2; y: parent.height/2
    Rectangle {
      id: rect
      width: 100; height: width; color: "red"
      anchors.centerIn: parent
    }
  }
  MouseArea {
    anchors.fill: parent
    onClicked: { empty.x = mouse.x; empty.y = mouse.y }
  }
}
```

The preceding code implements a simple scene with a red rectangle anchored to an empty item. Whenever the user clicks somewhere within the scene, the empty item is moved there, dragging along the rectangle. Let's see how to use the `Behavior` element to smoothly change the position of the empty item. The `Behavior` element is a property value source just like the `Animation` element itself; thus, it is easiest to use on the on-property syntax:

```
Item {
  id: rect
  x: parent.width/2; y: parent.height/2
  Rectangle {
    width: 100; height: width; color: "red"
    anchors.centerIn: parent
  }
  Behavior on x { NumberAnimation { } }
  Behavior on y { NumberAnimation { } }
}
```

By adding the two marked declarations, we define behaviors for properties `x` and `y` that follow animations defined by `NumberAnimation`. We do not include start or end values for the animation as these will depend on the initial and final value for the property. We also don't set the property name in the animation because by default, the property for which the behavior is defined will be used. As a result, we get a linear animation of a numerical property from the original value to the destined value over the default duration.

Using linear animations for real world objects rarely looks good. Usually, you will get much better results if you set an easing curve for the animation so that it starts slowly and then gains speed and decelerates just before it is finished.

Animations that you set on behaviors can be as complex as you want:

```
Behavior on x {
  SequentialAnimation {
    PropertyAction {
  target: rect; property: "color"; value: "yellow"
}
ParallelAnimation {
  NumberAnimation { easing.type: Easing.InOutQuad; duration: 1000
}

      SequentialAnimation {
        NumberAnimation {
          target: rect; property: "scale"
          from: 1.0; to: 1.5; duration: 500
        }
```

```
          NumberAnimation {
            target: rect; property: "scale"
            from: 1.5; to: 1.0; duration: 500
          }
        }
      }
      PropertyAction { target: rect; property: "color"; value: "red" }
    }
  }
```

The behavioral model declared in the last piece of code performs a sequential animation. It first changes the color of the rectangle to yellow using the `PropertyAction` element, which performs an immediate update of a property value (we will talk about this more a bit later). The color will be set back to red after, as the last step of the model. In the meantime, a parallel animation is performed. One of its components is a `NumberAnimation` class that executes the actual animation of the `x` property of `empty` (since the target and property of the animation are not explicitly set). The second component is a sequential animation of the `scale` property of the rectangle, which first scales the item up by 50 percent during the first half of the animation and then scales it back down in the second half of the animation.

Time for action – animating the car dashboard

Let's employ the knowledge we just learned to improve our car dashboard so that it shows some realism in the way the clocks update their values.

Open the dashboard project and navigate to the `dashboard.qml` file. Find the declaration of the `Needle` object, which is responsible for visualizing the speed of the vehicle. Add the following declaration to the object:

```
Behavior on rotation {
  SmoothedAnimation { velocity: 50 }
}
```

Repeat the process for the left clock. Set the velocity of the animation to `100`. Build and run the project. See how the needles behave when you modify the parameter values in spinboxes. Adjust the `velocity` of each animation until you get a realistic result.

What just happened?

We have set the property value sources on needle rotations that are triggered whenever a new value for the property is requested. Instead of immediately accepting the new value, the `Behavior` element intercepts the request and starts the `SmoothedAnimation` class to gradually reach the requested value. The `SmoothedAnimation` class is an animation type that animates numeric properties. The speed of the animation is not determined by its duration, but instead a `velocity` property is set. This property dictates how fast a value is to be changed. However, the animation is using a non-linear path—it first starts slowly, then accelerates to the given velocity and near the end of the animation, decelerates in a smooth fashion. This yields an animation that is attractive and realistic and at the same time, is of shorter or longer duration, depending on the distance between the starting and ending values.

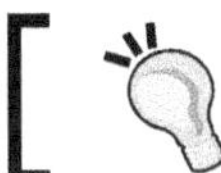

You can implement custom property value sources by subclassing `QQmlPropertyValueSource` and registering the class in the QML engine.

States and transitions

When you look at real world objects, it is often very easy to define their behavior by extracting a number of states the object may take and describing each of the states separately. A lamp can be turned either on or off. When it is "on" it is emitting light of a given color, but it is not doing that when in the "off" state. Dynamics of the object can be defined by describing what happens if the object leaves one of the states and enters another one. Considering our lamp example, if you turn the lamp on, it doesn't momentarily start emitting light with its full power, but rather the brightness of the light gradually increases to reach its final power after a very short period.

Qt Quick supports *state-driven* development by letting us declare states and transitions between them for items. The model fits the declarative nature of Qt Quick very well.

By default, each item has a single anonymous state and all properties you define take values of the expressions you bind or assign to them imperatively based on different conditions. Instead of this, a set of states can be defined for the object and for each of the state properties of the object itself; in addition, the objects defined within it can be programmed with different values or expressions. Our example lamp definition could be similar to:

```
Item {
  id: lamp
  property bool lampOn: false
  Rectangle {
    id: lightsource
    anchors.fill: parent
    color: transparent
  }
}
```

We could, of course, bind the `color` property of `lightsource` to `lamp.lampOn ? "yellow" : "transparent"`, but instead we can define an "on" state for the lamp and use a `PropertyChanges` element to modify the rectangle color:

```
Item {
  id: lamp
  property bool lampOn: false
  // …
  states: State {
    name: "on"
    PropertyChanges {
      target: lightsource
      color: "yellow"
    }
  }
}
```

Each item has a `state` property that you can read to get the current state, but you can also write to it to trigger transition to a given state. By default, the `state` property is set to an empty string that represents the anonymous state. Note that with the preceding definition, the item has two states—the "on" state and the anonymous state (which in this case is used when the lamp is off). Remember that state names have to be unique as the `name` parameter is what identifies a state in Qt Quick.

To enter a state, we can, of course, use an event handler fired when the value of the `lampOn` parameter is modified:

```
onLampOnChanged: state = lampOn ? "on" : ""
```

Such imperative code works, but it can be replaced with a declarative definition in the state itself:

```
State {
  name: "on"
  when: lamp.lampOn
  PropertyChanges {
    target: lightsource
    color: "yellow"
  }
}
```

Whenever the expression bound to the `when` property evaluates to `true`, the state becomes active. If the expression becomes `false`, the object will return to the default state or will enter a state for which its own `when` property evaluates to `true`.

To define more than one custom state, it is enough to assign a list of state definitions to the `states` property:

```
states: [
  State {
    name: "on"
    when: lamp.lampOn
  },
  State {
    name: "off"
    when: !lamp.lampOn
  }
]
```

The `PropertyChanges` element is the most often used change in a state definition, but it is not the only one. In exactly the same way that the `ParentChange` element can assign a different parent to an item and the `AnchorChange` element can update anchor definitions, it is also possible to run a script when a state is entered using the `StateChangeScript` element. All these element types are used by declaring their instances as children in a `State` object.

The second part of the state machine framework is defining how an object transits from one state to another. Similar to the `states` property, all items have a `transitions` property, which takes a list of definitions represented by the `Transition` objects and provides information about animations that should be played when a particular transition takes place.

A transition is identified by three attributes—the source state, the destination state, and a set of animations. Both the source state name (set to the `from` property) and the target state name (set to the `to` property) can be empty, in which case they should be interpreted as "any". If a `Transition` exists that matches the current state change, its animations will be executed. A more concrete transition definition (which is one where `from` and/or `to` are explicitly set) has precedence over a more generic one.

Suppose that we want to animate the opacity of the lamp rectangle from `0` to `1` when the lamp is switched on. We can do it as an alternative to manipulating the color. Let's update the lamp definition:

```
Item {
  id: lamp
  property bool lampOn: false
  Rectangle {
    id: lightsource
    anchors.fill: parent
    color: "yellow"
    opacity: 0
```

```
    }
    states: State {
      name: "on"
      when: lamp.lampOn
      PropertyChanges {
        target: lightsource
        opacity: 1
      }
    }
    transitions: Transition {
      NumberAnimation { duration: 100 }
    }
  }
```

The transition is triggered for any source and any target state—it will be active when the lamp goes from the anonymous to the "on" state, as well as in the opposite direction. It defines a single `NumberAnimation` element that lasts for 100 miliseconds. The animation does not define the target object nor the property it works on; thus, it will be executed for any property and any object that needs updating as part of the transition—in the case of the lamp, it will only be the `opacity` property of the `lightsource` object.

If more than one animation is defined in a transition, all animations will run in parallel. If you need a sequential animation, you need to explicitly use a `SequentialAnimation` element:

```
Transition {
  SequentialAnimation {
    NumberAnimation { target: lightsource; property: "opacity";
    duration: 200 }
    ScriptAction { script: console.log("Transition has ended") }
  }
}
```

> States are a feature of all `Item` types as well as its descendent types. It is, however, possible to use states with elements not derived from the `Item` object by using a `StateGroup` element, which is a self-contained functionality of states and transitions with exactly the same interface as what is described here regarding `Item` objects.

More animation types

The animation types we discussed earlier are used for modifying values of types that can be described using physical metrics (position, sizes, colors, angles). But there are more types available.

The first group of special animations consists of the `AnchorAnimation` and `ParentAnimation` elements.

The `AnchorAnimation` element is useful if a state change should cause a change to defined anchors for an item. Without it, the item would immediately snap into its place. By using the `AnchorAnimation` element, we trigger all anchor changes to be gradually animated.

The `ParentAnimation` element, on the other hand, makes it possible to define animations that should be present when an item receives a new parent. This usually causes an item to be moved to a different position in the scene. By using the `ParentAnimation` element in a state transition, we can define how the item gets into its target position. The element can contain any number of child animation elements that are going to be run in parallel during a `ParentChange` element.

The second special group of animations is action animations—`PropertyAction` and `ScriptAction`. These animation types are not stretched in time, but rather perform a given one-time action.

The `PropertyAction` element is a special kind of animation that performs an immediate update of a property to a given value. It is usually used as part of a more complex animation to modify a property that is not animated. It makes sense to use it if a property needs to have a certain value during an animation.

The `ScriptAction` is an element that allows the execution of an imperative piece of code during an animation (usually at its beginning or end).

Quick game programming

Here, we will go through the process of creating a platform game using Qt Quick. It will be a game similar to Benjamin the Elephant from *Chapter 6, Graphics View*. The player will control a character that will be walking through the landscape and collecting coins. The coins will randomly be appearing in the world. The character can access highly placed coins by jumping. The more the character jumps, the more tired he gets and the slower he begins to move and has to rest to regain speed. To make the game more difficult, at times moving obstacles will be generated. When the character bumps into any of them, he gets more and more tired. When the fatigue exceeds a certain level, the character dies and the game ends.

Throughout this chapter as well as the previous one, we prepared a number of pieces we will be reusing for this game. The layered scene that was arranged when you learned about animations will serve as our game scene. The animated sun is going to represent the passing of time. When the sun sets, the time runs out and the game ends. The heartbeat diagram will be used to represent the character's level of fatigue—the more tired the character gets, the faster his heart beats.

There are many ways this game can be implemented and we want to give you a level of freedom, so this is not going to be a step-by-step guide on how to implement a complete game. At some points, we will be telling you to employ some skills you have already learned to perform some task without telling you how to do it. At others, we will provide broad descriptions and complete solutions.

Game loops

Most games revolve around some kind of game loop. It is usually some kind of function that is repeatedly called at constant intervals and its task is to progress the game—process input events, move objects around, calculate and execute actions, check win conditions, and so on. Such an approach is very imperative and usually results in a very complex function that needs to know everything about everybody (This kind of anti-pattern is sometimes called a *god object* pattern). In QML (which powers the Qt Quick framework), we aim to separate responsibilities and declare well-defined behaviors for particular objects. Therefore, although it is possible to set up a timer which will periodically call a game loop function, this is not the best possible approach in a declarative world.

Instead, we suggest using a natural time-flow mechanism already present in Qt Quick—one that controls the consistency of animations. Remember how we defined the sun's travel across the sky at the beginning of this chapter? Instead of setting up a timer and moving the object by a calculated number of pixels, we created an animation, defined a total running time for it, and let Qt take care of updating the object. This has the great benefit of neglecting delays in function execution. If you used a timer and some external event introduced a significant delay before the timeout function was run, the animation would start lagging behind. When Qt Quick animations are used, the framework compensates for such delays, skipping some of the frame updates to ensure that the requested animation duration is respected. Thanks to that, you will not have to take care of it all by yourself.

To overcome the second difficult aspect of a game loop—the god anti-pattern—we suggest encapsulating the logic of each item directly in the item itself the using states and transitions framework we introduced earlier. If you define an object using a natural time flow describing all states it can enter during its lifetime and actions causing transitions between states, you will be able to just plop the object with its included behavior wherever it is needed and thus easily reuse such definitions in different games, reducing the amount of work necessary to make the object fit into the game.

As for input event processing, a usual approach in games is to read input events and call functions responsible for actions associated with particular events:

```
void Scene::keyEvent(QKeyEvent *ke) {
  switch(ke->key()) {
  case Qt::Key_Right: player->goRight(); break;
  case Qt::Key_Left:  player->goLeft();  break;
```

```
    case Qt::Key_Space: player->jump();    break;
    // ...
    }
  }
```

This, however, has its drawbacks, one of which is the need to check events at even periods of time. This might be hard and certainly is not a declarative approach.

We already know that Qt Quick handles keyboard input via the `Keys` attached property. It is possible to craft QML code similar to the one just presented, but the problem with such an approach is that the faster the player taps keys on the keyboard, the more frequently the character will move, jump, or shoot. It isn't hard if it is done properly, though.

Time for action – character navigation

Create a new QML document and call it `Player.qml`. In the document, place the following declarations:

```
Item {
  id: player
  y: parent.height
  focus: true

  Keys.onRightPressed: x = Math.min(x+20, parent.width)
  Keys.onLeftPressed: x = Math.max(0, x-20)
  Keys.onUpPressed: jump()

  function jump() { jumpAnim.start() }

  Image {
    source: "elephant.png"
    anchors.bottom: parent.bottom
    anchors.horizontalCenter: parent.horizontalCenter
  }
  Behavior on x { NumberAnimation { duration: 100 } }
  SequentialAnimation on y {
    id: jumpAnim
    running: false
    NumberAnimation { to: player.parent.height-50; easing.type:
      Easing.OutQuad }
    NumberAnimation { to: player.parent.height; easing.type:
      Easing.InQuad }
  }
}
```

Next, open the document containing the main scene definition and declare the player character near the end of the document after all the background layers are declared:

```
Player {
  id: player
  x:40
}
```

What just happened?

The player itself is an empty item with a keyboard focus that handles presses of the right, left, and up arrow keys, causing them to manipulate the `x` and `y` coordinates of the player. The `x` property has a `Behavior` element set so that the player moves smoothly within the scene. Finally, anchored to the player item is the actual visualization of the player—our elephant friend.

When the right or left arrow keys are pressed, a new position for the character will be calculated and applied. Thanks to the `Behavior` element, the item will travel gradually (during one second) to the new position. Keeping the key pressed will trigger auto-repeat and the handler will be called again. In a similar fashion, when the spacebar is pressed, it will activate a prepared sequential animation that will lift the character up by 50 pixels and then move it down again to the initial position.

This approach works but we can do better. Let's try something different.

Time for action – another approach to character navigation

Replace the previous key handlers with the following code:

```
QtObject {
  id: flags
  readonly property int speed: 20
  property int horizontal: 0
}
Keys.onRightPressed: { recalculateDurations(); flags.horizontal = 1 }
Keys.onLeftPressed: {
  if(flags.horizontal != 0) return
  recalculateDurations()
  flags.horizontal = -1
}
Keys.onUpPressed: jump()
Keys.onReleased: {
  if(event.key == Qt.Key_Right) flags.horizontal = 0
```

```
    if(event.key == Qt.Key_Left && flags.horizontal < 0)
    flags.horizontal = 0
  }

  function recalculateDurations() {
    xAnimRight.duration = (xAnimRight.to-x)*1000/flags.speed
    xAnimLeft.duration  = (x-xAnimLeft.to)*1000/flags.speed
  }
  NumberAnimation on x {
    id: xAnimRight
    running: flags.horizontal > 0
    to: parent.width
  }
  NumberAnimation on x {
    id: xAnimLeft
    running: flags.horizontal < 0
    to: 0
  }
```

What just happened?

Instead of performing actions immediately, upon pressing a key, we are now setting flags (in a private object) for which direction the character should be moving in. In our situation, the right direction has priority over the left direction. Setting a flag triggers an animation that tries to move the character toward an edge of the scene. Releasing the button will clear the flag and stop the animation. Before the animation is started, we are calling the `recalculateDurations()` function, which checks how long the animation should last for the character to move at the desired speed.

If you want to replace keyboard-based input with something else, for example, accelerometer or custom buttons, the same principle can be applied. When using an accelerometer, you can even control the speed of the player by measuring how much the device is tilted. You can addtionally store the tilt in the `flags.horizontal` parameter and make use of that variable in the `recalculateDurations()` function.

Have a go hero – polishing the animation

What we have done is sufficient for many applications. However, you can try controlling the movement even more. As a challenge, try modifying the system in such a way that during a jump, inertia keeps the current horizontal direction and speed of movement of the character until the end of the jump. If the player releases the right or left keys during a jump, the character will stop only after the jump is complete.

Despite trying to do everything in a declarative fashion, some actions will still require imperative code. If some action is to be executed periodically, you can use the `Timer` parameter to execute a function on demand. Let's go through the process of implementing such patterns together.

Time for action – generating coins

The goal of the game we are trying to implement is to collect coins. We will spawn coins now and then in random locations of the scene.

Create a new QML Document and call it `Coin.qml`. In the editor, enter the following code:

```
Item {
  id: coin

  Rectangle {
    id: coinVisual
    color: "yellow"
    border.color: Qt.darker(color)
    border.width: 2
    width: 30; height: width
    radius: width/2
    anchors.centerIn: parent

    transform: Rotation {
      axis.y: 1

      NumberAnimation on angle {
        from: 0; to: 360
        loops: Animation.Infinite
        running: true
      }
    }
    Text {
      color: coinVisual.border.color
      anchors.centerIn: parent
      text: "1"
    }
  }
}
```

Next, open the document where the scene is defined and enter the following code somewhere in the scene definition:

```
Component {
  id: coinGenerator
  Coin {}
}

Timer {
  id: coinTimer
  interval: 1000
  repeat: true

  onTriggered: {
    var cx = Math.floor(Math.random() * scene.width)
    var cy = Math.floor(Math.random() * scene.height/3)
          + scene.height/2
    coinGenerator.createObject(scene, { x: cx, y: cy});
  }
}
```

What just happened?

First, we defined a new element type, `Coin`, consisting of a yellow circle with a number centered over an empty item. The rectangle has an animation applied that rotates the item around a vertical axis, resulting in a pseudo three-dimensional effect.

Next, a component able to create instances of a `Coin` element is placed in the scene. Then, a `Timer` element is declared that fires every second and spawns a new coin at a random location of the scene.

Sprite animation

The player character, as well as any other component of the game, should be animated. If the component is implemented using simple Qt Quick shapes, it is quite easy to do by changing the item's properties fluently, by way of using property animations (like we did with the `Coin` object). Things get more difficult if a component is complex enough that it is easier to draw it in a graphics program and use an image in the game instead of trying to recreate the object using Qt Quick items. Then, one needs a number of images—one for every frame of animation. Images would have to keep replacing one another to make a convincing animation.

Time for action – implementing simple character animation

Let's try to make the player character animated in a simple way. In materials that come with this book, you will find a number of images with different walking phases for Benjamin the Elephant. You can use them or you can draw or download some other images to be used in place of those provided by us.

Put all images in one directory (for example, `images`) and rename them so that they follow a pattern that contains the base animation name followed by a frame number, for example, `walking_01`, `walking_02`, `walking_03`, and so on.

Next, open the `Player.qml` document and replace the image element showing "`elephant.png`" with the following code:

```
Image {
  property int currentFrame: 1
  property int frameCount: 10
  source: "images/walking_"+currentFrame+".png"
  mirror: player.facingLeft

  anchors.bottom: parent.bottom
  anchors.horizontalCenter: parent.horizontalCenter
  Animation on currentFrame {
    from: 1
    to: frameCount
    loops: Animation.Infinite
    duration: frameCount*40
    running: player.walking
  }
}
```

In the root element of `Player.qml`, add the following properties:

```
property bool walking: flags.horizontal != 0
property bool facingLeft: flags.horizontal < 0
```

Start the program and use the arrow keys to see Benjamin move.

What just happened?

A number of images were prepared following a common naming pattern containing a number. All the images have the same size. This allows us to replace one image with another just by changing the value of the `source` property to point to a different image. To make it easier, we introduced a property called the `currentFrame` element that contains the index of the image to be displayed. We used the `currentFrame` element in a string forming an expression bound to the `source` element of the image. To make substituting frames easy, a `NumberAnimation` element was declared to modify values of the `currentFrame` element in a loop from `1` to the number of animation frames available (represented by the `frameCount` property), so that each frame is shown for 40 miliseconds. The animation is playing if the `walking` property evaluates to `true` (based on the value of the `flags.horizontal` element in the player object). Finally, we use the `mirror` property of the `Image` parameter to flip the image if the character is walking left.

The preceding approach works, but is not perfect. The complexity of the declaration following this pattern grows much faster than required when we want to make movement animation more complex (for example, if we want to introduce jumping). This is not the only problem, though. Loading images does not happen instantly. The first time a particular image is to be used, the animation can stall for a moment while the graphics get loaded, which might ruin the user experience. Lastly, it is simply messy to have a bunch of pictures here and there for every image animation.

A solution to this is to use **sprites**—geometrical animated objects consisting of small images combined into one larger image for better performance. Qt Quick supports sprites through its sprite engine that handles loading sequences of images from a sprite field, animating them and transitioning between different sprites.

In Qt Quick, a sprite is an image of any type supported by Qt that contains an image strip with all frames of the animation. Subsequent frames should form a contiguous line flowing from left to right and from top to bottom of the image. However, they do not have to start in the top-left corner of the containing image, nor do they have to end in its bottom-right corner—a single file can contain many sprites. A sprite is defined by providing the size of a single frame in pixels and a frame count. Optionally, one can specify an offset from the top-left corner where the first frame of the sprite is to be read from. The following diagram can be helpful in visualizing the scheme:

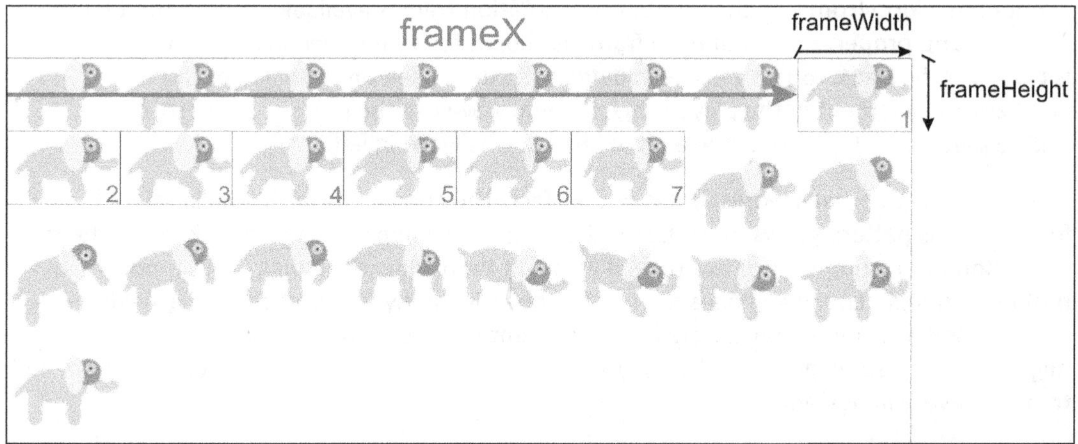

QML offers a `Sprite` element type with a `source` property pointing to the URL of the container image, a `frameWidth` and `frameHeight` element determining the size of each frame, and a `frameCount` element defining the number of frames in the sprite. Offsetting the image can be achieved by setting values of the `frameX` and `frameY` properties. In addition to this, some additional properties are present; the most important three are `frameRate`, `frameDuration`, and `duration`. All these serve to determine the pace of the animation. If the `frameRate` element is defined, it is interpreted as a number of frames to cycle through per second. If this property is not defined, then the `frameDuration` element kicks in and is treated as a period of time in which to display a single frame (thus, it is directly an inverse of the `frameRate` element). If this property is not defined, as well, the `duration` element is used, which carries the duration of the whole animation. You can set any of the three properties, and precedence rules (`frameRate`, `frameDuration`, `duration`) will determine which of them are going to be applied.

Time for action – animating characters using sprites

Let's wait no further. The task at hand is to replace the manual animation from the previous exercise with a sprite-based animation.

Open the `Player.qml` document, remove the whole image element responsible for displaying the player character:

```
AnimatedSprite {
  id: sprite
  source: "images/walking.png"
  frameX: 560
  frameY: 0
  frameWidth: 80
  frameHeight: 52
  frameCount: 7
  frameRate: 10
  interpolate: true
  width: frameWidth
  height: frameHeight

  running: player.walking
  anchors.bottom: parent.bottom
  anchors.horizontalCenter: parent.horizontalCenter

  transform: Scale {
    origin.x: sprite.width/2
    xScale: player.facingLeft ? -1 : 1
  }
}
```

What just happened?

We have replaced the previous static image with an ever-changing source with a different item. As the `Sprite` parameter is not an `Item` element but rather a data definition of a sprite, we cannot use it in place of the `Image` element. Instead, we will use the `AnimatedSprite` element, which is an item that can display a single animated sprite defined inline. It even has the same set of properties as the `Sprite` parameter. We defined a sprite embedded in `images/walking.png` with a width of `80` and a height of `52` pixels. The sprite consists of seven frames that should be displayed at a rate of 10 frames per second. The `running` property is set up similar to the original `Animation` element. As the `AnimatedSprite` element does not have a `mirror` property, we emulate it by applying a scale transformation that flips the item horizontally if the `player.facingLeft` element evaluates to `true`. Additionally, we set the `interpolate` property to `true`, which makes the sprite engine calculate smoother transitions between frames.

The result we are left with is similar to an earlier attempt, so if these two are similar then why bother using sprites? In many situations, you want more complex animation than just a single frame sequence. What if we want to animate the way Benjamin jumps in addition to him walking? Embedding more manual animations, although possible, would explode the number of internal variables required to keep the state of the object. Fortunately, the Qt Quick sprite engine can deal with that. The `AnimatedSprite` element we used provides just a subset of features of the whole framework. By substituting the item with the `SpriteSequence` element we gain access to the full power of sprites. In talking about `Sprite`, we didn't tell you about one additional property of the object, a property called `to` that contains a map of probabilities of transitioning from the current sprite to another one. By stating which sprites the current one migrates to, we create a state machine with weighted transitions to other sprites, as well as cycling back to the current state.

Transitioning to another sprite is triggered by setting the `goalSprite` property on the `SpriteSequence` object. This will cause the sprite engine to traverse the graph until it reaches the requested state. It is a great way to fluently switch from one animation to another by going through a number of intermediate states.

Instead of asking the sprite machine to gracefully transit to a given state, one can ask it to force an immediate change by calling the `SpriteSequence` class's `jumpTo()` method and feeding it with the name of the sprite that should start playing.

The last thing that needs to be clarified is how to actually attach the sprite state machine to the `SpriteSequence` class. It is very easy; just assign an array of the `Sprite` objects to the `sprites` property.

Time for action – adding jumping with sprite transitions

Let's replace the AnimatedSprite class with the SpriteSequence class in the Bejamin the Elephant animation, adding a sprite to be played during the jumping phase.

Open the Player.qml file and replace the AnimatedSprite object with the following code:

```
SpriteSequence {
  id: sprite
  width: 80
  height: 52
  anchors.bottom: parent.bottom
  anchors.horizontalCenter: parent.horizontalCenter
  currentSprite: "still"
  running: true

  Sprite {
    name: "still"
    source: "images/walking.png"
    frameCount: 1
    frameWidth: 80
    frameHeight: 52
    frameDuration: 100
    to: {"still": 1, "walking": 0, "jumping": 0}
  }
  Sprite {
    name: "walking"
    source: "images/walking.png"
    frameCount: 7
    frameWidth: 80
    frameHeight: 52
    frameRate: 10
    to: {"walking": 1, "still": 0, "jumping": 0}
  }
  Sprite {
    name: "jumping"
    source: "images/jumping.png"
    frameCount: 11
    frameWidth: 80
    frameHeight: 70
    frameRate: 4
```

```
      to: { "still" : 1 }
    }

    transform: Scale {
      origin.x: sprite.width/2
      xScale: player.facingLeft ? -1 : 1
    }
  }
```

Next, extend the `jumpAnim` object by adding the highlighted changes:

```
SequentialAnimation {
  id: jumpAnim
  running: false
  ScriptAction { script: sprite.goalSprite = "jumping" }
  NumberAnimation {
    target: player; property: "y"
    to: player.parent.height-50; easing.type: Easing.OutQuad
  }
  NumberAnimation {
    target: player; property: "y"
    to: player.parent.height; easing.type: Easing.InQuad
  }
  ScriptAction {
    script: { sprite.goalSprite = ""; sprite.jumpTo("still"); }
  }
}
```

What just happened?

The `SpriteSequence` element we have introduced has its `Item` elements-related properties set up in the same way as when the `AnimatedSprite` element was used. Apart from that, a sprite called "still" was explicitly set as the current one. We defined a number of `Sprite` objects as children of the `SpriteSequence` element. This is equivalent to assigning those sprites to the `sprites` property of the object. The complete state machine that was declared is presented in the following diagram:

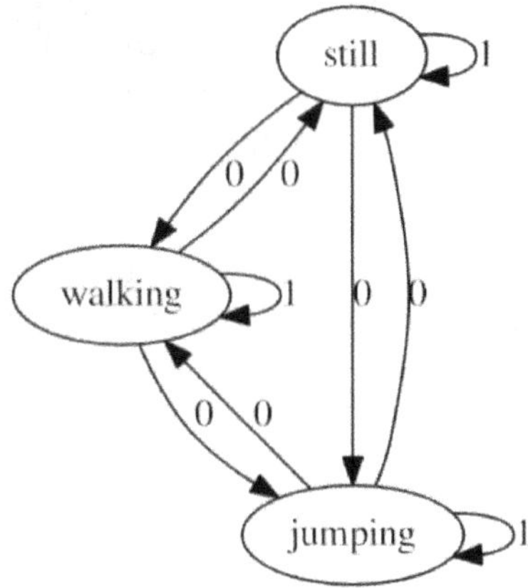

A sprite called "still" has just a single frame representing a situation when Benjamin doesn't move. The sprite keeps spinning in the same state due to the weighted transition back to the "still" state. The two remaining transitions from that state have their weights set to `0`, which means they will never trigger spontaneously, but they can be invoked by setting the `goalSprite` property to a sprite that can be reached by activating one of those transitions.

The sequential animation was extended to trigger sprite changes when the elephant lifts into the air.

Have a go hero – making Benjamin wiggle his tail in anticipation

To practice sprite transitions, your goal is to extend the state machine of Benjamin's `SpriteSequence` element to make him wiggle his tail when the elephant is standing still. You can find the appropriate sprite in the materials that come included with this book. The sprite field is called `wiggling.png`. Implement the functionality by making it probable that Benjamin spontaneously goes from the "still" state to "wiggling". Pay attention to ensure the animal stops wiggling and starts walking the moment the player activates the right or left arrow keys.

Parallax scrolling

We already discussed the useful technique of parallax scrolling in *Chapter 6, Graphics View*. Just to recapitulate, it gives the impression of depth for 2D games by moving multiple layers of background at a different speed depending on the assumed distance of the layer from the viewer. We will now see how easy it is to apply the same technique in Qt Quick.

Time for action – revisiting parallax scrolling

We will implement parallax scrolling with a set of layers that move in the direction opposite to the one the player is moving in. Therefore, we will need a definition of the scene and a moving layer.

Create a new QML Document (Qt Quick 2). Call it `ParallaxScene.qml`. The scene will encompass the whole game "level" and will expose the position of the player to the moving layers. Put the following code in the file:

```
import QtQuick 2.2

Item {
  id: root
  property int currentPos
  x: -currentPos*(root.width-root.parent.width)/width
}
```

Then, create another QML Document (Qt Quick 2) and call it `ParallaxLayer.qml`. Make it contain the following definition:

```
import QtQuick 2.2

Item {
  property real factor: 0
  x: factor > 0 ? -parent.currentPos/factor - parent.x : 0
}
```

Now, let's use the two new element types in the main QML document. We'll take elements from the earlier scene definition and make them into different parallax layers—the sky, the trees, and the grass:

```
Rectangle {
  id: view

  width: 600
  height: 380

  ParallaxScene {
    id: scene
    width: 1500; height: 380
    anchors.bottom: parent.bottom
    currentPos: player.x

    ParallaxLayer {
```

```
      factor: 7.5
      width: sky.width; height: sky.height
      anchors.bottom: parent.bottom
      Image { id: sky; source: "sky.png" }
    }
    ParallaxLayer {
      factor: 2.5
      width: trees.width; height: trees.height
      anchors.bottom: parent.bottom
      Image { id: trees; source: "trees.png" }
    }
    ParallaxLayer {
      factor: 0
      width: grass.width; height: grass.height
      anchors.bottom: parent.bottom
      Image { id: grass; source: "grass.png" }
    }

    Item {
      id: player
      // ...
    }
  }
}
```

What just happened?

The `ParallaxScene` element we implemented is a moving plane. Its horizontal offset depends on the character's current position and the size of the view. The range of scroll of the scene is determined by the difference between the scene size and the view size—it says how much scrolling we have to do when the character moves from the left edge to the right edge of the scene so that it is in view all the time. If we multiply that by the distance of the character from the left edge of the scene expressed as a fraction of the scene width, we will get the needed scene offset in the view (or otherwise speaking, a projection offset of the scene).

The second type—`ParallaxLayer` is also a moving plane. It defines a distance factor that represents the relative distance (depth) of the layer behind the foreground, which influences how fast the plane should be scrolled compared to the foreground (scene). The value of `0` means that the layer should be moving with exactly the same speed as the foreground layer. The larger the value, the slower the layer moves compared to the character. The offset value is calculated by dividing the character's position in the scene by the factor. Since the foreground layer is also moving, we have to take it into consideration when calculating the offset for each parallax layer. Thus, we subtract the horizontal position of the scene to get the actual layer offset.

Having the layers logically defined, we can add them to the scene. Each layer has a physical representation, in our case, static images containing textures of the sky, trees, and grass. Each layer is defined separately and can live its own life, containing static and animated elements that have no influence on remaining layers. If we wanted to render a sun moving from east to west, we would put it on the sky layer and animate it from one edge of the layer to the other with a long duration.

Have a go hero – vertical parallax sliding

As an additional exercise, you might want to implement vertical parallax sliding in addition to a horizontal one. Just make your scene bigger and have it expose the vertical scroll position in addition to the horizontal one reported by the `currentPos` element. Then, just repeat all the calculations for the `y` property of each layer and you should be done in no time. Remember that distance factors for `x` and `y` might be different.

Collision detection

There is no built-in support for collision detection in Qt Quick, but there are three ways of providing such support. First, you can use a ready collision system available in a number of 2D physics engines such as Box2D. Secondly, you can implement a simple collision system yourself in C++. Lastly, you can do collision checking directly in JavaScript by comparing object coordinates and bounding boxes.

Our game is very simple; therefore, we will use the last approach. If we had a larger number of moving objects involved in our game, then we would probably choose the second approach. The first approach is best if you have an object of non-rectangular shapes that can rotate and bounce off other objects. In this case, having a physics engine at hand becomes really useful.

Time for action – collecting coins

From Qt Creator's menu, access **File | New File or Project**. From **Qt Files And Classes**, choose the JS File template. Call the file "`collisions.js`". Put the following content into the document:

```
pragma library

function boundingBox(object1) {
  var cR = object1.childrenRect
  var mapped = object1.mapToItem(object1.parent, cR.x, cR.y,
    cR.width, cR.height)
  return Qt.rect(mapped.x, mapped.y, mapped.width, mapped.height)
}

function intersect(object1, object2) {
  var r1 = boundingBox(object1)
  var r2 = boundingBox(object2)
  return (r1.x <= r2.x+r2.width  && // r1.left <= r2.right
  r2.x <= r1.x+r1.width  && // r2.left <= r1.right
  r1.y <= r2.y+r2.height && // r1.top <= r2.bottom
  r2.y <= r1.y+r1.height)    // r2.top <= r1.bottom
}
```

Create another JS File and call it "`coins.js`". Enter the following:

```
import "collisions.js"

var coins = []

coins.collisionsWith = function(player) {
  var collisions = []
  for(var index = 0; index < length; ++index) {
    var obj = this[index]
    if(intersect(player, obj)) collisions.push(obj)
  }
  return collisions
}
```

```
coins.remove = function(obj) {
  var arr = isArray(obj) ? obj : [ obj ]
  var L = arr.length
  var idx, needle
  while(L && this.length) {
    var needle = arr[--L]
    idx = this.indexOf(needle)
    if(idx != -1) { this.splice(idx, 1) }
  }
  return this
}
```

Finally, open the main document and add the following `import` statement:

```
import "coins.js"
```

In the player object, define the `checkCollisions()` function:

```
function checkCollisions() {
  var result = coins.collisionsWith(player)
  if(result.length == 0) return
  result.forEach(function(coin) { coin.hit() })
  coins.remove(result) // prevent the coin from being hit again
}
```

Lastly, in the same player object, trigger collision detection by handling the position changes of the player:

```
onXChanged: { checkCollisions() }
onYChanged: { checkCollisions() }
```

In the `Coin.qml` file, define an animation and a `hit()` function:

```
SequentialAnimation {
  id: hitAnim
  running: false
  NumberAnimation {
    target: coin
    property: "opacity"
    from: 1; to: 0
    duration: 250
  }
  ScriptAction {
```

```
      script: coin.destroy()
    }
  }

  function hit() {
    hitAnim.start()
  }
```

What just happened?

The file `collisions.js` contains functions used to do collision checking. The first line of the file is a pragma statement noting that this document only contains functions and does not contain any mutable object. This is so that we can add a `.pragma library` statement, which marks the document as a library that can be shared between documents that import it. This aids in reduced memory consumption and improved speed as the engine doesn't have to reparse and execute the document each time it is imported.

The functions defined in the library are really simple. The first one returns a bounding rectangle of an object based on its coordinates and the size of its children. It assumes that the top-level item is empty and contains children that represent the visual aspect of the object. Children coordinates are mapped using the `mapToItem` element so that the rectangle returned is expressed in the parent item coordinates. The second function does a trivial checking of intersection between two bounding rectangles and returns `true` if they intersect and `false` otherwise.

The second document keeps a definition of an array of coins. It adds two methods to the array object. The first one—`collisionsWith`—performs a collision check between any of the items in the array and the given object using functions defined in `collisions.js`. That's why we import the library at the start of the document. The method returns another array that contains objects intersecting the `player` argument. The other method, called `remove`, takes an object or an array of objects and removes them from `coins`.

The document is not a library; therefore, each document that imports `coins.js` would get its own separate copy of the object. Thus, we need to ensure that `coins.js` is imported only once in the game so that all references to the objects defined in that document relate to the same instance of the object in our program memory.

Our main document imports `coins.js`, which creates the array for storing coin objects and makes its auxiliary functions available. This allows the defined `checkCollisions()` function to retrieve the list of coins colliding with the player. For each coin that collides with the player, we execute a `hit()` method; as a last step, all colliding coins are removed from the array. Since coins are stationary, collision can only occur when the player character enters an area occupied by a coin. Therefore, it is enough to trigger collision detection when the position of the player character changes—we use the `onXChanged` and `onYChanged` handlers.

As hitting a coin results in removing it from the array, we lose a reference to the object. The `hit()` method has to initiate removal of the object from the scene. A minimalistic implementation of this function would be to just call the `destroy()` function on the object, but we do more—the removal can be made smoother by running a fade-out animation on the coin. As a last step, the animation can destroy the object.

Notes on collision detection

The number of objects we track on the scene is really small, and we simplify the shape of each object to a rectangle. This lets us get away with checking collisions in JavaScript. For a larger amount of moving objects, custom shapes, and handling rotations, it is much better to have a collision system based on C++. The level of complexity of such a system depends on your needs.

Eye candy

A game should not just be based upon an interesting idea; it should not only work fluently on a range of devices and give entertainment to those people playing it. It should also look nice and behave nicely. Whether one is choosing from a number of similar implementations of the same game or wants to spend money on another similarly priced and entertaining game, there is a good chance the game she or he chooses will be the one that looks the best—having a lot of animations, graphics, and flashy content. We already learned a number of techniques to make a game more pleasing to the eye, such as using animations or GLSL shaders. Here, we will show you a number of other techniques that can make your Qt Quick applications more attractive.

Auto-scaling user interfaces

The first extension you might implement is making your game auto-adjust to the device resolution it is running on. There are basically two ways to accomplish this. The first is to center the user interface in the window (or screen) and if it doesn't fit, enable scrolling. The other approach is to scale the interface to always fit the window (or screen). Which to choose depends on a number of factors, the most important of which is whether your UI is good enough when upscaled. If the interface consists of text and non-image primitives (basically rectangles) or if it includes images but only vector ones or those with very high resolution, then it is probably fine to try and scale the user interface. Otherwise, if you use a lot of low resolution bitmap images, you will have to choose one particular size for the UI (optionally allowing it to downscale since the quality degradation should be less significant in this direction if you enable anti-aliasing).

Whether you choose to scale or to center and scroll, the basic approach is the same—you put your UI item in another item so that you have fine control over the UI geometry regardless of what happens to the top-level window. Taking the centered approach is quite easy—just anchor the UI to the center of the parent. To enable scrolling, wrap the UI in the `Flickable` item and constrain its size if the size of the window is not big enough to fit the whole user interface:

```
Item {
  id: window

  Flickable {
    id: uiFlickable
    anchors.centerIn: parent
    contentWidth: ui.width; contentHeight: ui.height

    width: parent.width >= contentWidth ? contentWidth : parent.width
    height: parent.height >= contentHeight ? contentHeight :
      parent.height

    UI { id: ui }
  }
}
```

You should probably decorate the top-level item with a nice background if the UI item does not occupy the full area of its parent.

Scaling seems more complicated, but with Qt Quick it is really easy. Again, you have two choices—either stretch or scale. Stretching is as easy as executing the `anchors.fill: parent` command, which effectively forces the UI to recalculate the geometry of all its items but possibly allows us to use the space more efficiently. It is, in general, very time-consuming for the developer to provide expressions for calculating the geometry of each and every element in the user interface as the size of the view changes. This is usually not worth the effort. A simpler approach is to just scale the UI item to fit the window, which will implicitly scale the contained items. In such an event, their size can be calculated relative to the base size of the main view of the user interface. For this to work, you need to calculate the scale that is to be applied to the user interface to make it fill the whole space available. The item has a scale of 1 when its effective width equals its implicit width and its effective height equals its implicit height. If the window is larger, we want to scale the item up until it reaches the size of the window. Therefore, the window's width divided by the item's implicit width will be the item's scale in the horizontal direction. This is shown in the following diagram:

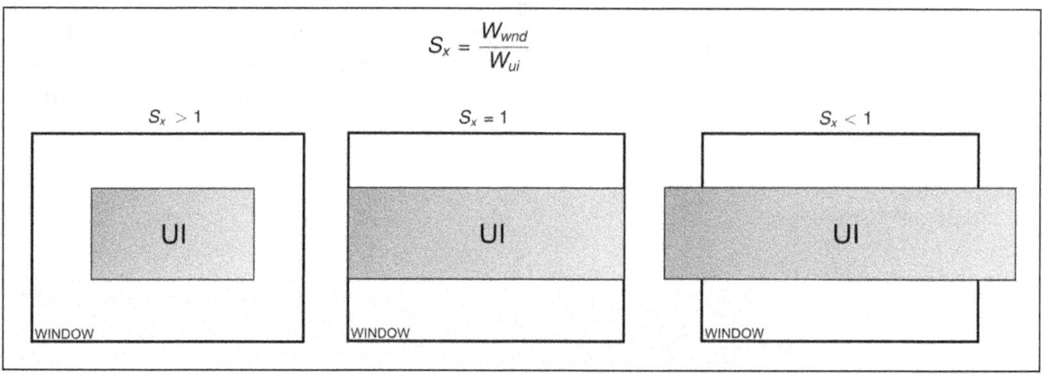

The same can be applied to the vertical direction, but if the UI has a different aspect ratio than the window, its horizontal and vertical scale factors will be different. For the UI to look nice, we have to take the lower of the two values—to only scale up as much as the direction with less space allows, leaving a gap in the other direction:

```
Item {
  id: window

  UI {
    id: ui

    anchors.centerIn: parent
    scale: Math.min(parent.width/width, parent.height/height)
  }
}
```

Again, it might be a good idea to put some background on the window item to fill in the gaps.

What if you want to save some margin between the user interface and the window? You could, of course, take that into consideration when calculating the scale (`(window.width-2*margin)/width`, and so on) but there is an easier way—simply put an additional item inside the window, leaving an appropriate margin, and put the user interface item in that additional item and scale it up to the additional item's size:

```
Item {
  id: window
  Item {
    anchors { fill: parent; margins: 10 }
    UI {
      id: ui

      anchors.centerIn: parent
      scale: Math.min(parent.width/width, parent.height/height)
    }
  }
}
```

When you scale elements a lot, you should consider enabling anti-aliasing for items that can lose quality when rendered in a size different than their native size (for example, images). This is done very easily in Qt Quick as each `Item` instance has a property called `antialiasing` which, when enabled, will cause the rendering backend to try to reduce distortions caused by the aliasing effect. Remember that this comes at the cost of increased rendering complexity, so try to find a balance between quality and efficiency, especially on low-end hardware. You might provide an option to the user to globally enable or disable anti-aliasing for all game objects or to gradually adjust quality settings for different object types.

Graphical effects

The basic two predefined items in Qt Quick are rectangle and image. One can use them in a variety of creative ways and make them more pleasant-looking by applying GLSL shaders. However, implementing a shader program from scratch is cumbersome and requires in-depth knowledge of the shader language. Luckily, a number of common effects are already implemented and ready to use in the form of the `QtGraphicalEffects` module.

To add a subtle black shadow to our canvas-based heartbeat element defined in the `HeartBeat.qml` file, use a code similar to the following that makes use of the `DropShadow` effect:

```
import QtQuick 2.0
import QtGraphicalEffects 1.0

Item {
  width: 1000; height: 600
  HeartBeat { id: hb; anchors.centerIn: parent; visible: false }
  DropShadow {
    source: hb
    anchors.fill: hb
    horizontalOffset: 3
    verticalOffset: 3
    radius: 8
    samples: 16
    color: "black"
  }
}
```

To apply a shadow effect, you need an existing item as the source of the effect. In our case, we are using an instance of the `HeartBeat` class centered in a top-level item. Then, the shadow effect is defined and its geometry follows that of its source by using the `anchors.fill` element. Just as the `DropShadow` class renders the original item as well as the shadow, the original item can be hidden by setting its `visible` property to `false`.

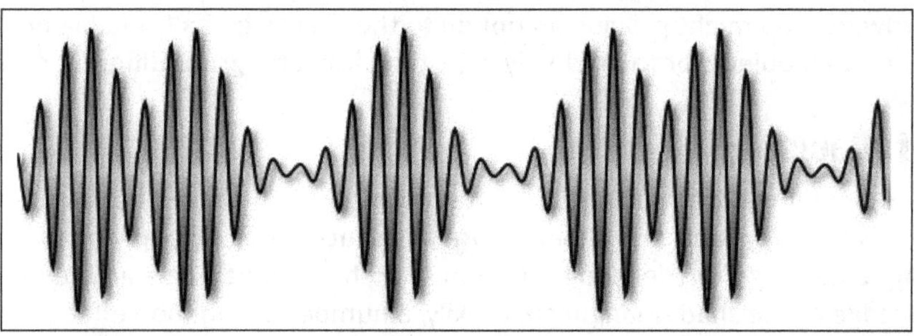

Most of the `DropShadow` class's properties are self-explanatory, but two properties—`radius` and `samples`—require some additional explanation. The shadow is drawn as a blurred monochromatic copy of the original item offset by a given position. The two mentioned properties control the amount of blur and its quality—the more samples used for blurring, the better the effect, but also the more demanding the computation that needs to be performed.

Speaking of blur, the plain blurring effect is also available in the graphics effects module through the `GaussianBlur` element type. To apply a blur instead of a shadow to the last example, simply replace the occurrence of the `DropShadow` class with the following code:

```
GaussianBlur {
  source: hb
  anchors.fill: hb
  radius: 12
  samples: 20
  transparentBorder: true
}
```

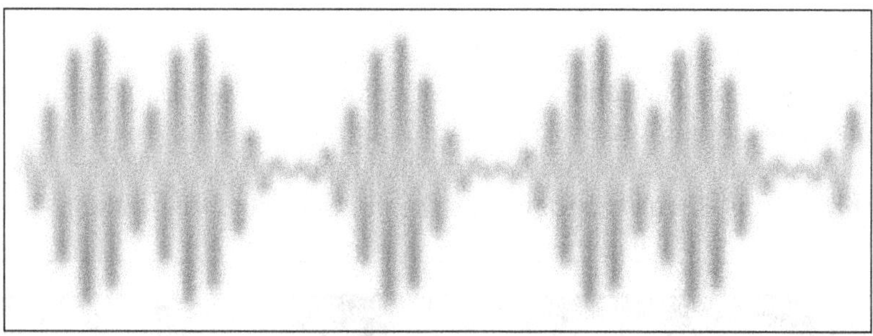

Here, you can see two earlier mentioned properties as well as a vaguely named `transparentBorder` one. Enabling this property fixes some artifacts on the edges of the blur and in general, you'll want to keep it that way.

Have a go hero – the blur parallax scrolled game view

The `blur` property is a very nice effect that can be used in many situations. For example, you could try to implement a feature within our elephant game whereby, when the user pauses the game (for example, by pressing the *P* key on the keyboard), the view gets blurred. Make the effect smooth by applying an animation to the effect's `radius` property.

Another interesting effect is `Glow`. It renders a colored and blurred copy of the source element. An example use case for games is highlighting some parts of the user interface—you can direct the user's attention to the element (for example, button or badge) by making the element flash periodically:

```
Badge {
  id: importantBadge
}
Glow {
  source: importantBadge
  anchors.fill: source
  samples: 16
```

```
    color: "red"

    SequentialAnimation on radius {
      loops: Animation.Infinite
      running: true

      NumberAnimation { from: 0; to: 10; duration: 2000 }
      PauseAnimation  { duration: 1000 }
      NumberAnimation { from: 10; to: 0; duration: 2000 }
      PauseAnimation  { duration: 1000 }
    }
  }
```

The complete module contains 20 different effects. We cannot describe each effect in detail here. Nevertheless, you can learn about it yourself. If you clone the module's source git repository (found under `git://code.qt.io/qt/qtgraphicaleffects.git`) in the `tests/manual/testbed` subdirectory of the cloned repository, you will find a nice application for testing existing effects. To run the tool, open the `testBed.qml` file with `qmlscene`.

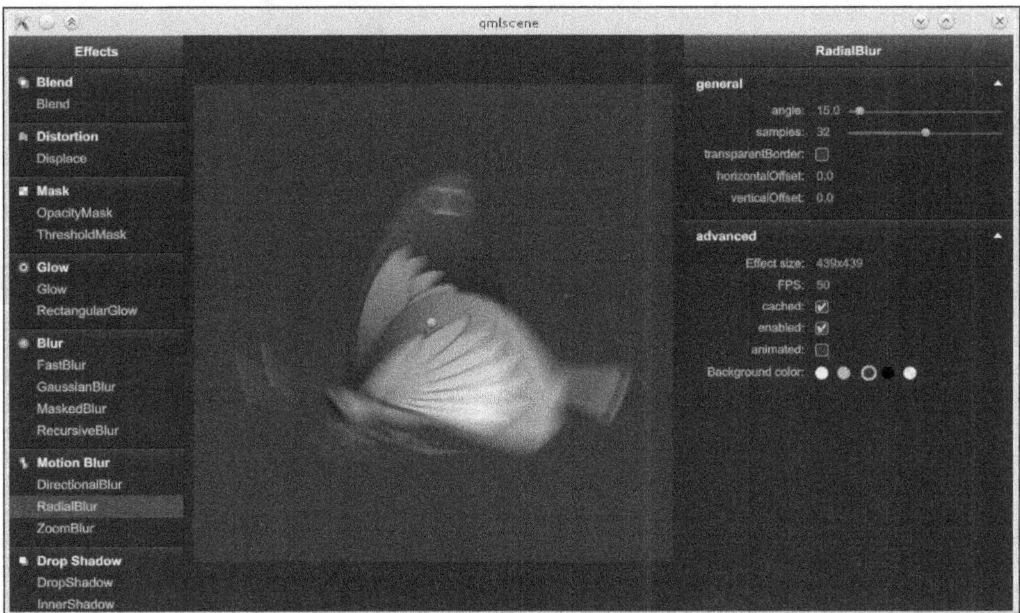

You can also access a complete list of effects and their short descriptions by navigating to the **GraphicalEffects** help page in the documentation.

Particle systems

A commonly used visual effect in systems such as games is generating a large number of small, usually short-lived, often fast-moving, fuzzy objects such as stars, sparks, fumes, dust, snow, splinters, falling leaves, or the like. Placing these as regular items within a scene would greatly degrade performance. Instead, a special engine is used which keeps a registry of such objects and tracks (simulates) their logical attributes without having physical entities in the scene. Such objects, called particles, are rendered upon request in the scene using very efficient algorithms. This allows us to use a large number of particles without having a negative impact on the rest of the scene.

Qt Quick provides a particle system in the `QtQuick.Particles` import. The `ParticleSystem` element provides the core for the simulation, which uses the `Emitter` elements to spawn particles. They are then rendered according to definitions in a `ParticlePainter` element. Simulated entities can be manipulated using the `Affector` objects, which can modify the trajectory or life span of particles.

Let's start with a simple example. The following code snippet declares the simplest possible particle system:

```
import QtQuick 2.0
import QtQuick.Particles 2.0

ParticleSystem {
  id: particleSystem
  width: 360; height: 360

  Emitter { anchors.fill: parent }
  ImageParticle { source: "star.png" }
}
```

The result can be observed in the following image:

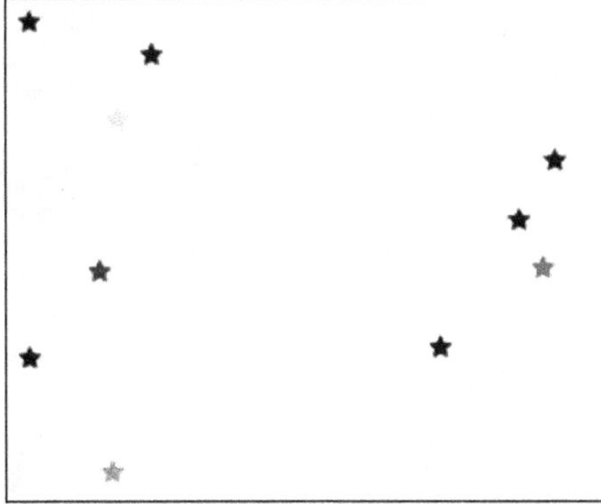

Let's analyze the code. After importing `QtQuick.Particles 2.0`, a `ParticleSystem` item is instantiated that defines the domain of the particle system. We define two objects within that system. The first object is the `Emitter` and defines an area where particles will be spawned. The area is set to encompass the whole domain. The second object is an object of the `ImageParticle` type, which is a `ParticlePainter` subclass. It determines that particles should be rendered as instances of a given image. By default, the `Emitter` object spawns 10 particles per second, each of which lives for one second and then dies and is removed from the scene. In the code presented, the `Emitter` and `ImageParticle` objects are direct children of the `ParticleSystem` class; however, this doesn't have to be the case. The particle system can be explicitly specified by setting the `system` property.

Tuning the emitter

You can control the amount of particles being emitted by setting the `emitRate` property of the emitter. Another property called the `lifeSpan` determines how many milliseconds it takes before a particle dies. To introduce some random behavior, you can use the `lifeSpanVariation` property to set a maximum amount of time (in milliseconds) the life span can be altered by the system (in both directions). Increasing the emission rate and life span of particles can lead to a situation in which a very large number of particles have to be managed (and possibly rendered). This can degrade performance; thus, an upper limit of particles that can concurrently be alive can be set through the `maximumEmitted` property:

```
ParticleSystem {
  id: particleSystem
  width: 360; height: 360

  Emitter {
    anchors.fill: parent
    emitRate: 350
    lifeSpan: 1500
    lifeSpanVariation: 400 // effective: 1100-1900 ms
  }
  ImageParticle { source: "star.png" }
}
```

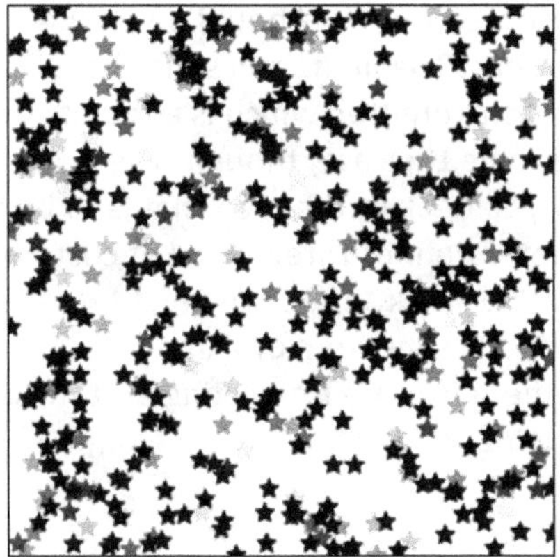

Tweaking the life span of particles makes the system more diverse. To strengthen the effect, you can also manipulate the size of each particle through the `size` and `sizeVariation` properties:

```
ParticleSystem {
  id: particleSystem
  width: 360; height: 360

  Emitter {
    anchors.fill: parent
    emitRate: 50
    size: 12
    sizeVariation: 6
    endSize: 2
  }
  ImageParticle { source: "star.png" }
}
```

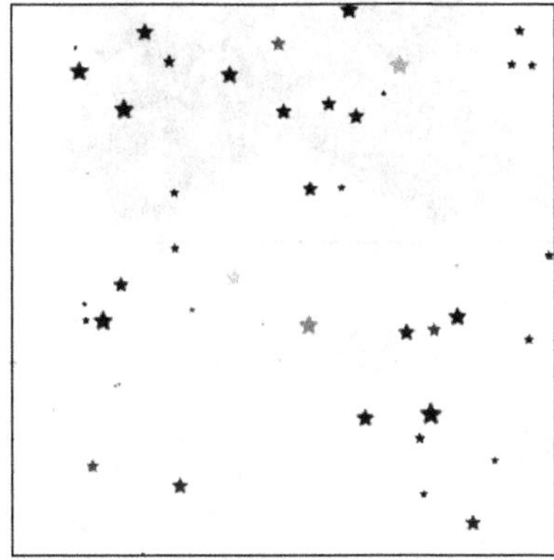

The range of functionality presented thus far should be enough to create many nice-looking and useful particle systems. The limitation so far has been that particles are emitted from the whole area of the emitter, which is a regular `QQuickItem` and thus is rectangular. This doesn't have to be the case, though. The `Emitter` element contains a `shape` property, which is a way to declare the area that is to be giving birth to particles. The `QtQuick.Particles` parameter defines three types of custom shape that can be used—`EllipseShape`, `LineShape`, and `MaskShape`. The first two are very simple, defining either an empty or filled ellipse inscribed in the item or a line crossing one of the two diagonals of the item. The `MaskShape` element is more interesting as it makes it possible to use an image as a shape for the `Emitter` element.

```
ParticleSystem {
  id: particleSystem
  width: 360; height: 360

  Emitter {
    anchors.fill: parent
    emitRate: 1600
    shape: MaskShape { source: "star.png" }
  }
  ImageParticle { source: "star.png" }
}
```

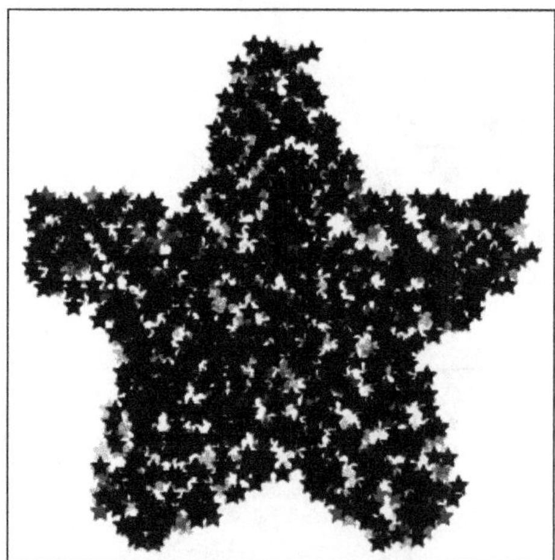

Rendering particles

Thus far, we have used a bare `ImageParticle` element to render particles. It is only one of three `ParticlePainters` available, with the others being `ItemParticle` and `CustomParticle`. But before we move on to other renderers, let's focus on tweaking the `ImageParticle` element to obtain some interesting effects.

The `ImageParticle` element renders each logical particle as an image. The image can be manipulated separately for each particle by changing its color and rotation, deforming its shape, or using it as a sprite animation.

To influence the color of particles, you can use any of the large number of dedicated properties—`alpha`, `color`, `alphaVariation`, `colorVariation`, `redVariation`, `greenVariation`, and `blueVariation`. The first two properties define the base value for respective attributes and the remaining properties set the maximum deviation of a respective parameter from the base value. In the case of opacity, there is only one type of variation you can use but when defining the color, you can either set different values for each of the red, green, and blue channels or you can use the global `colorVariation` property, which is similar to setting the same value for all three channels. Allowed values are any between the range of 0 (no deviation allowed) to 1.0 (100% in either direction).

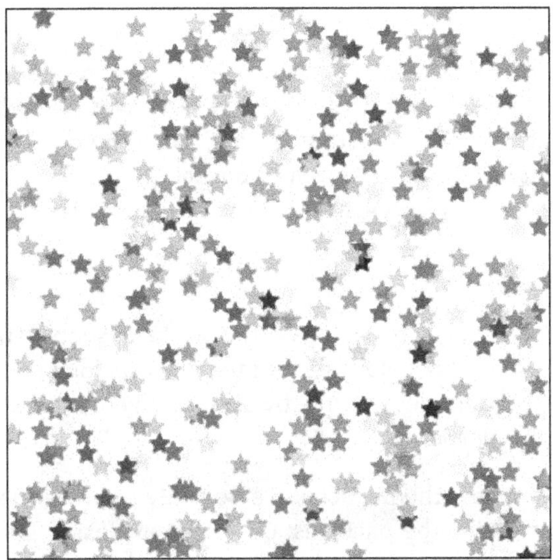

The properties mentioned are stationary—the particle obeys the constant value during its whole life. The `ImageParticle` element also exposes two properties, letting you control the color of particles relative to their age. First of all, there is a property called `entryEffect` that defines what happens with the particle at its birth and death. The default value is `Fade`, which makes particles fade in from 0 opacity at the start of their life and fades them back to 0 just before they die. You have already experienced this effect in all earlier particle animations we demonstrated. Other values for the property are `None` and `Scale`. The first one is obvious—there is no entry effect associated with particles. The second one scales particles from 0 at their birth and scales them back to 0 at the end of their life.

The other time-related property is `colorTable`. You can feed it with a URL of an image to be used as a one-dimensional texture determining the color of each particle over its life. At the beginning, the particle gets color-defined by the left edge of the image and then progresses right in a linear fashion. It is most common to set an image here containing a color gradient to achieve smooth transitions between colors.

The second parameter that can be altered is the rotation of a particle. Here, we can also either use properties that define constant values for rotation (`rotation` and `rotationVariation`) specified in degrees or modify the rotation of particles in time with `rotationVelocity` and `rotationVelocityVariation`. The velocity defines the pace or rotation in degrees per second.

Particles can also be deformed. The properties `xVector` and `yVector` allow binding vectors, which define distortions in horizontal and vertical axes. We will describe how to set the vectors in the next section. Last but not least, using the `sprites` property you can define a list of sprites that will be used to render particles. This works in a similar fashion to `SpriteAnimation`, described in an earlier section of this chapter.

Making particles move

Apart from fading and rotating, the particle systems we have seen so far were very static. While this is useful for making star fields, it is not useful at all for explosions, sparks, or even falling snow. This is because particles are mostly about movement. Here, we will show you two aspects of making your particles fly.

The first aspect is modeling how the particles are born. By that, we mean the physical conditions of the object creating the particles. During an explosion, matter is pushed away from the epicenter with a very large force that causes air and small objects to rush outwards at an extremely high speed. Fumes from a rocket engine are ejected with high velocities in the direction opposite to that of the propelled craft. A moving comet draws along a braid of dust and gases put into motion by the inertia.

All these conditions can be modeled by setting the velocity or acceleration of the particles. These two metrics are described by vectors determining the direction and amount (magnitude or length) of the given quantity. In Qt Quick, such vectors are represented by an element type called `StochasticDirection`, where the tail of the vector is attached to the object and the position of the head is calculated by the `StochasticDirection` instance. Since we have no means of setting attributes on particles because we have no objects representing them, those two attributes—`velocity` and `acceleration`—are applied to emitters spawning the particles. Because you can have many emitters in a single particle system, you can set different velocities and accelerations for particles of different origins.

There are four types of direction elements representing different sources of information about the direction. First, there is `CumulativeDirection`, which acts as a container for other direction types and works like a sum of directions contained within.

Then, there is `PointDirection`, where you can specify `x` and `y` coordinates of a point where the head of the vector should be attached. To avoid the unrealistic effect of all particles heading in the same direction, you can specify `xVariation` and `yVariation` to introduce allowed deviation from a given point.

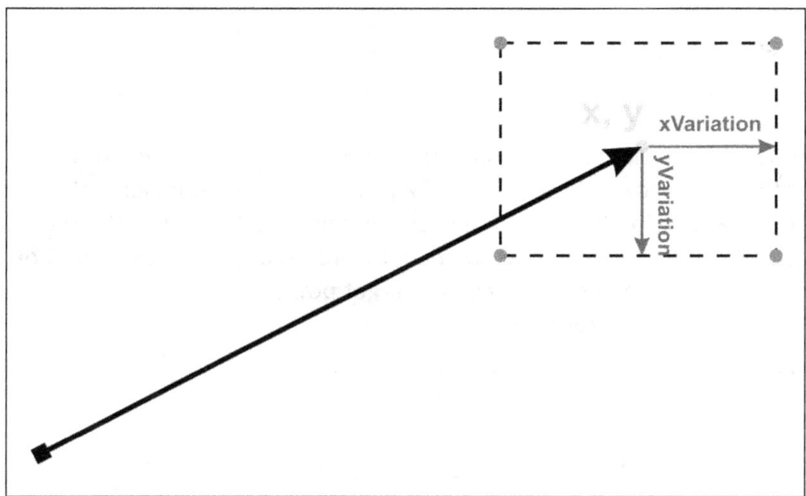

The third type is the most popular stochastic direction type—`AngleDirection`, which directly specifies the angle (in degrees clockwise from straight right) and magnitude (in pixels per second) of the vector. The angle can vary from the base by `angleVariation` and similarly, `magnitudeVariation` can be used to introduce variation to the length of the vector:

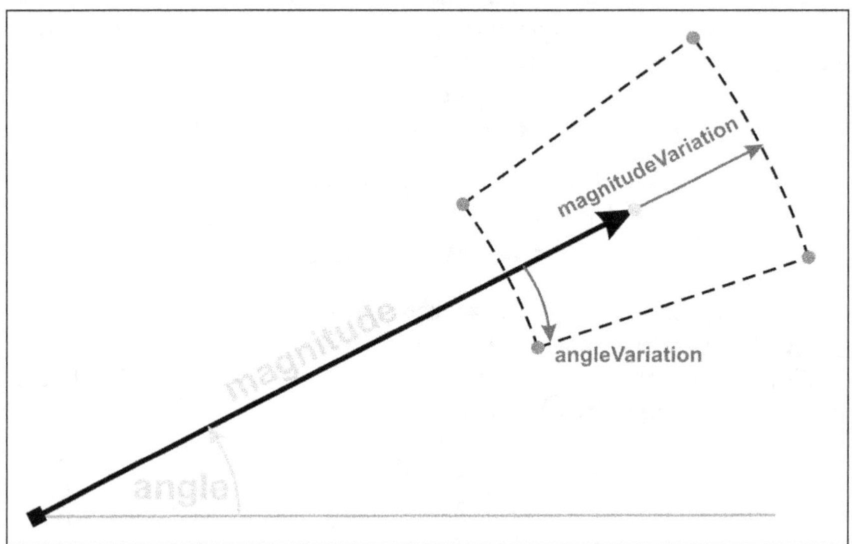

The last type is similar to the previous one. The `TargetDirection` vector can be used to point the vector toward the center of a given Qt Quick item (set with the `targetItem` property). The length of the vector is calculated by giving the `magnitude` and `magnitudeVariation`, and both can be interpreted as pixels per second or multiples of distance between the source and target points (depending on the value of the `proportionalMagnitude` property):

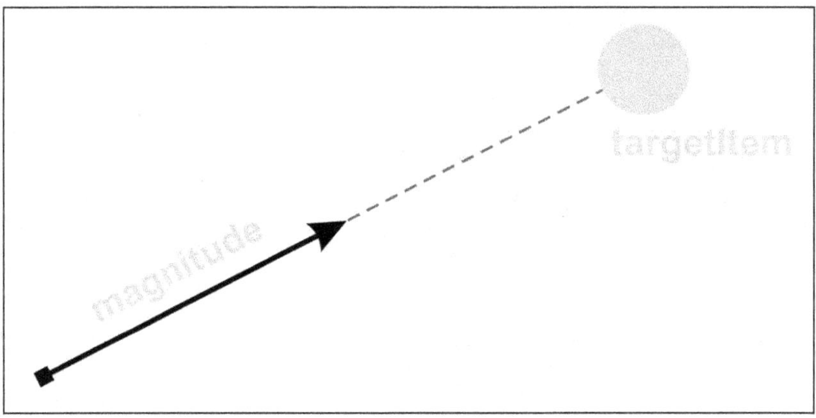

Let's get back to setting particle velocity. We can use the `AngleDirection` vector to specify that particles should be moving left, spreading at a maximum of 45 degrees:

```
Emitter {
  anchors.centerIn: parent
  width: 50; height: 50
  emitRate: 50

  velocity: AngleDirection {
    angleVariation: 45
    angle: 180
    magnitude: 200
  }
}
```

Setting acceleration works the same way. You can even set both the initial velocity and the acceleration each particle should have. It is very easy to shoot the particles in the left direction and start pulling them down:

```
Emitter {
  anchors.right: parent.right
  anchors.verticalCenter: parent.verticalCenter
  emitRate: 15
  lifeSpan: 5000

  velocity: AngleDirection {
    angle: 180
    magnitude: 200
```

```
    }
    acceleration: AngleDirection {
      angle: 90 // local left = global down
      magnitude: 100
    }
  }
```

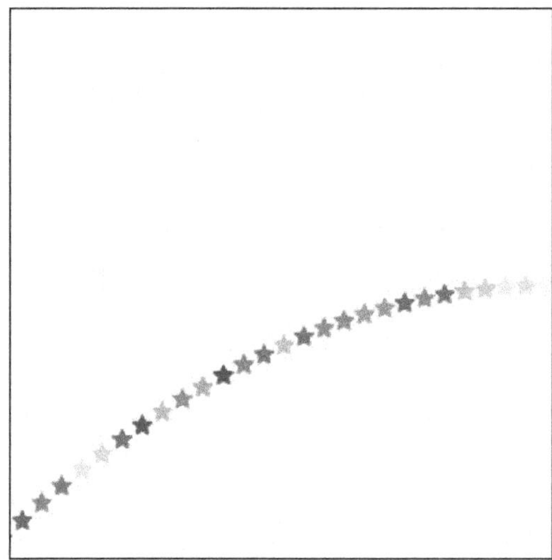

The `Emitter` element has one more nice property that is useful in the context of moving particles. Setting the `velocityFromMovement` parameter to a value different than `0` makes any movement of the `Emitter` element apply to the velocity of the particles. The direction of the additional vector matches the direction of the emitter's movement, and the magnitude is set to the speed of the emitter multiplied by the value set to `velocityFromMovement`. It is a great way to generate fumes ejected from a rocket engine:

```
Item {
  Image {
    id: image
    source: "rocket.png"
  }
  Emitter {
    anchors.right: image.right
    anchors.verticalCenter: image.verticalCenter
    emitRate: 500
    lifeSpan: 3000
    lifeSpanVariation: 1000
    velocityFromMovement: -20

    velocity: AngleDirection {
```

```
        magnitude: 100
        angleVariation: 40
      }
    }
    NumberAnimation on x {
      ...
    }
  }
```

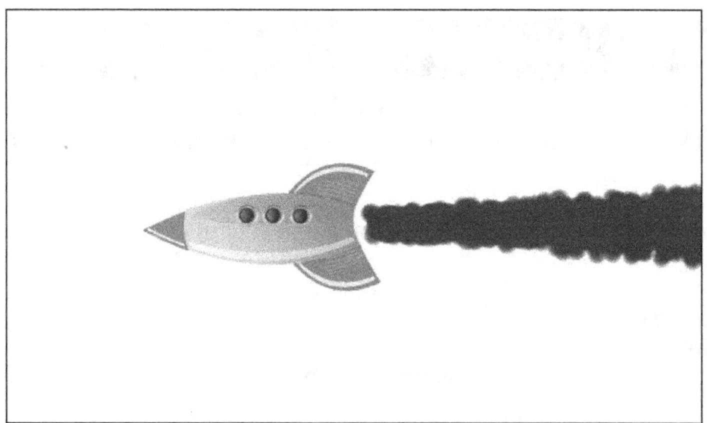

The second way of addressing the behavior of particles is to influence their attributes after they are born—in any particular moment of their life. This can be done using affectors. These are items inheriting affector, which can modify some attributes of particles currently traveling though the area of the affector. One of the simplest affectors is `Age`. It can advance particles to a point in their lifetime where they only have `lifeLeft` milliseconds of their life left.

```
Age {
  once: true
  lifeLeft: 500
  shape: EllipseShape { fill: true }
  anchors.fill: parent
}
```

Setting `once` to `true` makes each affector influence a given particle only once. Otherwise, each particle can have its attributes modified many times.

Another affector type is Gravity, which can accelerate particles in a given angle. Friction can slow particles down, and attractor will affect the particle's position, velocity, or acceleration so that it starts traveling toward a given point. Wander is great for simulating snowflakes or butterflies flying in pseudo-random directions.

There are also other affector types available, but we will not go into their details here. We would like to warn you, however, against using affectors too often—they can severely degrade performance.

Time for action – vanishing coins spawning particles

It is time now to practice our freshly acquired skills. The task is to add a particle effect to the game when the player collects coins. The coin will explode into a sprinkle of colorful stars when collected.

Start by declaring a particle system as filling the game scene, along with the particle painter definition:

```
ParticleSystem {
  id: coinParticles
  anchors.fill: parent // scene is the parent

  ImageParticle {
    source: "particle.png"
    colorVariation: 1
    rotationVariation: 180
    rotationVelocityVariation: 10
  }
}
```

Next, modify the definition of Coin to include an emitter:

```
Emitter {
  id: emitter
  system: coinParticles
  emitRate: 0
  lifeSpan: 500
  lifeSpanVariation: 100
  velocity: AngleDirection { angleVariation: 180; magnitude: 10 }
  acceleration: AngleDirection { angle: 270; magnitude: 2 }
}
```

Finally, the hit function has to be updated:

```
function hit() {
  emitter.burst(50)
  hitAnim.start()
}
```

What just happened?

In this exercise, we defined a simple particle system that fills the whole scene. We defined a simple image painter for the particles where we allow particles to take on all the colors and start in all possible rotations. We used a star pixmap as our particle template.

Then, an `Emitter` object is attached to every coin. Its `emitRate` is set to `0`, which means it does not emit any particles on its own. We set a varying life span on particles and let them fly in all directions by setting their initial velocity with an angle variation of 180 degrees in both directions (giving a total of 360 degrees). By setting an acceleration, we give the particles a tendency to travel toward the bottom edge of the scene.

In the hit function, we call a `burst()` function on the emitter, which makes it give instant birth to a given number of particles.

Summary

In this chapter, we have shown you how to extend your QML skills to make your applications dynamic and attractive. We've gone through the process of recreating and improving a game created earlier in C++ to familiarize you with such concepts as collision detection, state-driven objects, and time-based game loops. We also presented you with a tool in the form of `ShaderEffect`, which can serve as a means to create stunning graphics without compromising performance, and we taught you to use a particle system.

Of course, Qt Quick is much richer than all this, but we had to stop somewhere. The set of skills we have hopefully passed on to you should be enough to develop many great games. However, many of the elements have more properties than we have described here. Whenever you want to extend your skills, you can check the reference manual to see if the element type has more interesting attributes.

This concludes our book on game programming using Qt. We have taught you the general basics of Qt, described its widget realm to you, and introduced you to the fascinating world of Qt Quick. Widgets (including graphics view) and Qt Quick are the two paths you can take when creating games using the Qt framework. We have also shown you ways of merging the two approaches by making use of any OpenGL skills you might have, going beyond what Qt already offers today. At this point, you should start playing around and experimenting, and if at any point you feel lost or simply lack the information on how to do something, the very helpful Qt reference manual should be the first resource you direct yourself to.

Good luck and have lots of fun!

Pop Quiz Answers

Chapter 3, Qt GUI Programming

Pop quiz – making signal-slot connections

Q1	A slot
Q2	`connect(sender, SIGNAL(toggled(bool)), receiver, SLOT(clear()));` and `connect(sender, &QPushButton::clicked, receiver, &QLineEdit::clear);`

Pop quiz – using widgets

Q1	`sizeHint`
Q2	`QVariant`
Q3	It represents a functionality that a user can invoke in the program.

Chapter 4, Qt Core Essentials

Pop quiz – Qt core essentials

<table>
<tr><td>Q1</td><td>QString</td></tr>
<tr><td>Q2</td><td>((25[0-5]|2[0-4][0-9]|[01]?[0-9][0-9]?)(\.|$)){4}</td></tr>
<tr><td>Q3</td><td>XML</td></tr>
</table>

Chapter 6, Graphics View

Pop quiz – mastering Graphics View

Q1	You should know, for example, that there is a `QGraphicsSimpleTextItem` that you can use to draw a simple text and that you do not have to deal with `QPainter` yourself in these situations. You should further know that if you have a more complex text containing bold characters you can use `QGraphicsTextItem`, which is able of handling rich text.
Q2	The correct answers these questions pertain to the origin points of the different systems.
Q3	Be aware that `QObject` isn't restricted to the "world of widgets". You can also use it with items.
Q4	The catchword for the correct answer is Parallax Scrolling.
Q5	The correct answer will take into account how you can control the cache and how to affect which parts of the view are actually redrawn when an update is requested.

Chapter 7, Networking

Pop quiz – testing your knowledge

Q1	`QNetworkAccessManager`, `QNetworkRequest`, and `QNetworkReply`.
Q2	One has to use `QNetworkRequest::setRawHeader()` with the appropriate HTTP header field "Range".
Q3	`QUrlQuery`
Q4	One has to use `deleteLater()` not delete.
Q5	Both inherit `QAbstractSocket` which inherits `QIODevice`. `QIODevice` is itself also the base class of `QFile`. So the handling-files and sockets have much in common. Thus one does not have to learn a second (complex) API only to communicate with sockets.
Q6	`QUdpSocket`

Chapter 8, Scripting

Pop quiz – scripting

Q1	`QScriptEngine::evaluate()`
Q2	`QScriptValue`
Q3	`PyValue`
Q4	They contain all the variables defied within a function invocation so that a set of variables visible from within a script can be modified without affecting the global environment (called sandboxing).

Chapter 11, Miscellaneous and Advanced Concepts

Pop quiz – testing your knowledge

Q1	The suffix is `Reading`, for example, `QRotationReading`.
Q2	The class named `QSensorGestureRecognizer`.
Q3	It's the Qt Positioning module and you activate it by adding `QT += positioning` to the project fie.
Q4	One has to overload `QDebug& operator<<()`
Q5	It aborts the execution of the program if `condition` is `false` only if the program was built in the debug mode.

Index

D

E

J

K

L

M

O

R

S

X

Thank you for buying
Game Programming using QT

About Packt Publishing

Packt, pronounced 'packed', published its first book, *Mastering phpMyAdmin for Effective MySQL Management*, in April 2004, and subsequently continued to specialize in publishing highly focused books on specific technologies and solutions.

Our books and publications share the experiences of your fellow IT professionals in adapting and customizing today's systems, applications, and frameworks. Our solution-based books give you the knowledge and power to customize the software and technologies you're using to get the job done. Packt books are more specific and less general than the IT books you have seen in the past. Our unique business model allows us to bring you more focused information, giving you more of what you need to know, and less of what you don't.

Packt is a modern yet unique publishing company that focuses on producing quality, cutting-edge books for communities of developers, administrators, and newbies alike. For more information, please visit our website at `www.packtpub.com`.

About Packt Open Source

In 2010, Packt launched two new brands, Packt Open Source and Packt Enterprise, in order to continue its focus on specialization. This book is part of the Packt Open Source brand, home to books published on software built around open source licenses, and offering information to anybody from advanced developers to budding web designers. The Open Source brand also runs Packt's Open Source Royalty Scheme, by which Packt gives a royalty to each open source project about whose software a book is sold.

Writing for Packt

We welcome all inquiries from people who are interested in authoring. Book proposals should be sent to `author@packtpub.com`. If your book idea is still at an early stage and you would like to discuss it first before writing a formal book proposal, then please contact us; one of our commissioning editors will get in touch with you.

We're not just looking for published authors; if you have strong technical skills but no writing experience, our experienced editors can help you develop a writing career, or simply get some additional reward for your expertise.

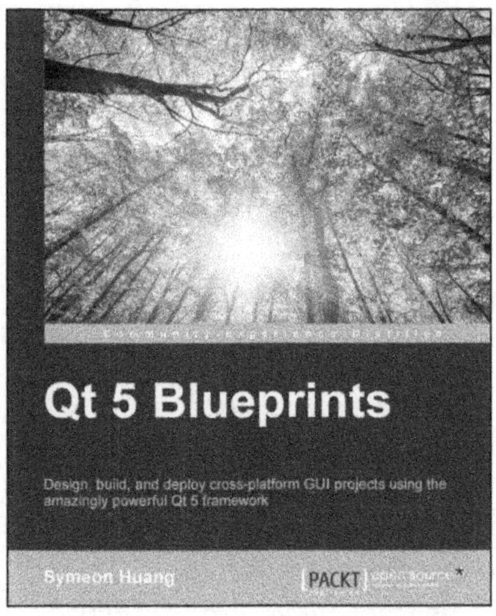

Qt 5 Blueprints

ISBN: 978-1-78439-461-5 Paperback: 272 pages

Design, build, and deploy cross-platform GUI projects using the amazingly powerful Qt 5 framework

1. Develop native graphical applications that can run anywhere with one of the world's best open-source frameworks.
2. Learn all about signals, slots, models, and views to design a robust structure for your application.
3. A comprehensive tutorial with step-by-step instructions to help you extend your applications across a wide domain.

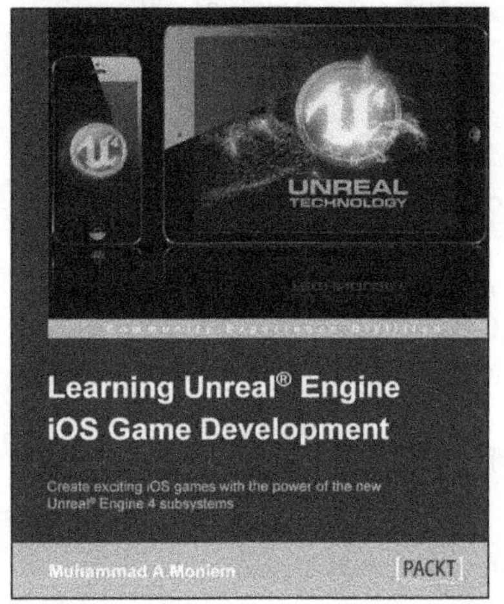

Learning Unreal® Engine iOS Game Development

ISBN: 978-1-78439-771-5 Paperback: 212 pages

Create exciting iOS games with the power of the new Unreal® Engine 4 subsystems

1. Learn each step in the iOS game development process, from start to finish.
2. Develop exciting iOS games with the Unreal Engine 4.x toolset.
3. Step-by-step tutorials to build optimized iOS games.

Please check **www.PacktPub.com** for information on our titles

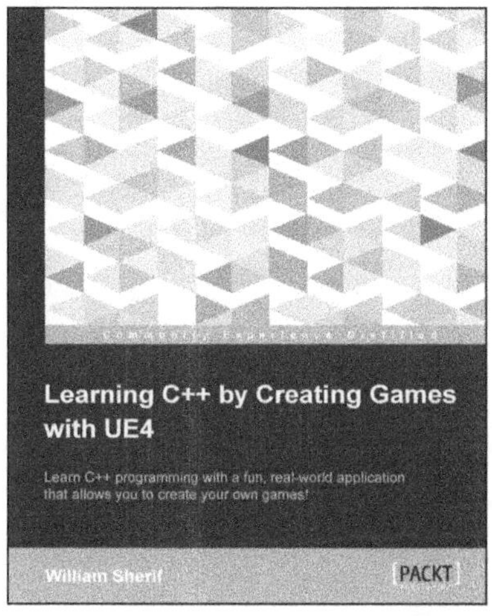

Learning C++ by Creating Games with UE4

ISBN: 978-1-78439-657-2 Paperback: 342 pages

Learn C++ programming with a fun, real-world application that allows you to create your own games!

1. Be a top programmer by being able to visualize programming concepts; how data is saved in computer memory, and how a program flows.
2. Keep track of player inventory, create monsters, and keep those monsters at bay with basic spell casting by using your C++ programming skills within Unreal Engine 4.
3. Understand the C++ programming concepts to create your own games.

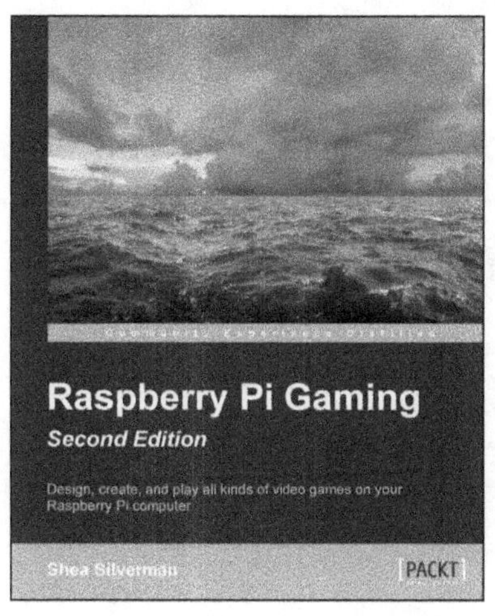

Raspberry Pi Gaming - Second Edition

ISBN: 978-1-78439-933-7 Paperback: 140 pages

Design, create, and play all kinds of video games on your Raspberry Pi computer

1. Program your very own video game on the Raspberry Pi using the Scratch programming language.
2. Install and manage your Raspberry Pi.
3. Set up your Raspberry Pi to play hundreds of retro and classic games.

Please check **www.PacktPub.com** for information on our titles

www.ingramcontent.com/pod-product-compliance
Lightning Source LLC
Chambersburg PA
CBHW080118220326
41598CB00032B/4884

* 9 7 8 1 7 8 2 1 6 8 8 7 4 *